INTRODUCTION TO
THE INTERNATIONAL HUMAN RIGHTS REGIME

THE RAOUL WALLENBERG INSTITUTE
HUMAN RIGHTS LIBRARY
VOLUME 14

Introduction to
the International Human Rights Regime

By

Manfred Nowak

MARTINUS NIJHOFF PUBLISHERS
LEIDEN / BOSTON

Published by:
Brill Academic Publishers
P.O. Box 9000, 2300 PA Leiden, The Netherlands
cs@brill.nl
http://www.brill.nl

Sold and distributed by:
Turpin Distribution Services Limited
Blackhorse Road
Letchworth
Herts SG6 1HN
United Kingdom

In North America:
Brill Academic Publishers
P.O. Box 605
Herndon, VA 20172
USA
cs@brillusa.com

A C.I.P. Catalogue record for this book is available from the Library of Congress.

Printed on acid-free paper.

ISBN 90-0413-658-4 (hardback)
      90-0413-672-x (paperback)
© 2003 Koninklijke Brill NV, Leiden, The Netherlands.

This is an updated English translation of the German *Einführung in das internationale Menschenrechtssystem* by Manfred Nowak, published in 2002 by Neuer Wissenschaftlicher Verlag GmbH, Wien/graz

Koninklijke Brill NV incorporates the imprint Martinus Nijhoff Publishers.

All rights reserved. No part of this publication may be reproduced, stored in a retrieval system, or transmitted in any form or by any means, electronic, mechanical, photocopying, microfilming, recording or otherwise, without written permission from the Publisher.

Authorization to photocopy items for internal or personal use is granted by Brill Academic Publishers provided that the appropriate fees are paid directly to The Copyright Clearance Center, 222 Rosewood Drive, Suite 910, Danvers MA 01923, USA. Fees are subject to change.

Printed and bound in The Netherlands.

CONTENTS

FOREWORD xiii

1. WHAT ARE HUMAN RIGHTS? 1

2. HISTORY OF HUMAN RIGHTS 9
- 2.1. Philosophical Foundations 9
- 2.2. Fundamental Rights and Constitutionalism 14
- 2.3. Historical Antecedents of the International Protection of Human Rights 16
- 2.4. The League of Nations 20
- 2.5. International Human Rights Law as a Reaction to National Socialism 21
- 2.6. Three Generations (Dimensions) of Human Rights as Ideological Concepts during the Cold War 23
- 2.7. All Human Rights for All: Universality, Indivisibility, Equality and Interdependence of Human Rights 25
- 2.8. From Promotion to Protection and Prevention 27

3. INTERNATIONAL HUMAN RIGHTS PROTECTION – CONTEXT AND CONCEPTIONS 33
- 3.1 Human Rights in Context 33
  - 3.1.1. Human Rights versus National Sovereignty 33
  - 3.1.2. Human Rights Protection – An Atypical Task of International Law 35
  - 3.1.3. Human Rights Protection: International and National Law 36
  - 3.1.4. Human Rights Law, Humanitarian Law, Refugee Law 38
  - 3.1.5. Human Rights and Peace 40
  - 3.1.6. Human Rights and Development 43
  - 3.1.7. Human Rights and Democracy, the Rule of Law, Good Governance and Popular Participation 45
- 3.2. Human Rights Theory 48
  - 3.2.1. Obligations of States to Respect, Fulfil and Protect Human Rights 48
  - 3.2.2. Horizontal Effects of Human Rights 51
  - 3.2.3. State Responsibility and Individual Responsibility 54
  - 3.2.4. Restrictions and Limitations of Human Rights 56
  - 3.2.5. The Principle of Proportionality and the Margin of Appreciation 59
  - 3.2.6. Prohibition of Discrimination 61

3.2.7. Right to Effective Remedy and Reparation for Human Rights Violations 63
3.2.8. Rules of Interpretation of Human Rights Treaties 64
3.3. Overview of the International Human Rights System 67

4. UNITED NATIONS 73
4.1. UN Charter 73
4.2. Universal Declaration of Human Rights (UDHR) 75
4.3. Human Rights Treaties and Monitoring Mechanisms 78
    4.3.1. International Covenant on Civil and Political Rights (CCPR) .. 78
    4.3.2. International Covenant on Economic, Social and Cultural Rights (CESCR) 81
    4.3.3. International Convention on the Elimination of All Forms of Racial Discrimination (CERD) 83
    4.3.4. Convention on the Elimination of All Forms of Discrimination against Women (CEDAW) 86
    4.3.5. Convention against Torture and Other Cruel, Inhuman or Degrading Treatment or Punishment (CAT) 88
    4.3.6. Convention on the Rights of the Child (CRC) 91
    4.3.7. Other Major UN Human Rights Treaties 94
    4.3.8. Treaty Monitoring Bodies 96
    4.3.9. State Reporting Procedure 97
    4.3.10. Complaints Procedure 99
    4.3.11. Inquiry Procedure 103
4.4. Charter Based Organs and Mechanisms 104
    4.4.1. Commission on Human Rights (CHR) 104
        4.4.1.1. General Remarks 104
        4.4.1.2. ECOSOC Resolution 1235 (XLII) of 6 June 1967 107
        4.4.1.3. ECOSOC Resolution 1503 (XLVIII) of 27 May 1970 108
        4.4.1.4. Country Specific Mechanisms 110
        4.4.1.5. Thematic Mechanisms 115
        4.4.1.6. Sub-Commission on the Promotion and Protection of Human Rights 117
    4.4.2. Commission on the Status of Women 119
    4.4.3. Commission on Crime Prevention and Criminal Justice 121
    4.4.4. Economic and Social Council (ECOSOC) 122
    4.4.5. Trusteeship Council 124
    4.4.6. General Assembly 125
    4.4.7. Security Council 129

Contents

4.4.8. Secretary General 131
    4.4.8.1. Structure of the Secretariat and Coordination Mechanisms 131
    4.4.8.2. Office of the High Commissioner for Human Rights in Geneva (UNHCHR) 133
    4.4.8.3. Division for the Advancement of Women (DAW), New York 134
    4.4.8.4. Centre for International Crime Prevention (CICP), Vienna 135
    4.4.8.5. Office of the High Commissioner for Refugees (UNHCR), Geneva 135
    4.4.8.6. United Nations Children's Fund (UNICEF), New York .. 137
    4.4.8.7. United Nations Development Programme (UNDP), New York 137
    4.4.8.8. Other Relevant UN Offices and Departments 138
4.5. UN Specialized Agencies 139
    4.5.1. 'The United Nations Family' 139
    4.5.2. International Labour Organization (ILO), Geneva 141
    4.5.3. UN Educational, Scientific and Cultural Organization (UNESCO), Paris 142
    4.5.4. World Health Organization (WHO), Geneva 143
    4.5.5. Food and Agriculture Organization (FAO), Rome 143
    4.5.6. World Bank and International Monetary Fund (IMF), Washington 144
    4.5.7. The World Trade Organization (WTO), Geneva 146
4.6. Main World Conferences 147
    4.6.1. Second World Conference on Human Rights, Vienna 1993 148
    4.6.2. Fourth World Conference on Women, Beijing 1995 150
    4.6.3. First World Social Summit, Copenhagen 1995 151
    4.6.4. Third World Conference Against Racism, Durban 2001 152

5. COUNCIL OF EUROPE (CoE)   157

5.1. The Three Pillars of the Council of Europe: Democracy, Rule of Law and Human Rights – Theory and Practice 157
5.2. European Convention on Human Rights 160
    5.2.1. The Traditional Concept of Civil and Political Rights 160
    5.2.2. Gradual Development of the Strasbourg Mechanism 161
    5.2.3. Inter-State Complaints Procedure 165
    5.2.4. Individual Complaints Procedure 168
5.3. European Social Charter (ESC) 173

5.4. European Convention for the Prevention of Torture (ECPT)	176
5.5. European Framework Convention for the Protection of National Minorities	179
5.6. European Charter for Regional and Minority Languages	181
5.7. European Convention on Human Rights and Biomedicine	181
5.8. European Commissioner for Human Rights	183
5.9. European Commission against Racism and Intolerance (ECRI)	184
5.10. Other Relevant Treaties and Mechanisms	185

6. ORGANIZATION OF AMERICAN STATES (OAS) — 189

6.1. From the Pan-American Union to the OAS	189
6.2. Purposes and Structures of the OAS	190
6.3. American Declaration of the Rights and Duties of Man	191
6.4. Charter Based Mechanisms	192
6.4.1. Inter-American Commission on Human Rights	193
6.4.2. Individual Complaints System (based on OAS Charter)	194
6.4.3. Country Reports	195
6.5. American Convention on Human Rights (ACHR)	196
6.5.1. Individual complaints procedure	197
6.5.2. Inter-state Complaints Procedure	198
6.5.3. Inter-American Court of Human Rights: Competence	199
6.5.4. Inter-American Court of Human Rights: Judgements on Individual Complaints	200
6.6. Other Relevant Treaties and Mechanisms	201

7. ORGANIZATION OF AFRICAN UNITY (OAU)/AFRICAN UNION (AU) — 203

7.1. Organization of African Unity (OAU)	203
7.2. African Union	204
7.3. Human Rights and Colonialism	205
7.4. African Charter on Human and Peoples' Rights	206
7.4.1. The African Concept of Individual and Collective Rights and Duties	207
7.4.2. African Commission on Human and Peoples' Rights	207
7.4.3. African Court on Human and Peoples' Rights (to be established)	208
7.4.4. Inter-State Complaints Procedure	209
7.4.5. Individual Complaints Procedure	210
7.5. Other Relevant Treaties and Mechanisms	211

CONTENTS

8. ORGANIZATION FOR SECURITY AND COOPERATION IN EUROPE (OSCE) — 215
- 8.1. From CSCE to OSCE — 216
- 8.2. The CSCE during the Cold War — 218
- 8.3. Human Dimension — 219
- 8.4. Human Dimension Mechanisms — 221
- 8.5. Charter of Paris for a New Europe — 222
- 8.6. The CSCE in Search of a New Identity — 223
- 8.7. The OSCE: Structures and Institutions — 224
- 8.8. Human Rights as Part of a Comprehensive Security Concept — 226
- 8.9. High Commissioner on National Minorities (HCNM) — 227
- 8.10. OSCE Representative on Freedom of Media — 228
- 8.11. Office for Democratic Institutions and Human Rights (ODIHR) — 229
- 8.12. OSCE Field Missions and Activities — 230

9. EUROPEAN UNION (EU) — 235
- 9.1. The Significance of Human Rights in the Process of European Integration — 236
- 9.2. Human Rights as Admission Criteria — 238
- 9.3. Human Rights within the EU — 228
   - 9.3.1. The Significance and Status of the European Convention on Human Rights (ECHR) — 239
   - 9.3.2. Jurisprudence of the European Court of Justice (ECJ) in Luxembourg — 239
   - 9.3.3. Asylum and Migration Policy — 240
   - 9.3.4. Protection against Discrimination in the European Union — 241
   - 9.3.5. European Monitoring Centre on Racism and Xenophobia (EUMC) — 242
- 9.4. Human Rights and EU External Relations — 242
   - 9.4.1. Common Foreign and Security Policy (CFSP) — 243
   - 9.4.2. Human Rights and Development Cooperation — 244
   - 9.4.3. Lomé Conventions and Cotonou Agreement — 245
   - 9.4.4. Human Rights Clauses in Bilateral Treaties of the EU — 246
- 9.5. Recent Developments — 246
   - 9.5.1. 'Leading by Example': A 'Human Rights Agenda' for the European Union for the Year 2000 — 247
   - 9.5.2. Vienna Declaration of the EU of 10 December 1998 — 248
   - 9.5.3. EU Annual Report on Human Rights — 248
   - 9.5.4. EU Charter of Fundamental Rights of 7 December 2000 — 249

10. EFFORTS OF OTHER REGIONAL ORGANIZATIONS TO PROTECT HUMAN RIGHTS   253
10.1. Organization of the Islamic Conference (OIC) 254
10.2. League of Arab States 255

11. NON-GOVERNMENTAL ORGANIZATIONS (NGOS)   257
11.1. NGOs as Part of Civil Society 257
11.2. Fact Finding and 'Mobilization of Shame' 258
11.3. The Contribution of NGOs to the Work of IGOs 259
11.4. UN Declaration on Human Rights Defenders 260
11.5. Well-Known International Human Rights NGOs 261

12. TRADITIONAL PROCEDURES AND MECHANISMS FOR THE INTERNATIONAL PROTECTION OF HUMAN RIGHTS   265
12.1. State Reporting Procedure 265
12.2. Inter-State Complaints Procedure 266
12.3. Individual Complaints Procedure 267
12.4. Inquiry Procedure 268
12.5. Other Forms of Fact-Finding, Investigation and Reporting 269
12.6. System of Visits 270

13. SHORTCOMINGS OF TRADITIONAL PROCEDURES AND NEW TRENDS IN THE INTERNATIONAL HUMAN RIGHTS REGIME   273

14. MECHANISMS FOR THE PREVENTION OF HUMAN RIGHTS VIOLATIONS   277
14.1. UN Preventive Deployment Force in Macedonia (UNPREDEP) ... 278
14.2. Burundi Field Mission of the UN High Commissioner for Human Rights (UNHCHR) 280
14.3. OSCE High Commissioner on National Minorities (HCNM) – Case Studies 282
14.4. UN Declaration and UN Working Group on Enforced Disappearances 283
14.5. Austria and the European Committee for the Prevention of Torture (CTP) 286

15. INDIVIDUAL CRIMINAL RESPONSIBILITY FOR SERIOUS HUMAN RIGHTS VIOLATIONS — 289

15.1. The Struggle against Impunity at the National Level: The 'Dirty War' in Argentina 290
15.2. The Principle of Universal Jurisdiction under the UN Convention against Torture (CAT): The Case of *Hissèin Habré* in Senegal 291
15.3. Diplomatic Immunity versus Criminal Responsibility: The Pinochet Case Before the British House of Lords 293
15.4. International Criminal Tribunal for the Former Yugoslavia (ICTY) 295
15.5. International Criminal Tribunal for Rwanda (ICTR) 297
15.6. The Long and Winding Road to the Adoption of the Rome Statute for an International Criminal Court (ICC) 298
15.7. International Criminal Court (ICC) 299
15.8. The Concept of Crimes against Humanity 301
15.9. Challenges for the ICC 302

16. HUMAN RIGHTS AND THE MAINTENANCE OF PEACE AND SECURITY — 307

16.1. Chapter VII UN Charter: Powers of the UN Security Council in the Event of a Threat to the Peace, Breach of the Peace or Act of Aggression 307
16.2. The Security Council and Human Rights 308
16.3. Sanctions of the Security Council under Article 41 312
16.4. Structure of the Dayton Peace Agreement for Bosnia and Herzegovina 315
16.5. UN Peacekeeping Force in Cyprus (UNFICYP) 319
16.6. UN Observer Mission in El Salvador (ONUSAL) 320
16.7. First Field Presence of the UN High Commissioner for Human Rights: UN Field Operation in Rwanda (HRFOR) 321
16.8. Between Peacekeeping and Protectorate: UN Transitional Authority in Cambodia (UNTAC) 322
16.9. Comprehensive Peace Operation: The International Community's Quasi Protectorate in Bosnia and Herzegovina 324
16.10. Self-Determination and UN Transitional Administration in East Timor (UNTAET) 326
16.11. Human Rights Protection by the Security Council as a Direct Consequence of International Peace Making: Case Study Iraq 328
16.12. Humanitarian Intervention for the Protection of Human Rights in 'Failed States': Case Study Somalia 330

16.13. The Tanzanian Intervention in Uganda in 1979: A 'Humanitarian Intervention'? 332
16.14. NATO Humanitarian Intervention for the Protection of Human Rights: Case Study Kosovo 334
16.15. Human Rights and the Fight against Terrorism: Case Study Afghanistan 336

17. CHALLENGES FOR THE FUTURE   339

ABBREVIATIONS   349
CASEBOX INDEX   353
NAME INDEX   355
SUBJECT INDEX   357

FOREWORD

This textbook is an updated English translation of my German *Einführung in das internationale Menschenrechtssytem*, published in September 2002 by the Neuer Wissenschaftlicher Verlag in Vienna. It was inspired by numerous discussions with law students and people I trained for human rights field missions. They generally agreed that the revolutionary developments in international human rights protection called for a textbook that was not too expansive, but still included both traditional human rights protection and modern trends, covering theory and practice, legal foundations and multidisciplinary aspects of human rights alike. To be consistent the book was to be written by one person and was also to address readers without legal background or human rights experience. It was to serve as a first introduction and a kind of red thread in the increasingly incomprehensible thicket of international human rights. Clearly one book alone cannot meet such high expectations. Whether or not my efforts have been worthwhile is for readers to decide and I gladly welcome any constructive criticism they may have.

In chapters 1 to 3, I shall attempt to give an introduction to the significance, history and framework of human rights and the legal dogmatics behind them. Following this, in chapters 4 to 10 I shall present the main bodies and procedures of human rights protection with the United Nations, the Council of Europe and other regional organizations, including the role of non-governmental organizations in chapter 11. I then venture to analyze (chapter 12) and review these critically (chapter 13). Major developments of recent years, such as measures for the prevention of human rights violations, the trend towards individual criminal responsibility, the shift of activities to the 'field', and the new role of human rights in maintaining world peace and international security are discussed and illustrated by case studies in chapters 14 to 16. As expected, the book ends with my personal reflections on the central challenges for the future of human rights protection.

I refrained from using footnotes and instead limited myself to internal references identified in parenthesis; at the end of each chapter there is a list of selected literature and relevant Internet links. I kept the text brief and simple to maintain the character of a first introduction, but I added a number of 'textboxes', 'lit boxes' and 'case boxes' to fulfil various roles throughout the book (all data as of May 2003, unless otherwise indicated):

- To draw the attention to important facts and issues
- To quote relevant normative principles and other original texts
- To illustrate structures and procedures
- To summarize the main facts of case studies
- To present statistics and tables
- To make bibliographical references
- To be used as overhead transparencies or similar tools for instruction

I tried to complement each of the chapters and subchapters 1 to 5 – on the theoretical background, the United Nations and the Council of Europe as the two main international organizations – with its own 'text box' as a sort of eye catcher. In chapters 6 to 16, I chose to present two different yet complementary approaches for each context. Again I tried to be brief in my general overview. Instead of subchapters I used boxes, each with its own structure. For specific information on the Inter-American Human Rights Commission, for example, one just needs to look up the apposite textbox (6.4.1.). To find out more about the significance of the Commission in the overall context of human rights protection with the OAS, there is the introduction to chapter 6.

The extensive 'case boxes' in chapters 14 to 16 are used to present concrete cases of preventive measures, application of international criminal law, humanitarian interventions and modern field operations in their context and all their complexity. I have added them, hoping not to confuse readers, but rather to give a more profound understanding of this highly complex matter.

This textbook would not have been possible without the support of many different individuals and institutions. Above all I would like to thank the staff of the Ludwig-Boltzmann-Institute of Human Rights at the University of Vienna who helped me prepare the 'boxes' and gave the necessary comments to make me reflect upon and improve the substance of my book. *Tanja Vospernik* was there from the very beginning to take care of the content and organizational issues. She prepared numerous overhead transparencies for my lectures in English and in German and many of the 'boxes' in the book are based on her work. During the final stages of the German version, *Helmut Sax* took over the main responsibility for reviewing, amending and revising the entire manuscript, the 'boxes', and the structure of the textbook. Both have been working for the institute for many years as legal researchers and I would like to thank them for their untiring commitment, their patience, competence, insistence and above all for the many scientific discussions we had in the course of the project. I also received many incentives and critical feedback from *Walter Suntinger* and *Ursula Kriebaum* who I prepared my lectures with.

During the early stages of the project, *Renate Frech, Sandra Horina, Julia Savage* and *David Dorrans*, amongst others, contributed towards preparing the 'boxes', while *Stefan Maier, Martin Reichardt* and *Severin Strohal* did an excellent job in correcting and editing the German text during the final stages. I would like to thank all of them for their valuable, competent and very often voluntary support.

The English translation of the German textbook was prepared by *Verena Tomasik*, with the assistance of *Elise Schopper*, in Vienna. In August 2002, I moved to Sweden in order to take up an Olof Palme Visiting Professorship on Human Rights and Humanitarian Law at the University of Lund. Again, I had the privilege of a very kind, constructive and professional support by the staff of the *Raoul Wallenberg Institute of Human Rights and Humanitarian Law*, above all by *Sadie O'Mahoney* who with great patience meticulously reviewed, corrected and updated the text. The final English language editing was done by *Christopher Cassetta*. Many late hours were contributed by *Carin Laurin* to adjust all textboxes and to prepare the layout for the camera-ready version. Last but not least I wish to thank

Foreword

the director of the Raoul Wallenberg Institute, *Gudmundur Alfredsson*, and Martinus Nijhoff Publishers, for publishing this book in the Raoul Wallenberg Institute Human Rights Library Series.

Financially the project was supported by the Austrian National Bank's Jubiläumsfond as well as by the Hermann und Marianne Straniak Foundation. I was also supported by the Freunde der Rechtswissenschaftlichen Fakultät (friends of the law faculty) of the University of Vienna and the Ludwig-Boltzmann Society. I want to express my sincere gratitude to all the above institutions without whose support, the project would not have been possible.

Finally, I would like to thank all the students whose discerning remarks initiated this book in the first place. I want to encourage them to be critical of this compilation of my efforts too. At any rate, I do hope the book will not only provide a first introduction to this fairly new multidisciplinary field for students of all faculties, but will also prove useful to those working in the 'field' and in other areas of international human rights protection. My aspiration is to give insight into a complex and fascinating phenomenon, which has revolutionized international relations in the course of more than half a century and has since come to provide the normative framework for a future 'world order'.

Lund/Vienna, May 2003   Manfred Nowak

1. WHAT ARE HUMAN RIGHTS?

Human rights must be considered one of the major achievements of modern day philosophy. Their moral fascination and revolutionary power have set the course of history over the past 250 years in many lasting ways. Their rightful claim today is to be the **only universally recognized system of values**, albeit one which, unlike ideologies or religions, is not closed in itself. It does not offer ready-made answers for any of life's countless questions, but instead provides a loosely knit network of minimum standards and procedural rules for human relations, all of which are equally applicable not only to governments, law enforcement bodies or the military, but in principle also to business enterprises, international organizations or private individuals.

The focus of human rights is on the **life and dignity of human beings**. A person's dignity is violated when they are subjected to torture, forced to live in slavery or poverty, i.e. without a minimum of food, clothing, and housing. Other economic, social and cultural rights, such as access to a minimum of education, medical care and social security, are as fundamentally important to a life in dignity as are respect of privacy and family life or personal freedom.

TEXTBOX 1

WHAT ARE HUMAN RIGHTS?

Descriptive, legal and philosophical approaches

1. Those fundamental rights, which empower human beings to shape their lives in accordance with liberty, equality and respect for human dignity.
2. The sum of civil, political, economic, social, cultural and collective rights laid down in international and regional human rights instruments, and in the constitutions of states.
3. The only universally recognized value system under present international law comprising elements of liberalism, democracy, popular participation, social justice, the rule of law and good governance.

These existential rights, which are essentially a manifestation of human dignity, provide the nucleus around which a number of other rights have been created, such as freedom rights (e.g. freedom of speech, conscience, religion, assembly and association), equality rights (equality before the law and equal protection of the law, protection against discrimination on the grounds of sex, race, colour, religion, ethnic or social origin, etc.), political rights (right to vote, equal access to public service, freedom to form a political party, right of petition, etc.), rights of economic life (right to own property, freedom of movement, right to work and free choice of employment, freedom to provide services), collective rights (the right of peoples to self-determination, protection of minorities and indigenous peoples, right to development, etc.), procedural rights (especially for administration of criminal

1. WHAT ARE HUMAN RIGHTS?

justice), or specific rights for children, the elderly, the sick, the disabled, aliens, asylum seekers as well as for other vulnerable groups. All of the above rights constitute **legal claims** whereby human beings are empowered to live in accordance with the principles of freedom, equality and human dignity. The Age of Enlightenment, by recognizing the rights of individuals within their community, was able to free human beings of the worldview prevalent in the Middle Ages, which was determined by duties alone. Human beings were made the subjects rather than the objects of legal systems, they were relieved of a life of submissiveness and vested with the rights of citizenship. This is the essential difference that distinguishes human rights from other value systems, religions in particular. It is this **process of emancipation, of empowerment** which makes up the revolutionary essence of human rights. Human beings who believe in the right to life or property have a fundamentally different conception of themselves from those who simply comply with the prohibition not to kill or steal. As obvious, natural and inherent to human beings as these rights may seem to many of us because of the dignity we are vested with, they continue to be **controversial** both in practice and in theory.

Many governments consider the protection of human rights a threat to their stability rather than the actual basis of their legitimacy, as postulated by none other than *John Locke*. While industrialized countries are increasingly guiding their foreign and development policies by human rights and are even attempting to justify wars such as the one witnessed in Yugoslavia, East Timor, Afghanistan and Iraq by human rights concerns, the countries which are directly affected, specifically those in Asia and the Islamic world, are increasingly regarding human rights as a system of values imposed upon them. Now that some international human rights treaties are recognized as binding by virtually all countries of the world, many governments are questioning the universality of human rights and are deploring the **neo-colonialist attitude of northern human rights policies.** Many enterprises and trans-national corporations too have come to see human rights as an unwanted harness used to restrict the scope of action granted to them in the course of neo-liberalism. Similar scepticism can be attributed to the World Bank and other international financial institutions, to religious and other institutions exerting power over human beings.

Examining the list of power holders, for whom human rights are nothing but a source of annoyance and considering the many serious violations of human rights systematically committed in almost all regions of the world, it may seem a little naive and frivolous to hail the victory of human rights. It is a conflict those committed to human rights work in the field and those engaged in scientific pursuits are painfully aware of in their daily work. The question arises whether this purported progress of human rights is witnessed only in the heads of a few human rights freaks (often referred to as 'do-gooders') or whether the spirit of the world as *Hegel* defined it is really inspired by human rights. If this was a purely philosophical system of values, a set of moral rules or simply one of many ideologies, a sceptical approach would be more than justified in view of the sad reality. Yet what we are dealing with is a **legally well-structured universal set of normative standards**. The roughly 200 countries of the world, which have recognized human rights as

1. WHAT ARE HUMAN RIGHTS?

legally binding in their constitutions or by ratification of treaties under international law, consider them standards of vital importance which all government actions are subject. It is this universal, normative element that essentially distinguishes human rights from other worldviews or value systems. Governments gradually accepted human rights as legal obligations, and during the 1993 Vienna World Conference on Human Rights, in fact abandoned the idea of human rights protection as being solely a matter of state sovereignty. At least in cases of gross or systematic human rights violations, the international community is legitimized and even called upon to intervene for the benefit of the victims against the governments or non-governmental forces held responsible.

Human rights must not be considered as a static system; their codification is an ongoing and never ending process both nationally and internationally. Human rights are usually established in **response to a specific threat or act of repression**. Freedom of religion for example, one of the first human rights to be phrased, was established in reaction to the powerful Catholic church in Europe and the religious wars and government coercions that the church provoked (*'cuius regio eius et religio'*). More recent human rights, such as the right to data protection and the right not to be subjected to enforced disappearance, were created in response to the dangers of modern information technology and the practices of Latin American military dictatorships in the 1960s and 1970s, where political opponents were detained *incommunicado* for many years and were made victims of enforced disappearance. The latest developments and threats, such as those presented by gene technology or biomedicine, no doubt necessitate the development of a further set of human rights. Whether or not these values, such as the prohibition of cloning human beings, will be phrased as human rights, will be for politics to decide. Once political decision makers have concluded that a specific right is important enough to be incorporated into national constitutions and/or international human rights treaties, it is recognized as a human right.

The **principle of universality does not in any way rule out regional or national differences and peculiarities**. What is universally valid is the principle of inalienable rights based on the dignity of human beings, as are certain minimum standards recognized by international customary or treaty law; these include the prohibition of torture and slavery, the prohibition of racial discrimination and apartheid, the right of peoples to self-determination or the minimum rights of children. Beyond that, of course, individual states or regional organizations are free to establish their own, higher standards or additional human rights. Thus, in the United States there exists a historically based human right to bear arms, yet unlike in Europe and most Latin American countries, there is no right to life or physical integrity that automatically includes a prohibition of the death penalty. In Africa, the peoples' collective rights, such as the right to development or the right to a healthy environment, by comparison play a far greater role than they do on other continents. Even identical wording does not preclude regional interpretations of standards when applied in practice. Thus, the European Court of Human Rights decided that corporal punishment, no matter how light, was degrading punishment and therefore

1. What Are Human Rights?

forbidden at all costs in Europe. This fairly strict standard does not seem to apply in some Islamic countries, who were successful in adding to article 1 of the 1984 UN Convention against Torture a clause which excludes from the definition of torture any pain or suffering arising only from 'lawful sanctions'. On the other hand, there can be no doubt that more draconic methods of corporal punishment amount to a violation of the universal prohibition of torture, cruel, inhuman or degrading treatment or punishment. It is not possible to draw a line that is valid for all times and regions, and each individual case would ultimately have to be clarified by the competent jurisdiction.

TEXTBOX 2

HUMAN RIGHTS TERMINOLOGY

Human rights (international law)	–	Fundamental rights (national constitutional law)
Human rights (for everyone)		Citizens' rights (for citizens)
Human rights (individual rights)	–	Peoples' rights (collective rights)

Finally, let me say a few words about **terminology**. I use the term '**human rights**' in a comprehensive legal sense, i.e. as the sum total of all subjective rights as laid down in national constitutions and/or international human rights documents. However, I am fully aware that the term may also be used, as implied by natural law, in a philosophical, and above all, a far less comprehensive sense. Thus the rights guaranteed by constitutional law are frequently referred to as '**fundamental rights**' and are clearly distinguished from the human rights anchored in international law. The more domestic bills of rights are in fact influenced by international human rights law, which often is directly incorporated into national constitutional law, the more this differentiation seems inappropriate. On the other hand, the European Union only in 2000 adopted a 'Charter of Fundamental Rights', which can be interpreted as a first step to a 'domestic' European bill of rights in a future European constitution.

The French 'Declaration des Droits de l'Homme et du Citoyen' of 1789 introduced a further distinction between human rights and **citizens' rights**. This made sense as long as many rights such as freedom of speech, of assembly and association, as well as freedom of movement were limited to citizens only, in other words as long as they were withheld from foreigners. Today, only a few, mainly political rights such as the right to vote are limited to only citizens and the term 'citizens' rights' has lost much of its relevance. Furthermore, the term human right does not in itself imply that such a right is applicable to all human beings alike. On the contrary, there are a number of human rights that are applicable only to certain groups of people, e.g. women, children and adolescents, the elderly, persons with disabilities, minorities or indigenous peoples, and, of course, there are those that apply to only foreigners or to only citizens.

The 1981 African Charter on Human and Peoples' Rights makes a clear distinction between individual human rights and **collective rights**. In literature as well there have been several attempts to limit the term human rights to individual rights only. Again, I find this restriction in terminology rather inappropriate. Of course, individual rights must be given priority. After all, it was the human rights concept which freed human beings from medieval subjugation and which placed the individual at the centre of the legal and social order. Nevertheless, it would be quite mistaken to pass off human rights as merely individual claims. Why indeed should religious associations, as legal persons, not enjoy freedom of religion? The same goes for other legal entities, groups and collectives: Political parties enjoy freedom of association, trade unions the right to organize and collective bargaining, media enterprises the right to freedom of expression and information, business corporations the right to property, minorities and indigenous peoples the special protection of the rights accorded to them, and peoples the rights to self-determination and development, just to mention a few examples. In other words: the term human rights applies equally to individual and collective rights, although not every human right allows by its very nature, to be extended to individuals, groups and legal entities alike. Some personal rights, such as the prohibition of torture and slavery, are strictly individual rights, whereas the right of peoples to self-determination is a purely collective right. For the majority of human rights, however, there are individual as well as collective claims to be asserted.

1. What Are Human Rights?

> CASEBOX 1
>
> ## Human Rights in Practice – Examples I
>
> Is the death penalty permissible under present international law? Article 2 ECHR; Article 6 CCPR; Article 4 ACHR; 6th and 13th AP ECHR; 2nd OP to CCPR; 1990 Protocol to ACHR; *Soering v. UK*; *Ng v. Canada*; *Errol Johnson v. Jamaica*; *State v. Makwanyane and Mchunu* (South African Constitutional Court)
>
> Is corporal punishment permitted? *Tyrer v. United Kingdom, Campbell and Cosans v. United Kingdom, Human Rights Committee General Comment No. 7(16), Osbourne v. Jamaica, Higginson v. Jamaica, Sooklal v. Trinidad and Tobago*
>
> What is torture? Article 1 CAT, *Ireland v. United Kingdom, Bleier v. Uruguay, Aksoy v. Turkey, Selmouni v. France*
>
> Which human rights are violated by an act of enforced disappearance? *Velasquez Rodriguez v. Honduras, Bautista v. Colombia, Kurt and Tas v. Turkey, Matanovic and Palic v. Republika Srpska*, UN Declaration on Enforced Disappearance
>
> What is the meaning of the principle of non-refoulement? Article 33 Geneva Refugee Convention; Article 3 CAT; Article 3 ECHR; Article 7 CCPR; *Motumbo v. Switzerland*
>
> Are there other provisions restricting the deportation of aliens? Article 8 ECHR; 4th AP to ECHR; Article 1 of 7th AP to ECHR; Article 12(4) and 13 CCPR; *Beldjoudi v. France; Nasri v. France; Stewart v. Canada*

1. What Are Human Rights?

> **CASEBOX 2**
>
> ### Human Rights in Practice – Examples II
>
> Are states permitted to prohibit homosexuality? *Dudgeon v. United Kingdom, Toonen v. Australia*
>
> Is there a human right to divorce? Article 12 ECHR; Article 5 of 7th AP to ECHR; *Johnston and Others v. Ireland*
>
> Is banishment to an island a deprivation of personal liberty? Article 5 ECHR; 4th AP to ECHR; *Guzzardi v. Italy*
>
> What are legitimate grounds for deprivation of personal liberty? Article 5 ECHR
>
> Does a public broadcasting monopoly violate freedom of information? Article 10 ECHR, *Informationsverein Lentia and Others v. Austria*
>
> Does the Turkish prohibition to wear a scarf (hijab) in public universities violate freedom of religion? Article 9 ECHR, Article 2 of 1st AP to ECHR, *Karaduman v. Turkey, Bulut v. Turkey*
>
> Is the public denial of the Nazi Holocaust protected by freedom of expression? Articles 19 and 20 CCPR, *Faurisson v. France*
>
> Does the right to education mean that states have to build and maintain schools? Article 2 of 1st AP to ECHR, Articles 13 and 14 CESCR, Article 29 CRC
>
> Is poverty a violation of human rights? Articles 2 and 11 CESCR; Draft UN Guidelines: A Human Rights Approach to Poverty Reduction Strategies
>
> Are states under an obligation to prohibit female genital mutilation? CEDAW, Declaration on Violence against Women, draft protocol to the Banjul Charta on the Rights of Women in Africa
>
> Do indigenous peoples have a right to enjoy their own culture? ILO Convention No. 169; Article 27 CCPR; *Kitok v. Sweden; Lubican Lake Band v. Canada; Mahuika et al. v. New Zealand*

1. What Are Human Rights?

> **LITBOX 1**
>
> ## Literature
> ### (Basic Documents)
>
> *Brownlie*, Ian and *Goodwin-Gill*, Guy (Eds.) 2002, Basic Documents on Human Rights, 4th ed., Oxford
>
> *Council of Europe* (Ed.) 2000, Human Rights in International Law, basic texts, 2nd ed., Strasbourg
>
> *Ermacora*, Felix, *Nowak*, Manfred and *Tretter*, Hannes 1993, International Human Rights, Documents and Introductory Notes, Vienna
>
> *Ghandhi*, P. R. (Ed.) 2000, Blackstone's International Human Rights Documents, London
>
> United Nations 1993, Human Rights: A Compilation of International Instruments, 2 volumes, New York
>
> *Wallace*, Rebecca, 2001, International Human Rights: Text and Materials, 2nd ed., London
>
> ## Internet
> ### (Human Rights Libraries)
>
> www1.umn.edu/humanrts/ – University of Minnesota Online Human Rights Library
>
> www.rwi.lu.se – Raoul Wallenberg Institute of Human Rights and Humanitarian Law
>
> http://sim.law.uu.nl/SIM/Dochome.nsf? Open – Netherlands Institute of Human Rights Documentation Site
>
> www.humanrights.at – Servicestelle Menschenrechtsbildung des Ludwig Boltzmann-Instituts für Menschenrechte
>
> www.bayefski.com – United Nations Treaties Database
>
> www.hri.ca/welcome.asp – Human Rights Internet
>
> www.law.harvard.edu/programs/HRP/Publications/research.html – Harvard Human Rights Program

2. History of Human Rights

2.1. Philosophical Foundations

The value system manifested in human rights is not a specifically European one, but is found in all major cultures and religions worldwide. Human life, dignity, freedom, equality and property were protected above all by moral commandments ('thou shalt not kill', 'thou shalt not steal'), standards of criminal law and justice maxims, such as the **Golden Rule** found in all religions.

TEXTBOX 3

THE GOLDEN RULE

Do naught to others which, if done to thee, would cause thee pain: this is the sum of duty (Hinduism)

What is hateful to you, do not to your fellow man. That is the entire law; all the rest is commentary (Judaism)

Do unto others as you would have them do unto you (Christianity)

No one of you is a believer until he desires for his brother that which he desires for himself (Islam)

Hurt not others in ways that you yourself would find hurtful (Buddhism)

However, the biggest achievement of the **Age of Enlightenment in Europe** and with it the **rationalistic doctrine of natural law** was to recognize individual human beings as subjects endowed with rights against the society and to place them at the centre of legal and social systems. The idea of the rights of the individual being natural, inherent and inalienable brought about a paradigm shift in the overall understanding of the state and its functions. This in turn was endorsed by the theory of the social contract. The state no longer drew its justification from mandates of divine order, whatever their makeup, but simply and solely from the need to protect the natural rights of the individual, i.e. the rights inherent in the nature of human beings, such as the right to life, liberty, property, security, happiness, etc. This theory, which has its roots in the teachings of *John Locke, Thomas Paine, Jean-Jacques Rousseau* and other philosophers of the 17th and 18th century, was the driving force behind the French and the American Revolutions and is clearly reflected in human rights documents of that time. The main schools of thought, upon which the classical human rights concept of the Age of Enlightenment (also known as the 1st generation, see 2.6. below) is founded, along with the rationalistic doctrine of natural law, are political liberalism and democracy. The principle of **democracy** is the embodiment of political freedom as coined in antiquity, i.e. the freedom of citizens to actively participate, most specifically to take part in political decision-making processes.

Liberalism, on the other hand, postulates the individualist civil freedom as fashioned by modern times, i.e. the freedom of individuals to fulfil themselves without interference from outside, e.g. from the state, the church, or from society. Liberal freedom has its natural limits, which are to respect the freedom of others, and legislators are called upon to determine these limits according to *Kant's* categorical imperative.

TEXTBOX 4

RATIONALISTIC DOCTRINE OF NATURAL LAW

John Locke (Two Treatises of Government, 1690, II, §§ 124, 123, 87)

'the great and chief end, therefore, of men uniting into commonwealths, and putting themselves under government, is the preservation of their property – that is, their lives, liberties and estates.'

American 'Declaration of Independence' 1776

'We hold these truths to be self-evident – that all men are created equal; that they are endowed by their creator with certain inalienable rights; that among these are life, liberty, and the pursuit of happiness. That, to secure these rights, governments are instituted among men deriving their just powers from the consent of the governed.'

French *Déclaration des droits de l'homme et du citoyen* 1789

Article II: *'Le but de toute association politique est la conservation des droits naturels et imprescriptibles de l'homme. Ces droits sont la liberté, la propriété, la sûreté et la résistance a l'oppression.'*

Liberal freedom, in human rights terms, is defined by the passive civil rights of non-interference (above all by the state), while the democratic freedom towards the state is defined by active political rights of participation. These civil and political rights were at the core of the classical human rights idea of the Age of Enlightenment which gained ground during the French and the American Revolution in the 18th century and the other bourgeois revolutions of the 19th century, and which is also manifested in the constitutions of that time.

2.1. PHILOSOPHICAL FOUNDATIONS

> **TEXTBOX 5**
>
> ### LIBERALISM
>
> **Immanuel Kant** (Über den Gemeinspruch 1793)
>
> 'Die Freiheit als Mensch, deren Prinzip für die Constitution eines gemeinen Wesens ich in der Formel ausdrücke: Niemand kann mich zwingen auf seine Art (wie er sich das Wohlsein anderer Menschen denkt) glücklich zu sein, sondern jeder darf seine Glückseligkeit auf dem Wege suchen, welcher ihm selbst gut dünkt, wenn er nur der Freiheit Anderer, einem ähnlichen Zwecke nachzustreben, die mit der Freiheit von jedermann nach einem möglichen allgemeinen Gesetze zusammen bestehen kann, (d.i. diesem Rechte des Anderen) nicht Abbruch thut.'
>
> **John Stuart Mill** (On Liberty 1859)
>
> 'The object of this essay is to assert one very simple principle, as entitled to govern absolutely the dealings of society with the individual in the way of compulsion and control, whether the means used be physical force in the form of legal penalties or the moral coercion of public opinion. That principle is that the sole end for which mankind are warranted, individually or collectively, in interfering with the liberty of action of any of their number is self-protection...Over himself, over his own body and mind, the individual is sovereign.'
>
> **French *Déclaration des droits de l'homme et du citoyen* 1789**
>
> Article IV: 'La liberté consiste à pouvoir faire tout ce, qui ne nuit pas à autrui; ainsi l'exercice des droits naturels de chaque homme n'a de bornes que celles, qui assurent aux autres membres de la société la jouissance de ces même droits. Ces bornes ne peuvent être déterminées que par la loi.'

Socialism's criticism of the classical human rights idea seizes on the civil rights of non-interference and the liberal concept of the separation of state and society these imply. The quintessence of civil human rights, according to *Karl Marx*, is the right to private property which is a breeding ground for unrestrained capitalism, and therefore, stands in the way of all other human rights, most particularly the right to equality. Socialist philosophers object to the liberal postulate of the separation of state and society (*Lassalle's* 'night-watchman state'), and in a countermove, they advance the socialist postulate of the unity of state and society, the reconciliation of individual and collective interests, the abolition of the human right to private property as well as the precedence of economic, social and cultural rights over civil and political rights. As long as there are homeless people in this world, the liberal right to protection of one's home to them means nothing but luxury. Consequently the state has to first make adequate provisions to ensure the social right to adequate housing for everyone. This also holds true for the priority of the cultural right to education (which includes the elimination of illiteracy) over the civil right to freedom of expression and information, and so on.

2. History of Human Rights

The economic, social and cultural rights, which the Russian and other socialist revolutions fought for as a means to achieve freedom through positive state action and which subsequently became a standard for the constitutions of socialist states, are frequently referred to as the second generation of human rights.

TEXTBOX 6

Democracy

Jean Jacques Rousseau (*Du contrat social* 1762)

I(8): *'On pourrait sur ce qui précède ajouter à acquis de l'état civil la liberté morale, qui seule rend l'homme vraiment maître de lui; car l'impulsion du seul appétit est esclavage, et l'obéissance à la loi qu'on s'est prescrite est liberté.'*

French *Déclaration des droits de l'homme et du citoyen* 1789

Article III: *'Le principe de toute souveraineté réside essentiellement dans la nation.'*

Article VI: *'La loi est l'expression de la volonté générale. Tous les citoyens ont droit de concourir personnellement ou par leurs représentants à sa formation.'*

The **conflicting ideologies** of the classical human rights concept in the West and the socialist human rights concept in the East, i.e. of the first two generations, proved a considerable hindrance to human rights and their philosophical and political development right up to the end of the Cold War. The international human rights idea, which took shape after the Second World War, most notably within the framework of the United Nations, was to provide a synthesis between the first two human rights generations. Yet to begin with, it was nothing more than a series of antagonistic ideas strung together. Their proponents showed little interest in a dialogue about a real synthesis and instead exploited human rights for their political gains. The only real incentives in those days came from the Southern hemisphere, particularly from Africa. Most of the former colonies fought for political independence from the European colonial powers by invoking the peoples' right to self-determination. They were supported in their endeavour by the League of Nations and the United Nations. Several other collective rights, such as the right of all peoples to equality, free disposition of their natural resources, a healthy environment, and above all the right to development were drawn up and proclaimed in response to the neo-colonial economic exploitation of the South. The main document in this context is the African Charter on Human and Peoples' Rights adopted in 1981 upon the initiative of prominent African philosophers and politicians. The collective rights of peoples contained in the Charter are also referred to as solidarity rights or human rights of the third generation.

The end of the Cold War and progressive globalization were instrumental in bringing to fruition the idea of **universalism**, which is one of the basic assumptions of human rights. Although the declarations of the French and American revolutions

2.1. PHILOSOPHICAL FOUNDATIONS

had already proclaimed the idea of freedom and equality for everyone, the classical human rights concept, de facto, only pertained to a small elite of white, male members of the bourgeoisie.

TEXTBOX 7

SOCIALISM

Karl Marx (Zur Judenfrage 1843)

'Vor allem konstatieren wir die Tatsache, dass die sogenannten Menschenrechte, die droits de l'homme im Unterschied von den droits du citoyen, nichts anderes sind als die Rechte des Mitglieds der bürgerlichen Gesellschaft, d.h. des egoistischen Menschen, des vom Menschen und vom Gemeinwesen getrennten Menschen.'

Friedrich Engels (Anti-Dühring, 1877/78)

'Die Proletarier nehmen die Bourgeoisie beim Wort: die Gleichheit soll nicht bloß scheinbar, nicht bloß auf dem Gebiet des Staates, sie soll wirklich, auch auf dem gesellschaftlichen, ökonomischen Gebiet durchgeführt werden.'

Constitution of the Union of Socialist Soviet Republics, 1936

Articles 118-132: First constitution with an elaborated catalogue of economic, social and cultural rights.

As *Karl Marx* and others like him rightly criticized, this idea of human rights was definitely compatible, both in practice and in its philosophical premises, with the idea of slavery, colonialism, suppression of women and the working classes. The socialist human rights concept on the other hand was intent on putting into practice real equality through state intervention. However, in subjecting the classical freedom rights to the social collective interests, they lost sight of the aspect of individual empowerment inherent in human rights. Socialist theory and practice dismissed the right of individual petition and to a remedy against human rights violations by the state, which meant that the human rights guaranteed by socialist constitutions were considered merely as principles of public order to be disposed of at the state's discretion. With the end of the Cold War the first chance for a real synthesis of the different human rights generations, as indicated by the Universal Declaration of Human Rights in 1948, materialized. Universalism proved the driving force for this new dialectic development in human rights.

An important forum for discussing the state of universal human rights in the post Cold War era was the second World Conference on Human Rights held in Vienna in 1993 (4.6.1.). Incidentally, the Conference almost failed because of the North-South conflict and the resistance of several Asian States to accept the universality of human rights. **'All human rights for all'**, the indicative motto of the NGO parallel activities in Vienna in 1993, became the United Nations' official motto for the human rights year 1998.

2. History of Human Rights

'All human rights for all' on the one hand refers to the indivisibility and interdependence of all human rights, i.e. the synthesis of different human rights concepts. Economic, social, cultural and collective human rights are as important and necessary as are civil and political rights. Real human rights protection can only be achieved through a well-balanced mix of different human rights that takes into account the right of individuals to non-interference and positive state action immanent in all human rights. Yet by the same token it also symbolizes the universality of human rights in the narrower sense, i.e. their validity in principle for all human beings, independent of gender, religion, race, colour, ethnic or social origin, nationality, sexual orientation, etc.

TEXTBOX 8

UNIVERSALISM

Universal Declaration Human Rights 1948

Preamble: 'Whereas recognition of the inherent dignity and of the equal and inalienable rights of all members of the human family is the foundation of freedom, justice and peace in the world...

The General Assembly proclaims this Universal Declaration as a common standard of achievement for all peoples and all nations...

Article 1: All human beings are born free and equal in dignity and rights. They are endowed with reason and conscience and should act towards one another in a spirit of brotherhood.'

Although the international community expressly recognized the indivisibility, interdependence and universality of human rights in the Vienna Declaration and its Programme of Action, it will take some time until these principles are implemented in practice and legally recognized by all states. Especially when Europe and the United States continue to exact high human rights standards from the countries of the South yet seem to get away with a very **one-sided interpretation of human rights** themselves, excluding economic, social, cultural and collective rights to a large extent. Besides, they are being very restrictive in their policies concerning aliens so as to retain comparatively high human rights standards for their own citizens.

2.2. Fundamental Rights and Constitutionalism

Up until the Second World War human rights standards were not developed within international law, but primarily within the framework of national constitutions. Human rights in the legal sense have only been in existence since the establishment of constitutions, in other words, the development of human rights is closely linked with the era of constitutionalism. The term used by national constitutions to describe

2.2. Fundamental Rights and Constitutionalism

these domestic human rights is *'Grundrechte'* (fundamental rights) in German, 'civil rights' or 'civil liberties' in English, and *'libertés publiques'* in French.

Constitutionalism, in turn, refers to a movement born out of the spirit of enlightenment to ensure that the state's main tasks and structures were **written down in a constitution,** which as the highest legal standard within the state, was considered binding and lasting. As a rule, constitutions consist of two distinct parts; a formal and a material one. The formal part contains rules concerning the highest bodies within the state, procedures of and the appointment of such bodies, as well as the main structural principles of the state (such as separation of powers, federalism or centralism, republic or monarchy, democratic or autocratic structures, etc.). The material part lays down the values, aims and objectives professed by the state, in other words, the objectives the state has defined for itself (the rule of law, democracy, social justice, good governance, environmental protection, neutrality, etc.) as well as fundamental rights. These bills of rights in the respective constitutions represent, therefore, an important indicator for those values that states wish to pursue and guarantee for their people.

The first comprehensive constitutions were the United States Federal Constitution of 1787, plus the first ten amendments of 1791 as a bill of rights, and the French Constitution of 1791 with the famous *Declaration des Droits de l'Homme et du Citoyen* of 1789 in its preamble. Trailblazers for European constitutions and fundamental rights development in the 19th century were the Belgian Constitution of 1831 and the German *Paulskirchenverfassung* of Frankfurt of 1848. For most socialist constitutions, it was the prototypical Soviet constitution of 1936. Many of the countries that achieved independence after the Second World War based their own bills of rights on the Universal Declaration of Human Rights of 1948. With a few exceptions, such as Bhutan, all countries of the world now have a written constitution and their own catalogue of fundamental rights. Some constitutions, such as the United States Federal Constitution, have proved remarkably stable and have lasted for centuries, while some countries like China proclaim a new constitution every time there is a major political change. Of course, every country has its own distinct bill of rights as well as its own internal mechanisms to ensure these fundamental rights. Nevertheless, there has been a clear **trend towards aligning national constitutions with international minimum standards** in recent years, which has partly been achieved by incorporating international human rights treaties. Many constitutions are also increasingly relying on particularly successful national institutions for the protection of fundamental rights such as constitutional courts, parliamentary committees, ombudsman institutions, and national human rights commissions.

2. History of Human Rights

TEXTBOX 9
Major Constitutions and Bills of Rights

- **United States of America**
  - 1776: Declaration of Independence as well as bills of rights in Virginia and other former British colonies
  - 1789/91: first 10 amendments to US Constitution of 1787
- **France**
  - 1789: *Declaration des droits de l'homme et du citoyen* as part of French constitutions since 1791
- **Belgium**: Constitution of 1831 as model for 19th century bills of rights
- **Germany**
  - *Paulskirchenverfassung* 1848
  - *Weimarer Reichsverfassung* 1919
  - *Bonner Grundgesetz* 1949
  - German Democratic Republic Constitutions of 1949 and 1968/74
- **Russia** (USSR)
  - 1917 'Declaration of the rights of the working and exploited people'
  - 1936 Stalin Constitution
  - 1977 Brezhnev Constitution
  - 1993 Yeltsin Constitution (Russian Federation)
- **China**: Constitutions of 1949, 1954, 1975, 1978 and 1982
- **India**: Constitution of 1950
- **Brazil**: Constitution of 1988
- **Uganda**: Constitution of 1995
- **South Africa**: 1994 interim Constitution, 1996 Constitution
- **European Union**: Charter of Fundamental Rights of 2000

2.3. Historical Antecedents of the International Protection of Human Rights

International law traditionally governs the relations between sovereign states and has, therefore, not been considered responsible for regulating the relations between states and their citizens or those among citizens. The latter are part of the individual state's sovereignty and, as such, are governed by national law (constitutional, administrative, penal and civil law). It is only since the Second World War, especially in reaction to the atrocities of National Socialism, that international law has come to regulate the rights of individuals in relation to their governments,

2.3. HISTORICAL ANTECEDENTS OF THE PROTECTION OF HUMAN RIGHTS

although many states still refuse to surrender this traditional part of their national sovereignty to international law. That is why the development of the international protection of human rights is an ongoing battle against national sovereignty (3.1.1.).

Up until the Second World War, international law was not responsible for the rights of individuals unless the interests of more than one state were concerned. This was true in particular in the case of foreigners for whom the state they are citizens of, has **protection power** vis-à-vis the state that exercises de facto power. Thus, if state A is prosecuting a case against citizens of state B for a crime they have committed in state A against citizens of state A, state B has a legitimate interest to ensure its citizens are not tortured and minimum rules for a fair criminal procedure are adhered to. State B's interest in exerting protective power is even more pronounced where certain groups of individuals are concerned, such as members of government, diplomats, soldiers, or other persons acting in state B on behalf of state A. This legitimate function of protective power, which is based on mutual interests (principle of reciprocity) led to the development of the right to immunity under international law as well as international humanitarian law. The right to **immunity** is first and foremost concerned with removing the persons concerned from the territorial sovereignty of the state they are in, while **international humanitarian law** has taken it upon itself to develop minimum rules for the treatment of persons in armed conflicts (originally only international ones), particularly for prisoners of war, wounded and sick persons and other combatants no longer involved in the conflict, as well as for civilians affected by military action.

TEXTBOX 10

INTERNATIONAL HUMANITARIAN LAW

- *Lieber Code* 1863 ('Instructions for the Government of Armies of the United States in the Field')
- Red Cross societies in Europe since 1863 – today 178 countries have national Red Cross and Red Crescent societies
- International Committee of the Red Cross 1875
- General Act and Declaration of Brussels 1890
- Geneva Conventions 1929
- Geneva Conventions 1949 and Additional Protocols 1977

These minimum standards are similar to human rights, but are applicable only during armed conflicts, and provided these conflicts are of an international nature, are based on the principle of reciprocity. In this they are essentially different from human rights. These minimum standards were primarily developed since the 1860's during the Red Cross Movement (*Henri Dunant*) in Europe (some also during the American Civil War – e.g. the Lieber Code) and have since been codified, amongst many other treaties, in the four Geneva Conventions of 1949 and the two Additional Protocols to the Geneva Conventions of 1977.

To this day the **International Committee of the Red Cross (or Red Crescent)**, a Swiss humanitarian organization with headquarters in Geneva, plays an outstanding role in supervising the implementation of international humanitarian law and providing humanitarian assistance.

TEXTBOX 11

EARLY TREATIES WITH HUMAN RIGHTS RELEVANCE
(FREEDOM OF RELIGION, PROTECTION OF MINORITIES, ECONOMIC AND SOCIAL RIGHTS)

- Augsburger Religionsfriede 1555
- Treaty of Westphalia 1648
- Treaty of Versailles 1871
- Peace treaties and minority protection treaties after World War I with Poland, the SHS Kingdom, Czechoslovakia, Austria, Bulgaria, Romania, etc.
- Peace Treaty of Versailles with Germany 1919: foundation of the League of Nations and the International Labour Office

---

The **protection of minorities** is a further historical antecedent of international human rights protection, which is also closely related to the protection power of national states. Ethnic, linguistic and religious minorities traditionally developed as new borders were drawn between states in the aftermath of wars. Typical examples are the collapse of the Ottoman Empire or the Austro-Hungarian monarchy, as well as the borders determined in the Peace Treaties of 1919/1920 (Peace Treaty of Versailles with Germany, Peace Treaty of Saint-Germain-en-Laye with Austria, Peace Treaty of Trianon with Hungary, Peace Treaty of Neuilly-sur-Seine with Bulgaria, Peace Treaty of Sèvres with Turkey). It was these peace treaties which led to the emergence of a German-speaking minority in Italy (South Tyrol), a Slovene minority in Austria (in Southern Carinthia, amongst others), a Hungarian minority in Slovakia and in Romania, an Albanian minority in Greece and a Greek minority in Albania, a Danish minority in Germany (Schleswig-Holstein), a German minority in Denmark, and so forth. As a rule, members of these minorities are citizens of the state they reside in, but are protected by the state of origin they associate with for ethnic, linguistic, religious and/or cultural reasons and which usually borders on the state they live in. Their protecting state feels responsible for ensuring their minority status is maintained and their cultural, linguistic, ethnic and/or religious identity is defended. As a consequence, bilateral agreements (e.g. for the Swedish minority on the Aaland islands which are part of Finland, or the so-called 'South Tyrol Package' between Austria and Italy) or multilateral peace treaties such as those after the First World War, are drawn up to secure minimum rights for the members of these minorities, including the right to use their own language in school, before state

2.3. HISTORICAL ANTECEDENTS OF THE PROTECTION OF HUMAN RIGHTS

authorities and courts, as well as for topographical designations. The League of Nations was partly entrusted with supervising the implementation of these rights (2.4.). The protection of minorities is also closely linked to the **peoples' right of self-determination**. It is true that the 14 Points Plan proposed by the former United States President *Woodrow Wilson* never really won recognition with his allies, France in particular. However, the right of self-determination did in some cases bring about the realignment of borders based on plebiscites, as in the case of the Eastern part of the Burgenland, which was ceded from Austria to Hungary in 1922. In the case of the former colonies of the Axis powers, the right of self-determination, supported by the League of Nations mandates system and the United Nations trusteeship system, eventually led to their independence.

In addition to bringing an end to the First World War and introducing provisions for the protection of minorities, the Peace Treaty of Versailles also created two international organizations which proved to be important for the development of the international protection of human rights: the **League of Nations** (2.4.) as predecessor of the United Nations, and the **International Labour Office** as predecessor of the International Labour Organization (4.5.2.), which today is one of the most effective specialized agencies of the United Nations for the protection of **economic, social and cultural rights**.

TEXTBOX 12

PROHIBITION OF SLAVERY AND THE SLAVE TRADE

- Private Anti Slavery Societies in Pennsylvania (1775) and other British colonies in North America, in London (1787), Paris and the USA (American Anti-Slavery Society 1833)
- British Act on the Abolition of the Slave Trade 1807
- Declaration on the Slave Trade adopted at the Vienna Congress of 1815
- Quintuple Treaty (London 1841/42) with 26 states parties
- Gradual abolition of slavery and the slave trade in most European and American states during the 19th century
- General Act of Berlin 1885
- General Act and Declaration of Brussels 1890
- Convention of Saint-Germain-en-Laye of 1919
- Slavery Convention 1926/27
- Supplementary Convention on the Abolition of Slavery, the Slave Trade, and Institutions and Practices Similar to Slavery 1956/57

Even centuries ago, some international treaties included human rights protective clauses. Thus, the *Augsburger Religionsfriede* of 1555 and the Treaty of Westphalia of 1648 contained provisions for the protection of **freedom of religion**.

Of particular interest for the early development of international human rights treaties is England's role in abolishing the **slave trade,** and ultimately, **slavery** itself. Despite the fact that these efforts were less of a human rights or humanitarian nature, but rather of an economic one (with the advance of capitalism in the 19th century, involuntary slave labour was replaced by 'voluntary' wage labour), the Declaration on the Slave Trade adopted at the Vienna Congress in 1815, as well as several bilateral treaties and the Quintuple Treaty of London of 1841 were nonetheless instrumental in gradually reducing and eventually abolishing slavery and the slave trade in the 19th century. Clearly this had to do with international law as the slave trade between European colonial powers, Africa and America undeniably included an international component and consequently the matter could hardly be considered a purely 'national one'. The Slavery Convention adopted under the auspices of the League of Nations in 1926, which strictly prohibits slavery and the slave trade, represents one of the first universal treaties for the protection of human rights under international law. Today, the prohibition of slavery has become customary international law and is considered to constitute ius cogens.

2.4. The League of Nations

The League of Nations was the first, potentially universal international organization and, as such, was justifiably considered the precursor to the United Nations. It was established in the **Peace Treaty of Versailles** of 1919 in reaction to the First World War and its main objective was to pre-empt another world war. Even though this objective was ultimately defeated because of the politics of National Socialism (Germany withdrew from the League of Nations in 1933), the League of Nations still contributed towards emphasizing the multilateral and legal aspects of international relations. Human rights protection was not among the tasks of the League of Nations, but its mandates and minority protection systems and the institution of international monitoring bodies did lay the foundations for a type of human rights protection as practised today by the United Nations and regional organizations.

According to article 22 of the Covenant of the League of Nations, the colonies of the Axis powers, i.e. of Germany and the Ottoman Empire, were divided into A, B, and C-Mandates depending on their 'stage of development' and were assigned to the League of Nations for a transition period until they were granted independence. Mandatory powers, England or France in most cases, were put in charge of the administration of these mandates. Mandate treaties were signed between the League of Nations and the Mandatory powers to lay down minimum rights for the people living in the territories under mandate.

Some of these minimum rights, such as the prohibition of torture, were not unlike human rights. The League of Nations appointed a **Mandate Commission** to supervise the regular reports submitted by the Mandate powers and to deal with petitions from individuals living in the territories under mandate. These activities represent the beginnings of the human rights state reporting and individual complaints procedure (12.1 and 12.3). Most A-Mandates, such as Iraq and Lebanon, were granted independence during the inter-war period, while B and C-Mandates, such as Togo and Cameroon, had to wait for the general decolonization movement after the Second World War to become independent. The C-Mandate Namibia, formerly German South-West Africa and the A-Mandate Palestine proved particularly critical cases. Due to the illegal occupation by South Africa, Namibia was granted independence as late as 1989, following massive pressure by the United Nations. Palestine became the state of Israel in 1949, yet to this day Palestinians are still fighting to have a state of their own.

TEXTBOX 13

LEAGUE OF NATIONS

- **Minority Protection**
  - Right of minorities and their members to submit petitions to the Minority Committee of the League of Nations: until 1938 roughly 650 petitions
  - Advisory opinions of the Permanent Court of International Justice: e.g. on minority schools in Albania 1935
- **Mandates System**
  - A-, B- and C- Mandates according to article 22 of the Covenant of the League of Nations
  - Reports from the Mandatory powers and petitions from individuals to the Mandate Commission of the League of Nations

---

Minority protection, as practiced by the League of Nations, is based on the peace treaties ending the First World War (2.3.). By signing these treaties, the Axis powers and/or their successor states, agreed to grant certain minimum rights to their minorities. A **Minority Committee** appointed by the League of Nations was to ensure that these commitments were adhered to under international law. By 1938, the Committee had handled approximately 650 petitions submitted by minorities or their members. The League of Nation's Permanent Court of International Justice, the predecessor to the International Court of Justice in The Hague, also repeatedly dealt with minority issues, e.g. in its advisory opinion of 1935 on minority schools in Albania.

2.5. International Human Rights Law as a Reaction to National Socialism

Up until the Second World War, international law did not regulate how sovereign states should treat their citizens or subjects (2.3.). International law provided that prisoners of war had a right to be protected from torture and to be treated with human dignity, yet by the same token states could go as far as committing **genocide** on 'their own' people without interference or reaction from outside. A frequently cited example in this context is the powerlessness of international diplomacy in the face of the Turkish genocide in Armenia in 1915. This double standard of morals was the result of the dogma of state sovereignty and the international principle of non-interference in national matters (3.1.1.). Regrettably, six million Jews became victims of the National Socialist genocide before a new way of thinking was introduced. The **Nazi Holocaust** was certainly not the result of the Second World War. It was a machinery of systematic discrimination and extermination, which had been planned carefully by the state and was directed against its own citizens because of their ethnic or religious background, sexual orientation (homosexuals), political conviction, or disabilities and so forth.

TEXTBOX 14

FROM THE HOLOCAUST TO HUMAN RIGHTS

1941 Atlantic Charter (*Roosevelt/Churchill*)

'Sixth, after the final destruction of the Nazi tyranny, the hope to see established a peace which will afford to all nations the means of dwelling in safety within their own boundaries, and which will afford assurance that all the men in all the lands may live out their lives in freedom from fear and want;'

1943 Moscow Declaration (*Roosevelt/Churchill/Stalin*)

'The United Kingdom, the United States and the Soviet Union have received from many quarters evidence of atrocities, massacres and cold-blooded mass executions which were being perpetrated by the Hitlerite forces in the many countries they have overrun and from which they are now being steadily expelled.'

1945 Preamble of the UN Charter

'We the Peoples of the United Nations determined to save succeeding generations from the scourge of war, which twice in our lifetime has brought untold sorrow to mankind, and to reaffirm faith in fundamental human rights, in the dignity and worth of the human person,...hereby establish an international organization to be known as the United Nations.'

1948 Preamble to the Universal Declaration of Human Rights

'Whereas disregard and contempt for human rights have resulted in barbarous acts which have outraged the conscience of mankind...'

It is true that scores of people were assassinated not before, but during the Second World War and many of them were citizens of occupied states, yet the fact remains that the holocaust was a national policy of systematic discrimination, racism and fascism. The **double standard of international law** at the time was made painfully clear because of the concomitant war crimes and atrocious violations of international humanitarian law. It was no longer compatible with moral standards to condemn the National Socialists for their war crimes, but at the same time to let the genocide of six million Jews go without criticism because it was considered a national matter.

2.6. THREE GENERATIONS OF HUMAN RIGHTS AS IDEOLOGICAL CONCEPTS DURING THE COLD WAR

The Western Allies, the United States in particular, entered the war not only to stop *Hitler's* wars of aggression, but also to intervene on humanitarian grounds. As early as 1941, *Franklin D. Roosevelt* and *Winston Churchill*, in the **Atlantic Charter**, had made the destruction of Nazi tyranny their declared war objective, partly on the basis of Roosevelt's 'freedom from fear and want'. The **United Nations** was founded immediately after the end of the Second World War to save succeeding generations from the scourge of further wars, but also to reaffirm people's faith in human rights and the dignity of the human person. Sadly though, the powerlessness of the United Nations (4.) as well as repeated genocides (e.g. in Tibet, Cambodia, Bosnia and Herzegovina or Rwanda) and human rights violations of the highest degree, have shown that it is still very difficult to break the dogma of national sovereignty with regard to human rights. Ultimately, this is what would be necessary to establish a functioning system of collective security and, thus, to guarantee all victims freedom from fear in the broadest sense. However, since the end of the Cold War, a wind of change is blowing through the system as interventions in Iraq, Somalia, Haiti, Bosnia and Herzegovina, Kosovo and East Timor have shown (16.).

2.6. Three Generations (Dimensions) of Human Rights as Ideological Concepts during the Cold War

The development of human rights, their philosophical foundations as well as their legal and factual realization, has been a dialectic and mostly revolutionary process (2.1.). Back in the 1970s, *Karel Vasak*, the Czech human rights expert, created the expression **'human rights generations'** to describe this intermittent process. Provided this term is not taken to imply that each succeeding generation is replaced by the one preceding it, it is frequently used to illustrate the debate on the ideology of human rights during the Cold War. Others have preferred using the term **human rights dimensions**.

TEXTBOX 15

THREE GENERATIONS/DIMENSIONS OF HUMAN RIGHTS

- Civil and political rights

Economic, social and cultural rights

- Collective rights

Of course, it would be rather simplistic to try and classify all human rights into three generations or dimensions, yet it is a clear reflection of the graphic human rights discussion carried on between the West, the East and the South. The states in the West liked to emphasize, and some are convinced to this day, that the **civil and political rights** of the first generation, i.e., the liberal rights of non-interference and the democratic participation rights inherent in the classical human rights concept, are the only real human rights in the sense of individual rights enforceable by law against the state. This restricted point of view is reflected in several Western constitutions, as well as in the liberal-constitutional theory of fundamental rights and the jurisprudence of many courts in Europe, the United States and other countries. It restricts human rights to the vertical relations between the state and the individual and to claims of the individual against state interference. In principle, it does not accept positive state obligations to protect and to fulfil human rights, nor the horizontal validity of human rights between individuals (so-called third party effect). The model relies on the classical human rights concept developed during the Age of Enlightenment, yet in doing so it overlooks the fact that the rationalist doctrine of natural law in particular considered the natural rights of human beings as effective against all types of interference, by state and non-state actors alike. In fact, this restriction of human rights to mere claims of non-interference only came about in the latter days of liberalism and legal positivism in the late 19th century and today is no longer sustainable. After all, all human rights are justiciable, obliging the state to respect (by non-interference), fulfil (by positive action) and to protect them against third parties (3.2.1.).

The socialist concept of the second generation is equally narrow-minded for it claims that civil and political rights would only aid and abet the capitalist interests of separating state and society. Accordingly, the only real human rights were those based on harmonization of individual and collective interests in socialist societies, in other words the **economic, social and cultural rights** as originally understood. Thus, the task of the state was to ensure the rights to work, social security, food, housing, health, education, etc. by granting positive benefits. Individual and legally enforceable claims against the state would therefore not only be superfluous, but actually run counter to the system. Furthermore, exercising such rights was not at the discretion of the individual, but in fact considered every citizen's duty (principle of the unity of rights and obligations). Thus, the right to work implied in a socialist economy also the duty to work, and even political freedoms, such as freedom of assembly, were to be exercised in conformity with collective interests of socialist society.

The third generation of the **collective rights of peoples** (of the South) tries to add a third dimension to human rights, which draws on the concept of universalism. Bearing in mind the fragility of human rights in the South, and in Africa in particular, which is due to a large extent to centuries of colonialism and imperialism, postulating individual rights at the national level only would hardly resolve the matter. International human rights protection, instead of being limited to international monitoring of states' observance of human rights, would have to ensure that the peoples of the South are granted collective solidarity rights vis-à-vis the peoples of the North. Article 28 of the 1948 Universal Declaration of Human Rights provides the basis for this third generation concept, stating that 'everyone is entitled to a social and international order in which the rights and freedoms set forth in this Declaration can be fully realized'. The main rights of the third generation are the right to self-determination, which is primarily interpreted as colonial peoples' right

2.7. UNIVERSALITY, INDIVISIBILITY, EQUALITY AND INTERDEPENDENCE OF HUMAN RIGHTS

to political independence from the European colonial powers and to free disposition of natural resources, as well as the right to self-determined development which is closely linked to the former.

The concept of the three generations finds its normative expression in the two UN International Covenants of 1966 (the Covenant on Civil and Political Rights and the Covenant on Economic, Social and Cultural Rights, including the right of self determination as laid down in article 1 of both Covenants), as well as in the 1981 African Charter on Human and Peoples' Rights. It provided the philosophical and historical foundation for discussions on human rights ideology during the Cold War, yet it lives on in the minds of many people and politicians. It has formally been replaced by the principles of indivisibility, equality, interdependence and universality of all human rights (2.7.), and still it will be a long time before the shortcuts and one-sided assumptions of this generations debate will be overcome.

2.7. All Human Rights for All: Universality, Indivisibility, Equality and Interdependence of Human Rights

During the Cold War, the question of human rights was essentially a political one. The **western industrialized states**, in establishing the European Convention on Human Rights, had installed a highly efficient regional protection and monitoring system for civil and political rights and took it upon themselves to criticize the socialist states and the South for their gross and systematic human rights violations. Starting in the 1970s, the Conference for Security and Cooperation in Europe (CSCE), (8.), along with the United Nations (4.), began to serve as a platform for the human rights clash between East and West. On a bilateral level, the United States, as well as several European donor states and the European Union (9.4.), as of the late 1970s, were using their development policies to extract human rights concessions (3.1.6.).

The East did try to counter by pointing to violations of economic, social and cultural rights (especially the right to work) in capitalist states, yet in the human rights debate it was on the defensive from the very start. For one thing, the human rights situation was much worse objectively, and for another, representatives of the **socialist human rights concept** resisted any progress in international human rights protection (including, economic, social and cultural rights) by rejecting any meaningful international monitoring mechanism and delivering a persistent running fight for state sovereignty.

No doubt, the South had gained a major victory for human rights in its **battle against colonialism** and **for self-determination**, yet its active human rights commitment for the longest time did not stretch beyond that very area. Up until the 1980s, the South only seemed interested in three issues in the human rights context: the battle against apartheid, in the southern part of Africa, the right of self determination for the Palestinian people and the right to development (previously, the right to a new international economic order). Colonialism was conveniently used as a scapegoat for most other human rights issues, especially in Africa. Because of this restrictive point of view, many 'home made' problems were suppressed and the

2. History of Human Rights

South too found itself in the defensive as far as the human rights debate was concerned. Furthermore, the two regional human rights protection systems for Latin America and Africa were a far cry from what was expected and in many respects did not meet any of the European standards. It was not until the 1980s and 1990s, as the military dictatorships in Latin America and apartheid in southern Africa were overcome, that the South too began setting incentives out of its own accord.

At about the same time, the socialist regimes in Central and Eastern Europe began to collapse, and these **'velvet revolutions'** were also considered a victory for human rights. As the Cold War ended and President *Gorbachev's* vision of a 'common European house' was taking root together with a 'new world order' based on the principle of human rights and democracy, the time seemed ripe for a new, dramatic development in global human rights politics. The 1993 **Vienna World Conference on Human Rights** was to set out the parameters for these new politics (4.6.1.)

TEXTBOX 16

1993 VIENNA DECLARATION AND PROGRAMME OF ACTION

4. 'The promotion and protection of all human rights and fundamental freedoms must be considered as a priority objective of the United Nations in accordance with its purposes and principles, in particular the purpose of international cooperation. In the framework of these purposes and principles, the promotion and protection of all human rights is a legitimate concern of the international community...'

5. 'All human rights are universal, indivisible and interdependent and interrelated. The international community must treat human rights globally in a fair and equal manner, on the same footing, and with the same emphasis. While the significance of national and regional particularities and various historical, cultural and religious backgrounds must be borne in mind, it is the duty of states, regardless of their political, economic and cultural systems, to promote and protect human rights and fundamental freedoms.'

However, the preliminary stage leading up to the conference soon showed that the sense of awakening borne in 1990 had evaporated into thin air. In Central and Eastern Europe the ideological void created by the collapse of socialism had been filled by a policy of aggressive nationalism, which caused the disintegration of Czechoslovakia, Yugoslavia and the Soviet Union, and even led to the genocide of Bosnian Muslims in the Balkans. At the same time, opponents of the idea of **universalism** serried ranks in the South, especially in Cuba, the Asian and the Islamic states. They unleashed a new North-South debate, accusing the industrialized states of abusing human rights to pursue their neo-liberalist and neo-colonial policies of dependence. If it had not been for the more than 1,500 non-governmental organizations (NGOs) both in the North and the South, which parallel to the conference were trying to push through the idea of **'all human rights for all'**, the world conference would have foundered because of the issue of universalism.

2.8. FROM PROMOTION TO PROTECTION AND PREVENTION

On the very last day, following tough negotiations, the 171 states were able to agree on the wording of the Vienna Declaration, which states that all human rights are **universal, indivisible, interdependent and interrelated**. Notwithstanding national and regional idiosyncrasies and differences in historical, cultural and religious backgrounds, all states are obligated to protect human rights and fundamental freedoms.

This very clear statement seems to have settled the debate on human rights ideology and generations, if only on paper (2.6.), as there is still a call for action both in the North and the South. At the same time, the Vienna Declaration also aimed to put an end to the tiresome dispute on state sovereignty (3.1) by identifying protection of human rights not only as a **legitimate concern of the international community**, but a **priority objective of the United Nations**. That was to once and for all knock the bottom out of the argument (brought forth by China amongst others) that human rights protection was an exclusively national matter under article 2(7) of the UN Charter. This definition is deliberately overlooked by many politicians yet provides the direct link to the last part of this chapter.

2.8. From Promotion to Protection and Prevention

There can be no doubt that the real aim of national and international human rights protection must be to prevent human rights violations as far as possible. *Mary Robinson*, former UN High Commissioner for Human Rights, quite rightly defined the **21st century** as the **century of prevention**. Looking at the numerous gross and systematic human rights violations committed at the beginning of this century in all parts of the world, however, this seems to be no more than wishful thinking.

Nevertheless, we must not forget that the international human rights regime, ever since the Second World War, has set a number of serious steps towards implementing that very ideal. The UN Charter, for one, does not mention protection of human rights, but rather their **promotion**. Promotion over protection was chosen carefully at the time because international measures for the protection of human rights would have been considered an inadmissible interference with national sovereignty. All that international law permitted were promotion measures upon the request of states or measures agreed upon by the states concerned, such as holding seminars, deploying experts or carrying out similar activities considered as advisory services.

International measures for the **protection** of human beings against actions taken by their governments in those days required further specifications under international treaty law. Thus, the international community, in the decades that followed, was bent on preparing internationally binding human rights standards. Based on the 1948 Universal Declaration of Human Rights, a considerable number of general and specific, universal and regional human rights conventions have been drafted, adopted, signed and ratified, and thus accepted as internationally binding during the second half of the 20th century. All countries of the world, by ratifying at least one if not several of these treaties, have obligated themselves internationally to respect, fulfil and protect the human rights contained therein (3.2.1.).

2. History of Human Rights

However, the term international human rights protection or **implementation** is only applicable in those cases where international bodies (political bodies of international organizations, experts bodies, or international courts) are granted the right to **monitor** compliance with these international obligations. It was the European Commission and the European Court of Human Rights who took on the pioneering role in international human rights protection. They had been established by the 1950 European Convention on Human Rights (ECHR) to decide in cases brought under inter-state and individual complaints (5.2.).

TEXTBOX 17

THE THREE P'S

- **Promotion**
  - Standard setting
  - Advisory services
  - Human rights education

- **Protection (including Enforcement)**
  - Individual complaints
  - Inter-state complaints
  - State reporting
  - Inquiry and investigation
  - Fact-finding
  - Human rights field monitoring
  - Condemnation
  - Sanctions
  - Humanitarian intervention

- **Prevention**
  - Early warning and early action
  - Conflict resolution
  - Preventive visits to places of detention
  - Preventive deployment of civilian and/or military field personnel
  - International criminal law

Such procedures and others like them, e.g. state reporting and inquiry procedures, were also developed by the UN and other regional international organizations on the basis of human rights treaties. However, some of them are directly based on the charter of the respective organization, as in the case of the UN or the Organization of American States (OAS), others again were developed as part of politically binding standards (CSCE/OSCE).

These international monitoring procedures can only be considered effective once a monitoring body's decision or recommendation can be **enforced** against the state concerned. This in fact continues to be the international human rights protection regime's main challenge, but also its biggest weakness.

2.8. From Promotion to Protection and Prevention

There are still very few ways of enforcing measures against the will of individual governments and those measures that are used are applied with great caution. They include, amongst others, exerting diplomatic and political pressure, expelling countries from international organizations, reducing or suspending development cooperation, as well as imposing economic and other sanctions and conducting humanitarian interventions (16.3.).

TEXTBOX 18

From Declarations to Enforcement of Human Rights

- **Declaration**

non-binding document/resolution of political bodies (UNGA, Parliamentary Assembly, etc.), e.g.
- Universal Declaration 1948
- American Declaration 1948

- **Convention/Covenant**

binding international treaty, e.g.
- UN Covenants 1966/76
- European Convention 1950/53
- American Convention 1969/78
- African (Banjul) Charter 1981/86

- **Implementation**

human rights treaty monitoring, e.g.
- complaints procedure
- reporting procedure
- inquiry procedure

- **Enforcement**

sanctions and enforced measures, e.g.
- expulsion from international organizations
- economic sanctions
- humanitarian interventions
- international criminal tribunals
- reduction or suspension of development cooperation, financial aid, etc.

Efficient prevention of human rights violations still has a long way to go (14.). Governments generally are not too enthusiastic on being accused of human rights violations, which is why objective fact-finding, publicity, and 'mobilization of shame' (Amnesty International) are still the most effective **prevention strategies**. The better human rights protection mechanisms and their enforcement are functioning in practice, the more they also yield a preventive (deterrent) effect. This holds true for traditional mechanisms, such as complaints procedures, and for more recent measures, such as imposing economic sanctions and the establishment of an International Criminal Court. Other methods include early warning systems (provided they are employed in combination with early action), preventive visits to places of detention (the European Committee for the Prevention of Torture), human rights educational activities or deployment of preventive field staff. In practice, however, it is difficult to mobilize the necessary financial and other resources, as long as 'nothing has happened', even though preventing a fire is always cheaper than having to extinguish one. Furthermore, there is still widespread belief that prevention measures, especially field operations, constitute a violation of national sovereignty.

2.8. FROM PROMOTION TO PROTECTION AND PREVENTION

> LITBOX 2
>
> ### LITERATURE
>
> *Alston*, Philip and *Steiner*, Henry (Eds.) 2000, International Human Rights in Context: Law, Politics, Moral: Text and Materials, 2nd ed., Oxford
>
> *Ermacora*, Felix 1974, 1983, 1994, Menschenrechte in der sich wandelnden Welt, 3 volumes, Wien
>
> *Hayden,* Patrick 2001, The Philosophy of Human Rights, New York
>
> ICRC 1999, Respect for International Humanitarian Law: Handbook for Parliamentarians, Geneva
>
> *Ishay*, Micheline 1997, The Human Rights Reader: Major Political Writings, Essays, Speeches, and Documents from the Bible to the Present, London
>
> *Lauren*, Paul Gordon 1998, The Evolution of International Human Rights, Visions Seen, Philadelphia
>
> *Leiser,* Burton and *Campbell*, Tom (Eds.) 2001, Human Rights in Philosophy and Practice, Ashgate
>
> *Lohmann*, Georg and *Gosepath*, Stefan (Eds.) 1998, Philosophie der Menschenrechte, Frankfurt
>
> *Nowak,* Manfred 1988, Politische Grundrechte, Vienna
>
> United Nations 1996, The League of Nations, 1920-1946: Organization and Accomplishments: A Retrospective of the First Organization for the Establishment of World Peace, New York
>
> *Wasserstrom*, Jeffrey, *Hunt*, Lynn, and *Young*, Marion B. (Eds.) 2000, Human Rights and Revolutions, Oxford

3. INTERNATIONAL HUMAN RIGHTS PROTECTION – CONTEXT AND CONCEPTIONS

3.1. Human Rights in Context

3.1.1 Human Rights versus National Sovereignty

The development of human rights to date very impressively illustrates the tensions between national sovereignty and international human rights protection. Before the Second World War it was practically unthinkable for international law to interfere with the relations between states and their citizens (2.3). In fact, it was not until the Nazi holocaust that a gradual turnaround in people's thinking set in (2.5). The UN Charter does emphasize the promotion of human rights as one of its goals, yet at the same time, in article 2(7), it stresses the **principle of non-intervention in domestic affairs** (4.1). This meant that while during the Cold War so-called 'advisory services' were admissible with the consent of the state concerned, the same was not true for measures of international human rights protection, which were not to be imposed against the will of the government concerned. Indeed, such measures had to be based on international treaty law, as a result of which innumerable human rights conventions were elaborated on at the universal and the regional level, the main conventions being equipped with international monitoring mechanisms established for that purpose. Thus, when the European Court of Human Rights, in a judgment based on an individual petition, determined that the Austrian state broadcasting monopoly conflicted with the right to freedom of information, as laid down in article 10 of the ECHR, then Austria was obliged to abolish that monopoly and could no longer argue that this was an unlawful or illegitimate interference with its national sovereignty, as the government had voluntarily accepted the jurisdiction of the European Court as final and binding. Apart from these treaty obligations, the **dogma of state sovereignty** has gradually lost ground since the late 1960s in other spheres too. Milestones in this direction, amongst others, have been the special procedures of the UN Commission on Human Rights, the Helsinki Final Act of 1975, the Vienna CSCE Final Document of 1989, as well as the Vienna Declaration and Programme of Action 1993.

Resolutions 1235 (XLVI) and 1503 (XLVIII) were issued by the **Economic and Social Council** of the United Nations (ECOSOC) to authorize the UN Commission on Human Rights to accept complaints from individuals and NGOs in the event of gross and systematic human rights violations, and further, to examine these situations in public and confidential proceedings and take the necessary decisions, regardless of whether the states involved have ratified any human rights conventions (4.4.1.). Since the early 1980s, a growing number of country specific and thematic working groups and special rapporteurs have been established to carry out fact-finding and reporting tasks.

With the **1975 Helsinki Final Act**, human rights were made an essential element of the CSCE's political negotiation process between the West and East,

3. INTERNATIONAL HUMAN RIGHTS PROTECTION – CONTEXT AND CONCEPTIONS

which ultimately was instrumental in bringing down the socialist regimes of Central and Eastern Europe (8). For all intents and purposes, the CSCE negotiations proved a catalyst in the gradual dismantling of the state sovereignty dogma in human rights matters, as upheld by the socialist states. The most visible sign of this development is the **conference on the 'human dimension'** agreed upon at the 1989 Vienna follow-up meeting (8.3).

Following the end of the Cold War, the United Nations, at the **Second World Conference on Human Rights**, endorsed international protection of human rights as its legitimate concern (2.7). Since then, it is no longer legitimate to apply article 2(7) of the UN Charter to human rights matters. In those cases where human rights violations are considered particularly serious, i.e. where they pose a threat to international peace and security, the **Security Council** itself may intervene and decide on binding measures in accordance with Chapter VII of the UN Charter. Examples of interventions like these are South Africa, Iraq, Haiti, Somalia, former Yugoslavia, and East Timor (16.).

TEXTBOX 19
HUMAN RIGHTS VERSUS NATIONAL SOVEREIGNTY

Human rights as goal of the United Nations (article 1 UN Charter)	**Sovereign equality of states** as basic principle of international law (article 2(1) UN Charter)
Protection of human rights - UN Commission on Human Rights, since 1967/1970: fact-finding, reporting and complaints procedures - 1975 Helsinki Final Act - 1993 World Conference on Human Rights ('legitimate concern') - Binding measures set by the UN Security Council	**Non-intervention in domestic affairs**, (article 2(7) UN Charter)

Despite these clear legal findings, most governments criticized by international organizations, other states or NGOs for violating human rights, still argue that such interventions are inadmissible interference in their domestic affairs. This is true not only for typical opponents of international human rights protection, such as China, Iran or Cuba, but ironically also for the United States or the European Union (EU) countries which, otherwise, like to interfere with other states human rights issues. No doubt it will take many serious efforts to develop a new political awareness for the fact that human rights protection is a legitimate concern of the international community.

3.1. HUMAN RIGHTS IN CONTEXT

3.1.2. Human Rights Protection – An Atypical Task of International Law

Classical international law determines relations amongst sovereign states. Its beginnings, like those of private law, are rooted in customary law, while today, relations between states are primarily determined through bilateral state treaties or multilateral agreements concluded in the framework of international organizations. International law essentially draws on the **principle of reciprocity**, i.e. the existence of mutual-joint interests. Thus, if France were to conclude a bilateral agreement with Senegal on the exchange of students and France were not to adhere to said agreement, e.g. by admitting fewer students than agreed, then as a rule, Senegal would respond by also admitting fewer French students or terminating the agreement altogether. Disputes might also be settled through arbitration or referred to the International Court of Justice in the Hague. Multilateral treaties such as the International Coffee Agreement may also provide for exclusion from the organization as a last sanction against violations.

In principle, this system also works for the protection of individual rights in the context of diplomatic immunity and international humanitarian law. In the event that a state restricts the immunity of diplomats on its territory in a way contrary to international law, or even goes so far as to arrest, ill-treat or expel them, it runs the risk of reciprocal treatment of its diplomatic staff. The principle of reciprocity also holds true for armed conflicts. Thus, once a state knows that one of its soldiers has been made prisoner of war of an enemy state, it will adhere to no less than the minimum international humanitarian laws required to protect that person and have them freed.

Human rights law on the other hand primarily deals with citizens of a single state, in which case the principle of reciprocity no longer takes effect. While it is true that states enter multilateral treaties with other contracting states – committing themselves to respect human rights – in reality it matters little to them whether or not the other parties actually adhere to them. Many states ratify human rights treaties for the simple reason of showing that they accept this unique and universally recognized value system, or for unrelated reasons such as receiving development aid if they do so. Yet, every time a situation occurs in a country where other states parties would be called upon to safeguard adherence to human rights standards (e.g. political unrest), such criticism of the country in question usually fails in the face of economic and strategic interests, which are not curtailed by human rights debates, as in the case of China. This is where non-governmental organizations (11.) and independent media come into play as they are capable of mobilizing the public and reporting to generate widespread attention and sometimes massive political pressure. However, most governments are willing to take further action against regimes disrespectful of human rights in extreme cases only, i.e. if such states are waging international wars or offering shelter to terrorists (e.g. Iraq 1990/91 or Afghanistan: 16.11. and 16.15.).

Given the fact that adherence to human rights treaties is not ensured by the principle of reciprocity, **collective monitoring and enforcement mechanisms** have to be introduced. To that end, international organizations consider it their duty to

3. International Human Rights Protection – Context and Conceptions

protect human rights (e.g. the UN, Council of Europe, OSCE, OAS and OAU) and have developed a comparatively complex system of international (intergovernmental) bodies and procedures.

	Textbox 20
International Human Rights Law	**Classical International Law**
Individuals as subjects of international law	Only states as subjects of international law
Network of objective obligations, the enforcement of which is not primarily in the interest of other states	Reciprocity – mutual rights, obligations and state interests
Enforcement rather through international bodies ('collective enforcement')	Enforcement rather through state (re-)action

However, bearing in mind that there will not be a 'world state' in the foreseeable future, with its own police force in place for compulsory enforcement of international law, the international human rights system will primarily have to trust in national legal protection systems, as it did before. In some exceptional cases it will also rely on a gradually emerging international solidarity for collective enforcement of elementary human rights.

3.1.3. Human Rights Protection: International and National Law

Historically seen, early human rights developed as part of national constitutional law (2.2.). Today, most states have a constitutional bill of rights, which includes a more or less refined national legal protection system, as the case may be. Admittedly though, since the Second World War, these domestic bills of rights are increasingly being determined by international law. In fact, nowhere else have international law and national constitutional law interacted as closely. For want of effective intergovernmental enforcement mechanisms, international human rights protection continues to rely on a functioning national human rights protection system. **Transformation** of international human rights standards into domestic law is largely left to national constitutional law.

International human rights treaties are considered national law equal to, or superior to, the constitution by virtue of express constitutional order in those states, which tend to abide by the theory of **monism** with preference to international law (e.g. the Netherlands), provided they have ratified such agreements and such agreements have been sufficiently determined (self-executing). Others, which according to the **dualist theory** strictly distinguish between international and national law (e.g. the United Kingdom), may not incorporate or transform international human rights treaties into national law except by express order from the national legislator.

3.1. HUMAN RIGHTS IN CONTEXT

Thus, for states parties to conform with international human rights treaties, there is no requirement to transform them word for word into national constitutional law but rather that all the obligations contained under international law are **implemented** under domestic law. Many states, especially those with a historically grown bill of rights (e.g. the United States and Germany), seem to be of the opinion that their bills of rights automatically meet the requirements of international human rights law or are superior to the latter.

TEXTBOX 21
INTERNATIONAL AND NATIONAL LAW

- Primary responsibility of national authorities
- Subsidiarity of international protection of human rights
- Effective remedy at national level
- Exhaustion of domestic remedies as condition for international complaints
- Obligation to implement international human rights through legislative and other measures
- Incorporation of human rights treaties in national law desirable, but not obligation

---

As a result, international human rights treaties are frequently implemented at the level of ordinary laws only. Whenever their conformity with national constitutional law is put in doubt, many states resort to reservations under international law (3.2.4.) instead of reforming their constitutional bills of rights. However, approaches like these tend to bring about different national standards and with them, enormous problems of interpretation.

For example, the European Convention on Human Rights (ECHR: 5.2.) originally was directly applicable in only a few states as most governments were convinced of the superior quality of their own, national civil rights standards. It was the jurisprudence of the European Court of Human Rights that finally made it clear that such assumptions were incorrect in many cases. However, as national (constitutional) courts were forbidden to directly apply the ECHR and repeal opposing national laws or at least, interpret them so as to conform with the Convention, time and again the European Court in Strasburg had to be resorted to for the necessary legislative reforms to become effective. Seeing as this double track of national and European human rights protection was turning out to be counterproductive, most states (most recently the United Kingdom with its *Human Rights Act 2000*) gradually began to incorporate the ECHR into their national laws.

With this **trend towards incorporation**, which is beginning to show effect with some UN human rights treaties too (e.g. the International Covenant on Civil and Political Rights 4.3.1), it is finally possible to establish a well-functioning division of labour between national and international human rights protection. In summary,

37

human rights that are codified in international treaties are to be protected first and foremost by the relevant **national legal protection institutions**. International courts of human rights and monitoring bodies are only appealed to as *ultima ratio*, i.e. in the event that the national legal process proves unsuccessful or the treaties are interpreted in conflicting ways.

3.1.4. Human Rights Law, Humanitarian Law, Refugee Law

These three areas of modern international law, while closely linked to each other, need to be distinguished systematically. **Protection of the individual** is a priority for all of them. **Human rights** are standards defined in international treaties and national bills of rights, and as such, in principle are applicable both in times of war and peace (but see the derogation provisions: 3.2.4.). **Humanitarian law** on the other hand, especially the four 1949 Geneva Red Cross Conventions and Additional Protocols of 1977, define minimum standards for international and non-international armed conflicts to protect combatants (especially when wounded or held as prisoners of war), as well as civilians affected by armed conflicts.

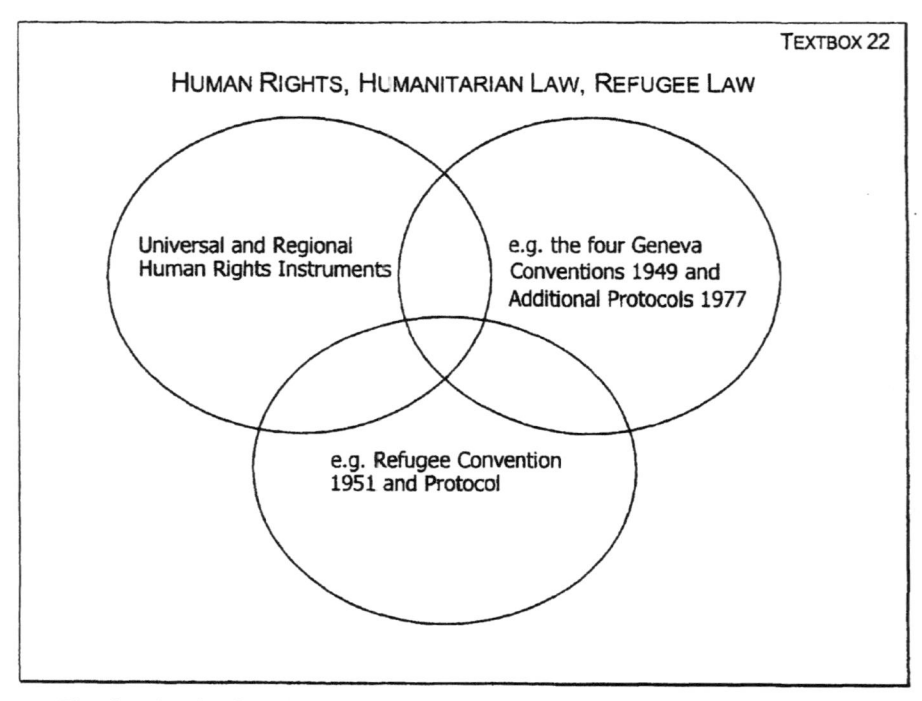

TEXTBOX 22

HUMAN RIGHTS, HUMANITARIAN LAW, REFUGEE LAW

- Universal and Regional Human Rights Instruments
- e.g. the four Geneva Conventions 1949 and Additional Protocols 1977
- e.g. Refugee Convention 1951 and Protocol

Yet despite the fact that human rights continue to be formally valid in times of armed conflicts, means of actual protection through national and international human rights bodies are rather limited. The International Committee of the Red Cross, on the other hand, because of its humanitarian role and consequently its

3.1. HUMAN RIGHTS IN CONTEXT

access to prisoners of war camps, has far more efficient means of protecting prisoners of war from arbitrary detention, torture or ill-treatment than national courts of an occupied state, the European or Inter-American Court of Human Rights, or the UN Committee against Torture. This is due to the fact that the principle of reciprocity under international law becomes effective in the event of international armed conflicts (3.1.2.).

Of course, **humanitarian law** only becomes effective in the event of **armed conflicts**. The main difficulty with this is how to distinguish between non-international armed conflicts, in which case the minimum standards of common article 3 of the four Geneva Conventions of 1949 and Protocol II of 1977 are applicable, and internal tensions, riots or actions by security forces to combat terrorism or guerrilla activities. In both cases, human rights tend to be restricted either legally or practically, yet only in the first case is this compensated, albeit partially, with the additional application of humanitarian law. Furthermore, most states, in fighting terrorism, are inclined not to consider relevant military action as armed conflicts in the sense of humanitarian law, as this would necessarily imply recognition of combatants and restrict their national sovereignty. The war rhetoric of the United States after the terrorist attacks of 11 September 2001 ('America at war' and 'war against terrorism') has done nothing to change this fundamental attitude of states.

Those most affected by a state of reduced international protection are civilians who are frequently involved in ethnically, religiously or politically motivated conflicts. In the event that the latter lead to violent displacements and the people concerned (so-called **internally displaced persons**) are unable to flee to another country, which in view of the rising number of violent internal conflicts and the unwillingness of traditional asylum countries to accept refugees is becoming more and more difficult, they have no recourse to protection under refugee law either. While article 14 of the Universal Declaration of Human Rights (4.2.) does mention the right of all persecuted persons to seek and enjoy asylum, this principle, in Europe at least, has not become part of internationally binding treaty law (but see article 18 of the non-binding EU Charter of Fundamental Rights, article 22(7) of ACHR and article II of the 1969 OAU Convention Governing Specific Aspects of Refugee Problems in Africa).

International refugee law only applies to recognized refugees and, in some cases, to asylum seekers too. Refugees as defined by the 1951 Geneva Refugee Convention are persons who, for well-founded fear of being persecuted on for reasons of race, religion, nationality, membership of a particular social group or political opinion, have fled to another country to seek asylum and who have been recognized by the competent authorities of that country as refugees under this Convention. Yet, with the growing immigration pressure on rich industrialized countries and the increasing xenophobia in these countries in recent decades, their willingness to accept migrants and refugees has diminished drastically. As a result, not only have immigration and alien laws become more stringent, but asylum and refugee laws have also been affected substantially. As immigration was made more difficult, persons who left their country for other, mainly economic reasons or because of social need (so-called 'economic refugees') also availed themselves of asylum procedures. This, in turn, meant that asylum laws were made even more stringent and persecuted persons have great difficulty being recognized as refugees. Spiralling restrictions play into the hands of organized crime or more specifically organized human trafficking, which is capitalizing enormously on the misery of persecuted persons. As a result, only a small minority of persecuted persons and refugees in this world are really protected by international refugee law.

Recognized refugees in the sense of the Convention, on the other hand, are equal in principle to the citizens of the receiving state with regard to the right to choose their place of residence, and other human rights such as with rights of equal access to education, work, social security and the courts. In particular, the state granting them asylum is responsible for protecting them from persecution, and for not expelling or returning them to the persecuting state (**principle of *non-refoulement***), as well as for granting them social support and integration aid should they need it.

Along with the refugee law under the Geneva Convention, which is based on the principle of individual asylum procedures, in the light of recent humanitarian crises (e.g. Bosnia and Herzegovina and Kosovo) a system of **temporary protection** on humanitarian grounds has developed in Europe particularly. This system provides that, instead of assessing individual asylum applications and granting refugee status to individuals, entire groups of individuals from these states are taken in collectively to be granted protection from persecution until they can safely return. Their status, however, is vested with far fewer minimum rights than the status of refugee as recognized under the Convention, and the fact that it is restricted in time and is followed by their repatriation creates additional uncertainties, and raises difficult political and social issues.

The **United Nations High Commissioner for Refugees** was established in Geneva in 1951 to support refugees and asylum seekers. It has since become the world's largest humanitarian organization and today increasingly takes care of displaced persons as well (4.4.8.5.).

3.1.5. Human Rights and Peace

Securing international peace and protecting human rights are major tasks of the international community. They have gradually come close to each other over the past decades and today are considered complementary. There are two reasons for this essentially. Firstly, the way human rights are threatened has changed. While in the early days human rights were threatened primarily by military dictatorships as in Latin America, or by totalitarian regimes as in Eastern Europe, most human rights violations today are witnessed in the context of armed conflicts. The latter are frequently motivated ethnically or religiously, yet in most cases they are far more deeply rooted in policies of discrimination or other systematic human rights violations. Thus, generally speaking armed conflicts are best prevented by adequate measures of human rights protection.

3.1. HUMAN RIGHTS IN CONTEXT

Secondly, the definitions for peace and international security have gradually been expanded. While peace used to be understood in a negative sense as absence of war, ever since the end of the Cold War a positive and **comprehensive concept of peace and security** has been developed that also includes human rights, the rule of law and democracy. In other words, dictatorships, which are suppressing their own civil society in general and their political opposition in particular and are systematically violating human rights, are considered a threat to peace and international security even if they do not pose an immediate danger of war to other states. Ensuring peace and security therefore is no longer primarily the responsibility of the military, but rather constitutes a complex task that is brought about effectively only through the concerted efforts of different parts of society. This is true both for national and international peace and security.

TEXTBOX 23
HUMAN RIGHTS AND PEACE

- Negative *versus* positive concept of peace
- Human rights as ingredient of peace – peace as condition for human rights
- Human rights violations as threat to international peace and security – 'humanitarian intervention'
- Human rights as essential components of peace-keeping/peace-building operations
- Human rights: an obstacle in peace negotiations?

This shift in the way peace and security are perceived, is best seen with the development of the UN **peacekeeping operations** (16.). Typical examples of classical operations during the Cold War are the operations on the Golan Heights and in Cyprus. From today's point of view there is no peace to keep there (after all, there are no peace treaties), but instead only armistice agreements, i.e. the absence of armed disputes. This task is carried out by lightly armed (blue helmet) soldiers positioned along the demarcation line between the two hostile parties. Their function is to observe whether armistice is obeyed or not. They may act as mediators in the event of minor violations, but for their own safety have to be withdrawn in the event of major violations. Other tasks such as creating the necessary requirements for sustainable peace are not within their competence.

The latter tasks are essentially those of a new generation of **peacekeeping and peace-building operations** such as those witnessed in the last decade of the 20th century in Cambodia, El Salvador, Guatemala, Haiti, Bosnia and Herzegovina, Kosovo, East Timor, Sierra Leone and other countries. These are based either on peace treaties brought about with the help and/or the pressure of the international community, or at least on preliminary treaties which provide for the conclusion of permanent peace treaties during the peace operations. Along with the military element (which is granted either by traditional, lightly armed blue helmets or combat

41

troops) this also calls for the deployment of police units and civilians. The police units generally recruited through the UN have the task of monitoring, training, supporting and, if necessary, reorganizing the national police force. The **civilian component** is responsible primarily for setting up democratic structures in accordance with the rule of law and human rights. Civilian tasks include carrying out and monitoring democratic elections, strengthening independent media and democratic parties, as well as setting up operational legal and administrative systems with their own bodies for the protection of human rights (administrative and human rights courts, ombuds institutions, national human rights commissions, truth commissions, etc.).

Given the fact that gross and systematic human rights violations today are considered a threat to international security, the UN Security Council, in accordance with Chapter VII of the UN Charter, is also entitled to impose **measures of constraint** against the governments concerned. Thus, it may exert diplomatic and political pressure, impose economic sanctions (arms embargo, boycotting air traffic and other means of transport and communication, and comprehensive economic embargo), and even carry out armed humanitarian interventions. These measures of constraint, too, have only become possible since the end of the Cold War, both from the political and the military point of view. Naturally, they are only applied as *ultima ratio*, i.e., in the event that other measures directed at protecting collective security, which have less of an impact on the sovereignty and territorial integrity of the states concerned, have proved futile. In the last decade of the 20th century, such **peace making and peace-enforcement operations** were carried out against Iraq (in 1991), Somalia, Haiti, Bosnia and Herzegovina (albeit only after the summer of 1995), the Federal Republic of Yugoslavia, East Timor, amongst others. The NATO air raids against Yugoslavia in the spring of 1999 were the cause of much controversy in this context, which from the political and the moral point of view were widely supported inasmuch as they were to prevent further systematic human rights violations and even genocide in Kosovo, but in the absence of a Security Council mandate must be qualified as a violation of international law (16.14). The Kosovo crisis and the United States-led war against the Saddam Hussein regime in Iraq in 2003 vividly show the limitations of the current concept of collective security in the context of gross and systematic human rights violations. If the UN does not want to leave humanitarian interventions to the United States, NATO or other military alliances, they will have to carry out a massive reform of structures in the Security Council and establish permanent UN military structures (in particular, a rapid intervention force) at the same time.

By the same token, during the last decade of the 20th century, the Security Council did set some very innovative steps towards **prevention** of armed conflicts and serious human rights violations. These include, amongst others, installing relevant early warning systems (which all too often were not followed by early action), deploying military units to prevent the spreading of armed conflicts (e.g. UNPREDEP in Macedonia: 14.1.), setting up commissions of experts to examine crimes under international law, as well as establishing international ad hoc tribunals

3.1. HUMAN RIGHTS IN CONTEXT

for criminal prosecution of war crimes, genocide and crimes against humanity in the former Yugoslavia and Rwanda (14., 15.).

3.1.6. Human Rights and Development

As peace securing, **development cooperation** as well, in the course of the past thirty years, has increasingly been merged with the tasks of human rights protection. Up until the 1970s, development essentially stood for industrialization and economic growth. This was based on the slightly naive idea that the so-called 'underdeveloped' states of Africa, Asia and Latin America had to be brought up to the economic standard of the industrialized North (Western Europe and North America). Development cooperation mainly focused on large industrialization and infrastructure projects, such as high-performance roads, industrial complexes, dams and similar projects of prestige. Not surprisingly, this form of development cooperation was primarily to the benefit of the corporations of the North and the political and economic elites of the South, and not so much to that of the general public in the so-called 'developing countries'. On the contrary, the gap between rich and poor widened and the spiral of 'overdevelopment and underdevelopment' accelerated, with stark contrasts between North and South, but also inside the societies of the South.

TEXTBOX 24

HUMAN RIGHTS AND DEVELOPMENT

- Human right to development *versus* human rights based development cooperation
- Development as a process for the realization of human rights
- Human rights as indivisible, universal rights
- Democracy, popular participation, good governance
- Human rights mainstreaming
- Prevention of poverty as a bridge between human rights and development

---

Bilateral and multilateral development policies (particularly those of the OECD, the EU and the UNDP) tried to counteract this by continuously establishing and revising development theories and strategies. Thus, they suggested overcoming the dependency of the South as revealed by the dependence theory (e.g. by improving the terms of trade and increasing prices for raw materials), including large numbers of the population in the development process (popular participation), emphasizing self-reliance in development, promoting the idea of sustainable development, and giving priority to poverty reduction as an over-arching principle of development cooperation.

3. INTERNATIONAL HUMAN RIGHTS PROTECTION – CONTEXT AND CONCEPTIONS

Since the late 1970s, several scholars and politicians of the South tried to establish the stagnating development issue as part of the modern human rights discourse by propagating a **human right to development**. In 1981, the African heads of state and government, under article 22 of the African Charter on Human and Peoples' Rights, espoused the collective right of all peoples (meaning in particular the citizens of African states) to economic, social and cultural development, and consequently the duty of all states (meaning, in particular, those of the North) to secure the use of that right through appropriate bilateral and multilateral measures. Not surprisingly, the states of the North were not willing to accept such a duty derived from a regional human rights treaty. Decidedly more caution was used in phrasing the **UN Declaration on the Right to Development** proclaimed by the UN General Assembly in 1986 (which nevertheless did not prevent the United States as the only state from voting against it). It defines the right to development as an 'inalienable human right by virtue of which every human person and all peoples are entitled to participate in, contribute to, and enjoy economic, social, cultural and political development, in which all human rights and fundamental freedoms can be fully realized'. According to the Declaration, the right to development is both an individual and a collective right, even so its article 2 defines the human person as the central subject of development, as an active participant and beneficiary alike. The duties of states (e.g. to devise appropriate national development policies) are primarily addressed to governments of receiving states, however, donor states too are called upon to cooperate and create international conditions for the promotion of the right to development. It is interesting to note that promotion, strengthening, as well as indivisibility and interdependence of all human rights were considered important elements of the right to development, even then. These concepts were also the main focus of the debate on universalism during the Second UN World Conference on Human Rights in 1993 (4.6.1.) and were incorporated into the **Vienna Declaration and Programme of Action** agreed upon with the consent of 171 states (including the United States). Article 5 of the Declaration sets out that all human rights are universal, indivisible, interdependent and interrelated. According to article 8, 'democracy, development and respect for human rights and fundamental freedoms are interdependent and mutually reinforcing', whereas under article 10, the World Conference reaffirms the right to development as defined in the 1986 Declaration on the Right to Development as an integral part of fundamental human rights. The Vienna Programme of Action as the basis of the UN Human Rights Programme after the Cold War, dedicated a separate chapter (articles 66 to 77) to the correlation between development, democracy and human rights.

Parallel to the demands of the South for a human right to development, as of the early 1980s, the majority of donor countries (especially the Scandinavian countries, the Netherlands and Canada, with the EU following suit) were becoming convinced that development cooperation was not to be granted irrespective of the human rights situation in the receiving countries. This meant, on the one hand, that donor states were entitled to suspend or even freeze development cooperation in the face of drastic deterioration of the human rights situation in their partner countries (so-called **'negative conditionality'**), while development projects were increasingly aimed at creating the necessary requirements for promoting and securing human rights (so-called **'positive measures'**). This new policy was revolutionary, particularly with regard to civil and political rights (implementation of projects to strengthen structures of democracy and the rule of law, i.e. elections, promotion of independent media, democratic parties, independent judiciary, as well as a civil service and police force respectful of human rights). As expected, it was reproached as interference with national affairs, or rather 'neo-colonialism based on human rights'.

This struggle over policies between the right to development advocated by the South and development cooperation contingent upon human rights stressed by the donor states of the North was, on the whole, diffused by a number of factors. For one thing, the UN Development Programme witnessed a paradigm shift towards **human development** in the early 1990s. UNICEF reoriented its policies on the basis of the Convention on the Rights of Child adopted in 1989, and the 1993 Vienna World Conference managed finally to grind out a compromise. This demonstrates that, on closer inspection, the different concepts are less antagonistic than their proponents in the North and the South pretend. Upon examination of the 1986 UN Declaration on the Right to Development the basic philosophy of development has changed fundamentally. Industrialization and economic growth, which used to be the objective of development, were gradually replaced by extensive realization of human rights, implying civil and political, as well as economic, social and cultural rights. Countries are no longer considered 'highly developed' simply because they have positive macro-economic statistics, but because of the number of people who have access to efficient education and health care, work, food, housing, social security, democratic governance, independent courts and a critical civil society and are able to live in safety and without discrimination; in other words, when **poverty** has been fought successfully and 'all human rights for all' (the NGO motto of the Vienna World Conference) have been implemented to the greatest extent possible. In practice, however, it will take some time for both the development agencies in the North and the political elites in the South to digest this **new development paradigm**.

3.1.7. Human Rights and Democracy, the Rule of Law, Good Governance and Popular Participation

Human rights and **democracy** are closely related to each other. Even though there is no binding definition of 'democracy' under international law, it is generally understood as a type of governance, which unlike autocracy (dictatorship), puts into effect the will of the people to the highest degree possible (sovereignty of the people), so as to meet or at least come close to the ideal of political freedom (the individual's self-determination through political participation) and political equality. As the European Court of Human Rights emphasizes in its jurisprudence, democratic societies also, and especially, call for pluralism and tolerance towards minorities and outsiders, which means that they must not become 'tyrannies of the majority'. As to the practical application of democracy, there are different forms such as the so-called people's democracy (based on the principle of the bound mandate), the plebiscitary or direct democracy (extensive direct decision-making on the part of the people as in the Swiss municipalities and cantons), as well as the representative or indirect democracy, where the people delegate most of their power of decision to freely elected representatives (members of parliament) by means of a free mandate. Representative democracy in turn distinguishes between parliamentary democracy as in the United Kingdom (sovereignty of the parliament, including the right to dismiss the government by a vote of no confidence), and presidential democracy as in the United States where the president, who has been elected by the people, is independent of parliament (congress) and has extensive competencies. Most modern states since the collapse of the model of socialist people's democracies have chosen the western model of **pluralistic representative democracies** as a form of governance.

The concept of democracy provides one of the philosophical foundations of human rights (2.1.). The ideal of political (democratic) freedom corresponds to the category of **political participation rights** in the narrower sense, i.e. the general right to take part in the conduct of public affairs either directly or through freely elected representatives (article 25 CCPR), the right of voting and being elected, the right to participate in popular referenda, the right of equal access to public offices, as well as the right of petition. Yet, the **political freedoms** as well (freedom of expression, media, information, association, assembly, trade union rights and in a wider sense also freedom of religion and belief, art and science) are indispensable if democracies are to work. Restrictions and limitations of the exercise of these political freedoms are usually only permitted to the extent of being 'necessary in a democratic society' (e.g. articles 9-11(2) ECHR), i.e. required by a pressing social need and proportionality. The democratic ideal of political equality and tolerance towards minorities is reflected in the right to equality before the law and equal protection of the law including a comprehensive prohibition of discrimination and protection against discrimination (article 26 CCPR), as well as different types of minority protection. Ultimately, the peoples' right of self-determination, by virtue of which all peoples may freely determine their political status (article 1 of the two UN Covenants), may also be considered a comprehensive guarantee of democratic governance. It has convincingly been argued to deduct a general **human right to democracy** from the sum of the above-mentioned rights.

The term **rule of law** (in the formal sense) refers to states whose legal systems, unlike those of police states, are well defined and have appropriate facilities in place to secure and adhere to statutory provisions. Above all, the rights and duties of persons must be defined with sufficient precision and their implementation must be secured through appropriate institutions, especially judicial ones. In other words, the rule of law essentially provides for **legal certainty** (predictability, transparency), as well as legal (judicial) protection and is to guard people against arbitrariness from the police and others. The Anglo-American terms rule of law and due process also

3.1. HUMAN RIGHTS IN CONTEXT

include a substantive aspect of justice and humaneness, which is to protect people from states of injustice in disguise (e.g. National Socialism).

As with human rights and democracy, the essential elements of the rule of law are reflected in today's human rights treaties. The **procedural guarantees** for the administration of civil and criminal justice (right to fair trial: e.g. article 14 CCPR) adopted from Anglo-American law constitute the core content of the rule of law.

TEXTBOX 25

HUMAN RIGHTS AND DEMOCRACY, THE RULE OF LAW, GOOD GOVERNANCE AND POPULAR PARTICIPATION

- **Democracy**
  - 'Rule by the people' (demos – kratos)
  - Ideal of identity between those who govern and those who are governed (*Rousseau*)
  - Right of peoples to internal self-determination
  - Political participation (in conduct of public affairs, elections, access to public offices/service), political freedoms (freedom of expression, information, media, association, assembly, freedom to form a political party)
  - Tolerance, pluralism, protection of minorities, equality and protection against discrimination are essential elements of modern democracies

- **Rule of law**
  - Legal certainty (legality, predictability, transparency)
  - Effective legal (judicial) remedy, procedural guarantees

- **Good governance**
  - Concept shaped in development context
  - World Bank concept: accountability, transparency, rule of law in public sector, prevention of corruption
  - EU concept: broader, includes democracy, civil society, human rights

- **Popular participation**
  - Concept shaped in development context
  - Grassroots involvement (the people) in decision-making at all levels
  - Human right to take part in conduct of public affairs, freedom of expression, association, assembly, right to vote

---

The principle of legality is embodied in the limitation clauses whereby restrictions of human rights are admissible only on the grounds of predictable and transparent legal provisions, which are in accordance with minimum standards of the rule of law (3.2.4.). The concept of the rule of law is also expressed in the provisions set out to ensure that people affected by human rights violations are granted the right to an **effective remedy before national and international courts** and similar human rights monitoring bodies, as well as the right to reparation (3.2.7.)

3. INTERNATIONAL HUMAN RIGHTS PROTECTION – CONTEXT AND CONCEPTIONS

While it is true that certain human rights, in the short term at least, may well be practiced by non-democratic regimes or regimes which are not subject to the rule of law, it is still safe to say that **democracy, the rule of law and human rights are contingent upon each other**. It is an empirical fact that well-functioning democracies governed by the rule of law are usually better able to protect human rights than autocratic police states. By the same token, past experience with processes of democratization has shown that the more human rights are accepted or gained, the more open states necessarily become towards democracy and the rule of law. The fact that human rights, democracy and the rule of law are inseparably linked to each other was first recognized in Western Europe, where in fact these three elements were made inalienable conditions for membership in the Council of Europe (5.1.), and later on, the European Union (9.2.). With the fall of the Iron Curtain, these three values were also established as the foundation of the CSCE/OSCE process, as laid down in the 1990 Paris Charter for a New Europe (8.5.). In addition, the Vienna Declaration adopted at the Second UN World Conference on Human Rights in 1993 (4.6.1) expressly defines democracy, development and human rights as interdependent and mutually strengthening concepts.

As a result of the above, human rights and democracy have increasingly become the target and main objective of modern day development cooperation (3.1.6.). This trend was first made evident with the claim for **popular participation**, i.e. participation of the majority of people in an ever more self-determined development process, and was complemented in the 1990s by the concept of **good governance**. The latter, in the eyes of the World Bank (4.5.6.), primarily refers to the rule of law, transparency and responsibility of the public sector (including the fight against corruption), while the EU pursues a wider concept based on the participation of civil society and the establishment of democratic and human rights structures within the development process (9.4.2.). Regardless of how these concepts are perceived, they both strongly favour the kind of development that will pave the way for democracy and human rights.

3.2. Human Rights Theory

3.2.1. Obligations of States to Respect, Fulfil and Protect Human Rights

In the early days it was assumed, in accordance with *Georg Jellinek's* status theory (status negativus = liberal rights of non-interference, status activus = democratic participation rights, status positivus = social rights requiring positive state action) and the theory of the three generations of human rights (2.6.), that states, with regard to civil rights, were merely obliged not to intervene whereas concerning economic and social rights they were obliged to perform positive services only. Only since it was made apparent that human rights are indivisible and interdependent (2.7.) it has gradually become accepted that in principle states are obliged to respect, fulfil and protect all human rights.

3.2. HUMAN RIGHTS THEORY

The **obligation to respect** human rights refers to the obligation to refrain from state intervention, provided the latter is not admissible under any relevant legal limitations and reservations clauses (3.2.4.). Unjustified interventions are considered violations of the human right in question. Thus, the right of life corresponds to the state's obligation not to kill; the right to physical and mental integrity corresponds to the state's obligation not to torture; the right to vote corresponds to the obligation not to arbitrarily exclude anyone from democratic elections; while the rights to employment, health and education correspond with the state's obligation not to arbitrarily exclude anyone from the labour market, the health care and the educational system. As the state withdraws from areas relevant for human rights, e.g. by privatizing and outsourcing the health care, educational system, refugee care, security and prison administration, and leaves them for the free market to take over, opportunities for direct state intervention and consequently the state's obligation to respect such rights are diminished. Yet, at the same time relevant obligations to fulfil and to protect increase, which means that extensive transfer of human rights obligations to private persons may result in violation of the relevant human rights.

The **obligation to fulfil** human rights refers to the state's obligation to take legislative, administrative, judicial and practical measures necessary to ensure that the rights in question are implemented to the greatest extent possible.

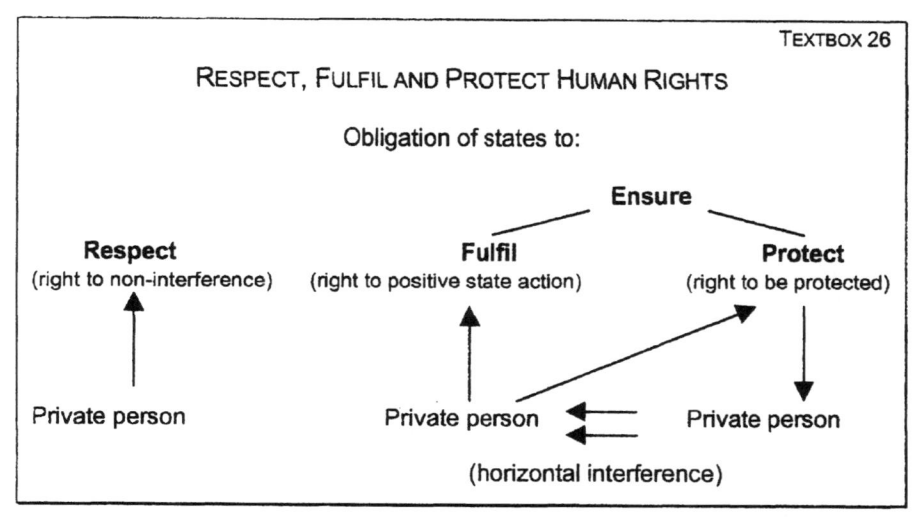

TEXTBOX 26

RESPECT, FULFIL AND PROTECT HUMAN RIGHTS

Obligation of states to:

Ensure

| **Respect** | **Fulfil** | **Protect** |
| (right to non-interference) | (right to positive state action) | (right to be protected) |

Private person | Private person ⟵ Private person

(horizontal interference)

Special emphasis in this context is placed on the concept of prevention (2.8.). Thus, the police force ought to be equipped and trained to take action against violent demonstrators or criminals (including everything from traffic offences to acts of terrorism) efficiently and professionally, employing the most lenient and suitable means of command and force possible in a given situation. If persons arrested are granted the legal and practical right to contact a person of their confidence (a lawyer, medical doctor or the consulate of their home country) immediately after their arrest, there is far less of a risk of them being ill-treated or made to disappear than if subject to extended *incommunicado* detention, i.e. detention without contact to the outside world. All of the rights need to be closely defined in a respective legal framework and in many cases concrete domestic structures of implementation need to be created or at least legally determined.

Thus, the right of equal access to a court inclusive of the relevant procedural guarantees during civil and criminal proceedings (article 6 ECHR; article 14 CCPR) calls for establishment of a sufficient number of courts, employment and training of independent judges, execution of fair and public proceedings, as well as a series of additional legal, administrative and judicial guarantees. The same is true for the right to vote and the corresponding obligation to create electoral offices and organize voting procedures which are in accordance with the principles of universal, equal, secret, free and democratic suffrage, at least as far as possible. Similarly, the right to work, social security, health and education requires the state to issue laws and establish a suitable administration of the labour market, and of social, health and educational services that will enable people to have non-discriminatory access to the labour market, hospitals, medical services, schools, universities and appropriate social institutions.

However, this does not mean that all the above-mentioned institutions have to be run by the state. The more structures with human rights relevance are left to the free market, the greater the state's obligation to ensure that the socially weak, the poor, children, the elderly, people with disabilities, foreigners and other endangered or disadvantaged groups, have access to the services they need. It takes several factors to define whether actual non-compliance with a positive obligation to fulfil is no longer justifiable and, therefore, constitutes a violation of the human right in question. These include amongst others: issues of state priority (political programme, distribution of existing resources), issues of economic reasonableness (especially with cost-intensive rights such as the rights to a fair trial, education or health, standards must be higher in rich industrialized countries than in the poorest of states; see articles 2(1) and 3 of CESCR), current social developments (e.g. political or economic crises), measures of **progressive realization** of human rights as well as the concrete facts of the individual case. These factors need to be weighed both in advance to assess the consequences of planned measures (impact assessment), as well as in retrospect during an objective (ideally a judicial) monitoring and accountability procedure. This is why it is imperative for economic, social and cultural rights to be recognized as 'justiciable' (2.7.) and subject to judicial or quasi-judicial assessment at the national and international levels. In no case are states allowed to take retrogressive measures which deprive people of the **core content** (minimum threshold) of human rights.

The **obligation to protect** human rights also requires positive state action, yet it is different from the above-mentioned obligations to fulfil inasmuch as it aims to **avoid human rights violations** by private persons. Although recognized in principle, the actual extent to which the state is to protect private persons is highly controversial and unclear in theory and practice as yet. Naturally, it is closely linked to the question of whether human rights are also effective at the horizontal level, however, it is not to be confused with what is known as 'the third party effect'. Nevertheless, the state's obligation to protect will be dealt with in the following chapter on horizontal effects of human rights.

3.2.2. Horizontal Effects of Human Rights

Due to their historical and philosophical origins, human rights are understood as being **'effective all-round'**, i.e. as a protection against all and any potential violators (2.1.). With the influence of liberalism in Europe and North America in the 19th century, this perception was, on the whole, lost and the constitutional protection of human rights was in fact reduced to mere claims against state interference. Only recently, in view of the development of international human rights law, the original broad understanding is gradually returning to our minds.

Violence in the family is an excellent example of this change in thinking. For the longest time, because of the influence of liberalism, domestic violence against women and children was considered a private matter protected by the human right of privacy against state interventions, as effected by the police and the courts in particular. As a result, rape in the family in many states was not punished and police and court officials refused to act as arbitrators in family disputes. It was the women's movement that pointed out with some vehemence that violence in the family was endemic to all societies of the world and that ultimately it did not matter to the women or children concerned whether they were abused at the police station or in their own homes, by their husbands, partners or fathers.

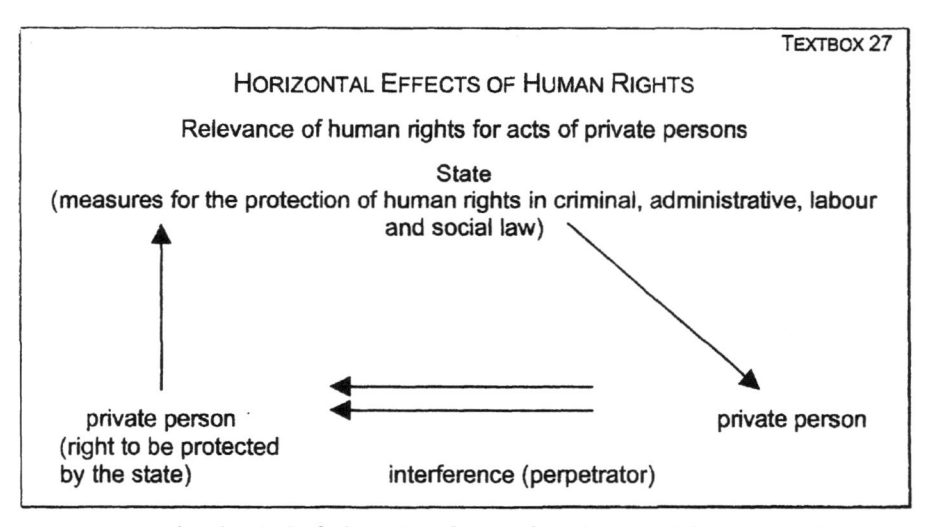

TEXTBOX 27

HORIZONTAL EFFECTS OF HUMAN RIGHTS

Relevance of human rights for acts of private persons

State
(measures for the protection of human rights in criminal, administrative, labour and social law)

private person
(right to be protected
by the state)

interference (perpetrator)

private person

As a result, the belief that this form of 'private' violence constitutes an interference with the human right to physical and mental integrity, gradually gained ground. During the Second UN World Conference on Human Rights (4.6.1.) the United Nations, in article 38 of the 1993 Vienna Programme of Action, stressed the importance of working towards the 'elimination of violence against women in public and private life' and in the same year adopted the **Declaration on the Elimination of Violence against Women**. In March 1994, the UN Human Rights Commission appointed a Special Rapporteur on Violence against Women (4.4.1.5.) to supervise compliance with the Declaration. In April 2002, the Commission recommended a fundamental international study on violence against children. According to the UN Committee on the Rights of the Child, violence against children in the family (e.g. corporal punishment by the parents) is an express violation of article 19 of the UN Convention on the Rights of the Child.

Most states are beginning to take legal and other measures to protect women and children from abuse. In Austria for example, under the Act on Domestic Violence in 1996/97, violent persons can be restrained by police or court order for the protection of their family and prevented from entering their home. The example of 'violence in the family' shows like no other, the shift of paradigms in international and national human rights law. Even classical civil rights, such as the prohibition of torture, are no longer limited to state actions. Of course, there is nothing new about this perception, as we know from the early development of human rights (2.3.). In the 17th and 18th century Europe, freedom of religion emerged as one of the first human rights as a reaction to the power of the Catholic Church over the individual. Similarly, the gradual prohibition of slavery and serfdom during the 19th century was never aimed at restricting state interference. On the contrary, governments intervened in order to liberate human beings from the traditional power of private slave-owners, slave traders and feudal landowners. Thus, human rights are directed both at violations by the state (the vertical level) and by private persons (the horizontal level), i.e. they are also effective at the horizontal level.

A totally different matter is the issue of **enforceability** (both at the national and the international level), which all too often is confused with the horizontal effect and as a result triggers debates on the effect on the third party. Of course, under **national law** there are a number of different bodies and procedures that are employed depending on whether human rights are violated by state bodies or private persons. Whenever a person regains their property by the judgment of a civil court, or a thief is convicted by a criminal court, the procedures and decisions taken by state bodies are enforcements of the human right to property at the national level similar to the decisions of constitutional courts declaring expropriation by the state as contrary to the right to property. Human rights perception that reduces protection of human rights to public law and its relevant bodies creates the false impression that only states can be accused of human rights violations.

International law on the other hand constitutes a legal order that essentially is valid between sovereign states only. Even though human rights are an exception only insofar as individuals are recognized as bearers of rights, the corresponding duty bearers are states (to some extent international organizations as well), which means that private persons are usually not directly obliged by international human rights treaties to act or refrain from acting. International criminal law alone may

3.2. HUMAN RIGHTS THEORY

subject individual perpetrators (persons responsible for having committed gross and systematic human rights violations, independent of whether they acted as state bodies or private persons) to responsibility (3.2.3., 15.). But the classical international procedures for the protection of human rights, such as the state reporting, complaints and inquiry procedures are exclusively directed at states. While the European and Inter-American courts of human rights are able to identify as part of their investigation competence which individuals are responsible for which human rights violations, their judicial decision that certain human rights have been violated, however, is exclusively directed at states. The cause of violation may consist in actions effected by state bodies or in refraining from effecting the necessary obligations to protect or fulfil human rights. In the event of slavery, serfdom, or violence in the family, the procedural matter is not the concrete violation by private persons, but the question alone of whether the state concerned has violated its positive obligation to protect, i.e. whether that state is responsible for the violation.

This **accountability** on the one hand depends on the type of human right concerned, and on the other, what measures the state has taken to protect against violations by private persons in general, and in individual cases. Naturally, this positive obligation to protect is strongest with serious human rights violations and also includes national criminal law. States with no or insufficient penal provisions against murder, genocide, torture, slavery, incitement to racial hatred, arbitrary detention or enforced disappearance, and where such serious human rights violations are actually committed by private persons, are in breach of their obligation to protect the respective human rights as well as the general **human right to personal security** (e.g. article 9 CCPR). The obligation to protect may, of course, also be exercised under private law (e.g. under matrimonial, family or property law), labour law, social welfare law or administrative law, as well as through actual measures. Thus, the right to work obliges states to establish appropriate labour laws and labour jurisdiction so as to protect employees against private employers' discriminating dismissals. Freedom of assembly also obliges states to protect peaceful demonstrators against violent counter-demonstrators. The right to vote obliges states to avert pressure and threats from private persons during elections, e.g. by ensuring a secret ballot. Ultimately, states are relatively free to decide how to meet their respective obligation to protect human rights on the horizontal level (3.2.5.). What matters is that they reasonably exercise that obligation.

In the German-speaking world, the debate on the so-called '**third party effect of human rights**' caused much upheaval and also some confusion. The term 'third party effect' (*Drittwirkung*) as such is rather confusing, because it is based on the false assumption that, in principle, human rights are directed against states only and it would take complicated procedures of interpretation to have them recognized as being effective against a third party, too. Furthermore, the discussion only addresses a comparatively unimportant part of the issue, which is whether human rights are valid under private law.

53

3.2.3. State Responsibility and Individual Responsibility

As mentioned above, according to traditional international law, only sovereign states (and some intergovernmental organizations) can be held directly responsible for human rights violations. Non-state actors (such as rebels, guerrilla organizations, transnational corporations and criminal organizations) or individuals are not answerable to such violations. Whenever non-state actors are found to violate human rights, only the states concerned are liable to legal action (that is, if the violation is attributable to them because they tolerated or indirectly supported it) and may be obliged to put an end to such violations by taking appropriate national measures. This would be the case with death squads associated with the military, but not with guerrilla activities, organized crime or transnational corporations, which are difficult to control, if at all. As the process of globalization under the conditions of neo-liberalism tends to further increase the power of non-state actors (in particular transnational corporations and organized crime) at the expense of governmental power (privatisation, de-regulation, phenomenon of so-called 'failed states', especially in Africa), such limitations of international law pose a serious structural problem and at the same time are a major challenge for the international human rights system of the 21st century.

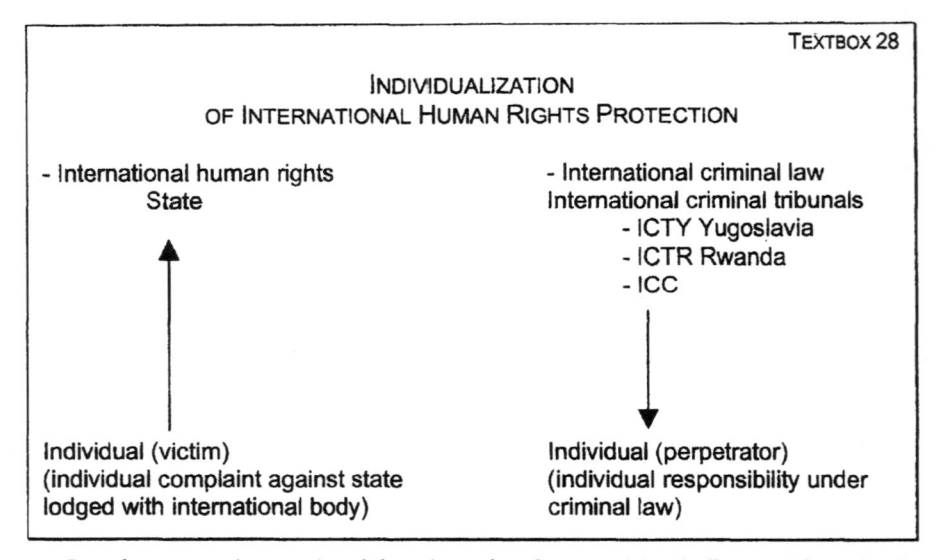

TEXTBOX 28

INDIVIDUALIZATION OF INTERNATIONAL HUMAN RIGHTS PROTECTION

- International human rights
State
	- International criminal law
	International criminal tribunals
	   - ICTY Yugoslavia
	   - ICTR Rwanda
	   - ICC

↑	↓
Individual (victim) (individual complaint against state lodged with international body)	Individual (perpetrator) (individual responsibility under criminal law)

In other areas international law has already met this challenge. Thus, in the event of non-international armed conflicts, international humanitarian law, in accordance with article 3 of the four Geneva Conventions of 1949 and the second Additional Protocol of 1977, is binding for non-state combatants (3.1.4.). International criminal law, which used to be applicable to armed international conflicts only, i.e. to war criminals responsible for serious international humanitarian law violations (Nuremberg and Tokyo criminal tribunals after the

3.2. Human Rights Theory

Second World War) is now also closely related to human rights law. As most human rights violations today occur in the context of armed conflicts (carried out for ethnic, religious or nationalist reasons) human rights protection is ever more closely linked to international humanitarian law (3.1.5.). As a result, international criminal law is now also applicable to gross and systematic human rights violations.

The most recent development of international criminal law began in 1993 with the establishment of an **International Criminal Tribunal for the Former Yugoslavia** by the UN Security Council. While this is responsible only for crimes carried out in the context of specific armed conflicts (Croatia 1991 and 1995, Bosnia and Herzegovina 1992 to 1995, Kosovo 1998 and 1999, Macedonia 2001), its competence is not restricted to war crimes, but also includes genocide and crimes against humanity (15.8.). **The International Criminal Tribunal for Rwanda** created by the UN Security Council in 1994 is the competent court for genocide, crimes against humanity and grave breaches of international humanitarian law in the context of the 1994 genocide, regardless of whether the events are termed as armed conflicts or not (15.5.). The establishment of a permanent **International Criminal Court** (15.6.) by the Rome Statute in 1998 proved a further step in the development of international criminal law, away from international humanitarian law. Thus, only war crimes and the crime of aggression have anything to do with armed conflicts. Genocide (in accordance with the 1948 UN Genocide Convention) and crimes against humanity, on the other hand, may also occur in times of peace and correspond to the most serious human rights violations. According to article 7 of the Statute of Rome 'crimes against humanity' include murder, torture, rape, enslavement, apartheid, enforced disappearances and other serious violations of the right to personal freedom, provided such crimes are committed as part of a widespread or systematic attack on civilians. Even though the term 'human rights' was avoided in the Statute, the crimes indicated in it are, in fact, nothing less than the most gross and systematic human rights violations. International criminal law has therefore become one of the potentially most effective means of implementing human rights and, in addition, has complemented the international responsibility of states with that of individual perpetrators (military and civilians, heads of state and guerrilla leaders, business and mafia bosses, terrorists and freedom fighters).

Persons accused of human rights crimes may not only be held responsible by international tribunals (whose competence, as with the ICC, in many cases is of a subsidiary nature only), but by domestic criminal courts as well, given the fact that serious human rights violations such as genocide, arbitrary executions, torture and rape are also considered crimes under national criminal law. In fact, states are obliged under international law to establish apposite penal provisions. According to the principle of territoriality, responsibility primarily lies with those states on whose territory the crimes were committed. In addition, states may exercise jurisdiction in case their citizens are involved in such crimes as perpetrators or victims. In practice, however, most states (above all where human rights were systematically violated) have not lived up to their responsibility under criminal law (practical **impunity** (*impunidad*) for serious human rights violations). Several human rights treaties such as the 1984 UN Convention against Torture, therefore, introduced the principle of **universal jurisdiction**, i.e. the competence and obligation of all states parties to detain suspicious persons and subject them to their own criminal jurisdiction in the event that the governments primarily responsible do not meet their obligations. It was not until the apprehension of the former Chilean dictator *Pinochet* by British police in October 1998 and the now well-known decision of the House of Lords, depriving him of his immunity as former head of state, that a new era began where impunity might gradually disappear (15.3.).

Yet, responsibility for human rights violations under criminal law is not the only manifestation of this current trend towards 'individualization of human rights'. Naturally, perpetrators, just like other persons, may (and indeed should) also be held responsible under civil, disciplinary or administrative law, which of course is primarily a national matter and competent governments are given fairly free play to act. Most recent discussions and developments in jurisprudence concerning the **right to an effective remedy** (3.2.7.), however, have shown that pressure from the international community is increasing. Furthermore, the possibilities of (international) **private law** have hardly been recognized as yet. As with environmental offences, victims of human rights violations are free to file injunctive or compensatory suits under civil law or assert other legal claims for redress independent of national borders. This possibility has hardly been resorted to, so far, which is partly due to the fact that the actual material and immaterial damage of human rights violations is difficult to calculate. However, if a victim of torture along with compensation for pain and suffering from the perpetrator, demanded payment for all social, medical and psychological rehabilitation expenses incurred by years of medical and psychological treatment and were actually adjudged these by the court, this could have a far more deterrent effect than any half-hearted penal and disciplinary state measures directed at the perpetrator. The collective claims successfully filed by lawyers of holocaust victims, more than half a century after the Nazi crimes (against banks and other private companies), and legal action recently taken before United States courts, against transnational corporations under the Alien Tort Claims Act, are evidence that a new way of thinking is emerging (17.).

3.2.4. Restrictions and Limitations of Human Rights

Only few human rights, such as the prohibition of torture or slavery are considered **absolute** or **unlimited**. In the event that an act of ill-treatment committed by a law enforcement officer meets the criteria defined under article 1 of the 1984 UN Convention against Torture (4.3.5.) with regard to the intensity of the physical and mental pain inflicted and the intention and the purpose pursued, this act of torture represents a violation of the human right not to be tortured, irrespective of theoretically valid moral reasons to justify it (e.g. the act of torture was committed to extort information on a bomb, the diffusion of which had saved many lives). In other words, international law in the case of this particularly condemnable human rights violation decided in favour of protecting the physical and mental integrity to prevent any strategies of justification on the part of the state. At the less serious level, i.e. the

3.2. Human Rights Theory

level of cruel, inhuman or degrading treatment, interpretation is of course a question of what is considered cruel, inhuman or degrading in each case. Every time the police arrest a person against his or her own will and every time police forcefully disperse a demonstration, they are in fact using force and thereby potentially interfering with the human right to physical integrity. When they do so in accordance with the proportionality principle, choosing the most lenient means possible (e.g. by using physical force instead of making use of firearms) and observing moderation, their treatment cannot by considered cruel or inhuman. By the same token, comparatively minor interventions, and even verbal injuries, may be considered degrading and, therefore, violations of this human right if it turns out that they were not necessary (3.2.5.).

The example shows that human rights in general cannot be considered absolute, but only have **relative validity** and that interferences with human rights are only regarded as violations when they are not justified. International human rights treaties are vested with a variety of means to **legally restrict human rights**. As the example of cruel and inhuman treatment shows, limitations of human rights begin with the definition of their respective **scope of application**. Not every act of police force is regarded as inhuman treatment; not every demonstration (especially those that are not peaceful) is protected by the freedom of assembly; and not every limitation of what we consider our own sphere of freedom is considered an interference with the human right to personal liberty. Generally, though, the scope of application of international human rights tends to be interpreted in a broad sense, which means that the argument put forward by several states, claiming that specific measures did in no way infringe upon human rights (e.g. for lack of intention), in most cases no longer holds true. Once a human right has been encroached upon, however, this is generally considered as **interference**, the admissibility of which needs to be assessed on the basis of the following limitation criteria.

TEXTBOX 29

Examining Human Rights Cases

- Scope of application – does the measure involve a human right?
- Interference – does the measure interfere with a human right?
- Justification – are there grounds for justifying an interference, provided the proportionality principle has been applied? Without justification (lawful restriction), an interference amounts to a violation.

As with international law in general, states parties to international human rights treaties are entitled to make **reservations and declarations of interpretation** at the time of signature, accession or ratification in order to limit or at least clarify their respective legal obligations. It is only with such exceptional cases as article 4 of the 6th Additional Protocol to the ECHR with regard to the prohibition of capital punishment that such reservations are expressly excluded.

Some treaties such as article 57 of the ECHR expressly allow reservations while limiting them to specific acts or measures of the state concerned so as to avoid reservations of a more general nature that tend to be very popular with many states. In the event that a treaty does not contain any relevant provisions, article 19 of the 1969 Vienna Convention on the Law of Treaties (VCLT) becomes effective which states that reservations not compatible with the aim and purpose of the treaty in question must be dismissed. It is up to the other states parties (e.g. by objections to specific reservations) and international treaty monitoring bodies (the European and the Inter-American Courts of Human Rights or the UN Human Rights Committee), to decide about the compatibility and validity of a specific reservation under international law.

Should these bodies arrive at the conclusion that a specific reservation is not compatible, it is declared null and void and the treaty is applied to the relevant state party as if the reservation had never been made. Thus, the UN Human Rights Committee decided that the reservation submitted by the United States, claiming that contrary to article 6(5) of the CCPR, minors could be executed, was not valid – yet to this day the United States government has not accepted that decision.

TEXTBOX 30

RESTRICTIONS AND LIMITATIONS OF HUMAN RIGHTS

- **Few absolute human rights**

  - Prohibition of torture
  - Prohibition of slavery
  - Recognition as a person before the law
  - Freedom of conscience

- **Most human rights can be limited under certain circumstances**

  - Reservations under international law
  - Derogation in state of emergency
  - Prohibition of abuse
  - Limitation clauses
  - Principle of proportionality

In the event of a **state of emergency** threatening the life of a nation (e.g. wars, serious violence, or natural disasters), states parties may seize measures based on express emergency clauses in many human rights treaties (e.g. article 4 CCPR; article 15 ECHR; article 27 ACHR) to **derogate** specific treaty obligations, in other words they may to some extent and for a certain period of time unilaterally set aside human rights. The relevant monitoring bodies also assess the admissibility of such measures. Particular rights such as the prohibition of torture and slavery or the prohibition of retroactive penal laws, as well as to some extent the right to life, personal liberty, freedom of religion and belief, are considered rights resistant to emergency which may not be limited even in the event of war.

3.2. HUMAN RIGHTS THEORY

The **prohibition of abuse** (article 5(1) CCPR; article 17 ECHR) represents a limitation, inasmuch as individual persons or groups must not exercise human rights (above all the political freedoms of expression, assembly and association) to the end of violating the human rights of others (the right to life and physical integrity or the rights of minorities and other discriminated groups). In the event of serious abuse (e.g. racist or religious indoctrination, war propaganda) states are even obliged to limit certain human rights in order to protect the human rights of others (article 20 CCPR; article 4 CERD; on the state's obligation to protect, 3.2.2.).

As a rule, states are free to decide to what extent and with what means to restrict human rights, provided they adhere to the conditions laid down in the relevant **limitation clauses**. One example is the lawful restriction of the freedom of expression and information under article 19(3) CCPR. The latter points out that the exercise of these rights carries with it special duties and responsibilities. To fulfil this responsibility, states are expressly authorized to interfere under certain circumstances: each and every interference must be provided for by law (as a rule by an act of parliament), it must serve a specific purpose (respect of the rights or the reputations of others, protection of national security, public order, health and morals), and must be necessary for the protection of these private and public interests. Evidently these interests (especially those of public order and morals) are defined rather vaguely and leave a wide margin of appreciation and assessment for the limitation of human rights by governments. This margin, however, is limited by the criterion of necessity, i.e. proportionality, so as to prevent abuse. It is a tricky tightrope walk between international (universal and regional) human rights protection and national sovereignty (e.g. for the protection of national peculiarities), which will be dealt with in the following chapter.

3.2.5. The Principle of Proportionality and the Margin of Appreciation

Human rights are international norms, which lay down regional (as in the case of Europe, America and Africa) and universal minimum standards for coexistence of people as well as for the relations between states and the people living within their territory. It seems that with the Vienna World Conference on Human Rights (4.6.1.), the political dispute on the universality of human rights (2.7.) was in principle settled and their universal validity recognized by all states. However, the 1993 Vienna Declaration also emphasizes the need to take into account national and regional peculiarities of peoples derived from their religious and cultural traditions. The best normative way for states to do this is using their competence to implement, regulate and, if necessary, restrict human rights in their domestic legal system in accordance with the respective limitation clauses.

Based on the limitation clauses of the ECHR, the European Court of Human Rights developed the doctrine of a **fairly wide margin of appreciation**, which of course is applicable to other areas, as well. Wherever governments are convinced that specific national values or traditions are threatened by the extensive application of international human rights standards and restrict certain rights in the form of a law that is clear and foreseeable for those it affects, such limitations are generally accepted if justified by preservation of public order or similar reasons.

Wherever governments convincingly argue for the need for such limitations during international monitoring procedures, especially during individual complaints procedures, the relevant monitoring bodies will generally be inclined to give precedence to national sovereignty over excessive interpretation of international standards. This is true even more for states forbearing their positive obligation to protect and ensure than for those actively interfering with human rights. Economic reasons in particular are usually respected, as many states are unable to make the investments necessary to fully ensure certain rights. In fact there are different standards for poorer and richer states in this context.

On the other hand, the **principle of proportionality** has the function to avoid abuse by states. Governments with the intent to directly interfere with rights such as privacy, freedom of religion, expression and assembly not only have to legitimately justify their action but they actually have to prove that their intervention is necessary for the protection of the respective interests.

TEXTBOX 31

THE PRINCIPLE OF PROPORTIONALITY

- The measure – aim relation
- Aptitude of measure
- Necessity of measure
- Final balancing of interests ('necessary in a democratic society' – 'pressing social need')

The European Court of Human Rights in this context developed the criterion of **pressing social need,** as a requirement for justifying restrictions. Some limitation clauses (article 21 CCPR; article 8(1) CESCR; articles 8-11(2) ECHR; articles 15 and 16(2) ACHR) place special emphasis on the requirement of necessity by introducing the argument of the **democratic society,** which means that the governments concerned must prove that even a democratic society based on the principles of openness and tolerance cannot possibly accept the way some human rights are exercised. This is all the more difficult if the same behaviour is tolerated or accepted by other (comparable) societies. Thus, the Irish government in the ECHR case of *Norris* was not able to prove that a general penal prohibition of homosexuality (an interference with the right to privacy in accordance with article 8(2) ECHR) was really necessary to protect morals (especially Catholic morals) in a democratic European society of the late 20th century.

Norris, as the similar cases of *Dudgeon* v. *the United Kingdom* and *Modinos* v. *Cyprus*, is also a good illustration of how interferences with human rights are closely examined on the basis of the proportionality principle. For one thing, the actual interference must present a **suitable** means of achieving a purpose (in this case protection of morals), which in the case of penal prohibition of homosexuality is certainly true. For another, interferences are only proportional if they represent the **most lenient** means of achieving said purpose. To demonstrate that a general penal prohibition really was the most lenient means, the respective government would have to prove that all other legal and factual measures (e.g. not recognizing homosexual partnerships under family law, penal measures for the protection of children and young persons, educational measures, etc.) would not be sufficient or effective. Finally, all interferences must observe **moderation,** i.e. the sentence imposed or to be imposed on the applicant must be in proportion to the purpose of the interference (in the *Norris* case the protection of Catholic morals).

Thus, the proportionality principle serves as a measure of the necessity of interferences in the context of limitation clauses. In addition, it is one of the main principles used to balance between international human rights standards and national sovereignty, i.e. the implementation or lack of implementation of human rights by individual states. Essentially the proportionality principle is to protect against arbitrary state conduct. In fact the **prohibition of arbitrariness,** which equally refers to the states' obligation to respect, fulfil and protect human rights (3.2.1.) runs through the entire human rights system (e.g. articles 6(1), 9(1) and 17(1) CCPR). The most important expression of the prohibition of arbitrariness is the prohibition of discrimination, which is the subject of the following chapter. After all, human rights limitations, which discriminate against certain groups of people (in our case homosexuals), never qualify as proportional.

3.2.6. Prohibition of Discrimination

The prohibition of discrimination is part of the **human right of equality** (article 26 CCPR), yet at the same time it is a principle applicable to all human rights alike. After all, international human rights protection was established in reaction to the systematic discrimination practiced by National Socialists (2.5.). One of the main aims of the United Nations, therefore, is to counteract all types of discrimination. This is reflected in the 1948 Convention on Genocide, the 1965 Convention on the Elimination of All Forms of Racial Discrimination (4.3.3.), the 1979 Convention on the Elimination of All Forms of Discrimination against Women (4.3.4.), the successful battle against Apartheid in Southern Africa, as well as several other measures. Most general human rights treaties include a so-called **accessory prohibition of discrimination** (e.g. article 2 in both UN Covenants; article 2 CRC; article 14 ECHR; article 1 AHRC; article 2 of the African Charter) whereby all states parties commit themselves to ensure the rights of the relevant treaties for everyone without any discrimination whatsoever, and furthermore to counteract certain forms of distinction which because of past experience are highly disapproved of, such as distinctions on the grounds of race, colour, language, birth and religion, gender, national or social origin. More recently, other distinction criteria such as sexual orientation, age, disability, and belonging to national minorities were also declared highly condemnable (e.g. article 13 EC Treaty).

However, distinctions for the above mentioned and other reasons are only considered discrimination if they cannot be objectively, i.e. reasonably justified. Of course, it is difficult to say which differences are **objectively justified** as far as human rights are concerned, because they always depend on the **societal values**, which again may change with time, place, culture, religion, etc. The **status of women**, for example, has changed fundamentally over the course of the past century. As a result, distinctions which not too long ago were deemed to be objectively justified (e.g. in the enjoyment of rights to vote, work, education, social security, etc.), today are generally considered discriminatory. Particularly in this field, however, there are enormous differences in perception between fairly emancipated societies such as Sweden, and traditionally Islamic societies like Saudi Arabia. Enforcing the universal prohibition of discrimination while simultaneously respecting cultural and religious traditions is no doubt a very difficult and sensitive task for international human rights monitoring bodies to accomplish.

TEXTBOX 32
PROHIBITION OF DISCRIMINATION

- Equality and non-discrimination as pillars of human rights protection
- Equality in fact demands equality in law
- Difference in facts demands differentiation in law
- Highly disapproved distinction criteria: race, colour, sex, religion, language, national and social origin, sexual orientation, age, disability, belonging to a minority/indigenous group
- Distinctions based on reasonable and objective grounds do not constitute discrimination
- Principle of proportionality as the test for the reasonableness of distinctions

---

Therefore, the UN Human Rights Committee, in the Dutch social security cases, decided that traditional gender-specific distinctions in the pension and social insurance laws (based on the 'breadwinner' concept) constituted violations of article 26 CCPR. At the same time, the question arises as to whether this measure also applies to traditional societies where women are discriminated against in much more serious ways (ritual killings, female genital mutilation (FGM), polygamy, forced marriage, strict dress regulations for religious reasons, prohibition of occupation).

The prohibition of discrimination is particularly important in the context of **economic, social and cultural rights**, because disadvantaged groups, such as women, ethnic or religious minorities, homosexuals or persons with disabilities are discriminated against especially when trying to access the labour or housing market, educational and health care institutions, as well as social services. As the case law of the Human Rights Chamber for Bosnia and Herzegovina (16.9.), which found in many cases systematic discrimination in the enjoyment of the rights to work,

3.2. HUMAN RIGHTS THEORY

housing or social security, illustrates, the prohibition of discrimination is also used as a means to overcome the still widespread assumption that such rights are not 'justiciable' (2.6., 3.2.1.).

3.2.7. Right to Effective Remedy and Reparation for Human Rights Violations

Similar to the prohibition of discrimination, the right to a remedy before domestic authorities in the event of human rights violations, as laid down in general human rights treaties (article 2(3) CCPR; article 14 ECHR; article 25 ACHR; article 26 of the African Charter), is also an accessory provision, i.e. it can only be invoked in conjunction with another human right. The **right to a remedy** guarantees a procedural and a substantive claim. At the **procedural level** states commit themselves to establishing suitable institutions to take decisions on alleged human rights violations during a procedure determined by the rule of law.

TEXTBOX 33
RIGHT TO REMEDY AND REPARATION FOR HUMAN RIGHTS VIOLATIONS

- Right to effective remedy at the national level, e.g. article 2(3) CCPR; article 13 ECHR
- Access to justice
- Adequate, effective and prompt reparation (right to reparation)
- Access to factual information concerning violations (right to the truth)
- State obligation to investigate and punish perpetrators
- Are amnesty provisions permissible?

Forms of Reparation
(*Van Boven/Bassiouni* – Guidelines)

- **Restitution**: restitution of property, release of prisoners
- **Compensation**: for material and immaterial damage
- **Rehabilitation**: legal, psychological, medical and social measures, e.g. rehabilitation of torture victims
- **Satisfaction**: truth commission, criminal persecution of perpetrators, apology
- **Guarantees of non-repetition**: e.g. amendments in the law

---

It is primarily judicial bodies (ordinary courts, constitutional and human rights courts), which decide on the complaints of victims of alleged human rights violations. Penal and civil courts may also grant legal remedy, as do ombuds institutions, national human rights commissions, equal opportunity bodies and other similar institutions. What is important in all this is that the victims of alleged human rights violations themselves may initiate such procedures, because exhaustion of domestic remedies is one of the prerequisites for admitting international human rights complaints (12.3.). This corresponds to the general principle of international law whereby legal remedy against human rights violations is primarily to be ensured at the **national level**, while international bodies are to provide subsidiary remedy only.

At the substantive level, the right to a remedy shall provide **reparation** to victims of human rights violations. What victims perceive as reparation is different in each case and largely depends on the type and gravity of the human rights violation, but also on the way the persons affected perceive justice. In many cases the mere fact that a human rights violation has been recognized as such by a court or truth commission is considered sufficient satisfaction. In those cases where **restitutio in integrum** is possible (e.g. restitution of expropriated property, release of prisoners, reemployment of previously dismissed persons, granting access to courts, a home, educational and health care institutions), this is of course the best form of reparation along with **provisional/interim measures** for the prevention of imminent human rights violations (non-execution of a death penalty, an eviction or deportation decision).

There are many human rights violations already committed (genocide, arbitrary execution, torture, unlawful dispersal of demonstrations) where restitution is no longer possible. Other ways of reparation have to be found, such as financial **compensation** for the material and immaterial damage suffered, **rehabilitation** (e.g. medical, psychological or social care of victims of torture), as well as other forms of **satisfaction** (public apologies, guarantees of non-repetition, changes in the law, social services for the victims or surviving dependents). For cases of serious human rights violations, truth commissions, criminal investigations as well as appropriate penal, civil, and disciplinary **measures against the individual perpetrators** are increasingly considered as adequate forms of reparation (3.2.3.).

As with the procedural component again the principle holds true that reparation ought to be ensured primarily by national bodies, taking into account that for some human rights violations, such as arbitrary detention and for miscarriages of justice, the right to compensation is actually part of the respective human right (e.g. articles 9(5) and 14(6) CCPR). International human rights courts have a subsidiary role and are partially entitled to award compensation and other forms of reparation (article 41 ECHR; article 63 ACHR; article XI of Annex 6 of the Dayton Peace Agreement for Bosnia and Herzegovina).

In practice the right to legal remedy has been neglected for some time, but is now becoming increasingly important in the case law of international human rights bodies, as well through the current efforts of the UN Commission on Human Rights to draft guidelines on the right to remedy and reparation. Reparation for past human rights violations (slavery, colonialism, racism) played a particularly controversial role during the preparations for the 2001 World Conference against Racism in Durban (4.6.4.).

3.2.8. Rules of Interpretation of Human Rights Treaties

As with all international treaties, interpretation of human rights treaties is primarily subject to the rules of interpretation as laid down under article 31 of the Vienna

3.2. HUMAN RIGHTS THEORY

Convention on the Law of Treaties (VCLT), which states that treaties are to be interpreted 'in good faith in accordance with the ordinary meaning to be given to the terms of the treaty in their context and in the light of its object and purpose'. The general linguistic usage (**ordinary meaning of a term**) may only be deviated from if the parties involved have intended a special meaning. For **systematic interpretations** (terms in their context) it is necessary not only to consider the entire text of a treaty including its preamble and annexes, but the deeds and agreements between the parties relating to the treaty, as well as all subsequent agreed **practices in the application of the treaty**.

Supplementary means of interpretation (the **travaux préparatoires** in particular) may only be resorted to in accordance with article 32 VCLT where the general rules of interpretation leave the meaning ambiguous or obscure, or lead to a result that is manifestly absurd or unreasonable. Essentially the emphasis is on interpreting treaties under international law in the light of their **object and purpose**. Where different yet authentic linguistic versions deviate from each other, precedence is to be given to the version that comes closest to the object and purpose of the treaty as a whole. With human rights treaties, naturally the main object is for states parties to protect the rights set out in the treaties. Especially with human rights treaties, however, it is often difficult to say whether interpretations, that limit the protection of human rights, are still in harmony with the object and purpose of the treaty as a whole.

TEXTBOX 34

RULES OF INTERPRETATION OF HUMAN RIGHTS TREATIES

- Interpretation 'in light of object and purpose'
- Dynamic interpretation (living instrument)
- *Effet utile* ('not theoretical and illusory, but practical and effective')
- Autonomous interpretation
- Restrictive interpretation of national human rights limitations
  - In dubio pro libertate et dignitate
  - Proportionality principle
  - Prohibition of discrimination

Thus, the UN Human Rights Committee decided in the case of *Kennedy v. Trinidad and Tobago* in 1999, that the object and purpose of the 1st Optional Protocol to the CCPR was to monitor the obligations of the treaty by an individual complaints procedure. Consequently, a reservation that excludes a particular group of persons (i.e. prisoners sentenced to death) from the right to file an individual complaint was not reconcilable with the object and purpose of the 1st Optional Protocol to the CCPR. International monitoring bodies are generally of the opinion that in **cases of doubt as to object and purpose, interpretation should favour the protection of the individual**, i.e. their freedom and dignity (*in dubio pro libertate et* *dignitate*). This is why limitation clauses (3.2.4.), in case of doubt, are to be interpreted restrictively taking into account the proportionality principle (3.2.5.) as well as the prohibition of discrimination (3.2.6.)

This pro human rights interpretation maxim provides the basis for a number of more specific interpretation rules, which, among others, the European Court of Human Rights developed during its many years of practice with the ECHR and which today in principle are recognized for all human rights treaties. These rules include the **principle of dynamic interpretation**. Back in 1978, the Court decided in the case *Tyrer v. the United Kingdom* that even fairly mild corporal punishment as still practiced then with adolescents on the Isle of Man, had to be considered a degrading punishment and therefore a violation of article 3 of the ECHR. It was then that the Court first introduced the formula of the ECHR as a living instrument not to be interpreted separately from the circumstances at the time. In other words, once terms such as torture, inhuman and degrading treatment or punishment change their meaning in the everyday usage of European societies, it is no longer admissible to rigidly stick to the meaning of a term coined in 1950 when most European states still did not consider corporal punishment degrading.

In 1979, a judgment was rendered in the case of *Airey v. the Republic of Ireland*, which concerned the question of whether, from the right to fair trial as laid down in article 6 of the ECHR, it was possible to derive the right of access to a court, whereby states parties would have a positive obligation to ensure that right. Since then, the Court has been using the interpretation rule of the '*effet utile*', which means that the Convention does not guarantee rights which are theoretical and illusory but those which are practical and effective. Thus, the Irish government in the concrete case of a procedure for legal separation of a marriage, would have had to make available to the applicant legal aid, irrespective of the fact that such claims, under the Convention, are explicitly intended for criminal proceedings only. Although the ECHR repeatedly refers to national legal systems (as with the limitation clauses), the terms for defining the scope of application of specific rights must be interpreted autonomously if protection is not to remain illusory. Interpretation of the terms 'civil rights and obligations' and 'criminal charge' as in article 6(1) of the ECHR, for example, cannot be subject to the meaning of these terms under civil and penal law of the states parties or the competence of national courts. After all, the purpose of a human right of access to an independent tribunal is to define at the level of international law which matters are too important to be decided on by an administrative authority bound by instructions, and rather have to be taken before an independent and impartial court. A treaty, however, will have to use fairly vague terms to arrive at such definitions. Ultimately the Court itself has to give an **autonomous interpretation** of the meaning of 'civil rights and obligations' and 'criminal charge'. This in fact required extensive changes in the laws in continental European states with a highly developed system of administrative law and administrative procedures not subject to judicial review, and therefore was the cause of heavy criticism on the part of governments and scholars.

3.3. Overview of the International Human Rights System

When we speak about the international human rights system we usually intend the standards, bodies and procedures under international law developed by intergovernmental organizations to protect human rights. Yet, at the bilateral level as well, governments, in their foreign, economic and development policies, are increasingly exerting pressure on other governments to respect their obligations concerning international human rights. The influence of **non-governmental human rights organizations** (NGOs) such as Amnesty International or Human Rights Watch must not be underestimated. Both by themselves and as the driving force behind the intergovernmental human rights system, they embody the human rights conscience of the international community and represent an important element of the international civil society (11.). The following overview is, however, limited to the main characteristics of **intergovernmental organizations**, which have defined the protection of human rights as a major task of theirs and are trying to enforce that protection with multilateral bodies and treaties.

Universal human rights protection is carried out by the **United Nations** and its specialized agencies (4.). Not only did the United Nations develop the majority of international human rights standards (treaties, declarations, bodies of principles, guidelines and other instruments of international 'soft law'), but they also created a complex system of universal bodies and procedures to monitor compliance with human rights. Their strength lies not so much in the procedures for enforcement of international treaties (human rights covenants and special conventions), but rather in the activities of their political bodies (especially the General Assembly and the Human Rights Commission), also referred to as **multilateral diplomacy;** of particular significance in this context are the special procedures, i.e. the different thematic and country-specific working groups, experts and special rapporteurs. During the past decade, the Security Council has increasingly become involved in the human rights process, as with the establishment of a new generation of complex peace operations (16.) or the development of the international criminal law applied in ad hoc tribunals (15.4, 15.5.). The growing importance of human rights after the Cold War was further emphasized by the establishment of the UN High Commissioner for Human Rights in Geneva. Various special programmes (e.g. UNDP, UNICEF) and legally independent specialized agencies (e.g. ILO, UNESCO, WHO, FAO) were installed to support practical field operations, especially those for the implementation of economic, social and cultural rights.

Unlike the United Nations most **regional organizations** are primarily occupied with enforcing human rights treaties. One of the pioneers in this was the **Council of Europe,** which adopted the European Convention on Human Rights in 1950 (5.2.). While in the beginning the intergovernmental element prevailed (inter-state complaints, decisions taken by the Committee of Ministers), ultimately the system of **individual complaints** asserted itself. The latter may be filed with an independent (since 1998 also a permanent and professional) European Court of Human Rights against all member states of the Council of Europe. The procedural right of victims of alleged human rights violations to bring an action against their governments before an international court, though a trademark of the Council of Europe, is limited to civil and political rights only, and to the mere ascertainment of human rights having been violated. The Court cannot oblige states to undertake measures of reparation (3.2.7.) beyond those of a (usually quite modest) financial compensation. The second innovation introduced by the Council of Europe is a preventive system of visits to all places of detention to be carried out by the European Committee for the Prevention of Torture to avert acts of torture and ill-treatment.

The second most important regional organization is the **Organization of American States (OAS),** which since the Second World War, has also developed a system of inter-state and individual complaints to be filed before independent expert bodies (6.). The latter system, however, is less efficient than that of the Council of Europe. Most complaints are brought before the Inter-American Commission on Human Rights, and the Inter-American Court, by comparison, has decided in only a few cases. The Organization's authority over its member states also leaves a lot to be desired. Indeed, the Commission's country reports seem to have more of an impression on the governments concerned. The reasons for this apparent failure of the Inter-American human rights system are manifold: the political, social and economic heterogeneity of the OAS states, the stark differences in poverty among the states linked to the lack of political willingness to protect human rights. Another factor is the dominant and highly controversial role played by the United States. On the one hand, the United States and its doctrine of 'national security' has been directly or indirectly responsible for some of the worst human rights violations in Chile and other Latin American countries. While strongly criticizing and sanctioning left wing governments (such as Cuba or the former Sandinista government in Nicaragua) for their human rights violations, the United States government has so far declined to ratify the American Convention on Human Rights and to recognize the jurisdiction of the Inter-American Court of Human Rights based in San Jose, Costa Rica.

The third organization to be discussed is the **Organization of African Unity** (OAU) or **African Union** (7.), which is also grappling with a lack of political willingness to enforce human rights. While it is true that several well-known politicians, in reaction to numerous gross and systematic human rights violations, adopted the African Charter on Human and Peoples' Rights in 1981 that was ratified by almost all African States, actual acceptance or regional human rights protection among the political and economic elites of the continent is rather low. The African Charter's main merit is the recognition of **collective solidarity rights** of the 'third generation' (2.6.). Its enforcement system (complaints system) is still very weak, but is to be improved by the decision to establish an African Court on Human Rights in 1997.

Asia, because of the enormous heterogeneity of its states, and also because of a widespread scepticism towards international human rights protection, has not developed a regional organization or regional human rights system. The few half-hearted sub-regional efforts (such as those made by the Arab League: 10.2.) have

3.3. OVERVIEW OF THE INTERNATIONAL HUMAN RIGHTS SYSTEM

not made a difference either. This is highly regrettable inasmuch as Asian states have also shown the highest reluctance to ratify universal human rights treaties.

European human rights systems are applied in Asia only in some areas of the former Soviet Union. The Russian Federation and some of the Caucasian republics (just like Turkey and Cyprus) are subject to the system of the Council of Europe and the jurisdiction of the European Court of Human Rights. All successor states of the Soviet Union, including the Central Asian Republics (as well as Canada and the USA) belong to the **Organization for Security and Cooperation in Europe** (OSCE, 8.). During the Cold War, the latter was simply a conference (CSCE) based on politically binding documents (1975 Helsinki Final Act), that nevertheless contributed substantially towards strengthening human rights in Socialist states and ultimately also towards bringing down 'real socialism' in Europe and the Soviet Union. Based on a **comprehensive security concept**, whereby human rights and democracy are understood as essential elements of security in Europe, the OSCE succeeded in creating a new identity for itself after the Cold War. Today, most of the OSCE's human rights activities, apart from a permanent political discourse on human rights and a comparably effective system of protection of minorities through the 'silent diplomacy' of the OSCE High Commissioner on National Minorities, are concentrated on field operations as in Bosnia and Herzegovina and Kosovo.

While protection of human rights in member states is not one of the designated tasks of the **European Union** (EU), it does seem justified, in the light of current developments, to dedicate a separate chapter (9.) to this central organization of the European unification process. It is true to say that ever since the 1998 Treaty of Amsterdam, the EU, as a supranational institution, has been postulating human rights, democracy, the rule of law and liberty as its central values, which need to be respected by states wishing to accede to the Union and whose systematic violation by member states may be reprimanded with sanctions. During the Nice summit of December 2000, the EU actually agreed upon a Charter of Fundamental Rights, albeit a non-binding one for the time being. Furthermore, the EU has declared human rights essential elements of its common foreign and development **policy in respect of third countries** and in doing so has made itself a key player in the political human rights scene of the United Nations and the OSCE.

3. INTERNATIONAL HUMAN RIGHTS PROTECTION – CONTEXT AND CONCEPTIONS

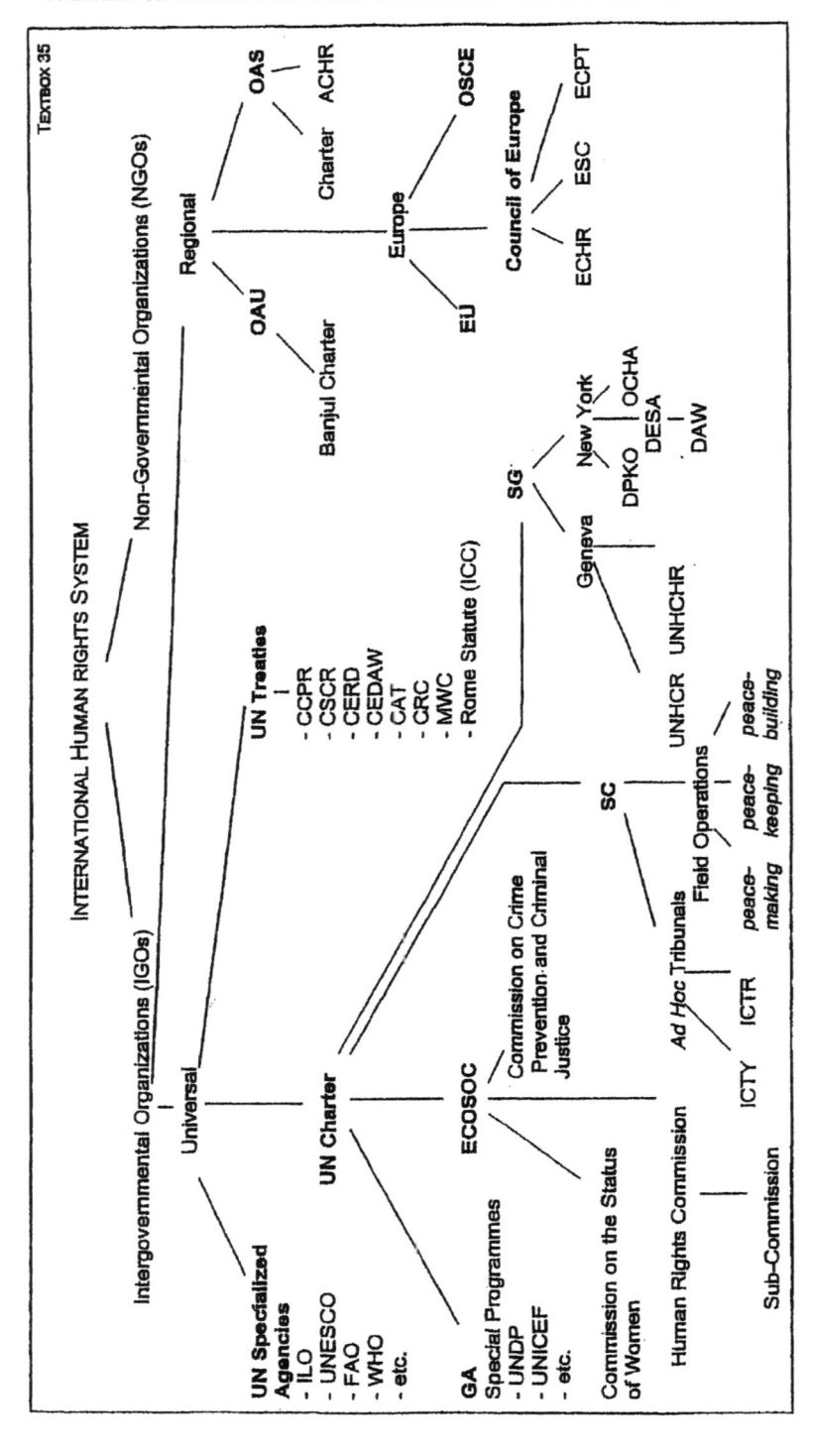

Textbox 35

INTERNATIONAL HUMAN RIGHTS SYSTEM

- Intergovernmental Organizations (IGOs)
- Non-Governmental Organizations (NGOs)

Universal

- UN Specialized Agencies
  - ILO
  - UNESCO
  - FAO
  - WHO
  - etc.

- UN Treaties
  - CCPR
  - CSCR
  - CERD
  - CEDAW
  - CAT
  - CRC
  - MWC
  - Rome Statute (ICC)

UN Charter

- GA
  - Special Programmes
    - UNDP
    - UNICEF
    - etc.
  - Commission on the Status of Women
  - Human Rights Commission
    - Sub-Commission

- ECOSOC
  - Commission on Crime Prevention and Criminal Justice

- SC
  - Ad Hoc Tribunals
    - ICTY
    - ICTR
  - Field Operations
    - peace-making
    - peace-keeping
    - peace-building
  - UNHCR

- SG
  - Geneva
    - UNHCHR
  - New York
    - DPKO
    - OCHA
    - DESA
    - DAW

Regional

- OAS — Charter, ACHR
- OAU — Banjul Charter
- Europe
  - EU
  - OSCE — ECPT
  - Council of Europe — ECHR, ESC

3.3. Overview of the International Human Rights System

LITBOX 3

LITERATURE
(GENERAL TEXTBOOKS)

Boven, Theo van 1995, General Course on Human Rights, in: Collected Courses of the Academy of European Law, Volume 4/2, The Hague

Buergenthal, Thomas 1995, International Human Rights in a Nutshell, 2nd ed., St. Paul

Claude, Richard and *Weston*, Burns (Eds.) 1992, Human Rights in the World Community: Issues and Action, 2nd ed., Philadelphia

Donelly, Jack 1998, International Human Rights, 2nd ed., Boulder

Dunner, Tim und *Wheele*, Nicholas (Eds.) 1999, Human rights in global politics, Cambridge

Falk, Richard 2000, Human Rights Horizons: The Pursuit of Justice in a Globalizing World, New York

Goldewijk, Berma Klein et al. 2002, Dignity and Human Rights: the Implementation of Economic, Social and Cultural Rights, Antwerp

Hannum, Hurst (Ed.) 1999, Guide to International Human Rights Practice, 3rd ed., New York

Hanski, Raija and *Suksi*, Markku (Eds.) 1999, An Introduction to the International Protection of Human Rights: A Textbook, 2nd ed., Turku

Hastrup, Kirsten (Ed.) 2001, The Human Rights on Common Ground: The Quest for Universality

Henkin, Louis and *Hargrove*, John (Eds.) 1994, Human Rights: An Agenda for the Next Century, Washington D.C.

Lijnzaad, Liesbeth 1994, Reservations of UN Human Rights Treaties: Ratify and Ruin, Dordecht

Newman, Frank und *Weissbrodt*, David 1996, International Human Rights, 2nd ed., Cincinnati

Provost, Rene 2002, International Human Rights and Humanitarian Law, Cambridge

Ramcharan, Bertram G. 2002, Human Rights and Security, The Hague

Rehman, Javaid 2003, International Human Rights Law: a Practical Approach, Harlow

Sano, Hans-Otto and *Alfredsson*, Gudmundur 2002, Human Rights and Good Governance, The Hague

Sen, Amartya 2001, Development as Freedom, Oxford

Smith, Rhona 2003, Textbook on International Human Rights, Oxford

Steiner, Henry und *Alston,* Philip 2000, International Human Rights in Context: Law, Politics, Morals, Texts and Materials, 2nd ed., Oxford

Symonides, Janusz (Ed.) 1998, Human Rights: New Dimensions and Challenges, Ashgate/Paris

Symonides, Janusz (Ed.) 2000, Human Rights: Concept and Standards, Aldershot

4. UNITED NATIONS

4.1. UN Charter

The United Nations Organization (UNO, UN) was founded in 1945 as the successor organization to the League of Nations (2.4.) upon the initiative of the victorious powers of the Second World War and in reaction to the sufferings caused by the war and National Socialism. With the accession of East Timor and Switzerland in 2002, the UN now has 191 member states, which essentially, but with a few exceptions (such as Taiwan) include all sovereign states of the world. The main objectives of the UN, along with maintaining international peace and security, are to achieve international cooperation, development and human rights, as laid down in article 1 of the UN Charter. All the same, the Charter does not mention protection, but only promotion of human rights (2.8.), and none of the UN's principal organs have actually been established to deal exclusively with this issue. It is the chapter on international economic and social cooperation, which regulates promotion of and universal respect for human rights, and consequently the Economic and Social Council (ECOSOC), which, along with many other tasks, is primarily responsible for human rights issues. However, it soon delegated this duty to the **Commission on Human Rights** (4.4.1.) established in accordance with article 68, which de facto acts as a principal body, while requiring formal approval from ECOSOC in all its decisions.

For many years, the Commission took the term '**promotion of human rights**' far too literally, considering every action that went beyond advisory services (e.g. delegating experts and organizing seminars upon the invitation of individual states) as inadmissible interference with the domestic jurisdiction of states in accordance with article 2(7) of the Charter (3.1.1.) ('no power to take action doctrine', 4.4.1.1.). The UN's main achievement, especially that of the Commission, in the first decades of its existence, therefore was to set standards, i.e. to carry out a comprehensive **universal codification of human rights,** which was largely completed by the end of the Cold War.

Apart from the International Bill of Human Rights, which consists of the 1948 Universal Declaration of Human Rights and the two 1966 International Covenants, the United Nations established an extensive network of special conventions, bodies and procedures to monitor adherence to these treaty obligations (4.3.), which in many cases exceed the standards of comparable treaties at the regional level.

While to this day there is no international court of human rights that would compel states to meet their treaty obligations by internationally binding judgments, the significance of this universal codification process as the foundation of a world order rooted in the principles of the rule of law, democracy and human rights must not be underestimated.

4. United Nations

> **TEXTBOX 36**
>
> ## UN Charter
>
> ### Purposes of the United Nations (article 1)
>
> 2. To develop friendly relations among nations based on respect for the principle of equal rights and self-determination of peoples, and to take other appropriate measures to strengthen universal peace;
> 3. To achieve international co-operation in solving international problems of an economic, social, cultural or humanitarian character, and in promoting and encouraging respect for human rights and for fundamental freedoms for all without distinction as to race, sex, language, or religion;
>
> ### General Assembly (article 13)
>
> 1. The General Assembly shall initiate studies and make recommendations for the purpose of:
> a) promoting international co-operation in the political field and encouraging the progressive development of international law and its codification;
> b) promoting international co-operation in the economic, social, cultural, educational, and health fields, and assisting in the realization of human rights and fundamental freedoms for all without distinction as to race, sex, language, or religion.
>
> ### International Economic and Social Co-operation (articles 55 and 56)
>
> The United Nations shall promote…'universal respect for, and observance of, human rights and fundamental freedoms for all, without distinction as to race, sex, language, or religion.'
> 'All Members pledge themselves to take joint and separate action in co-operation with the Organization for the achievement of the purposes set forth in Article 55.'
>
> ### ECOSOC (articles 62 and 68)
>
> The Economic and Social Council 'may make recommendations for the purpose of promoting respect for, and observance of, human rights and fundamental freedoms for all.'
> The Economic and Social Council 'shall set up commissions in economic and social fields and for the promotion of human rights;'
>
> ### International Trusteeship System (article 76)
>
> The basic objectives of the trusteeship system '…shall be to encourage respect for human rights and for fundamental freedoms for all without distinction as to race, sex, language, or religion, and to encourage recognition of the interdependence of the peoples of the world;'

Along with this codification process under international law, the Human Rights Commission, from the late 1960s onwards, established a number of **thematic and country-specific mechanisms** (special rapporteurs, working groups, etc.) and procedures for the worldwide protection of human rights (4.4.1.), which are based directly on the UN Charter and increasingly diffused the argument of inadmissible interference in national matters (at least with gross and systematic human rights violations). This gradual development was endorsed by the express recognition of the legitimacy of international measures for the protection of human rights during the 1993 Vienna World Conference on Human Rights (4.6.1.). At the same time, the **UN High Commissioner for Human Rights** (4.4.8.2.) was established, hailing a new era for the UN human rights system, which from promotion and protection was to move on to international enforcement, and finally, to the prevention of human rights violations (2.8.).

With these new tasks of enforcement and prevention, human rights have moved closer, and are in fact inseparably linked to the UN's other main objectives which are those of **securing peace** and **development** (3.1.5. and 3.1.6.). Human rights protection is no longer a case for the conference rooms of Geneva and New York, but is increasingly becoming a field operation. This is illustrated by a new generation of peace operations (16.), a new philosophy of development cooperation based on the human being (3.1.6, 4.4.8.7.), preventive field operations of the High Commissioner for Human Rights (14.2.), a new type of humanitarian relief operations, as well as humanitarian interventions for the protection of human rights. International criminal law, which after the Cold War was suddenly aroused from its long sleep, no longer serves international humanitarian law only, but has become a main pillar of international human rights protection (15.). Human rights are the only normative basis for a new world order, and as such have permeated almost all fields of activity of the United Nations. Many of its bodies that used to act primarily on humanitarian grounds, such as the United Nations Children's Fund (UNICEF) (4.4.8.6.), today have found a new and more solid legal foundation in the relevant human rights treaties, such as the Convention on the Rights of the Child (4.3.6.). This **mainstreaming of human rights** is also reflected in the fact that virtually all of the UN's principal organs, including the Security Council (4.4.7.), have now assumed some of the tasks of human rights protection. With this integration function, human rights are gradually assuming the significance the authors of the UN Charter and the Universal Declaration of Human Rights intended for them, but which then got lost in the times of the Cold War.

4.2. Universal Declaration of Human Rights (UDHR)

The UN Charter did not define the term 'human rights', but rather presupposed it. The first task of the Human Rights Commission founded in 1946 was, therefore, to develop a universally valid definition. The idea was to proceed in three successive steps: to pronounce a non-binding **declaration** as a basis for a legally binding **convention**, and create international **implementation** mechanisms (2.8.). Looking back, it is quite remarkable that in the course of two years the international community was able to agree on a universal declaration, while the adoption of two human rights covenants took two decades and their efficient implementation is still pending. This success is due on the one hand to the personal commitment of individual delegates in the Human Rights Commission like *Eleanor Roosevelt*

(United States) and *René Cassin* (France), but also to the fact that the international community in the 1940s was fairly small, and rigid ideological differences had yet to surface.

While the Universal Declaration of Human Rights of 10 December 1948 (UDHR) primarily reflects the human rights concept of the Age of Enlightenment, in other words, the 'first generation' of civil and political rights (articles 1 – 21), it is remarkable that at the time of its drafting, the 'second generation' of human rights (economic, social and cultural rights) was accepted more or less on equal footing with the first generation by western states (2.6.). In doing so, they pre-empted the doctrine of interdependence and indivisibility of all human rights, which was not formally recognized until the 1993 Vienna World Conference, and in fact, is still a matter of controversy for most industrialized countries (2.7.). More surprising still, the states at the time, obviously still under the shock of the Nazi holocaust, recognized in article 28 that everyone was entitled to a 'social and international order in which the rights and freedoms set forth in this Declaration can be fully realized'. This regulation today not only provides the basis for the 'third generation' of collective rights, but also is considered the foundation for the legitimacy of the international human rights regime in general. The Declaration still includes rights, which were not codified in the two subsequent UN Covenants, such as the right of asylum (article 14) and the right to property (article 17). On the other hand, it does not include peoples' right of self-determination and protection of minorities, which prompted the Soviet Union and its allies to abstain from voting at the General Assembly.

Even though the Universal Declaration – which is formally a resolution of the General Assembly – is not binding under international law, it still represents an **authoritative interpretation of the term 'human rights' in the UN Charter**, and thus can be considered indirectly constituting international treaty law. All human rights activities and mechanisms of the Human Rights Commission and other bodies of the United Nations, which are directly based on the Charter, refer to the Universal Declaration as universally recognized standards by all states. Furthermore, many African and Asian states, which gained their independence after 1948, refer to the Declaration in their constitutions, thus emphasizing its moral, political and legal significance.

No doubt some of its provisions, such as the prohibition of torture and slavery, today enjoy the status of customary international law, yet despite certain legal opinions to the contrary, it is still doubtful whether the Declaration as a whole can be considered as having achieved this status. However, with the increase in ratifications of the two UN Covenants, this academic debate on the status of the Declaration in international law is gradually losing ground.

4.2. Universal Declaration of Human Rights

TEXTBOX 37

Universal Declaration of Human Rights (UDHR)
GA Res. 217 A (III), 10 December 1948

- Most fundamental international human rights document
- Not binding, but parts constitute customary international law
- Authoritative interpretation of the term 'human rights' in the UN Charter
- Incorporated in many national constitutions and referred to in many international human rights treaties
- Includes civil, political, economic, social and cultural rights

Preamble

Whereas recognition of the inherent dignity and of the equal and inalienable rights of all members of the human family is the foundation of freedom, justice and peace in the world,

Whereas disregard and contempt for human rights have resulted in barbarous acts which have outraged the conscience of mankind, and the advent of a world in which human beings shall enjoy freedom of speech and belief and freedom from fear and want has been proclaimed as the highest aspiration of the common people,

Whereas it is essential, if man is not to be compelled to have recourse, as a last resort, to rebellion against tyranny and oppression, that human rights should be protected by the rule of law,

Now, therefore,

The General Assembly,

Proclaims this Universal Declaration of Human Rights as a common standard of achievement for all peoples and all nations, to the end that every individual and every organ of society, keeping this Declaration constantly in mind, shall strive by teaching and education to promote respect for these rights and freedoms and by progressive measures, national and international, to secure their universal and effective recognition and observance, both among the peoples of Member States themselves and among peoples of territories under their jurisdiction.

Article 28

Everyone is entitled to a social and international order in which the rights and freedoms set forth in this Declaration can be fully realized.

4. UNITED NATIONS

4.3. Human Rights Treaties and Monitoring Mechanisms

4.3.1. International Covenant on Civil and Political Rights (CCPR)

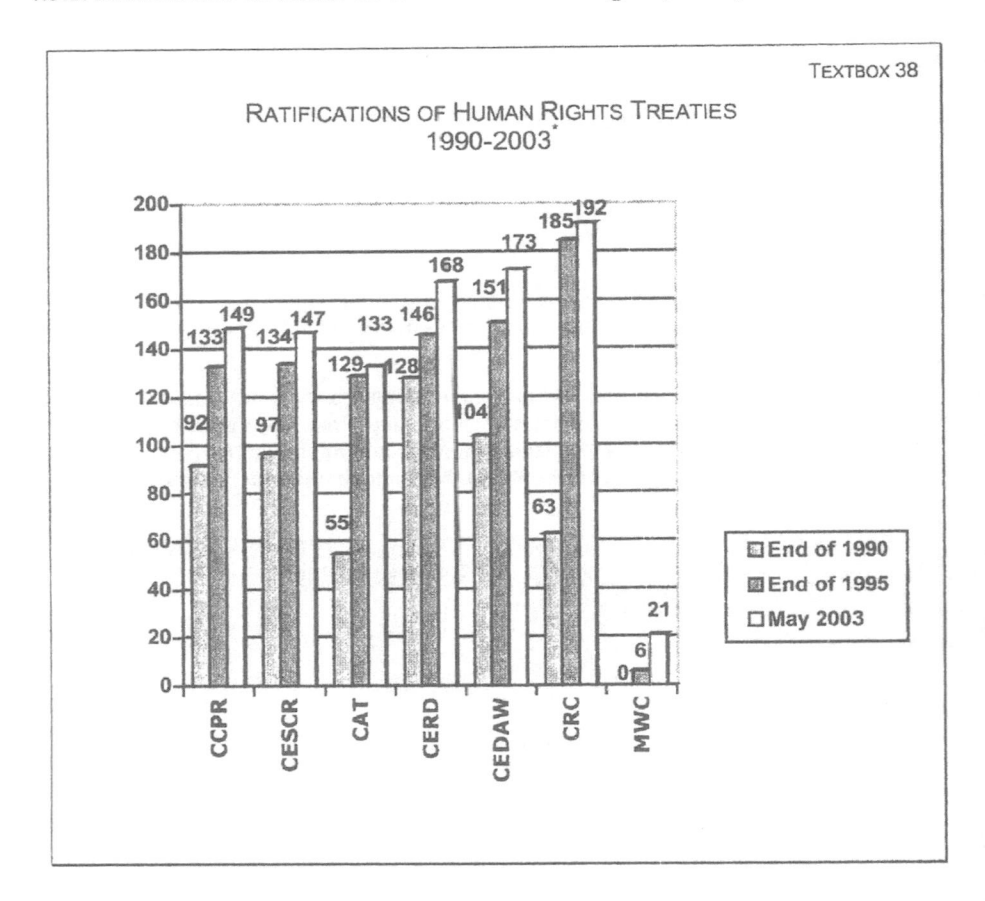

> TEXTBOX 38
>
> **RATIFICATIONS OF HUMAN RIGHTS TREATIES 1990-2003**[*]
>
> | Treaty | End of 1990 | End of 1995 | May 2003 |
> |---|---|---|---|
> | CCPR | 92 | 133 | 149 |
> | CESCR | 97 | 134 | 147 |
> | CAT | 55 | 129 | 133 |
> | CERD | 128 | 146 | 168 |
> | CEDAW | 104 | 151 | 173 |
> | CRC | 63 | 185 | 192 |
> | MWC | 0 | 6 | 21 |

As soon as the Universal Declaration was completed, the Human Rights Commission set out to prepare an internationally binding human rights convention, as well as the apposite mechanisms for monitoring its observance. In 1951, however, the western states succeeded in demanding a division of the Declaration into **two different treaties** on the 'model of the Council of Europe'. This momentous decision was taken against the resistance of socialist states, which had insisted on the interdependence and indivisibility of all human rights (2.7.). The West essentially justified their demand for division by arguing that economic, social and cultural rights were only 'programmatic rights', which could not establish any directly enforceable international obligations and consequently could not be made

---

[*] Migrant Workers Convention came into force on 1 July 2003.

4.3. HUMAN RIGHTS TREATIES AND MONITORING MECHANISMS

'justiciable'. The socialist states, while emphasizing the indivisibility of human rights, as a matter of principle (2.6.) rejected any form of international monitoring.

Given these differences of opinion it was, of course, exceptionally difficult to draw up a universal human rights convention inclusive of effective implementation procedures during the Cold War. While the Council of Europe succeeded in adopting a treaty with an (optional) judicial complaints mechanism for the classical civil rights within the course of a year (ECHR 1950, 5.2.), it took the United Nations almost two decades to adopt the two UN Covenants in 1966 and a further ten years to put them into force in 1976. The Human Rights Commission had submitted draft proposals to the General Assembly in 1954, which the General Assembly then worked on for more than ten years. Whereas the wording of the two Covenants was finally approved by consensus, the two Optional Protocols of 1966 and 1989 were not.

The **International Covenant on Civil and Political Rights** (CCPR) in substance corresponds to the European and the American Conventions on Human Rights in many points. Because of the resistance of the socialist states, the CCPR does not contain the right to property, while some rights, such as the right to personal liberty and privacy, are not regulated with the same amount of detail as in the two regional conventions. On the other hand, the Covenant contains a number of rights that do not appear in the 1950 version of the ECHR. These shortcomings in the ECHR were partly corrected with the Additional Protocols No. 1 (right to vote), No. 4 (freedom of movement and prohibition of detention for debt), No. 7 (minimum guarantees against expulsion of aliens, some procedural guarantees for criminal proceedings, equality of husband and wife), as well as No. 12 (independent prohibition of discrimination). Nevertheless, to this day, the Covenant goes beyond the scope of the ECHR, inasmuch as it also contains the right of self-determination of peoples (article 1), rights of persons belonging to minorities (article 27), a general right to equality (article 26), minimum rights for children (article 24), the right to recognition as a legal person (article 16), as well as prohibition of propaganda for war and incitement to national, racist and religious discrimination, hostility or violence (article 20). Ultimately, political rights (article 25), protection of the family (article 23), minimum guarantees for detained persons (article 10) and the limitations on the death penalty in article 6, also exceed comparable standards in the ECHR. The prohibition of the death penalty is regulated more stringently in the 2nd Optional Protocol to the Covenant of 1989 than in the equivalent 6th Additional Protocol to the ECHR of 1983. However, a further 13th Additional Protocol to the ECHR was adopted as late as May 2002, which now provides for a comprehensive prohibition of the death penalty in times of war and peace in Europe.

While the Covenant in substance provides a broader scope of application than the ECHR or the ACHR, the **international monitoring system** compared to that of the two regional Conventions leaves a lot to be desired. Until today, i.e. 13 years after the end of the Cold War, the United Nations has not been able to decide on the establishment of an **international court of human rights**. Rather, monitoring of the observance of the states' parties human rights treaty obligations is incumbent upon international bodies of experts (the Human Rights Committee in the case of the CCPR) who are not in a position to render legally binding decisions. In fact, the only mandatory monitoring system is the **state reporting procedure** (4.3.9.), the inter-state complaints procedure and the individual complaints procedure are only optional. That the Human Rights Committee is at all competent to decide on individual complaints (4.3.10) was a last minute diplomatic achievement of a few states in 1966. Just before a vote had been taken in the General Assembly, they proposed to move this controversial procedure to a separate (1st) Optional Protocol. The latter was eventually adopted together with the Covenant by a vote of 66 to 2 (Niger and Togo), with 38 abstentions (from socialist states in particular).

TEXTBOX 39

INTERNATIONAL COVENANT ON CIVIL AND POLITICAL RIGHTS
(CCPR)

GA Res. 2200A (XXI) of 16 December 1966
Entry into force: 23 March 1976
149 states parties

Contents

- Contains essential civil and political rights including the right of self-determination (article 1), right to equality and non-discrimination (article 26), rights of persons belonging to minorities (article 27) and prohibition of propaganda for war and incitement to discrimination, hostility or violence (article 20).

- Second Optional Protocol, aiming at the abolition of the death penalty (GA Res. 44/128 of 15 December 1989, entry into force on 11 July 1991; 49 states parties)

Monitoring

- Human Rights Committee: 18 experts

- State reporting procedure – mandatory (article 40): country-specific recommendations

- General comments: essential interpretative views, 29 to date

- Inter-state communication procedure (article 41); no cases to date

- Individual communication procedure under the 1st Optional Protocol to the CCPR (1966/76, 104 states parties): similar to the procedure before the European Court of Human Rights, total cases (as of May 2003) 1171, 273 cases pending, 580 inadmissible and discontinued cases

---

In practice, the **Human Rights Committee** has become a **quasi-judicial monitoring body** for state reporting and individual complaints procedures. Its decisions, from a quality point of view, are comparable to those of the European and

4.3. HUMAN RIGHTS TREATIES AND MONITORING MECHANISMS

the Inter-American Courts of Human Rights. Yet, despite their high quality such decisions are not legally binding and no political body at the United Nations (not even the Human Rights Commission) feels responsible for exacting the enforcement of these decisions from the states concerned. This lack of political *follow-up* may be one of the reasons why the Human Rights Committee, in its 25 years of existence, has received barely more than 1,000 individual complaints, which means on average approximately 10 complaints for each state party to the 1st Optional Protocol.

4.3.2. International Covenant on Economic, Social and Cultural Rights (CESCR)

The **International Covenant on Economic, Social and Cultural Rights** (CESCR) was adopted by the General Assembly in 1966, at the same time as the CCPR, and also entered into force in 1976. Most states ratified both Covenants simultaneously in order to underline their interdependence. Only a few states restricted the ratification so far to one of the two treaties, such as the United States (CCPR) and China (CESCR). The CESCR constitutes the most important international treaty for the codification of the 'second generation' of human rights (2.6.) and includes the main **economic rights** (right to work, right to fair and favourable working conditions, freedom to form and join trade unions, right to strike), **social rights** (protection of the family, maternity protection, protection of children and juveniles, right to social security, right to an adequate standard of living including food, clothing, and housing, right to health), as well as **cultural rights** (right to education and participation in cultural life, protection of intellectual property). Furthermore, it also includes the right of all peoples to self-determination, a comprehensive accessory prohibition of discrimination, as well as emphasis on gender equality.

Although both Covenants are equal in principle, the wording chosen for the state obligations in terms of domestic implementation under article 2(1) of the CESCR is far weaker than that of the CCPR. States are merely obliged to take steps with a view to achieving progressively the full realization of the rights recognized in the Covenant. In fact, the wording was frequently interpreted as referring to **obligations of conduct** only and not to obligations of result, and states were only obliged to achieve **progressive implementation** of economic, social and cultural rights.

Some political and academic commentators even went so far as to maintain that with human rights of the 'second generation', there was no indication that these were actually individual, enforceable rights and, therefore, states could not possibly violate such rights. This assumption, however, was refuted by the recognition of indivisibility and interdependence of all human rights, as well as by successive state practice (2.7.). The Committee on Economic, Social and Cultural Rights specified, in a general comment on this issue, that 'progressive implementation' also produced direct and immediately effective obligations for the states: observance of the prohibition of discrimination, preservation of standards already achieved, as well as the obligation to take concrete, effective and target-oriented steps towards rapid realization of these rights.

For **developing countries** article 2(3) has set aside the possibility to limit these rights to their own citizens. This implies that industrialized countries and other states with suitably developed economies, in granting economic, social and cultural rights, in principle may not distinguish between their own citizens and those of other countries. Article 2(1), which expressly refers to international assistance and cooperation of an economic and technical nature, also implies some obligation on the part of industrialized countries to help ensure worldwide minimum economic, social and cultural rights by taking the necessary steps in development cooperation.

TEXTBOX 40

INTERNATIONAL COVENANT ON ECONOMIC, SOCIAL AND CULTURAL RIGHTS (CESCR)

GA Res. 2200A (XXI) of 16 December 1966
Entry into force: 3 January 1976
147 states parties

Contents

- Right of peoples to self-determination – article 1

- Basic state obligation differs from CCPR – article 2:
- To take steps, individually and through international assistance and co-operation
- To the maximum of its available resources
- With a view to achieving progressively the full realization of the rights recognized in the Covenant
- By all appropriate means

- Most economic, social and cultural rights including:
- Right to work – article 6
- Right to an adequate standard of living – article 11
- Right to education – article 13

Monitoring

- Committee on Economic, Social and Cultural Rights (not provided in the treaty, established by ECOSOC, Res.1985/17): 18 experts

- State reporting procedure – mandatory (articles 16, 17): country-specific recommendations

- General comments: essential interpretative views, 15 to date

- No Individual communication procedure, draft Optional Protocol under deliberation

---

The real weakness of the CESCR lies in its **international monitoring mechanism**. Article 16 merely provides for a mandatory procedure for monitoring **state reports**, and, moreover, this task was delegated to the Economic and Social Council, i.e. one of the principal political organs of the United Nations. It was clear from the outset that the procedure would not be successful and the Economic and Social Council in 1985 finally passed a resolution to establish a body of experts similar to other treaty monitoring bodies. The **Committee on Economic, Social and Cultural Rights** made up of 18 independent experts, like the Human Rights Committee, has since turned the reporting procedure into an efficient monitoring procedure. It has integrated non-governmental organizations into the process of state reporting and by issuing general comments, particularly on the rights to food, housing, education, health, and water has contributed enormously to the interpretation of these rights and the corresponding treaty obligations. More recently, the Committee has also dealt with these rights in the context of development issues and the fight against poverty.

Ultimately, however, a complaints procedure seems to be more effective to monitor observance of states parties' obligations and to provide concrete interpretations of the significance of individual rights than a mere state reporting procedure. Consequently, the Committee, following many discussions, prepared a draft **optional protocol to the CESCR**, which the Human Rights Commission has been deliberating on for several years now. While at the 1993 Vienna World Conference on Human Rights (4.6.1.), states expressly endorsed such an **individual communication procedure**, it seems that, especially industrialized countries, are blocking the adoption of the optional protocol with highly questionable ideological arguments. Much work needs to be done at the United Nations in convincing them to really accept the equal value of economic, social and cultural rights instead of just paying them lip service.

4.3.3. International Convention on the Elimination of All Forms of Racial Discrimination (CERD)

Given the fact that the United Nations was founded in reaction to National Socialism, protection against discrimination and especially the fight against racial discrimination has always been at the core of UN human rights activities. This emphasis is made evident, amongst others, with the establishment of a Sub-Commission to the Human Rights Commission (which to begin with, was dedicated to prevention of discrimination and protection of minorities, 4.4.1.6.) and also with the fight against Apartheid in southern Africa. Not surprisingly, therefore, the first convention to have its own monitoring mechanism is dedicated to this issue. It should be noted in the context that the term 'race' today is considered void of substance, since there are no human 'races'; still, it is used in many international treaties and documents in connection with measures for the prevention of racism.

The **International Convention on the Elimination of All Forms of Racial Discrimination** (CERD), adopted one year before the two Covenants, not only prohibits any racial discrimination in the narrower sense, but also any distinction based on race, colour, descent, national or ethnic origin, which has the purpose or effect of impairing the enjoyment of human rights. Article 5 contains a mini-catalogue of civil, political, economic, social and cultural rights which states parties must undertake to prohibit and eliminate racial discrimination. The catalogue also includes the express right of access to any places and services intended for use by the general public (even if privately owned), such as means of transport, hotels, restaurants, cafés, theatres and parks (article 5 (f)), which groups of persons discriminated against were excluded from most frequently.

TEXTBOX 41

INTERNATIONAL CONVENTION ON THE ELIMINATION OF ALL FORMS OF RACIAL DISCRIMINATION (CERD)

GA Res. 2106A (XX) of 21 December 1965
Entry into force: 4 January 1969
168 states parties

Contents

- Definition – article 1: racial discrimination shall mean:
- Any distinction, exclusion, restriction or preference
- Based on race, colour, descent or national or ethnic origin
- Which has the purpose or effect of nullifying or impairing the recognition, enjoyment, or exercise...of human rights and fundamental freedoms

- Not applicable between citizens and non-citizens – article 1(2)

- Affirmative action is permissible (special measures taken for the sole purpose of securing adequate advancement of certain racial or ethnic groups or individuals) – article 1(4)

- States undertake:
- To punish those responsible for racial discrimination – article 4
- To guarantee the right of everyone, without distinction as to race, colour, etc., to equality before the law, notably in the enjoyment of specified rights – article 5
- To assure to everyone within their jurisdiction effective protection and remedies against any acts of racial discrimination – article 6

Monitoring

- Committee on the Elimination of Racial Discrimination: 18 experts

- State reporting procedure – mandatory (article 9): country-specific recommendations

- General Recommendations: essential interpretative views, 28 to date

- Inter-state communication procedure: mandatory (article 11); not effective, no cases to date

- Individual communication procedure: optional (following state declaration, article 14). In place since 1982, 42 declarations, 28 cases in total, 2 case pending. States may establish a special national body to receive and examine complaints.

4.3. HUMAN RIGHTS TREATIES AND MONITORING MECHANISMS

Any form of segregation, such as the former United States policy of 'separate but equal' and the Apartheid policy in southern Africa, is condemned (article 3). The only exceptions are distinction between citizens and aliens, as well as temporary special measures of affirmative action for the benefit of certain racial or ethnic groups (i.e. protection of minorities), which had been victims of racial discrimination in the past.

Along with a comprehensive prohibition of racial discrimination the Convention contains a number of positive obligations to fulfil and protect for the currently 168 states parties. States undertake to punish individuals and organizations responsible for **racial incitement** and propaganda (article 4) and to assure comprehensive protection and remedies against racial discrimination, including compensation for damages before national tribunals for everyone concerned (article 6). In the field of education, teaching, culture and information, immediate and effective measures are to be adopted with the result of preventing discrimination, while tolerance between peoples and ethnic groups is to be promoted (article 7).

The **Committee on the Elimination of Racial Discrimination** established in 1970 is the first UN human rights treaty monitoring body, which played a pioneering role in developing a procedure to monitor periodic **state reports**. The reporting cycle provided for in article 9(1) soon proved impracticable (one initial report one year after entry of force, thereafter every two years) and in fact resulted in regular violations of the states' obligation to report, while creating excess workloads for the Committee and rather superficial monitoring of the reports. The Committee, in its rule of procedure, consequently limited the obligation to report periodically, and instead gave priority to emergency reports requested from states parties in certain cases. Yet, despite these efforts, the monitoring procedure before the Committee on the Elimination of Racial Discrimination is considered fairly inefficient compared to those before other treaty monitoring bodies.

The ineffectiveness of the Committee is reflected particularly in the lack of acceptance for the two complaints procedures. Despite the fact that article 11 is the only provision in all of the UN treaties to include a **mandatory inter-state communication procedure**, and racial discrimination has assumed epidemic proportions in many states parties (such as Rwanda 1994, or Bosnia and Herzegovina between 1992 and 1995), not one of the 168 contracting states has so far availed themselves of the inter-state communication procedure to fight such gross and systematic human rights violations or even just to draw international attention to such violations.

The **optional individual communication procedure** in accordance with article 14 is not enjoying too much popularity either. While the Convention entered into force as early as 1969, due to the comparatively quick ratification process, however, recognition of the Committee to examine individual complaints did not take place until 1982, when eventually, ten states parties had submitted the necessary declarations to initiate the procedure. Meanwhile, more than 40 states have recognized the Committee's competence, however the total number of individual complaints brought before the Committee in the past 20 years is no more than 28 (mostly from European states), i.e. barely one complaint worldwide each year. Of course, these figures are by no means a reflection of reality and racial discrimination continues to be one of the most serious human rights violations in all regions of the world.

4.3.4. Convention on the Elimination of All Forms of Discrimination against Women (CEDAW)

Discrimination against women is just as common and universal a phenomenon as racial discrimination. The United Nations has always given precedence to the human rights of women and the fight against gender-based discrimination, as illustrated by the establishment of the Commission on the Status of Women in 1946 (4.4.2.), the adoption of the Conventions on the Political Rights of Women in 1952, the Nationality of Married Women in 1957, the Consent to Marriage in 1962, as well as the various Women's World Conferences and Decades (4.6.2.), the adoption of the Declaration on the Elimination of Violence against Women in 1993 and the appointment of a Special Rapporteur on these issues by the Human Rights Commission. The most important and effective legal protection by far in this context was the adoption of the **Convention on the Elimination of All Forms of Discrimination against Women** (CEDAW) in 1979.

Discrimination against women means any 'distinction, exclusion or restriction made on the basis of sex which has the effect or purpose of impairing or nullifying the recognition, enjoyment or exercise by women of human rights and fundamental freedoms' (article 1). States parties are also encouraged to adopt special temporary measures aimed at accelerating de facto equality between men and women (**affirmative action**, article 4).

Along with a comprehensive prohibition of discrimination against women (article 2) the Convention contains a series of detailed provisions and **positive state obligations to fulfil**, the purpose of which are to eliminate discrimination against women in political and public life (part II), in economic, social and cultural life (part III), as well as equality before the law, including matrimonial and family law (part IV). Special provisions refer to the abolition of trafficking in women, exploitation of prostitution (article 6) and promoting the rights of women in rural areas (article 14). Overall, the states parties are obliged to take suitable steps to bring about a change in social and cultural behavioural patterns of women and men, to remove practices based on stereotyped roles of women and men, and to ensure that joint responsibility of women and men for the upbringing and development of their children is recognized (article 5).

Unlike the Convention on the Elimination of All Forms of Racial Discrimination (4.3.3.), CEDAW does not expressly mention segregation for reasons of gender – as provided for in some Islamic states (e.g. Saudi Arabia, Afghanistan under the Taliban regime). It also does not expressly guarantee access to quasi-public places and services and does not oblige states to prohibit sexist propaganda or sexist organizations under criminal law. While, under article 16, it obliges states parties to eliminate discrimination against women in matters relating

4.3. HUMAN RIGHTS TREATIES AND MONITORING MECHANISMS

to marriage and family relations, it does not expressly prohibit violence in the family. The international monitoring mechanism of the Convention was also, for many years, inferior to that of the Convention on the Elimination of All Forms of Racial Discrimination.

TEXTBOX 42

CONVENTION ON THE ELIMINATION ALL FORMS OF DISCRIMINATION AGAINST WOMEN (CEDAW)

GA Res. 34/180 of 18 December 1979
Entry into force: 3 September 1981
173 states parties

Contents

- Basic principle: elimination and prohibition of all discrimination against women – article 2

- Affirmative action is permissible – article 4

- Provisions on women's political rights (articles 7 – 9); social and economic rights (articles 10 – 14); equality before the law and family rights (articles 15 – 16); special provisions on trafficking in women (article 6) and rights of rural women (article 14).

Monitoring

- Committee on the Elimination of Discrimination Against Women: 23 experts

- State reporting procedure – mandatory (article 18): country-specific recommendations

- General Recommendations: essential interpretative views, 24 to date

- No Inter-state communication procedure

- Individual communication procedure under the 1st OP to CEDAW: GA Res. 54/4 of 6 October 1999, entry into force on 22 February 2000, 51 states parties, no cases decided to date

- Inquiry procedure under the same 1st OP to CEDAW in cases where the Committee has received reliable information of gross and systematic violations (OP article 8); possible to opt out at ratification (OP article 10); one case pending

---

The **Committee on the Elimination of Discrimination against Women** is composed of 23 experts (mainly women). In the early days, it was responsible only for the monitoring of state reports. The open and constructive attitude of members of the Committee and state delegations during the **state reporting procedure** was highly conducive to setting a number of relevant legal standards and practical steps to improve the status of women.

4. UNITED NATIONS

The CEDAW Committee's success was also instrumental in adopting an optional protocol during the General Assembly in 1999, which provides for an **individual communication procedure** and an **inquiry procedure** on the model of the UN Convention against Torture (4.3.5.). The Optional Protocol entered into force in December 2000; first complaints are not expected until individuals have exhausted all domestic remedies.

4.3.5. Convention against Torture and Other Cruel, Inhuman or Degrading Treatment or Punishment (CAT)

Torture is one of the most serious human rights violations and in fact constitutes a **direct attack on human dignity**. Although officially abolished under the influence of the Age of Enlightenment, and like slavery prohibited without exception by customary international law and in many general human rights treaties, it went through a veritable 'renaissance' during the 20th century. Virtually no government will admit to acts of torture, yet according to non-governmental organizations like Amnesty International, whose highest priority is the abolition of torture, systematic torture is practiced throughout the world in approximately 50 per cent of all states. This is why in the 1970s, it became clear that fighting torture required special measures that went beyond mere prohibitions under international law and their monitoring through traditional international procedures. The Council of Europe introduced new standards by establishing a system of preventive visits to places of detention (5.4. and 14.5.). The United Nations, in turn, contributed to the worldwide combat against torture by appointing a Special Rapporteur against Torture (4.4.1.5.), setting up a special fund for victims of torture, as well as adopting a separate **Convention against Torture and other Cruel, Inhuman or Degrading Treatment or Punishment** in 1984.

Article 1 of the Convention gives a fairly narrow and somewhat controversial **definition of torture:**

> 'For the purposes of this Convention, the term "torture" means any act by which severe pain or suffering, whether physical or mental, is intentionally inflicted on a person for such purposes as obtaining from him or a third person information or a confession, punishing him for an act he or a third person has committed or is suspected of having committed, or intimidating or coercing him or a third person, or for any reason based on discrimination of any kind, when such pain or suffering is inflicted by or at the instigation of or with the consent or acquiescence of a public official or other person acting in an official capacity. It does not include pain or suffering arising only from, inherent in or incidental to lawful sanctions.'

This implies that torture, according to this definition,
- cannot be committed through negligence;
- cannot be committed by private persons;

4.3. HUMAN RIGHTS TREATIES AND MONITORING MECHANISMS

- requires a certain degree of intensity in intentionally inflicting suffering;
- cannot be committed without purpose (e.g. by mere sadism).

Apart from this limitation to state officials, it is the last sentence provided in the definition of torture in article 1 CAT, 'the **lawful sanctions clause**', which is considered a concession to some states, mainly Islamic, causing most controversies.

TEXTBOX 43

CONVENTION AGAINST TORTURE AND OTHER CRUEL, INHUMAN OR DEGRADING TREATMENT OR PUNISHMENT (CAT)

GA Res. 39/46 of 10 December 1984
Entry into force: 26 June 1987
133 states parties

Contents

- Definition of torture – article 1
- State obligations to prevent torture (articles 2, 10, 11, 15, 16)
- State obligations to provide remedies and reparation (articles 12, 13, 14)
- Non-refoulement principle (article 3)
- Punishment of perpetrators:
- All acts of torture must be offences under domestic criminal law (article 4)
- Universal jurisdiction (articles 5 to 8): principle 'aut dedere aut judicare'

Monitoring

- Committee against Torture: 10 experts
- State reporting procedure – mandatory (article 19)
- General Comments: essential interpretative views, 1 to date
- Inter-state communications: optional (article 21); no cases to date
- Individual communications: optional (article 22); total cases 221, 54 cases pending
- Inquiry procedure: mandatory (article 20) with opting-out possibility (article 28); total cases 7, 5 reports published
- 1st Optional Protocol 2002 (GA Res. 57/199 of 18 December 2002, not yet in force): system of preventive visits to places of detention (based on the ECPT model)

The purpose of the clause was above all to exclude some types of corporal punishment provided for in criminal law from being a prohibited form of torture. However, this limitation needs to be interpreted restrictively if states are not to bypass the international prohibition of torture through 'legalization' of specific methods of torture, as called for repeatedly in the fight against terrorism, especially after the events of 11 September 2001. The Convention contains a number of obligations for states parties to prevent torture (e.g. by appropriate training of law enforcement personnel and systematic reviewing of interrogation methods) and ensure comprehensive remedies and reparation (including rehabilitation and compensation).

Such obligations refer not only to the acts of torture described above but even to less serious forms of cruel, inhuman or degrading treatment or punishment (article 16(1)). Yet the Convention's most important objective by far is that of **criminal prosecution of torture** in the narrower sense. All states parties have committed themselves to recognizing all acts of torture as offences under criminal law and must provide for appropriate punishment which takes into account the gravity of the offence. Moreover, what is so revolutionary about the Convention is that it is the first international human rights treaty to embody the principle of **universal jurisdiction** (articles 5(2), 6 – 9; see 15.2.). Whenever a person suspected of having committed an act of torture is present on the territory of a state party (irrespective of the nationality of perpetrator or victim, or of the scene of the crime), the authorities of that state (even without a request for extradition from the other state) are obliged to initiate a provisional investigation and take the suspect into custody or otherwise ensure their physical presence until criminal or extradition proceedings are commenced. If there is satisfaction after the examination of information that torture was committed, the state, in accordance with the principle of '*aut dedere aut iudicare*', either has to extradite that person to another state (e.g. either the state of the scene of torture, or the national state of the perpetrator or the victim) or undertake to prosecute the suspect under its own criminal proceedings. The latter is most likely to be the case if due to the **principle of non-refoulement** (article 3), it is not possible to extradite the suspect, or if there is a risk that they will not be brought before a tribunal in the relevant state because they are immune or are protected from criminal prosecution by a special amnesty law or by the political circumstances prevailing there.

International monitoring of the observance of treaty obligations is incumbent upon the **Committee against Torture** (article 17), which is made up of 10 independent experts. Apart from the mandatory state reporting procedure and the optional inter-state and individual complaint procedures an **ex-officio inquiry procedure** was introduced in article 20 as a further innovation of this Convention. Its purpose is to deal with those cases where there is reliable information which appears to contain well founded indications that systematic torture is being practiced in one of the states parties. This procedure is mandatory but may be opted out of (only at the time of signing or ratifying the Convention) by way of a special reservation in accordance with article 28. On-site visits, which are part of this procedure, may only be conducted with the express agreement of the state party concerned (4.3.11.).

4.3. HUMAN RIGHTS TREATIES AND MONITORING MECHANISMS

Back in 1980, Costa Rica submitted a proposal to the UN Human Rights Commission to introduce a **system of preventive visits to places of detention as an instrument of torture prevention**. As the system would provide for visits to places of detention without the specific consent of the states concerned, it was strongly resisted by many states on the basis that it would infringe upon state sovereignty (3.1.1.). The Council of Europe took a first step towards implementation of such a system by adopting the European Convention for the Prevention of Torture (ECPT) in 1989 (5.4., 14.5.), which other regional organizations (above all the OAS) were supposed to follow. However, the Inter-American Convention against Torture (6.6.) of 1994 hardly exceeds the scope of the UN Convention, and the efforts of the UN Human Rights Commission to introduce a universal system of preventive visits on the basis of the ECPT were protracted for many years. It was only in April 2002 that the Commission finally agreed on a compromise. The Optional Protocol to CAT was adopted by the General Assembly in December 2002 and provides for the establishment of a Sub-Committee on Prevention of the Committee against Torture consisting of 10 (later: 25) experts. The Sub-Committee on Prevention will organize a universal programme of preventive visits to places of detention, but most of these visits will, in practice, be carried out by independent national preventive mechanisms, which the states parties to the OP have agreed to establish.

4.3.6. Convention on the Rights of the Child (CRC)

'Children are not *made* human beings, they are *born* human beings' in the words of the early 20th century Polish pedagogue *Janusz Korczak*. These young people have the right to claim from their environment, respect and recognition of their abilities, **promotion and protection**, self-esteem and participation, without having to have attained the age of majority first. Given the fact that 'minimum age' does not feature in the Universal Declaration of Human Rights, most general human rights, such as the prohibition of torture or the right to health, are valid for children and adults alike (exceptions apply, for example, to the right to vote, the right to work, and the right to marry).

Basic recognition of children's rights is not diminished by the fact that some of them are tied to the level of children's individual development (e.g. freedom of association, freedom of assembly). The exploitation of children for economic purposes in textile factories, sexual violence, trafficking and forced prostitution of girls and extensive exclusion of young people from decision-making processes are, however, attacks upon the dignity and integrity of children, which are insufficiently covered by general human rights treaties. Hierarchical relationships between parents and their children, characterized by dominance and subordination, as well as a lack of opportunities to develop social skills, are often the root causes for children and young people becoming victims of violence, exploitation, neglect, discrimination and other human rights violations by governments, private persons, and not least by parents or close relatives.

For all of the above reasons, the United Nations decided as early as 1959 to adopt a Declaration on the Rights of the Child that consisted of ten principles; very soon though it became clear that only a legally binding convention geared to the **specific needs of children** would offer sufficient protection.

TEXTBOX 44

CONVENTION ON THE RIGHTS OF THE CHILD (CRC)

GA Res. 44/25 of 20 November 1989
Entry into force: 2 September 1990
192 states parties (no ratifications yet by Somalia and the USA)

Contents

- Includes children's civil, political, economic, social and cultural rights in the areas of *provision* (e.g. adequate standard of living), *protection* (e.g. from violence or exploitation) and *participation* (e.g. in the family, at school, in society)
- Four basic principles:
- Best interest of the child shall be a primary consideration in all actions concerning children (article 3)
- Prohibition of discrimination (article 2)
- Right to life and development of the child to the maximum extent (article 6)
- Right to participation (article 12)
- Optional Protocol on the involvement of children in armed conflicts: GA Res. 54/263 of 25 May 2000; entry into force 12 February 2002; 52 states parties
- Optional Protocol on the sale of children, child prostitution and child pornography: GA Res. 54/263 of 25 May 2000; entry into force 18 January 2002; 51 states parties

Monitoring

- Committee on the Rights of the Child: 10 experts (number of experts to be increased to 18 after entry into force of a respective treaty amendment of 7 November 1995)
- State reporting procedure – mandatory (article 44)
- General Comments: essential interpretative views, 4 to date
- No Inter-state communication procedure
- No Individual communication procedure
- Days of General Discussion: annual Experts Forum
- Active involvement of NGOs and UNICEF

It took ten years of intensive work at the Human Rights Commission, with the active participation of non-governmental organizations and UNICEF, before the General Assembly adopted a comprehensive treaty on 20 November 1989, which entered into force within less than a year. Today, the Convention on the Rights of the Child

4.3. HUMAN RIGHTS TREATIES AND MONITORING MECHANISMS

is the only human rights treaty signed by all states of the world (only two ratifications by Somalia and the United States are still outstanding).

Article 1 of the Convention defines a '**child**' as every human being below the age of 18 years (unless under the law applicable to the child, majority is attained earlier), which means that it is applicable to children and juveniles alike. It is unique inasmuch as it claims to encompass all life situations of young people from the human rights point of view.

It is the first treaty covering civil, political, economic, social and cultural human rights on an equal level in one document; it attempts to meet the different needs of children and juveniles not only by establishing special guarantees for the protection of children (e.g. from violence in the family or at school, from abuse, exploitation, neglect or unacceptably poor circumstances), but also by protecting children in the development of their identity, autonomy and active participation in social life (e.g. by the right to privacy, freedom of expression, information, religion, association and assembly or by the right to be heard in judicial proceedings). It also provides for positive obligations of states to ensure adequate standards of living, access to education, health institutions, social security, etc. These three elements – **protection, participation, and provision** – are often referred to as 'the three p's' in children's rights.

The **UN Committee on the Rights of the Child** has made the extensive prohibition of discrimination (article 2), the right to life and best possible development (article 6), the right to participation (article 12) and the principle of comprehensive orientation towards the best interest of children (article 3(1)) the four General Principles of the CRC.

Finally, the Convention also tries to find a balance in the sensitive triangle of children-parents-state. Article 5 recognizes the primary **responsibility of parents** to care for and raise their children, while the state is allocated a subsidiary responsibility for protection and welfare (article 3(2)). Still, the Convention is very clear on the point that parents' responsibility does not give them any absolute rights, but only such rights as are beneficial to the child, meaning that parents 'provide, in a manner consistent with the evolving capacities of the child, appropriate direction and guidance in the exercise by the child of the rights recognized in the present Convention' (article 5).

The catalogue of rights set out in the Convention corresponds with the universal human rights in many areas and in addition, also includes a number of **rights specific to children**. Of particular importance in this context are the rights to non-arbitrary separation from their parents (article 9), protection against the illicit transfer and non-return of children abroad (article 11), family reunification (article 10), as well as protection against abuse of (inter-country) adoptions (article 21). Furthermore, the Convention puts forward the principle that both parents are jointly responsible for the upbringing and development of their children and calls upon states to provide appropriate assistance and sufficient child-care facilities and services (article 18). Article 31 lays down the independent right of children to rest and leisure, to engage in play and recreational activities. Special rights are ensured for children with disabilities (article 23), refugees (article 22) and children belonging to minorities or indigenous peoples (article 30). Article 40 sets out standards for juvenile criminal law, which are to take into account social reintegration and promotion of children.

Special emphasis is placed on the rights to protection from all forms of exploitation (economic, sexual and other forms of exploitation, child trafficking, abuse of narcotic drugs). This was further highlighted by the adoption of the **Optional Protocol on the Sale of Children, Child Prostitution, and Child Pornography** in May 2000. The CRC's obligations to fight child labour was complemented by the **ILO Convention No. 182 on the Worst Forms of Child Labour** in 1999.

Protection of children in the context of armed conflicts has been the cause of many political controversies. Back in 1989, the states were unable to agree on a general prohibition of child soldiers because of the resistance of the United States and some other governments, but instead stipulated a special age limit of 15 years (article 38(2)) as the smallest common denominator. As this age limit falls below the standards already achieved in international humanitarian law (3.1.4), a further **Optional Protocol on the Involvement of Children in Armed Conflicts** was adopted in May 2000, which provides for the prohibition to participate in hostilities and compulsory recruitment into the armed forces for all persons who have not attained the age of 18 years.

International monitoring of compliance with treaty obligations is incumbent upon the **Committee on the Rights of the Child** (article 43), which currently consists of ten independent experts and is limited to monitoring **state reporting** (article 44). In practice, however, the Committee has made this a fairly efficient procedure and, vested with a special authorization for international cooperation in article 45, has also actively and systematically involved UNICEF (4.4.8.6.), as well as national and international NGOs (11.) in the examination of state reports.

4.3.7. Other Major UN Human Rights Treaties

The above-mentioned six 'core' conventions are the only UN human rights treaties endowed with independent monitoring mechanisms operating at present. On 1 July 2003, the **International Convention on the Protection of the Rights of All Migrant Workers and Members of their Families** of 1990 (Migrant Workers Convention, MWC) entered into force, which also provides for the establishment of a separate 'Migrant Workers Committee' of 10 experts (after the 41st ratification by a state, the committee will increase to 14 members) competent to examine state reports (mandatory), inter-state and individual communications (optional). This seventh 'core' human rights treaty contains a comprehensive list of civil, political, economic, social and cultural rights of migrant workers and their families, but most industrialized states, where migrant workers actually live (often under deplorable conditions), have denied accepting any obligations under this treaty. As of 31 May 2003, a total of 21 states have ratified the Migrant Workers Convention, among

4.3. HUMAN RIGHTS TREATIES AND MONITORING MECHANISMS

them only Azerbaijan and Bosnia and Herzegovina as members of the Council of Europe.

The 1973 International Convention on the Suppression and Punishment of the Crime of Apartheid (**Apartheid Convention**) also had its own committee of three representatives of states to examine state reports (article IX). However, it discontinued its work when Apartheid in South Africa was brought to an end.

TEXTBOX 45

OTHER MAJOR UN HUMAN RIGHTS TREATIES

(indicating years of adoption and entry into force)

- Slavery Convention (1926/27)
- Protocol amending the 1926 Slavery Convention (1953/53)
- Supplementary Convention on the Abolition of Slavery, the Slave Trade, and Institutions and Practices Similar to Slavery (1956/57)
- Convention on the Prevention and Punishment of the Crime of Genocide (1948/51)
- Four Geneva Conventions on Humanitarian Law (1949/50)
- Two Protocols Additional to the Geneva Conventions (1977/78)
- Convention Relating to the Status of Refugees (1951/54)
- Protocol Relating to the Status of Refugees (1967/67)
- Convention on the Political Rights of Women (1952/54)
- Convention Relating to the Status of Stateless Persons (1954/60)
- Convention on the Reduction of Statelessness (1961/75)
- Convention on Consent to Marriage, Minimum Age for Marriage and Registration of Marriages (1962/64)
- International Convention on the Suppression and Punishment of the Crime of Apartheid (1973/76)
- International Convention on the Protection of the Rights of All Migrant Workers and Members of Their Families (1990/2003)

For further treaties of specialized agencies (e.g. ILO) see 4.5.

In addition to these 'core' conventions, the United Nations and its specialized agencies have adopted a large number of binding treaties, non-binding declarations and so-called soft law standards (bodies of principles, guidelines, codes of conduct, standard minimum rules, etc.) for human rights, international humanitarian law and refugee law. These are designed for the protection against discrimination, slavery and forced labour, the rights of prisoners, rights during criminal proceedings, rights to social and economic development, nationality, human rights of women and the right to self-determination and related fields.

With these international instruments, the UN has created a formidable normative framework of universal minimum standards. Although the human rights codification process can be considered as largely completed, the Human Rights Commission is continuing its standard setting activities in order to meet new challenges or to improve international monitoring mechanisms.

At present, inter-sessional working groups have been set up to draft a binding treaty on enforced disappearances and an Optional Protocol to the CESCR introducing an individual complaints procedure in the field of economic, social and cultural rights. However, the biggest challenge for UN human rights protection is not so much to prepare new standards or perfect existing ones, but to put them into practice and have them effectively monitored and enforced internationally.

4.3.8. Treaty Monitoring Bodies

All of the treaty monitoring bodies of the 'core' conventions are **independent bodies of experts**. In those cases where they also decide on complaints (i.e. with the exception of the Committee on Economic, Social and Cultural Rights and the Committee on the Rights of the Child), they can be regarded as **quasi-judicial bodies**. Apart from the Committee on Economic, Social and Cultural Rights, which is not provided for in the Covenant and which is elected by ECOSOC, members are elected by the states parties for the duration of four years and may be re-elected. Their work for the Committees is usually done on an honorary and voluntary basis.

The number of weeks in session is partly defined in the Convention, in practice however, it depends on the specific amount of work and the financial means available. The minimum is two weeks per year (which, de facto, was for a long time the case with the CERD and CEDAW Committees), but may extend to up to three sessions of three weeks each. Sessions are usually held in New York or Geneva. With the exception of the Committee on the Elimination of Discrimination against Women whose secretariat is supplied by the Division for the Advancement of Women in New York (4.4.8.3.), secretarial support of the treaty monitoring bodies is provided by the **UN Office of the High Commissioner for Human Rights** in Geneva (4.4.8.2.). The question is of course whether this separation still makes sense in view of the 'gender mainstreaming' policy and now that the complaints and inquiry procedure based on the Optional Protocol to CEDAW has entered into force.

Political observers and scholars frequently criticize the large number and proliferation of UN **treaty monitoring bodies** and their overlapping functions. Issues of racial discrimination, discrimination against women and rights of the child, are not only examined by the relevant special committees on the basis of respective state reports, but also by the Human Rights Committee and the Committee on Economic, Social and Cultural Rights. At the same time, it is only legitimate to wonder why individual and inter-state complaints procedures in Europe, Latin America and shortly in Africa too, may be brought before an independent regional court of human rights, while the establishment of an International Court of Human Rights at the United Nations has not even been seriously considered so far. It may well be worth thinking about reducing the current experts bodies to two full-time

4.3. HUMAN RIGHTS TREATIES AND MONITORING MECHANISMS

bodies in the medium term. A permanent Human Rights Committee might be in charge of examining, every four or five years, one consolidated report per state covering all human rights treaties ratified by that state. In addition, a permanent International Court of Human Rights should be established in order to render legally binding judgments on inter-state and individual complaints relating to various human rights treaties, as well as to conduct ex-officio inquiry procedures with on-site inspections in case of gross and systematic human rights violations.

4.3.9. State Reporting Procedure

The only mandatory monitoring procedure provided for in all 'core' treaties is that of examining state reports. Each treaty provides that states submit **initial reports** on the steps they have taken to implement the rights recognized by the treaty within one or two years of the entry into force of the treaty, to be followed by **regular periodic reports** every two to five years. The reports are to point to progress, as well as to problems and difficulties that may arise in the context of implementation of the treaty. They are also to include sufficient legal, statistical and other accurate information as may be useful for the Committees in gaining a comprehensive impression of the human rights situation and implementation of the relevant treaty at the domestic level.

Ideally such reports should be the result of a **comprehensive national discussion process,** which parliament, national human rights institutions, such as ombuds institutions and human rights commissions, as well as civil society as a whole are actively involved in, rather than being prepared behind closed doors by government officials only. After all, comprehensive, critical and objective human rights assessment, which is the real objective of every state reporting procedure, is only possible if all those concerned are actually consulted.

In **practice**, though, **reports are prepared** in many different ways. Few governments have gone to the trouble to make critical and comprehensive assessments of their own human rights situation. As a rule, preparing reports is considered an onerous obligation that is dealt with in the simplest and most general way possible and frequently causes long delays. Actively involving civil society in the process is the exception.

The task of the **treaty monitoring bodies** is to **critically examine** the state reports in **public session**. Although not expressly provided in the treaties, the Racial Discrimination Committee and the Human Rights Committee already during the 1970s have adopted the practice of requesting states to delegate high-ranking government representatives experienced in the matter and to have the reports examined in their presence only. In some cases (especially before the Committee on Economic, Social and Cultural Rights) special UN agencies, such as the ILO, UNESCO, the WHO, and FAO, are also called in to participate in the examination of state reports. UNICEF is particularly important for the Committee on the Rights of the Child.

4. UNITED NATIONS

TEXTBOX 46

OVERSIGHT OVER UN TREATY MONITORING SYSTEM

Treaty	Date of adoption/entry into force of the treaty	Treaty Monitoring Body	Number of experts	Elected by	State reporting	Inter-state complaints	Individual complaints	Inquiry procedure
CERD	21.12.1965/ 4.1.1969	Committee on the Elimination of Racial Discrimination	18	States Parties	Art 9 mandatory	Arts 11, 12, 13 mandatoryl	Art 14 optional	
CCPR	16.12.1966/ 23.3.1976	Human Rights Committee	18	States Parties	Art 40 mandatory	Arts 41, 42 optional	First Optional Protocol	
CESCR	16.12.1966/ 3.3.1976	Committee on Economic, Social and Cultural Rights	18	ECOSOC (1985)	Arts 16, 17 mandatory		Draft Optional Protocol	
CEDAW	18.12.1979/ 3.9.1981	Committee on the Elimination of Discrimination against Women	23	States Parties	Art 18 mandatory		Optional Protocol	Optional Protocol Arts 8, 10 (opting out possibility)
CAT	10.12.1984/ 26.6.1987	Committee against Torture	10	States Parties	Art 19 mandatory	Art 21 optional	Art 22 optional	Arts 20, 28 mandatory with opting out possibility
CRC	20.11.1989/ 2.9.1990	Committee on the Rights of the Child	10 (18)	States Parties	Art 44 mandatory			
MWC	18.12.1990/ 1.7.2003	Committee on the Protection of All Migrant Workers and Members of their Families	10 (14)	States Parties	Art 73 mandatory	Art 76 optional	Art 77 optional	

98

4.3. HUMAN RIGHTS TREATIES AND MONITORING MECHANISMS

As non-governmental organizations are not expressly mentioned in the treaties, some governments and committee members (e.g. in the Human Rights Committee) originally tried to exclude representatives of these organizations from the state reporting procedure. This effort failed because today national and international NGOs have a decisive role to play, providing relevant information to the experts (e.g. 'shadow reports' as an alternative to state reports), and sometimes are officially invited to participate in treaty body discussions. Media representatives are also admitted to the examination of reports.

Though not without controversy initially, it soon became common practice for the Committees to draw up their **concluding observations and recommendations for the relevant states** and publish them in their annual reports after the reports have been examined adversarially, which usually takes place in a constructive atmosphere. Governments are expected to pay heed to these recommendations and give an account of their state of implementation in the follow-up report. NGOs also play an important monitoring role in this, particularly at the national level. If the situation in a particular country is found to be highly unsatisfactory, the Committees will make use of their right to request supplementary or so-called **emergency reports** (e.g. the Racial Discrimination Committee) from those governments.

TEXTBOX 47

STATE REPORTING PROCEDURE

- Initial, periodic and supplementary (e.g. emergency) reports
- Preparation of the report at the domestic level (NGO input?)
- Public examination by the treaty monitoring body (informal role of NGOs)
- Concluding observations (country-specific) and general comments (published in the annual report)
- Follow-up (important role of NGOs)

Based on their experience with the state reporting procedure Committees also publish **general comments** (article 40(4) CCPR; article 19(3) CAT; article 45(d) CRC) or **general recommendations** (article 19 CESCR; article 9(2) CERD; article 21(1) CEDAW) on specific provisions in the treaties, which in many cases take several years to draft and adopt by consensus. Along with the decisions taken during the complaints procedures, these general comments and recommendations constitute the main source of interpretation for the rights and other provisions contained in the respective treaties.

4.3.10. Complaints Procedure

Given that complaints procedures interfere with states' sovereignty far more than state reporting procedures, only some of the 'core' treaties provide for them, usually on an **optional basis**, i.e. based on states express recognition by way of declaration or ratification of an optional protocol. Although the complaints procedure was designed on the model of the ECHR, relevant UN treaties use a much softer terminology. The term 'complaint' is replaced by 'communication', applicants are referred to as 'authors', and decisions are considered 'final views' so as not to create the impression of being binding judgments.

Inter-state complaints procedures are provided for in four treaties (article 11 CERD, article 41 CCPR, article 21 CAT, article 76 MWC). Though mandatory in the Racial Discrimination Convention, not a single state within the United Nations has so far availed itself of this procedure. This is due to the fact that governments, without violations of their own interests (as would be the case if the rights of their citizens or persons belonging to minorities which they feel responsible for are violated), are not particularly keen to act 'only' in the interest of human rights and to make as 'unfriendly' a move as to file a human rights complaint against another state. Even under the ECHR, inter-state complaints are rarely raised unless a state's interests have been violated. On the other hand, the insignificance of inter-state complaints with the UN may also be due to the fact that the procedure itself is not laid down efficiently in any of the relevant treaties.

TEXTBOX 48

INDIVIDUAL COMPLAINTS BEFORE UN TREATY MONITORING BODIES
(1976 – May 2003)

Treaty	number of cases registered	number of cases decided on the merits
• CCPR	1,171	418
• CAT	221	74
• CERD	28	14
• CEDAW	0	0
• MWC	0	0

Individual complaints procedures are purely optional. They are partly governed by the relevant treaties themselves (article 14 CERD, article 22 CAT, article 77 MWC) or by separate optional protocols (CCPR and most recently CEDAW as well). Another optional protocol is currently being prepared for the CESCR. In practice, the most important individual complaints procedure is that before the **Human Rights Committee** of the CCPR. Despite initial resistance from the former socialist states, the Committee succeeded in painstakingly developing this procedure into a quasi-judicial procedure on the model of the ECHR. The decisions of the Committee, while not legally binding, are built up and argued like judgments and delivered to the states parties with specific recommendations. Although the 1st Optional Protocol to the CCPR has been ratified by more than 100 states, less than 1200 individual complaints have been registered and less then 500

4.3. HUMAN RIGHTS TREATIES AND MONITORING MECHANISMS

decided on the merits in the 25 years of its existence. Many complaints, however, have resulted in significant decisions, which frequently go beyond comparable jurisprudence of the European or the Inter-American Court of Human Rights.

The individual complaints procedure in accordance with article 22 of CAT, has so far been recognized by 51 states. Approximately 220 complaints have been put before the **Committee against Torture**. Many of these complaints, however, do not refer to specific allegations of torture as such, but to violations of the **principle of non-refoulement** under article 3 of CAT by European states that had expelled or were in the process of expelling aliens to states where they are likely to be tortured. Individual complaints procedures before the **Committee on the Elimination of Racial Discrimination** have only marginal significance, with less than 30 registered cases to date.

Unlike the ECHR or the ACHR, procedures before the UN Committees are based exclusively on **written information**. In the absence of oral hearings or information gathered during on-site visits, these written submissions by the two parties are highly important. Should the relevant governments fail to cooperate, any well-founded submissions by the applicants are generally considered conclusive. Procedures are split into admissibility procedures and proceedings on the merits, though frequently a single decision is taken on the two parts. Complaints are dismissed as inadmissible if domestic remedies have not been exhausted, if they are not compatible with the provisions of the relevant treaty or if they are insufficiently substantiated. In principle only individuals (and groups of individuals in the case of CERD) are entitled to submit a complaint, but not legal entities and non-governmental organizations as under the ECHR, ACHR and African Charter.

In the event that a treaty is found to have been violated, usually decisions also contain an appropriate **recommendation for reparation**. Unlike the European or the Inter-American Court of Human Rights, the UN treaty monitoring bodies are not authorized to render legally binding judgments, compensation or reparation to victims of human rights violations. The **follow up** of decisions by treaty monitoring bodies is just as weak. While the UN Committees report to the ECOSOC or directly to the General Assembly, none of the UN's political bodies including the Human Rights Commission, feels responsible for effectively monitoring implementation of the treaty bodies' decisions at the national level. Thus the experts' bodies have taken it upon themselves to carry out the *follow-up* during the state reporting procedure, with variable success to date.

4. UNITED NATIONS

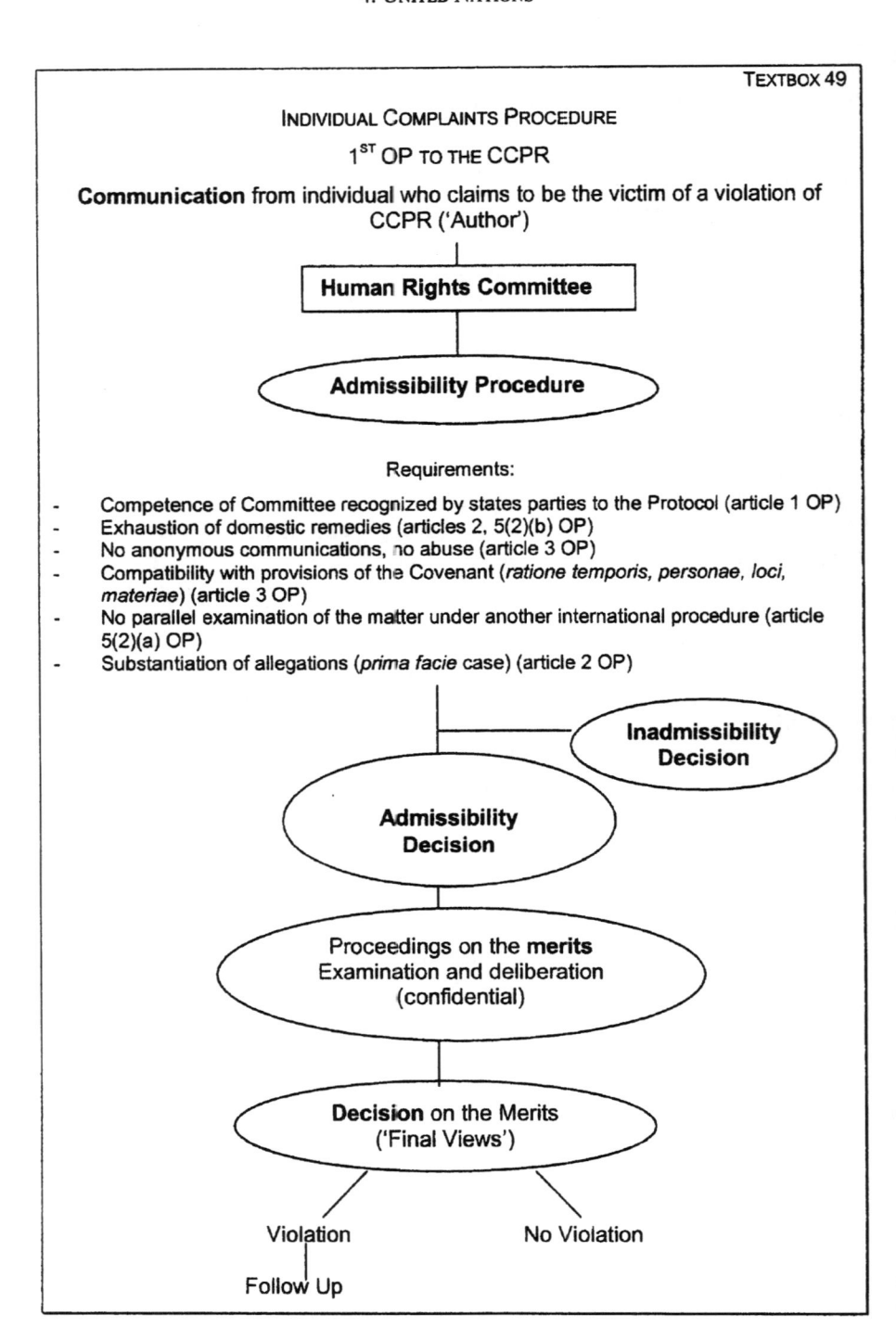

> **TEXTBOX 49**
>
> INDIVIDUAL COMPLAINTS PROCEDURE
> 1ST OP TO THE CCPR
>
> **Communication** from individual who claims to be the victim of a violation of CCPR ('Author')
>
> → **Human Rights Committee**
>
> → **Admissibility Procedure**
>
> Requirements:
> - Competence of Committee recognized by states parties to the Protocol (article 1 OP)
> - Exhaustion of domestic remedies (articles 2, 5(2)(b) OP)
> - No anonymous communications, no abuse (article 3 OP)
> - Compatibility with provisions of the Covenant (*ratione temporis, personae, loci, materiae*) (article 3 OP)
> - No parallel examination of the matter under another international procedure (article 5(2)(a) OP)
> - Substantiation of allegations (*prima facie* case) (article 2 OP)
>
> → **Admissibility Decision** — **Inadmissibility Decision**
>
> → Proceedings on the **merits** Examination and deliberation (confidential)
>
> → **Decision** on the Merits ('Final Views')
>
> → Violation / No Violation
>
> Follow Up

4.3. HUMAN RIGHTS TREATIES AND MONITORING MECHANISMS

4.3.11. Inquiry Procedure

The inquiry procedure is only provided for in article 20 of CAT and, as of 1999, in article 8 of the Optional Protocol to CEDAW. In both cases, procedures are **mandatory** for the states parties; however, it is possible to exclude application of the procedure by **opting out** at the time of signing or ratifying the Convention. During the 1980s a large number of chiefly socialist states opted out in accordance with article 28 of CAT only to withdraw their reservation later on. Of the 51 states parties to the Optional Protocol to CEDAW, only three made reservations to opt out in accordance with article 10 (Bangladesh, Belize and Cuba).

TEXTBOX 50

INQUIRY PROCEDURE

(Article 20 CAT)

Opting-out possibility at the time of signature or ratification (article 28)

Procedure

- Procedure initiated by the Committee against Torture on the basis of well-founded indications of the systematic practice of torture (information frequently provided by NGOs)
- Observations of the government concerned
- Confidential inquiry
- On-site visit to the country (with consent of the government concerned)
- Confidential report of the Committee with suggestions and observations
- Possible publication of summary account
- As of 2003, inquiry reports relating to Turkey, Egypt, Peru, Sri Lanka, Mexico and two further states (confidential as yet)

Contrary to the complaints procedure, the inquiry procedure is **ex-officio** initiated by the CAT and CEDAW Committees, provided they have received reliable and well-founded indications of serious or systematic practice of torture or forms of discrimination against women. The origin of such information is not specified, in most cases though it is derived from NGOs or media reports.

In a first step, the state concerned is asked to comment on the allegations. In the event that it is unable to sufficiently refute the accusations, the Committee may, in a second step, appoint one or more of its members to make a **confidential inquiry** that may be done **on site** with the prior consent of the government concerned. The Committee then sends a confidential report with recommendations to the government based on the results of the inquiry. It is also entitled to publish a summary account of the results in its annual report.

So far the Committee against Torture has initiated inquiries on systematic practice of torture in seven states parties and has published the results of five procedures (against Turkey, Egypt, Peru, Sri Lanka, Mexico). In four cases, the allegations of systematic torture were essentially proved, whereas in respect of Sri Lanka, the Committee did not confirm such systematic practice. The CEDAW Committee has initiated only one inquiry procedure to date, which is still confidential.

4.4. Charter Based Organs and Mechanisms

4.4.1. Commission on Human Rights (CHR)

4.4.1.1. General Remarks

To this day, the United Nations does not have a principal political organ in charge of human rights (no 'human rights council'). Instead the Economic and Social Council (ECOSOC, 4.4.4.), along with other duties, has been assigned this area of activities. According to article 68 of the UN Charter, it is authorized to entrust commissions with the care of its many tasks, among them 'in economic and social fields and for the promotion of human rights'. Consequently, it appointed a number of **regional and functional commissions** (e.g. on sustainable development) including three commissions directly responsible for human rights, the status of women (4.4.2.) and crime prevention and criminal justice (4.4.3.).

The Commission on Human Rights is by far the **most important UN body in the field of human rights**. It began work in 1946 and immediately turned to its first major task, which was that of defining human rights in a Universal Declaration of Human Rights (1948) and following this in an International Bill of Human Rights. In the beginning, the Commission did not have many member states and was guided mainly by public figures like *Eleanor Roosevelt* and *René Cassin*.

Over the years, the number of member states increased to 53 and with it, the political influence of governments and diplomats. In theory, the Commission is to serve the noble idea of human rights protection, in reality though, as one of the international community's political bodies it is made up of state representatives who ultimately act and decide on political criteria.

Nevertheless, NGOs, media and widespread public attention on the Commission ensure that it is not just political arguments that count. As a matter of fact, it is not only representatives from 53 states who come together at the Commission's annual six week session at the Palais des Nations in Geneva to exchange their ideas, but approximately 3,000 individuals who have an interest in human rights in one way or another: high-ranking politicians, diplomats, human rights experts, representatives from regional organizations, the media, persons belonging to indigenous groups and above all hundreds of human rights activists who, as NGO representatives, have been granted consultative status with ECOSOC. In other words the Human Rights Commission's sessions in March and April are a **mega human rights conference** with a colourful mix of NGO activists, victims of human rights violations,

4.4. CHARTER BASED ORGANS AND MECHANISMS

politicians, diplomats and experts discussing the human rights situation in virtually all states of the world, deliberating resolutions and drafting decisions. NGO representatives (and non-member states having observer status) are fully integrated in the Commission's work, they have the right of public speech, and like governments and experts, they may circulate written observations as UN documents in the official languages and are involved in drafting resolutions.

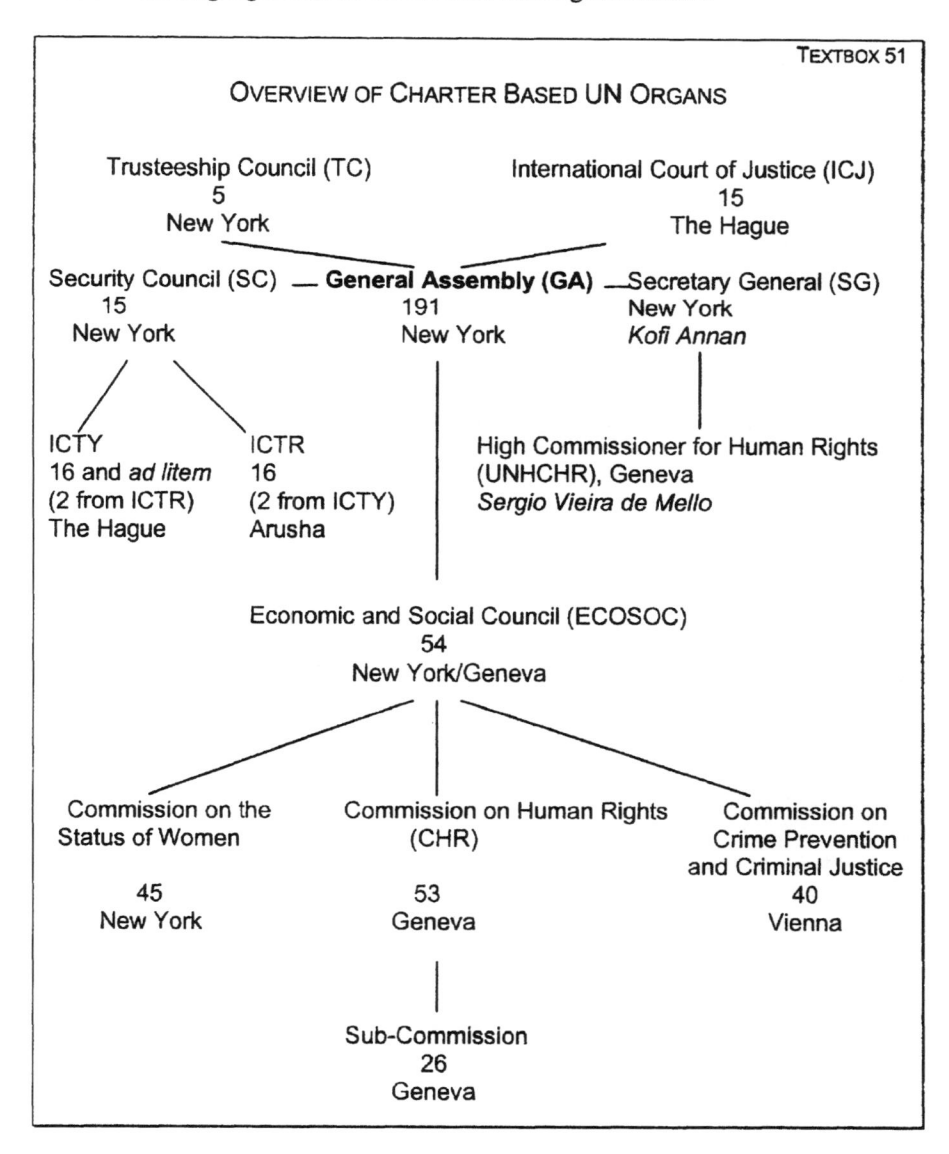

TEXTBOX 51

OVERVIEW OF CHARTER BASED UN ORGANS

Trusteeship Council (TC)
5
New York

International Court of Justice (ICJ)
15
The Hague

Security Council (SC) — **General Assembly (GA)** — Secretary General (SG)
15   191   New York
New York   New York   *Kofi Annan*

ICTY
16 and *ad litem*
(2 from ICTR)
The Hague

ICTR
16
(2 from ICTY)
Arusha

High Commissioner for Human Rights
(UNHCHR), Geneva
Sergio Vieira de Mello

Economic and Social Council (ECOSOC)
54
New York/Geneva

Commission on the
Status of Women

45
New York

Commission on Human Rights
(CHR)

53
Geneva

Commission on
Crime Prevention
and Criminal Justice
40
Vienna

Sub-Commission
26
Geneva

105

Observer states and NGOS are not granted the right to vote, which is exclusive to the 53 member states, and are also excluded from the few confidential sessions held under the '1503' procedure (4.4.1.3.). However, the Commission assumed these conference dimensions only gradually. In the first decades of the Cold War the '**no power to take action**' **doctrine** prevailed by which the Commission curtailed its own competences. It was argued that because the UN Charter did not speak of 'protection' but only of 'promotion' of human rights (2.8.), the Commission was in no way entitled to initiate steps that might interfere even the slightest bit with state sovereignty (3.1.1.).

TEXTBOX 52

UN COMMISSION ON HUMAN RIGHTS (CHR)

- Main political UN body in the field of human rights
- Established in 1946 (in accordance with article 68 of the UN Charter) as one of ECOSOC's functional commissions
- Presently 53 member states + observers from other states + IGOs and NGOs (some 3,000 delegates)
- Annual session for 6 weeks in Geneva (March/April)
- Emergency sessions: so far in relation to former Yugoslavia (2), Rwanda, East Timor and the occupied Palestinian territories
- No power to take action doctrine: promotion, standard setting, advisory services – up until the late 1960s
- Protection of human rights: resolutions, country-specific and thematic mechanisms and procedures – since then

---

The argument even referred to the discussion of human rights at the Commission. Discussing general human rights issues was tolerated, considering specific violations by individual states was not. Thus the Commission, up until the late 1960s restricted itself to setting promotion measures only, e.g. **advisory services** (e.g. holding seminars or appointing experts on the invitation of the governments concerned), as well as to **preparing an International Bill of Human Rights** and other binding human rights standards. For as the doctrine said, measures for the protection of human rights were only to be implemented on the basis of binding treaties and only for the states parties of these conventions (4.3.).

The 'no power to take action' doctrine was first undermined with the stance taken towards some pariah states. Ever since the massacre of Sharpeville in 1960, criticism of **South Africa's Apartheid politics** grew and not just for historical reasons (fight against National Socialist racism), but because its direct link to the decolonialization process was of special interest to the UN and was put on the agenda as a separate item. In 1967, a working group of five was appointed to examine the human rights situation in southern Africa and remained there until the

4.4. CHARTER BASED ORGANS AND MECHANISMS

end of Apartheid in South Africa in 1995. **Israel's human rights politics** were also put on the agenda following its occupation of Palestinian territory in 1967, and in 1973 after the coup of 11 September, **Chile** became the third pariah state to be put on the agenda as a separate item. Parallel to this, a general item was created on the basis of ECOSOC resolution 1235 from 1967, to allow discussions on human rights situations in all countries. This was later used as the legal basis for overcoming the 'no power to take action' doctrine and establishing specific measures of human rights protection at the Commission level (4.4.1.2.).

Given that the Commission only meets once a year in the spring, it can only react with delay to gross and systematic human rights violations occurring during late spring or summer. This is why eventually it was authorized by ECOSOC to call emergency sessions for urgent cases should the majority of member states so decide. The first **emergency session** was held in 1992 to deal with the particularly gross and systematic human rights violations in former Yugoslavia; sessions on Rwanda, East Timor and the Palestinian territories occupied by Israel followed suit.

4.4.1.2. ECOSOC Resolution 1235 (XLII) of 6 June 1967

As mentioned above (4.4.1.1.) Resolution 1235 was instrumental in overcoming the 'no power to take action' doctrine. Before that, the Human Rights Commission held the view that regardless of the thousands of human rights communications it received from victims or from NGOs acting on behalf of victims, according to the UN Charter it had no powers to take any relevant steps. The Economic and Social Council then passed **Resolution 728 F(XXVIII)** on 30 July 1959, requesting the UN Secretary General to prepare a non-confidential list of all general communications as well as a confidential list of all country-specific communications before each Commission session and to have these lists distributed to the members of the Commission. Country-specific communications were forwarded to the governments concerned for their comments. The Commission appointed an *ad-hoc* committee to examine these communications, but continued to hold the view that it was unable to take any other measures against the states concerned. Still, with Resolution 728 F, the groundwork had been laid for future distinction between a public procedure according to ECOSOC Resolution 1235 and a confidential procedure according to ECOSOC Resolution 1503 (4.4.1.3.), and despite the sustained resistance of many governments in the South and the East, a **first procedure for examining human rights complaints** had been established.

ECOSOC Resolution 1235 of 6 June 1967 was only made possible because of its association with the Commission's politics on Apartheid in southern Africa. It soon proved the basis for **public discussion and examination of gross and systematic human rights violations in all states** of the world. Firstly, the Economic and Social Council approved the Commission's decision to introduce a general item on the 'question of the violation of human rights and fundamental freedoms, including policies of racial discrimination and segregation and of apartheid in all countries, with particular reference to colonial and other dependent countries and territories' to the agenda. Although the wording chosen clearly reflected the concessions made to African and socialist states, it still meant that the West had succeeded in making public discussions of specific human rights violations in all states of the world possible under this item.

Secondly, the Commission and its Sub-Commissions were now entitled to examine information (from victims, NGOs, etc.) relevant to serious human rights violations based on the annual communications lists drawn up in accordance with Resolution 728 F. Again, express mention was given to the examples of Apartheid policy in South Africa and politics of racial discrimination as practiced by the white minority regime in Southern Rhodesia (today Zimbabwe). With this examination, the Commission was also empowered to make **thorough studies of situations,** which revealed a consistent pattern of human rights violations, and to report these to ECOSOC with relevant recommendations.

TEXTBOX 53

ECOSOC RESOLUTION 1235 (XLII) OF 6 JUNE 1967

- Human Rights Commission and Sub-Commission on the Promotion and Protection of Human Rights
  - Examination of information relevant to systematic human rights violations in public sessions
  - Thorough study of situations which reveal a consistent pattern of human rights violations
  - Report on the issue to ECOSOC

- Information may be submitted by
  - States
  - Members of the Sub-Commission
  - NGOs with consultative status

- Thorough studies may be conducted by
  - Working groups
  - Individual experts (special rapporteurs, representatives, envoys, etc.)
  - Secretary General

This authorization to make studies provides the legal basis for appointing country-specific and thematic **working groups** and **special rapporteurs** (4.4.1.4., 4.4.1.5.) who today are among the Commission's most effective remedies. The authorization to examine, however, does not cover individual cases, but **general situations of gross and systematic human rights violations** only.

4.4.1.3. ECOSOC Resolution 1503 (XLVIII) of 27 May 1970

Initially, the introduction of a **confidential procedure for examining communications of concrete human rights violations** in 1970 was hailed as a big success, particularly by NGOs, as it opened up new ways of having their communications examined in a formal procedure, including those against states which had not ratified a single human rights treaty. At the same time, the procedure gave an enormous boost to the Commission's Sub-Commission (4.4.1.6.). Over the years, however, seeing as the public procedure developed so rapidly (4.4.1.4., 4.4.1.5.) and there were increasing possibilities to bring complaints before independent treaty monitoring bodies (4.3.10.), this strictly confidential, highly complicated and time-consuming procedure lost much of its significance. Not even the reform initiated by ECOSOC Resolution 2000/3 of 16 July 2000 was able to eliminate the somehow anachronistic nature of this procedure.

TEXTBOX 54

ECOSOC RESOLUTION 1503 (XLVIII) OF 27 MAY 1970

'1503' Procedure revised by ECOSOC Resolution 2000/3 of 16 June 2000

- Confidential complaints procedure
- Communications by victims, other persons or NGOs may be addressed to the UN High Commissioner for Human Rights in Geneva
- Secretariat screens out manifestly ill-founded communications
- Sub-Commission: Working Group on Communications (meets annually immediately after the Sub-Commission) examines communications – where reasonable evidence of a consistent pattern of gross violations of human rights exists – referred to
- Human Rights Commission: Working Group on Situations (meets at least one month prior to the Commission) examines the particular country situations and decides whether or not to refer any of these situations to the Commission
- Commission takes a decision on
- Thorough study + report and recommendation to ECOSOC
- Whether to appoint an ad-hoc committee for investigation and/or special rapporteur
- Whether to transfer from 1503 to 1235 procedure ('to go public')
- Keep the situation under review
- Terminate/end the investigation
- Chair of the Commission announces the names of countries under examination

Up until the year 2000, the 1503 procedure included the full Sub-Commission and was even more complex and time-consuming

---

Just as the public procedure, the confidential procedure is also built on communications lists addressed to the Office of the High Commissioner for Human Rights in Geneva by victims, other persons or NGOs and compiled in accordance with the ECOSOC Resolution 728 F. Contrary to individual complaints procedures based on treaties so-called popular complaints, especially by NGOs, are also permitted, provided the relevant information is sufficiently substantiated to prevent abuse of the procedure for political purposes.

In the first step, a working group of the Sub-Commission (before 2000 the entire Sub-Commission in addition), examines all communications during the summer and refers those cases to the Commission which, according to the experts in the Working Group on Communications, 'appear to reveal a consistent pattern of gross and reliably attested violations of human rights and fundamental freedoms'.

The Commission no longer deals with individual cases, but only with **general situations** where there is a **systematic pattern of gross and reliably attested violations of human rights**. A separate Working Group on Situations performs a pre-examination following which the Commission meets in a confidential session to deliberate each situation. In the end, the Commission decides: whether to appoint an **ad hoc committee for investigation** or a **special rapporteur** for a more detailed investigation of the situation; whether to transfer the situation to the public procedure in accordance with Resolution 1235 (to go public); whether to suspend examination in view of an improvement of the situation; or whether to continue observing and examining the state concerned confidentially. The chair of the Commission communicates to the public only the names of the countries under investigation and does not provide any information on what the investigation refers to or what decisions the Commission has arrived at in the context.

Most states would rather not be exposed in a public procedure, by a resolution, or worse still by having a special rapporteur appointed to them, and are, therefore, willing to cooperate in confidential procedures and even to make some concessions to improve their human rights situation. This instrument of indirect pressure, i.e. of being able to switch to a public procedure should the government concerned not be willing to cooperate, is probably the main reason why this procedure has not been abandoned. As Textbox 55 illustrates, in quite a few cases (e.g. Afghanistan, Bolivia, Congo (Zaire), Equatorial Guinea, Haiti, Liberia, Myanmar, Rwanda, Somalia, Sudan), the investigation had been initiated in the 1503 procedure and was later transferred to the 1235 procedure. On the other hand, experience has shown that the confidential procedure is heavily politicized and many states whose governments were hardly inclined to improve the human rights situation (e.g. **Uganda** during the 1970s, **Paraguay** during the 1980s and **Chad** during the 1990s) were still dealt with in confidential procedures for many years.

4.4.1.4. Country Specific Mechanisms

ECOSOC Resolution 1235 expressly authorized the Commission to make thorough studies of situations where there is reasonable evidence of a systematic pattern of gross human rights violations. The Commission, in condemning a state by a separate resolution in this public procedure, expresses its provisional legal opinion that in the state concerned human rights have been grossly and systematically violated. Once an investigation has been done, the Commission decides on the basis of the results of that investigation whether such a violation is still and continues to be the case. If

4.4. CHARTER BASED ORGANS AND MECHANISMS

that is found to be so, the investigation is prolonged until the situation has noticeably improved and the state concerned has been removed from the 'black' list.

Of course, the Commission is not capable to conduct the **investigation** itself, but has to refer this task to the Secretary General, or to special envoys or special representatives appointed by the Secretary General. Recently, also the High Commissioner for Human Rights has been authorized to appoint a Personal Representative. The Commission may also appoint through its chairperson working groups, which regularly consist of five persons to represent the UN's five geopolitical regions, or independent experts or so-called special rapporteurs. In practice, it hardly matters what these experts are called.

Initially **working groups** were appointed to ensure some degree of geopolitical balance; such working groups included those already mentioned for southern Africa and the Palestinian territories occupied by Israel, as well as the working group for Chile in 1975. While the working group on South Africa continued to exist until the end of Apartheid in 1995, the working group on Chile was replaced by a special rapporteur in 1979. For Cuba too, the United States, on diplomatic grounds, initially proposed a working group 'only' which soon was replaced by a special rapporteur. As it turned out, Poland was the first state on the 'black' list directly under the influence of a superpower. In this case, the Commission resorted to the weakest of all possible solutions, which was to appoint a **special envoy**. Only two years later, the Commission, against all political resistance, succeeded in appointing a **special rapporteur** for Afghanistan to investigate and report on the gross human rights violations committed there by the Soviet Union.

The term '**independent expert**' instead of special rapporteur, usually indicates that a mandate does not or not primarily consist of investigating the human rights situation in the sense of Resolution 1235, but in dealing with aspects of technical cooperation and advisory services. One such example is **Equatorial Guinea** where due to gross human rights violations, a special rapporteur was appointed as early as 1979 who following some degree of improvement of the situation was replaced in 1980 by an independent expert appointed under the agenda item 'advisory services'. However, the situation deteriorated again and in 1993 another special rapporteur was appointed under the 1235 procedure, who was replaced in 1999 by a special representative of the Secretary General. In **Guatemala** with the first signs of a gradual peace process becoming evident, the special rapporteur there was replaced by a special representative of the Secretary General in 1986, and in 1987, an independent expert was appointed to support the peace process by measures of technical cooperation, especially in the field of human rights institution building (e.g. truth commissions). **Haiti** is a similar case, which since 1987 is subject to the regime of 'advisory services', but in the worst years of its military dictatorship (1992 to 1995) was monitored by a special rapporteur under the 1235 procedure.

COUNTRY SPECIFIC MECHANISMS

TEXTBOX 55

Country	Under confidential investigation by the Commission (Res. 1503)	Under public investigation by a special mechanism (Res. 1235, partly advisory services)*
Afghanistan	1981-84	1984-
Albania	1984-88, 95	
Antigua and Barbuda	1997	
Argentina	1980-84	
Armenia	1994-96	
Azerbaijan	1994-96	
Bahrain	1992-93	
Benin	1984, 85, 88	
Bolivia	1977-81	1981-83
Botswana	1997	
Brazil	1974-75	
Brunei Darussalam	1988-90	
Burundi	1974	1995-
Cambodia (Dem. Kamp.)		1993-
Central Africa	1980, 81	
Chad	1991-1999, 2002-03	2003
Chile	1975, 77, 81, 2000	1975-90
Congo (Zaire)	1985-93, 2000-01	1994-
Cuba		1988, 1990-98
Czech Republic	1997	
East Timor		1983, 1999-2002
El Salvador		1981-95
Equatorial Guinea	1976-79	1979-2002
Estonia	1994, 97	
Ethiopia	1978-81	
Gabon	1986	
Gambia	1997-99	
German Dem. Rep.	1981-83	
Germany	1994	
Grenada	1988	
Guatemala	1981	1983-98
Guyana	1974	
Haiti	1981-87, 89-90	1987-2003
Honduras	1988-89	
Indonesia	1974-75, 77-81, 83-85	
Iran	1974, 83	1984-2002
Iraq	1988-89	1991-
Israel (Occ. Palestine)		1993-
Japan	1981, 98	
Kenya	1993, 2000	
Korea (South)	1977-82	
Kuwait (Occupied)	1994	1991
Kyrgyzstan	1997-98	
Lao People's Democratic Republic	1995	
Latvia	1995, 97, 2000	

4.4. CHARTER BASED ORGANS AND MECHANISMS

Lebanon	1997	
Liberia	2002-03	2003-
Lithuania	1997	
Malawi	1977-79	
Malaysia	1984	
Maldives	2001	
Mali	1996	
Moldova	1995	
Mozambique	1981	
Myanmar (=Burma)	1979, 90-92	1992-
Nepal	1996, 99	
Nigeria	2002	1997-99
Pakistan	1984, 85, 88	
Paraguay	1978-90, 98	
Peru	1998	
Philippines	1984-86	
Poland		1982-85
Portugal (Territories)	1974	
Romania		1989-92
Rwanda	1993-95	1994-2001
Saudi Arabia	1995-98, 99	
Sierra Leone	1996-99	
Slovenia	1995, 96	
Somalia	1989-94	1993-
South Africa		1967-95
Sudan	1991-1993	1993-2003
Syrian Arab Republic	1989, 92, 97	
Tanzania (Zanzibar)	1974, 97	
Thailand	1995, 96	
Togo	2001-02	
Turkey	1983-86	
Uganda	1975-81, 95, 2000-01	
United Arab Emirates	2000	
UK (Northern Ireland)	1974	
United States	1997	
Uruguay	1978-85	
Uzbekistan	1996-97, 2003	
Venezuela	1982	
Viet Nam	1975, 94, 2000	
Yemen	1998, 99, 2000	
Yugoslavia (Former)		1992-
Zambia	2002	
Zimbabwe	2000	

* The investigation is conducted either by a Working Group or by individual experts (Special Rapporteur, Special Envoy, Special Representative, Independent Expert).

Quite evidently the governments concerned will do everything in their power not to be put on the **'black list' of countries investigated under the 1235 procedure**. Powerful states like China and Russia in particular, by exerting the necessary diplomatic and political pressure on member states, have so far successfully averted a conviction by the Commission, which decides by a simple majority of member states. Time and again, the UN has been accused of applying

113

double standards and of openly criticizing only smaller states for their human rights violations. As long as the Commission only had the three pariah states South Africa, Israel and Chile (4.4.1.4.) on its 'black list', such criticism was no doubt justified. It has to be said though, that the instrument of country-specific mechanisms has since been developed substantially and today's Commission lists of states subjected to investigations under public or confidential procedures give a fairly representative overview of gross and systematic human rights violations. Especially the country-specific reports prepared by special rapporteurs and other experts, generally speak very critically and objectively. Still, as long as the states to be investigated are selected by a political UN organ, political criteria will continue to play a significant role in this context.

The mandate of the working group on **South Africa** was with 28 years (1967-1995) the longest country-specific mechanism ever established by the Commission. **Equatorial Guinea** was under the observation of the Commission in the 1503 and 1235 procedures as well as by independent experts under the 'advisory services' for a total of 26 years (1976-2002). If one takes the 1503 and 1235 procedures (including advisory services) together, **Afghanistan** and **Haiti** have also been continuously under investigation for more than 20 years (since 1981). Usually, the confidential procedure lasted for only a few years and was then transferred to the public procedure. But some countries were under continuous examination in the 1503 procedure for a considerable period (in the case of Paraguay for 13 years) without ever 'going public'. Of all the other procedures brought to an end, those against **Iran, Chile, Guatemala** and **El Salvador** were definitely the longest. There is no question that in all of these countries, the monitoring by the Commission contributed to improving the human rights situation, although it took many years of long suffering to achieve. Whether or not this pressure will ultimately bare any fruits primarily depends on the political constellation and willingness to cooperate in the states concerned. Allowing experts of the Commission to enter the country for an on-site investigation is a clear indication of such willingness. South Africa, for example, in all the years under investigation, never granted the working group permission to enter the country, which meant that all investigations (especially the interrogation of witnesses and experts) were conducted in neighbouring states in southern Africa. Other states, such as **Iraq**, in principle refused to cooperate; generally though experts are able to conduct their fact finding missions in the states concerned undisturbed. In some cases they are supported in their tasks by one of the UN High Commissioner for Human Rights field operations, as first witnessed in former Yugoslavia and Rwanda, or by human rights field staff during peace-keeping operations as in El Salvador, Guatemala, Haiti or Cambodia (16.).

Originally the experts conducted a fact-finding mission only once a year plus additional investigations in Geneva and then submitted an annual report to the Commission. Since the end of the Cold War, human rights monitoring in the field has increased noticeably. The mandate of the special rapporteur in the **former Yugoslavia** is a good example of this trend. The former Polish Prime Minister, *Tadeusz Mazowiecki*, during an emergency session of the Commission in summer

4.4. CHARTER BASED ORGANS AND MECHANISMS

1992, was asked to conduct a first fact-finding mission within the course of a few weeks only and to report to the Commission without delay. In fact, the Commission convened a further emergency session on that subject in autumn 1992. *Mazowiecki* was also authorized to report to the General Assembly and the Security Council. With the support of several of the UN High Commissioner for Human Rights' field offices in the successor states of the former Yugoslavia, he was able to conduct regular fact finding missions on site and to write as many as 20 extensive reports in the three years until his resignation in summer 1995. This provided a very clear picture of the gross human rights violations committed at that time. Sadly, his resignation in reaction to the genocide in the Bosnian enclave Srebrenica, also shows the limitations of this instrument in view of the ruthless politics of ethnic cleansing and war against civilians. Ultimately, systematic human rights violations like these can only be stopped by more stringent measures and in some cases even by military humanitarian interventions as *ultima ratio* (16.14.) imposed by the international community. Nevertheless, *Mazowiecki's* critical and committed reports clearly achieved one objective, which was to convince the international community to intervene more forcefully and put an end to the genocide.

4.4.1.5. Thematic Mechanisms

While country-specific mechanisms generally investigate the human rights situation in a given country as a whole, thematic mechanisms deal with one specific, exceptionally serious human rights issue in **all countries of the world**. Originally, the legal basis for the appointment of thematic working groups, special rapporteurs, special representatives and other experts was also provided by ECOSOC Resolution 1235, which meant that they were only appointed for gross and systematic human rights violations. In the meantime, however, the instrument has proved highly efficient and is used for other items on the Commission's agenda as well.

The idea of thematic mechanisms was created in the context of enforced or involuntary disappearances of persons caused by police or the military in Latin America in the 1970s. The Chile working group made particular mention of the phenomenon and consequently two experts from the working group were appointed under a separate mandate to prepare a special report on disappeared persons in Chile. In other Latin American states, especially in Argentina, many political opponents of military dictatorships had disappeared, yet Argentina, for political reasons, was successful in avoiding a public country-specific special mandate being imposed. As a result, the Commission decided in 1980 to set up a **Working Group on Enforced or Involuntary Disappearances** with a universal mandate. The first thematic mechanism had been created, which by the way is still effective today, and in the more than 20 years of its existence, has dealt with approximately 50,000 individual cases of enforced disappearances in more than 90 states (14.4.).

In the years that followed, other thematic mechanisms, more specifically **special rapporteurs**, were established to deal with human rights violations such as **arbitrary executions, torture** or **religious intolerance**.

115

4. UNITED NATIONS

In 1991, a second **working group** was set up on the issue of **arbitrary detention**, but usually individual experts are employed as thematic mechanisms.

TEXTBOX 56

THEMATIC MECHANISMS

Mandate	Years	Measures
Enforced or involuntary disappearances	1980 -	Working Group
Extrajudicial, summary or arbitrary executions	1982 -	Special Rapporteur
Torture	1985 -	Special Rapporteur
Religious intolerance	1986 -	Special Rapporteur
Use of mercenaries	1987 -	Special Rapporteur
Sale of children, child prostitution and child pornography	1990 -	Special Rapporteur
Children in armed conflicts	1997 -	Special Representative
Arbitrary detention	1991 -	Working Group
Internally displaced persons	1992 -	Representative of the SG
Contemporary forms of racism	1993 -	Special Rapporteur
Right to freedom of opinion and expression	1993 -	Special Rapporteur
Missing persons in the territory of the former Yugoslavia	1994 – 1997	Expert
Independence of judges and lawyers	1994 -	Special Rapporteur
Violence against women	1994 -	Special Rapporteur
Toxic waste	1995 -	Special Rapporteur
Mass exoduses	1996 -	High Commissioner
Human rights and forensic science	1998 -	High Commissioner
Right to restitution, compensation and rehabilitation	1998 – 2000	Independent Expert
Human rights and extreme poverty	1998 -	Independent Expert
Right to development	1998 -	Independent Expert
Right to education	1999 -	Special Rapporteur
Human rights of migrant workers	1999 -	Special Rapporteur
Structural adjustment policies	2000 -	Independent Expert
Human rights defenders	2000 -	Special Representative
Right to adequate housing	2000 -	Special Rapporteur
Right to food	2000 -	Special Rapporteur
Legal issues concerning disappearances	2001-	Independent Expert
Human rights and fundamental freedoms of indigenous peoples	2001 -	Special Rapporteur
Draft OP to the CESCR	2001 -	Independent Expert
Right to health	2002 -	Special Rapporteur
Follow up to Durban	2002 -	Working Group
Discrimination of people of African descent	2002 -	Working Group

Over the past ten years, the number of thematic mechanisms has increased considerably, today many of them also deal with **economic, social and cultural rights** (e.g. rights to education, health, food and adequate housing), issues of

development policies (fighting poverty, right to development, structural adjustment policies), **violence against women, sale of children** or the human rights of **indigenous peoples**.

Most thematic mechanisms remain in force until the human rights problem has been resolved. Mandates of special rapporteurs or working groups are generally renewed for three years. Experts are not supposed to stay in the same function for more than six years. Only in exceptional cases, mandates are terminated such as the special process on missing persons in the former Yugoslavia (following the resignation of the independent expert in 1997) or the mandate on the right to restitution, compensation and rehabilitation. Of course, working methods differ for each mandate, yet some general remarks are valid for all of them. Each is dedicated to solving a particular human rights problem. For effectively addressing individual cases of human rights violations, **urgent actions** for direct intervention in burning issues (e.g. imminent risk of torture or execution) have proved particularly useful. Such actions of course require the close cooperation of professional NGOs, as well as a properly working information and communication structure. If due to successful NGO research, a government only one day after the secret arrest of a person, receives a notification from a UN special rapporteur requesting it urgently to stop torturing that person, release them from incommunicado detention, and to bring them before a judge, as a rule this is more likely to bring about the release of that person than an urgent action from Amnesty International or SOS Torture without the backing of the UN.

Apart from interventions for the solution of individual cases, thematic mechanisms are also engaged in **fact finding** missions to get a thorough idea of the extent of specific human rights issues worldwide, to address the root causes and to recommend ways and means of preventing or at least minimizing the extent of violations. Along with the necessary legal, administrative and political steps on the part of directly responsible governments thematic mechanisms today, especially in the context of economic, social and cultural rights, development, the rights of children, women and migrants, increasingly point to the international dimension of contemporary human rights issues and the growing responsibility of rich industrialized countries, transnational corporations and international financial institutions to pull their weight in solving these problems.

4.4.1.6. Sub-Commission on the Promotion and Protection of Human Rights

The Sub-Commission is the main institution created by the Commission on Human Rights and subordinate to it. It was established in 1947 as the 'Sub-Commission for the Prevention of Discrimination and Protection of Minorities' with the specific mandate to conduct studies related to discrimination in various fields. Over the years, the Sub-Commission has become a permanent advisory body for the Commission on all human rights issues and, in fact, in 1999 was renamed 'Sub-Commission on the Promotion and Protection of Human Rights'. It established six subsidiary working groups and its annual three-week session is held in Geneva every August.

4. UNITED NATIONS

The Sub-Commission is not composed of state representatives like the Commission but of (currently) 26 independent experts. It was envisaged as a kind of 'scientific' advisory body or **'think tank' for the Commission** to deal with difficult and labour-intensive tasks such as drafting standards, conducting comprehensive studies and sorting out thousands of individual communications. Past experience has shown, however, that the Sub-Commission has not always stuck to its purely advisory function but has sought an independent existence of its own. The 26 experts did not withdraw to their 'ivory tower' to draft standards and conduct studies, but for all intents and purposes, held a second human rights conference not unlike the sessions of the Commission in Geneva every summer. The same diplomats and NGO representatives would meet at the conference, discussing the same country situations and similar draft resolutions, the only difference being that only the experts and not the member states of the Commission on Human Rights had the right to vote.

TEXTBOX 57

SUB-COMMISSION ON THE PROMOTION AND PROTECTION OF HUMAN RIGHTS

- Main subsidiary body of the Commission on Human Rights; established in 1947 as Sub-Commission on Prevention of Discrimination and Protection of Minorities; name and functions changed by ECOSOC Res. 1999/256 of 27 July 1999.
- Composed of 26 independent experts
- Observers from other states, UN bodies and specialized agencies, IGOs and NGOs
- Annual session for three weeks in Geneva (August)

Main Functions

- To act as a 'think tank' of the Commission (undertaking studies, evaluating country situations, drafting standards, making recommendations to the Commission)
- Six working groups on:
- Communications (1503 procedure)
- Contemporary forms of slavery
- Indigenous populations
- Minorities
- Transnational corporations
- Administration of justice

This practice of the Sub-Commission to condemn states for human rights violations with its own resolutions and thus to copy the Commission, of course, also meant that its work was **politicized.** Some of its members were selected in a politically tainted manner, its experts were subjected to heavy political pressure, and its independence as a whole was undermined. Not surprisingly, therefore, its

4.4. CHARTER BASED ORGANS AND MECHANISMS

political component was increasingly exposed to criticism on the part of governments, NGOs and scholars. Thus, the Human Rights Commission and ECOSOC decided to launch a **comprehensive reform**, which included reducing the session time of the Sub-Commission from four to three weeks, changing its name, removing it from the 1503 procedure (but not its working group on communications), and curtailing its competences to treat country-specific situations. This reform was decided in July 1999 and took effect as of 2000.

Apart from this political component the Sub-Commission at all times adhered to its primary function as a think tank for the Commission in a most comprehensive way. It appointed several rapporteurs and drafted standards for the most diverse issues. Its working group on communications has a decisive function in the communications procedure according to ECOSOC Resolution 1503 (4.4.1.3.), which is to sort out thousands of communications and pick out those situations of gross and systematic human rights violations that are then submitted to the Commission for further treatment. The Sub-Commission also provides vital information for public procedures under Resolution 1235 (4.4.1.2.).

The **Sub-Commission's permanent working groups** on contemporary forms of slavery, minorities and indigenous populations have also contributed substantially to raising awareness for these issues. These working groups provide an ideal forum for NGO representatives, minorities and indigenous peoples to put forward and discuss their concerns informally with experts and government representatives. In 2002, the working group on transnational corporations submitted a draft for 'Human Rights Principles and Responsibilities of Transnational Corporations and Other Business Enterprises'.

4.4.2. Commission on the Status of Women

Just as the Human Rights Commission, the Commission on the Status of Women (CSW) was established in 1946 as a **functional commission of ECOSOC** in accordance with article 68 of the UN Charter. Today, it has 45 member states and is considered the principal political organ of the United Nations dealing exclusively with the **advancement of women**. All major women-specific treaties, including the Convention on the Political Rights of Women in 1952 and the Convention on the Elimination of All Forms of Discrimination against Women (CEDAW, 4.3.4.) in 1979, were drafted by the Commission, while all major measures for the advancement of women including preparation and follow-up to the four women's world conferences (4.6.2.) are carried out by the Commission.

Establishing a separate commission for the promotion of women's rights at the same level as the Human Rights Commission shows the political weight the United Nations has awarded to promoting the principle of gender equality and to equal rights between women and men. Its **separation from the Human Rights Commission** and thus from the mainstream of human rights protection, plus the fact that like the CEDAW Committee, it is not serviced by the Office of the UN High Commissioner for Human Rights in Geneva (4.4.8.2.), but by the Division for the Advancement of Women in New York (4.4.8.3.), has given rise to criticism. More than once the Commission was referred to as the Human Rights Commission's 'younger sister' with far less time in session (eight days as opposed to six weeks), fewer financial resources and less political attention from states or NGOs, all of which is reflected in the practical inefficiency of the Commission's individual complaints system that is built on the model of the 1503 procedure (4.4.1.3.). Besides, the Commission's activities for the longest time were not considered human rights activities in the narrower sense.

TEXTBOX 58

COMMISSION ON THE STATUS OF WOMEN

Established in 1946 as a functional commission of ECOSOC

45 member states elected by ECOSOC

Annual session for eight days in New York

Secretariat services are provided by the Division for the Advancement of Women (DAW), New York

Main Functions

- Preparing recommendations and reports for ECOSOC (on promotion of women's rights in the political, economic, civil, social and educational fields)
- Promotion of principle of equality between women and men
- Follow up to 1995 Fourth World Conference on Women in Beijing
- Individual petition system (similar to 1503 procedure)

In reaction to this criticism, the issue of equality of women over the past ten years was increasingly **integrated into the human rights mainstream**. The most visible evidence of this process was the strong representation of women-specific NGOs at the Second World Conference on Human Rights held in Vienna in 1993, which led to particular emphasis placed on the issue of 'human rights of women' in the Vienna Declaration (4.6.1.), the adoption of a Declaration on Violence against Women in that same year (3.2.2.), the appointment of a Special Rapporteur on Violence against Women by the Human Rights Commission in 1994, with the Office of the UN High Commissioner for Human Rights taking care of its secretarial work, and finally the 'mainstreaming' programme of action decided on at the Fourth World Conference on Women in Beijing in 1995, which is now the Commission's main working basis. It has been argued that, as the Fourth World Conference on Women was a logical consequence of this process, the Commission and the Division for the Advancement of Women ought to have been abolished and instead made part of the Human Rights Commission and the Office of the UN High Commissioner for Human Rights. Such a move would no doubt have created many synergies and would have helped to avoid double tracking in the treatment of individual complaints (following entry into force of the Optional Protocol to CEDAW in

2000). On the other hand, such integration may have risked losing or at least diminishing the significance awarded to equality of women until then.

4.4.3. Commission on Crime Prevention and Criminal Justice

The functional Commission on Crime Prevention and Criminal Justice (UN Crime Commission), established by the Economic and Social Council in 1992 as a successor to the Committee on Crime Prevention and Control created in 1971, is relevant to human rights protection for at least two reasons. Firstly, **organized international crime** and terrorism are becoming a major threat for human rights. Secondly, the Commission regularly drafts new human rights standards for the administration of criminal justice, which are then adopted as **international 'soft law'** at the UN Congress on the Prevention of Crime and the Treatment of Offenders that is held every five years. These standards bare reference to a number of human rights such as the right to life, the prohibition of torture, the right to personal liberty and the right to fair trial before an independent court, and in many cases are also adopted formally by ECOSOC or the General Assembly. They are a main source of interpretation for the application of relevant treaty norms, especially those of the CCPR.

TEXTBOX 59

COMMISSION ON CRIME PREVENTION AND CRIMINAL JUSTICE

Established in 1992 as a functional commission of ECOSOC

40 member states elected by ECOSOC

Annual session for 10 or 11 days in Vienna

Secretariat services are provided by the Centre for International Crime Prevention (CICP) in Vienna

Main Functions

- Policy guidance in the field of crime prevention and criminal justice
- Implementation of the UN Crime Prevention Programme
- Co-ordination of activities of the inter-regional and regional institutions on the prevention of crime and treatment of offenders
- Preparation and follow-up of the UN Congress on the Prevention of Crime and the Treatment of Offenders (every five years)
- Drafting of soft law standards

The Commission is composed of 40 member states, which meet annually in Vienna for a period of 10 or 11 days. Its secretarial services are provided by the Centre for International Crime Prevention located at the UN Office for Drug Control and Crime Prevention (ODCCP) in Vienna (4.4.8.4.).

4. UNITED NATIONS

Below is a list of **minimum standards** relevant to human rights drafted by the Commission on Crime Prevention and Criminal Justice or the Committee on Crime Prevention and Control over the years:
- UN Standard Minimum Rules for the Treatment of Prisoners of 1995 (ECOSOC Res. 663 C (XXIV) of 31 July 1957 and 2076 (LXII) of 13 May 1977)
  Code of Conduct for Law Enforcement Officials (GA Res. 34/169 of 17 December 1979)
  Safeguards guaranteeing the protection of the rights of those facing the death penalty (ECOSOC Res. 1984/50 of 25 May 1984)
  Basic Principles on the Independence of the Judiciary (GA Res. A 40/32 of 29 November 1985 and 40/146 of 13 December 1985)
  UN Standard Minimum Rules for the Administration of Juvenile Justice ('Beijing Rules', GA Res. A 40/33 of 29 November 1985)
  Declaration of Basic Principles of Justice for Victims of Crime and Abuse of Power (GA Res. A 40/34 of 29 November 1985)
  UN Standard Minimum Rules for Non-custodial Measures ('Tokyo Rules', GA Res. 45/110 of 14 December 1990)
  UN Guidelines for the Prevention of Juvenile Delinquency ('Riyadh Guidelines', GA Res. 45/112 of 14 December 1990)
  UN Rules for the Protection of Juveniles Deprived of their Liberty (GA Res. 45/113 of 14 December 1990)
  Basic Principles on the Use of Force and Firearms by Law Enforcement Officials (adopted by the 8th UN Congress on the Prevention of Crime and the Treatment of Offenders in Havana in 1990)
  Basic Principles on the Role of Lawyers (adopted by the 8th UN Congress on the Prevention of Crime and the Treatment of Offenders in Havana in 1990)
  Guidelines on the Role of Prosecutors (adopted by the 8th UN Congress on the Prevention of Crime and the Treatment of Offenders in Havana in 1990).

4.4.4. Economic and Social Council (ECOSOC)

The United Nations' principal task, apart from securing peace, is to promote international cooperation in economic and social matters. 'With a view to the creation of conditions of stability and well-being, which are necessary for peaceful and friendly relations among nations based on respect for the principle of equal rights and self-determination of peoples, the United Nations shall promote', according to article 55 of the UN Charter, higher standards of living, solutions of international problems and 'universal respect for, and observance of, human rights and fundamental freedoms for all without distinction as to race, sex, language, or religion.' The wording leaves no doubt that **the close interdependence between peace, development and human rights** (3.1.5. and 3.1.6.) had already been recognized by the time the world organization was founded. While the Security

4.4. CHARTER BASED ORGANS AND MECHANISMS

Council was entrusted with securing peace (4.4.7.), the other two main tasks of promoting development and human rights were summarized under the vague term 'International Economic and Social Cooperation' (Chapter IX) and assigned either to specialized agencies such as ILO, UNESCO, WHO or FAO (4.5.), or to the General Assembly (4.4.6.) and the Economic and Social Council 'under the authority of the General Assembly', in accordance with articles 56 to 60.

Thus, according to the UN Charter, the Economic and Social Council (ECOSOC) is the **principal UN organ established for the purpose of promoting human rights**. Its functions and powers are vaguely described in article 62 and include international economic, social, cultural, educational, health and other related matters. In addition, article 62(2) expressly entitles it to make recommendations 'for the purpose of promoting respect for, and observance of, human rights and fundamental freedoms for all'. To be able to fulfil these extensive tasks it is entitled, amongst others, to call international conferences, draft international conventions, conduct studies, prepare reports and make recommendations to the UN members and specialized agencies.

The 54 member states of ECOSOC meet annually for one substantive and one **organizational session** where they delegate most activities to those commissions, which ECOSOC was expressly authorized to set up in article 68. These currently include five **regional commissions** (e.g. the Economic Commission for Africa, or the Economic and Social Commission for Western Asia), as well as ten **functional commissions** most of which deal with human rights in one way or another (e.g. the Commission for Social Development which appointed a Special Rapporteur on Disability and also manages the follow up for the World Social Summit of 1995; and the Commission on Sustainable Development). Those most relevant for human rights protection, however, are the Commission on Human Rights, the Commission on the Status of Women and the Commission on Crime Prevention and Criminal Justice (4.4.1. to 4.4.3.).

The Commission on Human Rights is responsible for most of ECOSOC's human rights activities. As a subsidiary institution it may adopt its own substantive resolutions, but all decisions with organizational and especially financial implications require the formal consent of ECOSOC. Thus, the chair of the Commission may only appoint new special rapporteurs (4.4.1.4. and 4.4.1.5.) with prior approval of ECOSOC. Whether or not an NGO has the right to speak in the Commission also depends on the consultative status it has been granted by ECOSOC; every new declaration or convention drafted by the Commission must be approved by ECOSOC before it is finally adopted in the General Assembly. While ECOSOC generally considers this a mere formality and routinely confirms the Commission's decisions without major discussions, it may in certain cases cause unnecessary delays or may even be abused as a delay strategy.

Removing human rights matters from economic and social cooperation and creating a human rights council as a separate principal organ of the United Nations instead of the Human Rights Commission could solve the problem. The reform programme initiated by Secretary General *Kofi Annan* in 1997, however, aims at treating human rights as a cross-cutting issue to be mainstreamed into the UN's four main sectoral areas which are international peace and security, humanitarian affairs, development, and economic and social affairs (4.4.8.1.).

TEXTBOX 60

ECONOMIC AND SOCIAL COUNCIL (ECOSOC)

One of the principal UN organs established by the UN Charter (Chapter X)

54 member states elected by the General Assembly

'Substantive session' (annually, alternating between New York and Geneva) and 'organizational session' (New York)

Main Functions (article 62 UN Charter)

- Studies, reports and recommendations on economic, social and cultural matters
- Recommendations on promoting respect for, and observance of human rights for all
- Calling of international conferences
- Drafting conventions

Organization

ECOSOC has set up a number of subsidiary bodies, i.e. five regional and ten functional commissions to carry out year-round work:

Functional commissions:

- Statistical Commission
- Commission on Population and Development
- Commission for Social Development
- Commission on Human Rights
- Commission on the Status of Women
- Commission on Narcotic Drugs
- Commission on Crime Prevention and Criminal Justice
- Commission on Science and Technology for Development
- Commission on Sustainable Development
- UN Forum on Forests

4.4.5. Trusteeship Council

Paying heed to the **self-determination of peoples** as one of its main principles, the UN in its Charter also established an international trusteeship system (Chapter XII) to succeed the mandate system created by the League of Nations (2.4.). Along with furthering international peace, promoting the advancement of the inhabitants of the trust territories and their progressive development towards self-government or

4.4. CHARTER BASED ORGANS AND MECHANISMS

independence the trusteeship system, according to article 76(c) of the UN Charter, also served the purpose 'to encourage respect for human rights and for fundamental freedoms for all without distinction as to race, sex, language or religion, and to encourage recognition of the interdependence of the peoples of the world'.

Trust territories (former mandates such as the former German colonies in Africa, territories detached from the Axis powers as a result of the Second World War or territories voluntarily placed under the system) were under the administration of one or more states (usually a former colonial power such as the United Kingdom or France) or the UN itself based on individual trusteeship agreements.

TEXTBOX 61

TRUSTEESHIP COUNCIL

Officially suspended operation on 1 November 1994 due to the independence of Palau, the last remaining UN trust territory.

It consisted of the five permanent members of the UN Security Council

Its major functions were (article 76 UN Charter)

- Promotion of advancement of the inhabitants of trust territories (towards self-government or independence)
- Strengthening respect for human rights and fundamental freedoms

---

The General Assembly and the Trusteeship Council exercised the functions of the United Nations with regard to the above, including observance of human rights in the trust territories. The Trusteeship Council, in accordance with article 86 of the UN Charter, consisted of the **five permanent members of the Security Council** (4.4.7.). It suspended operation on 1 November 1994, as Palau, the last remaining trust territory, gained independence. The UN was instrumental in promoting the process of decolonialization (e.g. with the Declaration of the General Assembly of 14 December 1960 on the Granting of Independence to Colonial Countries and Peoples), and the trusteeship system contributed substantially to realizing the right to self-determination of peoples guaranteed under article 1 of the two UN Covenants as well as other human rights in the trust territories.

4.4.6. General Assembly

The General Assembly is the only organ that consists of all 191 UN member states (taking into account the accession of East Timor and Switzerland in 2002). It meets for its regular annual session in autumn in New York, as well as for special sessions upon request. The six main committees do most of its work. According to article 10 of the UN Charter, the General Assembly has the general competence to discuss all questions and matters within the scope of the Charter or relating to the powers and functions of any organ provided for in the Charter. The only exception is the priority granted to the Security Council under article 12; while the Security Council deals with a dispute, the General Assembly may not make any recommendations with regard to that dispute. Apart from that it is also responsible for maintaining international peace and according to article 11(3) is expressly entitled to call the attention of the Security Council (4.4.7.) to situations that are likely to endanger international peace. In the event that the Security Council, because of the veto of one of the permanent members, does not act upon this, the General Assembly may, in accordance with the well-known **'uniting for peace' resolution** of 1950, take action and make recommendations to the members for collective measures, including in the case of a breach of the peace the use of armed force.

TEXTBOX 62

GENERAL ASSEMBLY

Main deliberative organ composed of all (presently 191) member states of the UN

Decisions on important questions (peace and security, admission of new members, budgetary matters) require two-third majority; other questions can be decided by simple majority.

Regular annual session in New York (from third Tuesday in September until third week in December)

Special sessions (upon request of Security Council, majority of GA members)

Six main committees: Third Committee responsible for human rights (similar to Commission on Human Rights)

Main Functions

- Studies and recommendations concerning (article 13 UN Charter):
  - Promotion of international cooperation in economic, social and other fields
  - Realization of human rights and fundamental freedoms for all

- 'Uniting for peace' GA Res. 377 A (V) of 3 November 1950: the Assembly 'may take action if the Security Council, because of a lack of unanimity of its permanent members, fails to act in a case where there appears to be a threat to the peace, breach of the peace or act of aggression. The Assembly is empowered to consider the matter immediately with a view to making recommendations to Members for collective measures, including, in the case of a breach of the peace or act of aggression, the use of armed force when necessary.'

In the context of promoting international cooperation article 13(1)(b) of the UN Charter empowers the General Assembly to initiate studies and recommendations for the purpose of 'assisting in the realization of human rights and fundamental freedoms for all without distinction as to race, sex, language or religion'. The committee responsible for this issue is the **Third Committee,** which like the Human Rights Commission, discusses the situation of human rights in many states of the

4.4. CHARTER BASED ORGANS AND MECHANISMS

world and adopts country-specific and thematic resolutions as needed. Although the decisions taken by the General Assembly unlike those of the Security Council are not binding under international law, the General Assembly is still the main **legislative organ of the United Nations**. All major international standards including declarations and conventions for human rights are discussed in the Third Committee and adopted by the plenary after they have been drafted by other bodies, especially the Human Rights Commission or other functional commissions of ECOSOC. To become binding under international law, all treaties require ratification by the contracting states. New standards are generally accepted by consensus (which explains the extensive drafting periods), but where necessary, may also be decided with the simple majority of member states. A two-thirds majority, according to article 18, is only required for decisions on important questions, such as recommendations with respect to the maintenance of international peace, budgetary questions, election of members of other organs, admission of new members, expulsion of members or the suspension of the rights and privileges of membership.

Over the years, the General Assembly developed a widely branched system of permanent **programmes** (e.g. the development, food and environmental programmes), **funds** (e.g. the population fund or the children's fund), **offices of high commissioners** (e.g. for refugees and human rights), **research and educational institutions** (e.g. the University of the United Nations, as well as separate research institutes for the advancement of women or international crime prevention) and other **institutions** (e.g. the Centre for Human Settlements). Those that are of particular relevance to human rights will be dealt with below in the chapter on the Secretary General (4.4.8.).

In recent years, the General Assembly has increasingly resorted to **special sessions** on fundamental international issues, many of them the size of summit meetings. In September 2000, a special session was convened in New York to commemorate the new millennium (**'millennium summit'**), which just under 150 heads of state and government participated in. They adopted the UN Millennium Declaration on the main goals of human development at the beginning of the third millennium (Millennium Development Goals, MDG), which on the whole are identical to those of achieving fundamental human rights (right to education, health, etc.) and **fighting poverty**. Special sessions are also convoked as part of review processes. The latter have become popular tools for assessing international progress in the implementation of goals and decisions of earlier conferences and deciding on new programmes of action.

Thus, the General Assembly convened 12 years after the World Summit for Children of September 1990 to again review the situation of children worldwide. More than 70 heads of state and government, representatives from several hundred NGOs, and for the first time ever, over 300 children and juveniles in May 2002 participated in this **'Second World Summit for Children'**. Following some fierce controversy, especially on how to embody the rights of children, a final document ('A World for Children') was eventually adopted requiring governments to set targeted measures in the fields of education, health (particularly with regard to the

4. UNITED NATIONS

spreading of HIV/AIDS) and protection from violence, ill-treatment and exploitation.

TEXTBOX 63

MILLENNIUM DEVELOPMENT GOALS (MDG)

By the year 2015 all United Nations Member States have pledged to meet the following goals:

- **Eradicate extreme poverty and hunger**: Reduce by half the proportion of people living on less than a dollar a day and who suffer from hunger

- **Achieve universal primary education**: Ensure that all boys and girls complete a full course of primary schooling

- **Promote gender equality and empower women**: Eliminate gender disparity in primary and secondary education preferably by 2005, and at all levels by 2015

- **Reduce child mortality**: Reduce by two-thirds the mortality rate among children under five years-old

- **Improve maternal health**: Reduce by three-quarters the maternal mortality ratio

- **Combat HIV/AIDS, malaria and other diseases**: Halt and begin to reverse the spread of HIV/AIDS and the incidence of malaria and other major diseases

- **Ensure environmental sustainability**: Integrate the principles of sustainable development into country policies and programmes; reverse loss of environmental resources, reduce by half the proportion of people without sustainable access to safe drinking water, achieve significant improvement in lives of at least 100 million slum dwellers by 2020

- **Develop a global partnership for development**: Develop further an open trading and financial system that is rule-based, predictable and non-discriminatory. Includes a commitment to good governance, development and poverty reduction – nationally and internationally, address the least developed countries' special needs. This includes tariff- and quota-free access for their exports; enhanced debt relief for heavily indebted poor countries; cancellation of official bilateral debt; and more generous official development assistance for countries committed to poverty reduction. Address the special needs of landlocked and small island developing states. Deal comprehensively with developing countries' debt problems through national and international measures to make debt sustainable in the long term. In cooperation with the developing countries, develop decent and productive work for youth. In cooperation with pharmaceutical companies, provide access to affordable essential drugs. In cooperation with the private sector, make available the benefits of new technologies – especially information and communications technologies.

4.4. CHARTER BASED ORGANS AND MECHANISMS

4.4.7. Security Council

In order to ensure prompt and effective action by the United Nations, its members, in accordance with article 24 of the UN Charter, confer on the Security Council **'primary responsibility for the maintenance of international peace and security'**. The Security Council is organized so as to be able to carry out its functions in New York continuously (article 28). It is the only organ whose decisions are **internationally binding for all member states** (article 25). It is composed of 15 member states, with the five great powers emerging from the Second World, i.e. China, France, Russia, the United Kingdom, and the United States, designated as **permanent members** in accordance with article 23 of the UN Charter. The non-permanent members are elected by a two-thirds majority of the General Assembly for a term of two years. In accordance with article 27 decisions of the Security Council require a majority of nine votes with permanent members having a **veto right**.

All member states of the United Nations are obliged to settle their disputes by peaceful means and to refrain from the use of violence in accordance with articles 2 and 33 of the Charter. The only two exceptions are the individual and the collective **right to self-defence** in the event of an armed attack in the sense of article 51 (including terrorist attacks such as those on the World Trade Center in New York and the Pentagon in Washington on 11 September 2001, which the Security Council deems pertinent to that category), as well as **military sanctions** imposed by the Security Council in accordance with article 42. Apart from its powers to investigate disputes and make recommendations to solve these as laid down in Chapter VI of the Charter, the Security Council may also take concrete measures in accordance with **Chapter VII**. Firstly, it determines, in accordance with article 39, whether there is any threat to peace, breach of the peace or act of aggression. In the event that its recommendations or provisional measures are not complied with, it may decide on **peaceful sanctions** as defined in article 41, which include 'complete or partial interruption of economic relations and of rail, sea, air, postal, telegraphic, radio, and other means of communication, and the severance of diplomatic relations'. Should these measures not have the desired effect it may in accordance with article 42, 'take such action by air, sea or land forces as may be necessary to maintain or restore international peace and security'. This concept of **collective security**, however, still needs to be put into practice as the United Nations does not have any armed forces of its own. So far military sanctions have been limited to empowering states and military alliances, especially NATO, to conduct the necessary military operations on behalf of the United Nations.

Given that the Security Council is responsible exclusively for the maintenance of international peace and security, it has no explicit powers to protect human rights. As a matter of fact article 2(7) of the UN Charter, which prevents the United Nations from intervening in matters 'which are essentially within the domestic jurisdiction of any state', has traditionally been interpreted as a prohibition to interfere for the purpose of human rights protection (3.1.1.). Over the years, however, peace securing and human rights protection measures have merged closer (3.1.5.) and today it is no longer unusual for **gross and systematic human rights violations** to be considered a **threat to peace** subject to article 39.

TEXTBOX 64

SECURITY COUNCIL

Primarily responsible for the maintenance of peace and security

15 members (five permanent: China, France, Russian Federation, UK, US), functions continuously

Binding decisions upon member states: majority of nine votes, veto power of the five permanent members (article 27 UN Charter)

Special powers under Chapter VII

- Economic sanctions (article 41)
- Authorization of military force (article 42)
- Peace keeping operations (40 completed operations, 15 ongoing operations)
- International tribunals
- International Criminal Tribunal for the Former Yugoslavia: ICTY (SC Res. 808 of 1993)
- International Criminal Tribunal for Rwanda: ICTR (SC Res. 955 of 1994)

The Security Council started to develop such a strategy already during the Cold War with regard to the apartheid regimes of former Southern Rhodesia (today Zimbabwe) and South Africa. Given that the permanent members of the Security Council regularly exercised their veto right, however, the system of collective security generally did not work during the Cold War. It was not until the 1990s, that the Security Council started reacting to acts of aggression and breaches of or threats to peace by imposing economic and/or military sanctions. It first did so in reaction to the Iraqi attack on Kuwait, then later for example in Somalia, Haiti, former Yugoslavia, East Timor, Sierra Leone and Afghanistan. Even though the term 'human rights' is rarely used in relevant Security Council resolutions, many of its measures and humanitarian interventions also serve the purpose of protecting human rights (16.)

Apart from the sanctions imposed in accordance with Chapter VII of the UN Charter, the Security Council and the General Assembly have conducted **peace keeping operations** in more than 50 states, with human rights constituting an essential element in this new generation of comprehensive peace operations (16.) that have emerged since the end of the Cold War (e.g. in Cambodia, El Salvador, Guatemala, Haiti, Bosnia and Herzegovina, Kosovo, East Timor and Sierra Leone). The Security Council has developed a highly innovative interpretation of its powers for the maintenance of international peace and security as laid down in Chapter VII.

4.4. CHARTER BASED ORGANS AND MECHANISMS

It appointed **international criminal tribunals** for the former Yugoslavia and for Rwanda, giving vital incentive to the further development of international criminal law (15.). Following the attacks of 11 September 2001, it also decided a number of far-reaching measures to fight terrorism (16.15.).

4.4.8. Secretary General

4.4.8.1. Structure of the Secretariat and Coordination Mechanisms

The Secretary General is appointed by the General Assembly upon the recommendation of the Security Council for a five-year term. He or she is the head of an extremely complex administrative apparatus consisting of many different offices, departments, programmes, institutions and coordinating mechanisms. The UN Secretariat's headquarters is in **New York**, with additional main offices in **Geneva** (most human rights officials operate from here), **Vienna** and **Nairobi**.

TEXTBOX 65

UN SECRETARIES GENERAL TO DATE

- *Kofi Annan* (Ghana): since 1 January 1997
- *Boutros Boutros-Ghali* (Egypt): 1992 – 1996
- *Javier Pérez de Cuéllar* (Peru): 1982 – 1991
- *Kurt Waldheim* (Austria) : 1972 – 1981
- *U Thant* (Burma): 1961 – 1971
- *Dag Hammarskjöld* (Sweden): 1953 – 1961
- *Trygve Lie* (Norway): 1945 – 1952

Although the Secretary General is considered one of the principal organs of the United Nations, he has very few competences of his own. In accordance with article 99 of the UN Charter, he may bring to the attention of the Security Council any matter that in his opinion may threaten the maintenance of international peace and security.

The Secretariat traditionally consists of **departments** (for political affairs – DPA, for peace keeping operations – DPKO, for economic and social affairs – DESA, etc.) and **offices** (for legal affairs – OLA, for the coordination of humanitarian affairs – OCHA, for drug control and crime prevention – ODCCP, etc.), which in most cases are headed by an Under-Secretary General (USG). The Human Rights Centre in Geneva was turned into the Office of the High Commissioner for Human Rights between 1994 and 1997, its head becoming an Under-Secretary General as well (4.4.8.2.). With the **reform process** initiated many years ago and subsequently intensified by Secretary General *Kofi Annan* in 1997, a comprehensive restructuring set in, including establishment of a series of coordinating mechanisms. **Human rights** were redefined as a **cross-cutting issue** to be integrated into the four main sectoral areas by way of mainstreaming. Executive committees were appointed to coordinate the sectoral areas of humanitarian affairs, peace and security, development, and economic and social affairs, with the Office of the High Commissioner for Human Rights represented in all of them.

TEXTBOX 66

UN COORDINATION MECHANISMS

(selection)

- Four Executive Committees: Office of the High Commissioner for Human Rights in Geneva (UNHCHR), represented in all major UN sectoral areas ('cross-cutting issues', 'mainstreaming')
- Inter-Agency Standing Committee (IASC): 17 main humanitarian UN organizations in the field; chair: USG for humanitarian affairs; special working group: humanitarian actions and human rights
- United Nations System Chief Executive Board for Coordination (CEB): heads from 27 UN organizations, chaired by the Secretary General

---

It stands to reason that the UN Secretariat should have all of its activities closely linked to those of the '**UN family**' in the wider sense, i.e. to those of the relatively independent programmes and funds created by the General Assembly (4.4.6.), those of the legally independent specialized agencies (4.5.) including the international financial institutions (World Bank and International Monetary Fund), to the World Trade Organization, but also to those non-governmental organizations such as the Red Cross (11.). The **Inter-Agency Standing Committee** (IASC) chaired by the Under-Secretary General for Humanitarian Affairs (who is, at the same time, emergency relief coordinator and runs the Office for the Coordination of Humanitarian Affairs/OCHA) was created for that very purpose. It consists of 17 leading humanitarian institutions working at the operational level in the field, such as Offices of the UN High Commissioner for Refugees and Human Rights, UN programmes and funds like the Development and World Food Programmes, the Children's Fund and the Population Fund, specialized agencies such as the World Health Organization, the Food and Agricultural Organization or the World Bank, as well as non-governmental organizations such as the International Committee of the Red Cross (Red Crescent) and the International Organization for Migration. A separate working group deals with humanitarian actions and human rights. Yet another important coordinating instrument worth mentioning in this context is the **United Nations System Chief Executives Board for Coordination** (CEB, previously the Administrative Committee on Coordination, ACC) which is chaired by the Secretary General and includes currently directors or secretary generals of 27 organizations (i.e. all UN specialized agencies as well as international financial institutions, the World Trade Organization and all major UN funds and programmes with the exception of the Office of the UN High Commissioner for Human Rights).

4.4. CHARTER BASED ORGANS AND MECHANISMS

4.4.8.2. Office of the High Commissioner for Human Rights in Geneva (UNHCHR)

Time and again, states and NGOs called for the establishment of a separate UN High Commissioner for Human Rights (UNHCHR) on the model of the UN High Commissioner for Refugees (4.4.8.5.). Yet it took until the **Second World Conference on Human Rights** in 1993 (4.6.1.) for this demand to be put into practice (GA Res. 48/141 of 20 December 1993). In April 1994, *José Ayala Lasso*, former foreign minister of Ecuador, was appointed first high commissioner, to be succeeded in September 1997 by *Mary Robinson*, the former president of the Republic of Ireland, and in September 2002 by the Brazilian UN career diplomat and former head of the UN Transitional Administration for East Timor, *Sergio Vieira de Mello*. While *Ayala Lasso* had to build up the office and develop its activities under extremely difficult circumstances (handling of the genocide in Rwanda, lack of support by SG *Boutros Boutros-Ghali*, unclear relationship with the Human Rights Centre which continued to be headed by an Assistant SG, lack of financial resources), *Mary Robinson* benefited from the human rights mainstreaming initiated by SG *Kofi Annan* (4.4.8.1) and by the full integration of the Human Rights Centre into her office in 1997. She enjoyed the full support of the NGO community. During her five years in office, she took a strong stance on many controversial human rights issues, openly criticized many governments and made the Office of the High Commissioner widely known as an independent institution.

This change from being one of many departments of the UN Secretariat to becoming an Office of the High Commissioner for Human Rights has more than symbolic value. As a centre, it was a service institution for the UN's many human rights bodies (especially the Human Rights Commission and the treaty monitoring bodies), being an office of the high commissioner means having **functions of its own**. The High Commissioner for Human Rights in fact has the major responsibility for the entire UN human rights programme and should take an official position on all major human rights issues. He or she is responsible for human rights crisis management, developing different preventive measures and early warning systems, and organizing independent **human rights field presences** in presently 30 states (14.2., 16.7.). Beyond that, the High Commissioner is responsible for entrenching human rights in all UN peace keeping operations, conducting development cooperation programmes in the field of human rights and representing the human rights programme in the various UN coordinating mechanisms.

Even though the Office of the High Commissioner for Human Rights is still in the process of developing an independent profile and has many organizational, bureaucratic and financial problems to cope with, the first two High Commissioners did much to move human rights activities to the field and undertake practical steps towards peace and development cooperation. They succeeded in giving their office sustainable authority and creating a new foundation for the UN human rights programme.

Mary Robinson was hailed by the media and civil society for her open criticism of governments, including those of major powers such as the United States, China and the Russian Federation. At the same time, her frankness and commitment to human rights also meant loosing the support of many governments. Her successor, *Sergio Vieira de Mello*, is known for his diplomatic skills and good relations to most governments. His first year of office remained fairly low-key, even during the time of the United States led war against Iraq. He is faced with the difficult challenge of courageously defending human rights without unnecessarily offending governments.

TEXTBOX 67

CURRENT FIELD PRESENCES OF THE OFFICE OF THE HIGH COMMISSIONER FOR HUMAN RIGHTS (UNHCHR)

- Afghanistan
- Angola – in cooperation with UNOA, United Nations Office in Angola
- Azerbaijan
- Bosnia and Herzegovina
- Burundi
- Cambodia
- Cameroon – UNHCHR headquarters for Africa
- Central African Republic
- Chile
- Colombia
- Democratic Republic of Congo
- Eritrea – Ethiopia
- East Timor
- Ethiopia
- Georgia
- Guatemala
- Guinea Bissau – UNOGBIS, United Nations Peace-building Support Office in Guinea Bissau
- Lebanon
- Liberia
- Macedonia
- Mexico
- Mongolia
- Occupied Palestinian Territories – Gaza and the West Bank
- Serbia and Montenegro (including Kosovo)
- Sierra Leone – UNAMSIL, United Nations Mission in Sierra Leone
- Solomon Islands
- South Africa – in cooperation with UNDP, Southern Africa Regional Office
- Sudan
- Tajikistan
- Thailand

4.4.8.3. Division for the Advancement of Women (DAW), New York

While most human rights bodies and mechanisms including that of the Human Rights Commission's Special Rapporteur on Violence against Women have their secretarial work performed by the Office of the High Commissioner for Human

4.4. CHARTER BASED ORGANS AND MECHANISMS

Rights in Geneva, the Commission on the Status of Women (4.4.2.) and the Committee on the Elimination of All Forms of Discrimination against Women (4.3.4.), the two principal UN bodies for the protection of human rights of women, are taken care of by a separate Division for the Advancement of Women (DAW), which in turn is part of the Department of Economic and Social Affairs (DESA) in New York. Apart from taking care of the above organs and other more general activities for the advancement of women, the division primarily deals with coordinating and implementing the programme of action adopted at the fourth **World Conference on Women** in Beijing in 1995 (4.6.2.).

4.4.8.4. Centre for International Crime Prevention (CICP), Vienna

The Centre for International Crime Prevention (CICP) is responsible for providing secretarial services to the Commission on Crime Prevention and Criminal Justice (4.4.3.), as well as to the UN Congress on the Prevention of Crime and the Treatment of Offenders held every five years. It is part of the Office for Drug Control and Crime Prevention (ODCCP) in Vienna and has been in existence since 1948. Along with **'soft law' standards for criminal justice,** which directly refer to various human rights such as the right to life, personal liberty and security, the prohibition of torture and the right to fair trial before an independent court (4.4.3.), fighting **international organized crime** is increasingly becoming an issue of human rights protection. Gross human rights violations such as trafficking of women and children, forced prostitution and child pornography today are primarily products of organized crime.

4.4.8.5. Office of the High Commissioner for Refugees (UNHCR), Geneva

The Office of the UN High Commissioner for Refugees (UNHCR) in Geneva is currently the **biggest humanitarian organization worldwide**. It has a staff of more than 5,000 persons, most of them working in field offices and refugee camps in more than 120 states, granting support and protection to approximately 50 million **refugees and internally displaced persons** the world over. UNHCR activities include providing shelter and food, health care and educational measures as well as offering job opportunities, legal aid and social services. Apart from emergency relief for sudden refugees crises and medium term supply programmes (for refugees and internally displaced persons waiting for their situation to be solved), UNHCR also carries out integration programmes (in the asylum states), as well as repatriation and reintegration programmes in the home countries. UNHCR was founded by the General Assembly in 1951 to protect the approximately 1.2 million European refugees after the Second World War. Although the Office of the High Commissioner is formally an institution of the General Assembly and has to report to the General Assembly, over the years it has become practically independent and is monitored by its own executive committee of 57 member states. Shortly after its creation the General Assembly adopted the **1951 Geneva Refugee Convention,** which was originally designed for European post-war refugees only, but later on was extended by the 1967 Protocol to include other refugees as well.

Along with assisting refugees in the **individual asylum procedures** based on the Refugee Convention, the Office of the High Commissioner has in recent years been involved above all in implementing the state policy of **temporary protection** on a quota basis (e.g. for refugees from Bosnia or Kosovo), albeit without the legal status awarded to refugees under the Convention. UNHCR offices in asylum countries also contribute to monitor compliance with the **principle of non-refoulement** laid down in article 33 of the Refugee Convention, as well as in article 3 of the ECHR and article 3 of the CAT, which provides minimum protection from expulsion or deportation to the persecuting state.

TEXTBOX 68

UN OFFICE OF THE HIGH COMMISSIONER FOR REFUGEES (UNHCR)

- *Ruud Lubbers* (Netherlands): 2001 – current
- *Sadako Ogata* (Japan): 1990 – 2000
- *Thorvald Stoltenberg* (Norway): January 1990 – November 1990
- *Jean-Pierre Hocké* (Switzerland): 1986 – 1989
- *Poul Hartling* (Denmark): 1978 – 1985
- *Sadruddin Aga Khan* (Iran): 1965 – 1977
- *Félix Schnyder* (Switzerland): 1960 – 1965
- *Auguste R. Lindt* (Switzerland): 1956 – 1960
- *Gerrit Jan van Heuven Goedhart* (Netherlands): 1951 (year of foundation) – 1958
- *Fridtjof Nansen* (Norway): 1921 – 1930 (League of Nations High Commissioner for Refugees)

In article 1 of the 1951 Convention, **refugees** are defined as persons who for 'well-founded fear of being persecuted because of their race, religion, nationality, membership of a particular social group or political opinion, have left the country they are citizens of, and who are unable to or, owing to such fear, are unwilling to avail themselves of the protection of that country' (3.1.4.). **Internally displaced persons**, on the other hand, are persons who have all the characteristics of refugees, but who have not fled or have not been able to flee to another country. These definitions are fairly narrow and do not include persons who have fled their country because of war situations, natural disasters or for economic and social reasons. Instead what makes a person a refugee is the fact that they, as individuals, are persecuted for specific, mainly discriminatory reasons, i.e. that they are victims of gross and systematic human rights violations. Looking at statistics of the main refugee streams in the past decade, it is quite evident that most refugees are from countries or regions suffering from the most serious human rights violations (e.g. Afghanistan, Iraq, former Yugoslavia, Congo, Rwanda, Sierra Leone, Liberia). A comprehensive and proactive refugee policy should, therefore, not be limited to humanitarian aid only, but rather must get down to the root of the problem,

4.4. CHARTER BASED ORGANS AND MECHANISMS

practicing effective human rights protection in order to prevent refugee flows before they even start. *Sadako Ogata*, the predecessor to the present High Commissioner *Ruud Lubbers*, made first steps towards establishing preventive refugee politics. Secretary General *Kofi Annan* then continued by introducing the necessary coordinating and 'human rights mainstreaming' measures (4.4.8.1.) for humanitarian organizations, in particular, the Inter-Agency Standing Committee.

4.4.8.6. United Nations Children's Fund (UNICEF), New York

The United Nations Children's Fund (UNICEF) is yet another example of how human rights are increasingly mainstreamed into traditional humanitarian areas and organizations. UNICEF was founded by the General Assembly in 1946. In cooperation with governments, NGO's, national UNICEF committees and other NGO institutions, it has been carrying out humanitarian programmes for children in well over 160 states of the world ever since. Like other major UN programmes and funds, UNICEF has on the whole become independent and today is governed by an executive board consisting of 36 member states. Its current executive director, *Carol Bellamy*, manages to recruit large numbers of well-known artists, actors and politicians to engage in fundraising and other UNICEF activities.

With the **UN Convention on the Rights of the Child** (CRC) entering into force in 1990 (4.3.6.), UNICEF's role has changed fundamentally. Article 45 of the CRC awards UNICEF an essential function in international cooperation for the effective implementation of the Convention. UNICEF has understood this role as a mission to **reorganize its own mandate with a view to human rights**, which has had far-reaching synergy effects. With UNICEF, the Committee for the Rights of the Child has found a strong, internationally known partner with its own offices in more than 120 states, as well as its own concrete practical programmes, projects and measures to realize the rights of children. Reciprocally, UNICEF has received a solid legal framework for its activities, which is recognized as binding by practically all states of the world, and which UNICEF can rely on in the event of a dispute with any one government. Projects to fight child labour, child prostitution and other forms of exploitation of children, as well as projects for street children are no longer carried out for humanitarian reasons only, but have been given a concrete normative framework to implement human rights of children and to promote and monitor the international obligations of states. UNICEF with its new image has shown how recognizing human rights can trigger processes of empowerment and development.

4.4.8.7. United Nations Development Programme (UNDP), New York

While UNHCR and UNICEF have exemplified successful integration of human rights into traditional humanitarian affairs, the United Nations Development Programme (UNDP) shows how much human rights and development have merged in recent years (3.1.6.). Today the programme established by the General Assembly in 1965 is considered the **largest development organization,** with a wide range of development cooperation projects in roughly 170 states worldwide. Just as other programmes, the UNDP has essentially become independent and is governed by an executive body consisting of 36 donor and programme countries. Since the introduction of the coordinating measures inspired by Secretary General *Kofi Annan* (4.4.8.1.), the UNDP Administrator, *Mark Malloch Brown*, is now also chairman of the Executive Committee on Development Operations and the United Nations Development Group (UNDG), which other programmes and funds, such as the Children's Fund, or the Population Fund belong to as well. In addition, the Administrator presides over a worldwide system of so-called 'UN Resident Coordinators' whose task it is to coordinate the growing number of field activities.

The UNDP annual **Human Development Reports,** published since the early 1990s and drawing inspiration from the 1986 UN Declaration on the Right to Development, have been instrumental in establishing a new development theory. Rather than focusing on purely macroeconomic goals and targets and raising national incomes, UNDP's present policy is guided by the belief that development is ultimately 'a process of enlarging people's choices', i.e. a process of empowerment leading to the maximum enjoyment of basic human rights. This policy has been reinforced by the Millennium Development Goals (4.4.6.), which put **sustainable human development** at the heart of the global agenda and set clear targets for reducing poverty, hunger, disease, illiteracy and discrimination against women by 2015. **Eradication of poverty** has, thus, become the overarching goal of development. By addressing the root causes of poverty, which is one of the most serious and complex human rights violations, UNDP in fact has become one of the major human rights field organizations within the United Nations.

4.4.8.8. Other Relevant UN Offices and Departments

As mentioned above (4.4.6.), the General Assembly has established a large number of programmes, funds, conferences, centres, research and training institutions, which in one way or another are linked to the human rights programme defined as a crosscutting issue.

Some of these institutions were set up to support implementation of specific human rights, amongst them the World Food Programme (WFP) for the right to food and the UN Centre for Human Settlements (HABITAT) for the right to housing. Others such as the United Nations Volunteers (UNV) or the United Nations University (UNU) increasingly devote themselves to the furtherance of human rights. The following list of institutions shows the complexity of activities at the United Nations.

4.5. UN SPECIALIZED AGENCIES

TEXTBOX 69
OTHER RELEVANT UN INSTITUTIONS
- United Nations Centre for Human Settlements (HABITAT)
- United Nations Conference on Trade and Development (UNCTAD)
- United Nations Development Fund for Women (UNIFEM)
- United Nations Environment Programme (UNEP)
- United Nations Institute for Disarmament Research (UNIDIR)
- United Nations Institute for Training and Research (UNITAR)
- United Nations International Drug Control Programme (UNDCP)
- United Nations Population Fund (UNFPA)
- United Nations Research Institution for Social Development (UNRISD)
- United Nations University (UNU)
- United Nations Volunteers (UNV)
- World Food Programme (WFP)

4.5. UN Specialized Agencies

4.5.1. 'The United Nations Family'

Unlike the programmes, funds, centres, conferences, offices of high commissioners, and other institutions set up by the General Assembly (4.4.6.), which from a legal point of view are part of the United Nations Organization and which are, therefore governed by the UN General Secretariat in one way or another (4.4.8.), the UN specialized agencies are **legally independent international organizations** with their own charters, bodies and member states. Nevertheless, they belong to what is commonly known as the 'UN family', and are rarely distinguished from the United Nations.

Consequently article 57 of the UN Charter provides that the specialized agencies 'having wide international responsibilities in economic, social, cultural, educational, health, and related fields, shall be brought into relationship with the United Nations'. These relationships are defined in agreements with the **Economic and Social Council** in accordance with article 63 of the UN Charter. Thus, ECOSOC also has primary responsibility for coordinating the activities of specialized agencies and their integration into the activities of the United Nations, e.g. by regular reports or their right to participate in the administration of UN organs (4.4.4.). The Standing Administrative Committee is responsible for implementing the agreements between the UN and its specialized agencies. In addition the

4. UNITED NATIONS

Secretary General has set up his own coordinating mechanisms such as the United Nations System Chief Executives Board for Coordination and the Inter-Agency Standing Committee to harmonize the activities of the 'UN family' members and avoid double tracking (4.4.8.1.).

TEXTBOX 70

MAIN UN FAMILY MEMBERS

Organization	Seat	Head
FAO Food and Agriculture Organization	Rome	*Jacques Diouf* (Senegal)
IFAD International Fund for Agricultural Development	Rome	*Lennart Bage* (Sweden)
IMF International Monetary Fund	Washington	*Horst Köhler* (Germany)
IAEA International Atomic Energy Agency	Vienna	*Mohamed El Baradei* (Egypt)
ILO International Labour Organization	Geneva	*Juan Somavía* (Chile)
UNDP United Nations Development Programme	New York	*Mark Malloch Brown* (UK)
UNESCO United Nations Educational, Scientific and Cultural Organization	Paris	*Koichiro Matsuura* (Japan)
UNHCHR United Nations High Commissioner for Human Rights	Geneva	*Sergio Vieira de Mello* (Brazil)
UNHCR United Nations High Commissioner for Refugees	Geneva	*Ruud Lubbers* (Netherlands)
UNICEF United Nations Children's Fund	New York	*Carol Bellamy* (USA)
UNIDO United Nations Industrial Development Organization	Vienna	*Carlos Magarinos* (Argentina)
World Bank	Washington	*James Wolfensohn* (Australia/USA)
WHO World Health Organization	Geneva	*Gro Harlem Brundtland* (Norway)

Some agencies' activities like those of the ILO, UNESCO, FAO, or WHO are directly linked to certain human rights, mostly of an economic, social or cultural

4.5. UN SPECIALIZED AGENCIES

nature. Other specialized agencies concerned with development, such as UNIDO or IFAD, also contribute in one way or another to the realization of human rights. Though still highly controversial in practice, the same is true in principle, for the international financial institutions known as Bretton Woods institutions, i.e. the World Bank Group and the International Monetary Fund, and to a minor degree, also for the World Trade Organization.

4.5.2. *International Labour Organization (ILO), Geneva*

The International Labour Organization, seated in Geneva, was founded in 1919 as part of the Peace Treaty of Versailles (2.3.). Aside from being the oldest UN specialized agency, it is also by far the most important human rights organization in the field of **economic rights**.

TEXTBOX 71

MAIN ILO CONVENTIONS

Forced Labour Convention, 1930/32 (No. 29) (161 ratifications)

Freedom of Association and Protection of the Right to Organize Convention, 1948/50 (No. 87) (142 ratifications)

Right to Organize and Collective Bargaining Convention, 1949/51 (No. 98) (152 ratifications)

Equal Remuneration Convention, 1951/53 (No. 100) (161 ratifications)

Abolition of Forced Labour Convention, 1957/59 (No. 105) (159 ratifications)

Discrimination (Employment and Occupation) Convention, 1958/60 (No. 111) (158 ratifications)

Indigenous and Tribal Peoples' Convention, 1989/91 (No. 169) (17 ratifications)

Worst Forms of Child Labour Convention, 1999/2000 (No. 182) (137 ratifications)

'Fundamental ILO conventions' (core agreements) are based on the four basic principles of the ILO: Freedom of Association and Right to Tariff Negotiations, Abolition of Child Labour and Prohibition of Discrimination in Employment and Occupation

---

In the course of its more than 80 years of existence the ILO not only established an impressive number of almost 200 international conventions and just as many non-binding standards (declarations, recommendations, etc.), but also developed several human rights monitoring procedures that have since served as a model for the United Nations, the Council of Europe and other international organizations.

Many conventions have laid down and furthered the development of international minimum standards for economic and social rights. Such standards include the right to work and protection from discrimination in occupation, the right to strike, the right to form trade unions, the right to collective bargaining, the right to social security, as well as the prohibition of forced and child labour and the rights of indigenous peoples. Even though the ILO is composed of (currently) 175 member states, its governing body (56 members) and other bodies, unlike with other international organizations, is not composed of government representatives only, but of representatives from employers' and workers' associations as well (an overall ratio of 2:1:1 respectively). This **tripartite system** is largely credited for making the ILO so well balanced and efficient. Secretarial services are provided by the International Labour Office in Geneva under the direction of *Juan Somavía* from Chile.

The ILO's **state reporting system** is different from that of the United Nations (4.3.9.) and other organizations inasmuch as, in accordance with the ILO Constitution, it is applicable to all ILO Conventions without distinction, even to those that have not been ratified by member states. It is this obligation of states to be answerable to the competent ILO bodies even for justifying non-ratification of particular conventions, which has no doubt resulted in a high degree of ratifications of ILO conventions. The ILO is one of the organizations, in which along with the **individual complaints procedure** (e.g. in the field of freedom of association) the **inter-state complaints procedure** is also of some relevance.

4.5.3. UN Educational, Scientific and Cultural Organization (UNESCO), Paris

The UN Educational, Scientific and Cultural Organization, founded in 1945 and seated in Paris, is the main specialized agency for **cultural rights,** and in particular for the right to education and the right to participation in cultural and scientific life. As the ILO, UNESCO has established relevant international standards (especially the 1962 Convention against Discrimination in Education), as well as separate human rights bodies and procedures for monitoring adherence to these standards in its (currently) 188 member states. Such procedures include, amongst others, **state reporting** and **complaints procedures** before the Committee on Conventions and Recommendations (CCR). The general conference held every two years in Paris elects the executive body of 58 representatives from member states. Its current Executive Director, *Koichiro Matsuura* from Japan, has been in office since 1999.

This specialized agency has a fully functioning and extensive network of educational institutions consisting of approximately 5,700 UNESCO schools, more than 400 UNESCO chairs at universities, 5000 UNESCO clubs, national committees and 580 associated NGOs. This network has proved a valuable asset in human rights education in schools, universities and other institutions. UNESCO is also playing a vital role in the **UN Decade for Human Rights Education,** which was launched in 1995 and will run through to 2004. In addition, the UN Decade for a **Culture of Peace** and Non-violence for the Children of the World (2001-2010), for which UNESCO is the lead agency, has done much to link peace education to human rights education.

In April 2000, the **World Education Forum** was held in Dakar, Senegal, with more than 1,100 participants adopting the Dakar Framework for Action. Signatories committed themselves to achieving education for all (for everyone to have access to and complete free and compulsory primary education) by the year 2015. Follow-up to the Framework for Action and relevant implementation measures is also carried out by UNESCO.

4.5.4. World Health Organization (WHO), Geneva

The World Health Organization established in 1945 and based in Geneva has 192 member states, which is more than the United Nations. It is the main authority on implementation of the social **human right to health,** which is closely linked to the right to an adequate standard of living and the right to food. The right to health is not to be understood as the right to be healthy, but as the right to the enjoyment of a variety of facilities, goods, services and conditions necessary for the realization of the highest attainable standard of health. The WHO's Constitution defines health as a state of complete physical, mental and social well-being and not merely as the absence of disease or infirmity. WHO functions include: coordinating international health work, assisting governments in strengthening national health services and related education, initiating campaigns to eradicate epidemic, endemic and other diseases, and conducting programmes and projects of health care in many countries of the world. Its **global programme on AIDS/HIV** gained international reputation and is important not only from the point of view of the medical measures it pursues, but also because of the human rights approach it has taken and the tireless efforts to point out the dangers of discriminating against HIV positive persons and persons suffering from AIDS.

The World Health Assembly held annually in Geneva elects the executive board, which consists of 32 representatives from member states. *Gro Harlem Brundtland* of Norway has been head of the secretariat with its 3,500 health and other experts since 1998.

4.5.5. Food and Agriculture Organization (FAO), Rome

The **right to adequate food** and **eradication of hunger** are closely linked to the right to health and adequate living standards. The Food and Agriculture Organization seated in Rome has been dedicated to this primary goal in the fight against poverty since its foundation in 1945. It is one of the **largest specialized UN agencies** whose functions include amongst others raising the level of nutrition, improving agriculture productivity, ensuring fair distribution of food and improving living conditions for the rural population through appropriate measures and implementation of concrete programmes and projects.

The FAO works in close cooperation with other relevant UN programmes, su.. as the World Food Programme (WFP) and the UN Environment Programme, as well as with programmes and institutions concerned with development cooperation, in particular the UNDP. A specific priority of FAO is encouraging sustainable agriculture and rural development, a long-term strategy for increasing food production and food security while conserving natural resources for future generations. The overarching goal of **food security** is defined as the access of all people at all times to the food they need for an active and healthy life. At the World Food Summit in 1996, more than 100 heads of state or government adopted the Rome Declaration on World Food Security and decided to reduce by half the number of undernourished people by the year 2015, a target, which has been reaffirmed in the Millennium Development Goals (4.4.6.)

The currently 183 member states plus the EU as a member organization meet at the FAO Conference in Rome every two years. They elect the council, which consists of 49 representatives from member states. *Jacques Diouf* from Senegal has been Head of the Secretariat with more than 4000 employees since 1994.

4.5.6. World Bank and International Monetary Fund (IMF), Washington

The World Bank, established in Bretton Woods in 1944, and the International Monetary Fund (IMF), are the two main **international financial institutions** (IFIs). Strictly speaking, the World Bank consists of five closely linked institutions with the International Bank for Reconstruction and Development (IBRD) and the International Development Association (IDA) forming the core of the **World Bank Group**. The IBRD receives most of its budget from international financial markets and has been set up to grant loans and to conduct development programmes in middle-income and creditworthy poorer countries. The IDA, on the other hand, is financed by contributions from industrialized countries. Its task is to grant interest-free credits and other financial aid to the 78 poorest countries. The total annual volume of credits and donations from the IBRD and the IDA in recent years has amounted to approximately USD 20 billion. The World Bank Group has 184 member states. The five largest 'shareholders' are France, Germany, Japan, the United Kingdom and the United States. These states have the most influence, each represented by an Executive Director on the 24-member board. *James D. Wolfensohn* (United States) has been President of the World Bank since 1995, and *Horst Köhler* from Germany has been Managing Director of the IMF since 2000.

The original mandate for the World Bank and the IMF did not make any reference to human rights, but mainly consisted in stabilizing international financial markets (IMF) and avoiding world economic depressions through adequate monetary and economic control instruments. Human rights at that time were still considered political goals, which were not supposed to interfere with economically oriented decision-making processes.

In actual fact though, strict distinction between economy, finances, development and human rights is no longer justified (3.1.6.). The rigid **structural adjustment programmes** (SAPs) defined by the two financial institutions to achieve budget and economic growth objectives have had devastating effects on the human rights situation in many development countries. Cuts in social expenditures have been felt by the poorest of the poor, consequently, both the World Bank and the IMF have come under intense criticism from the international civil society. It has held these two institutions accountable for the rise in poverty, and for several human rights violations committed in connection with the building of dams and other oversized status projects.

4.5. UN SPECIALIZED AGENCIES

Since the 1990s, a **new way of thinking** has been gaining ground here, too. Although human rights are still dismissed as 'political elements' formally (especially by the IMF), in substance, not even the IFIs can continue to ignore the need for politics based on internationally recognized human rights. Aside from the heavy criticism from NGOs, three main factors have been responsible for this change in thinking: the shift of the development paradigm from a primarily macro-economic one towards 'human development' based on the needs and rights of human beings (3.1.6., 4.4.8.7.), the growing importance of reducing poverty through sustainable development policies, and the structural reform of the United Nations obliging all areas of the United Nations and its specialized agencies to work towards mainstreaming human rights (4.4.8.1.). Even if the 'Bretton Woods institutions' have been awarded a special role in the overall scenario, they are still part of the 'UN family' and have to comply with these requirements. The **Millennium Declaration,** announced by UN heads of governments and states on 8 September 2000 (4.4.6.), which amongst other things provides for reducing by half the number of people living in extreme poverty by the year 2015, has been recognized by the World Bank and the IMF as fundamental to their activities.

As a first reaction to the growing NGO-criticism, the World Bank established in 1993 an **Inspection Panel**, which deals with complaints of individuals alleging to be directly and adversely affected by a Bank-financed project. Most complaints so far investigated by the Inspection Panel refer to non-compliance with environmental and social operational policies. Although not directly related to human rights, the respective conclusions and recommendations of the Inspection Panel serve as a quality control instrument and improves the transparency of the Bank's policies.

During the late 1990s, the international financial institutions have drawn up a **Comprehensive Development Framework** (CDF) identifying poverty reduction as the new and overarching goal of their activities. Since December 1999, the preparation of so-called **Poverty Reduction Strategy Papers** (PRSPs) has been serving as one of the main tools in this framework. The idea behind them is for poor and heavily indebted countries to develop long-term strategies to gradually reduce poverty of their own accord and to commit themselves to achieving the goals set out in the respective PRSPs. Even though human rights have so far hardly been integrated explicitly into the PRSP process, many of the goals set out in the PRSPs, such as easier access to educational, judicial and health care systems are in harmony with achieving economic, social and cultural rights and to some extent civil and political rights as well. Focusing on the poorest while ensuring that the PRSPs are the result of a country-driven process developed with the participation of all, including the poor, is also in accordance with human rights objectives. Since the start of the initiative as many as 26 states have presented full PRSPs and an additional 45 states have presented interim PRSPs. Once the World Bank or the IMF have recognized these, they use them as a basis for **debt relief** as part of the Debt Initiative for Heavily Indebted Poor Countries (HIPCs), as well as for granting loans and financing development programmes. The PRSP strategy is highly regarded as a major and promising new initiative for the reduction of poverty. Other international organizations such as the UNDP or the OECD as well as bilateral state development agencies in Canada, Denmark, France, the Netherlands, the United Kingdom and others have started using it as a basis for their bilateral development programmes. The Office of the High Commissioner for Human Rights, upon the initiative of the UN Committee on Economic, Social and Cultural Rights (4.3.2.), in September 2002 has published a set of 'Draft Guidelines: A Human Rights Approach to Poverty Reduction Strategies' with the aim of integrating human rights into the PRSP concept.

4.5.7. The World Trade Organization (WTO), Geneva

The World Trade Organization established in 1994 to succeed the General Agreement on Tariffs and Trade (**GATT**) is the only global international organization dealing with the rules of trade between nations. According to its own website, its main function is 'to ensure that trade flows as smoothly, predictably and freely as possible', and its goal is 'to help producers of goods and services, exporters, and importers conduct their business'. Although the WTO participates in the United Nations Chief Executives Board for Coordination (4.4.8.1.), it is, strictly speaking, not a specialized agency of the United Nations and, therefore, not formally answerable to the UN human rights regime as are the members of the UN Family, including the World Bank and the IMF.

In recent years, the WTO has become the most prominent **symbol of globalization in times of neo-liberalism**, associated with all the human rights violations this entails. Consequently it has also been receiving the brunt of criticism from the international civil society, which all too often is simply dismissed as being 'anti-globalization'. Such criticism, however, is not aimed at globalization as such, but rather at the way it is practiced as a primarily economic phenomenon characterized by deregulation and privatization, and leaning towards practically unlimited liberalization of world trade and international financial markets. Transnational corporations (TNCs) are the ones who benefit most from this trend. Their turnovers are often many times bigger than the gross domestic products of small countries, yet it seems almost impossible to tie them to any international human rights commitments (3.2.2.). On the downside, states are gradually shunning their legal and political responsibility for human rights violations committed on economic grounds. The only way to compensate for the apparent lack of legal protection and effective remedies would be for global political organizations to take responsibility for the observance of international human rights standards and to impose them on the new global players, including transnational corporations and intergovernmental organizations, including the WTO. Voluntary codes of conduct, as increasingly adopted by private business companies in reaction to criticism for human rights abuses, such as exploiting child labour, are only a first step in that direction. They are encouraged by such 'soft law' instruments as the UN Global Compact, the OECD Guidelines for Multinational Enterprises and the draft 'Human Rights Principles and Responsibilities for Transnational Corporations and Other Business Enterprises' elaborated by the UN Sub-Commission (4.4.1.6.) in 2002.

While WTO's preambular agreement mentions a number of values such as raising the standard of living, ensuring full employment and promoting sustainable development, it makes **no reference to human rights**. On the contrary, the WTO goes out of its way to stress that the politics and control instruments set out in its various agreements, e.g. the Agreement over Trade Related Aspects of Intellectual Property Rights (TRIPS), the Agreement on Trade Related Investment Measures (TRI), the Agreement on Government Procurement (AGP), or the Agreement on Technical Barriers to Trade (TBT), are 'neutral with regard to human rights', and that it (the WTO) must not be held responsible for any human rights violations that might occur during implementation of the said agreements. Human rights obligations of UN member states, in accordance with article 103 of the UN Charter, are given priority over contracting obligations arising from WTO agreements, however, economically weak states in particular do not have sufficient conflict solution capacities to handle the situation and the WTO's dispute settlement bodies are not bound by any human rights standards.

The Ministerial Conference of currently 146 member states meets every two years (most recently in 1999 in Seattle and in 2001 in Doha) to elect the General Council, which also acts as the main Dispute Settlement Body (DSB). Every state that feels its rights under the WTO agreements infringed upon may have an independent dispute settlement committee appointed for that matter. *Supachai Panitchpakdi* from Thailand has been appointed Director General of the WTO as from September 2002.

Given that human rights are currently the only universally recognized value system (1.) and as such provide the normative framework for an urgently needed global political order, the WTO, like the World Bank and the IMF (4.5.6.), will have to embark upon a process of redefining its politics in accordance with minimum human rights standards. Formally recognizing the WTO as a UN specialized agency in accordance with articles 57 and 63 of the UN Charter, and thus subjecting it to a policy of human rights mainstreaming, would be a first step in that direction.

4.6. Main World Conferences

During the past decade, states had high hopes that the vast problems caused by rapid globalization and the new political scenario after the Cold War would be solved through major conferences under the auspices of the United Nations. As early as 1990, dozens of heads of state and government met at the first World Summit for Children in New York to adopt a programme of action to improve children's living conditions. The Earth Summit of Rio in 1992 was the first major environmental conference in this context.

The 1993 World Conference on Human Rights in Vienna and other conferences on specific issues, were expected to come up with a new world order based on human rights. Although many of the objectives set out in the respective programmes of action, and many of the final documents solemnly adopted by the worlds' leaders might seem almost revolutionary, their implementation was less so and instead has had a rather sobering effect on people's minds.

> **TEXTBOX 72**
>
> **MAIN WORLD CONFERENCES AND FOLLOW UP**
>
> World Summit for Children, New York 1990
> UN Special Session on Children, New York 2002
>
> UN Conference on Environment and Development, Rio de Janeiro 1992
> UN Special Session – Earth Summit (Rio+5), New York 1997
> World Summit on Sustainable Development, Johannesburg 2002
>
> World Conference on Human Rights, Vienna 1993
>
> International Conference on Population and Development, Cairo 1994
> UN Special Session (Cairo+5), New York 1999
>
> World Summit for Social Development, Copenhagen 1995
> UN Special Session for Social Development and Beyond, Geneva 2000
>
> World Conference on Women, Beijing 1995
> UN Special Session (Beijing+5), New York 2000
>
> UN Conference on Human Settlements (HABITAT II), Istanbul, 1996
> UN Special Session (Istanbul+5), New York 2001
>
> World Congress against Commercial Sexual Exploitation of Children, Stockholm 1996
> Second World Congress against Commercial Sexual Exploitation of Children, Yokohama 2001
>
> World Food Summit, Rome 1996
> World Food Summit, Rome 2002
>
> UN Millennium Summit, New York 2000
>
> World Conference against Racism, Durban 2001

4.6.1. Second World Conference on Human Rights, Vienna 1993

From the 1950s onward, international progress in human rights was hindered for many years by the East-West conflict and its tendency to politicize human rights (2.6.). When the CSCE solemnly declared the **end of the Cold War** in the 1990 Charter of Paris, hailing in a new era of democracy, rule of law and human rights for all of Europe (8.5.), many politicians and political observers saw in these intertwined values (3.1.7.) the basis for a **new world order** to be implemented without delay.

Twenty-five years after the first World Conference on Human Rights in Teheran in 1968, a new universal human rights compact was to be negotiated in Berlin, the capital of a reunified Germany and symbol of new cooperation between East and West. Yet the largest human rights conference ever in the history of mankind was barely being prepared when the initial euphoria gave way to crisis

4.6. MAIN WORLD CONFERENCES

management. The last-minute cancellation on the part of the German government and the hasty transfer to Vienna showed only too clearly that the East-West conflict had been replaced by a new, North-South conflict, most conspicuously so in the debate on the **universality of human rights** (2.7.). The countries of the South feared, not without reason, that the development initiatives and investments of the West would be shifted to the Central and Eastern European countries for the most part, and that the concurrent human rights rhetoric and politics of the North would create new dependencies for the South, new conditionality for development cooperation, and eventually end up as a 'neo-colonialism in the name of human rights'. Many dictatorships, especially in Asia and the Islamic world, used the debate on universalism to try and deny human rights their legitimacy as a basis for a new world order and to sabotage general efforts to strengthen international human rights protection.

The second World Conference on Human Rights held in Vienna from 14 to 25 June 1993, stood on shaky legs right up to the last minute because of this newly emerged North-South conflict. It was also overshadowed by the tragic events of the genocide in Bosnia and Herzegovina continuing to unfold only several hundred kilometres southeast of Vienna (16.9.). Looking back it seems almost a miracle that against all odds **171 heads of state and government** managed to pass the extensive Vienna Declaration and Programme of Action and thus lay the groundwork for a new and future-oriented UN human rights programme approved by consensus. This success is due not only to the commitment and diplomatic skills of many human individuals actively involved in the drafting process, but also to the pressure of more than **1,500 non-governmental organizations,** which under the banner of 'all human rights for all' were able to push through long-standing demands and which demonstrated the growing power of a globally networked civil society.

The **Vienna Declaration and Programme of Action** contains a number of quite specific objectives and recommendations, some of which have been implemented since. These include amongst others: improving the human rights of women, as expressed in the Optional Protocol to CEDAW (4.3.4.) and the Declaration and appointment of a Special Rapporteur on Violence against Women (3.2.2.); strengthening the human rights of the child through universal ratification of CRC (4.3.6.) and support of the fight against exploitation of children, i.e. against particularly dangerous forms of child labour, child prostitution or child soldiers; improving the rights of minorities, indigenous peoples and persons with disabilities; setting effective measures against racial discrimination, ethnic cleansing and other excessive forms of intolerance; combating torture, e.g. through adoption of the Optional Protocol to CAT for a universal system of visits to places of detention (4.3.5. and 14.1.), combating the phenomenon of enforced disappearances; strengthening the international implementation of economic, social and cultural rights by drafting an optional protocol to the CESCR in order to allow individual complaints procedures under that Covenant (4.3.2.); adopting the declaration on the protection of 'human rights defenders' (11.4.); consolidating and coordinating the UN treaty monitoring bodies (4.3. and 12., 13.); declaring the Decade of Human

Rights Education (1995 to 2004) and creating a permanent International Criminal Court (15.6.).

Given the controversial events in the past, special emphasis needs to be placed on the express affirmation that **all human rights are universal, indivisible and interdependent,** irrespective of national, regional, or other peculiarities, and that international protection of human rights is a legitimate task of the international community (2.7.). By the same token, the United Nations for the first time ever unanimously (including the United States) recognized the human right to development and declared reduction of poverty and indebtedness a human rights goal (3.1.6.). Finally, the World Conference decided to establish the post of a **United Nations High Commissioner for Human Rights**, a demand made by Amnesty International and other NGOs, which was heavily contested to the very end. This most significant of all items under the Vienna Declaration with regard to further development of the entire UN human rights programme and implementation of the above recommendations was formally adopted by the General Assembly in December 1993 (4.4.8.2.). The activities of the three High Commissioners to date have proved that this organizational reform was more than a symbolic renaming of the former Human Rights Centre in Geneva, as some critics had characterized it. This new office, in addition to providing secretarial services to the different human rights bodies of the United Nations, has its own tasks to fulfil, such as issuing official statements on major human rights issues worldwide, coordinating all UN human rights activities and mainstreaming human rights, as well as shifting human rights to the field. The UN Office of the High Commissioner draws its political legitimacy and substance from the Vienna Declaration and Programme of Action, a major political document that will prove its worth in the future development of the UN human rights programme.

4.6.2. Fourth World Conference on Women, Beijing 1995

Furtherance of the status of women and the fight against their discrimination cannot be treated separately from human rights; human rights of women are in fact a central element of international human rights protection. The strong position of women-specific NGOs at the 1993 Vienna World Conference on Human Rights, and subsequent incorporation of major women-specific issues into the Vienna Declaration, gave ample proof of these politics. **Gender mainstreaming with a view to human rights** ('women's rights are human rights') was further intensified under the pressure of several thousand NGO representatives at the fourth World Conference on Women held in Beijing from 4 to 15 September 1995.

The Chinese organizers imposed a number of bureaucratic hurdles and kept NGO activities separate from the actual conference (NGO Forum 'look at the world with women's eyes' in Huairou) to diminish the influence of NGOs, yet they could not stop human rights issues such as universality of (women's) human rights, measures against discrimination of women and fighting violence against women including traditional practices like female genital mutilation (FGM) from being the main focus of discussion and of the **Beijing Platform for Action**. The conference also called for concrete measures to improve international monitoring of the CEDAW through introduction of a complaints and inquiry mechanism, both of which have since been implemented with the adoption of the Optional Protocol to CEDAW in 1999 (4.3.4.).

Unlike earlier world women's conferences (Mexico City 1975, Copenhagen 1980, Nairobi 1985) the conference in Beijing was more issue-related and less under the influence of the North-South conflict. It was generally agreed that most of the goals set out in the future strategies of Nairobi in 1985 had not been achieved and that the human rights approach was far more promising than the traditional development policy one. During the Special General Assembly on Beijing+5 held in New York from 5 to 9 June 2000 some of the successes of this human rights approach were reaffirmed, such as express recognition of **female genital mutilation** as a human rights violation.

4.6.3. First World Social Summit, Copenhagen 1995

No doubt much has been done, especially since the end of the Cold War, to stress the fact that **economic, social and cultural human rights** are indivisible from, and equal to, civil and political rights (2.6. and 2.7.). Yet few of the industrialized countries have come to accept this new way of thinking and, in fact, many governments still believe that this 'second generation of human rights' is not justiciable in practice. Bringing about an optional protocol to the CESCR that would introduce an international individual complaints procedure for these rights has proved a real struggle, despite the express recommendations of the Vienna Declaration (4.3.2., 4.6.1.). Much the same can be said for the relationship between human rights and development (3.1.6.). It is hardly revolutionary to say that in the final analysis, the goals of development processes are virtually identical to the realization of human rights for all. However, efforts to integrate the human rights approach into the development strategies of states and relevant international organizations, from the Organization for Economic Cooperation and Development (OECD) in Paris to the World Bank in Washington, have come up against widespread fear and obstruction.

The first World Social Summit held in Copenhagen from 6 to 12 March 1995, like the Vienna World Conference on Human Rights before it, contributed substantially to raising the awareness about the **correlation between poverty, development and human rights** as well as the need for better protection of economic, social and cultural rights. For the first time ever, reduction of worldwide poverty was recognized as one of the overriding goals of development and human rights policies. It was this new awareness, which eventually convinced the World Bank and the International Monetary Fund to introduce their 'poverty reduction strategy papers' (PRSPs) and thus make **reduction of poverty** in conjunction with debt relief for the heavily indebted poor countries (HIPC-Initiative) the main focus of their new and comprehensive development framework (CDF) (4.5.6.). Other organizations such as the UN Development Programme (4.4.8.7.) or the OECD, in their new development and poverty reduction strategies, also make reference to the goals and human rights obligations set out in the **Copenhagen Declaration on Social Development**.

For the United Nations, the World Social Summit saved as a catalyst for a number of important developments. It contributed to an upgrading of the **Commission for Social Development** as one of the main functional commissions of the Economic and Social Council (4.4.4.). The call for a right to individual complaints under the CESCR was renewed and the ILO adopted a special convention in 1999 on the worst forms of child labour. In September 2000, the heads of state and government of the United Nations solemnly adopted the **United Nations Millennium Declaration** (4.4.6.), which amongst others provides for a drastic reduction of poverty by the year 2015.

4.6.4. Third World Conference Against Racism, Durban 2001

Racism, nationalism, xenophobia, religious and other forms of intolerance have been on the rise in all parts of the world, especially since the end of the Cold War. They have caused a number of ethnic and religious conflicts, wars and genocide, as in Bosnia and Herzegovina or Rwanda, and consequently must be considered among the most urgent human rights issues to be dealt with today (5.5.). Not surprisingly, therefore, great hopes were placed in the third World Conference against Racism, the first major UN conference of the new millennium, held in Durban from 31 August to 8 September 2001. It was envisaged to develop a comprehensive set of measures for preventive action against racism, xenophobia and similar types of discrimination and human rights violations. **South Africa**, having suffered from a racist regime of apartheid for many decades, and having achieved a peaceful transition from a white minority regime to a democratic government with the help of the United Nations, seemed the perfect host country for this conference.

Ultimately, however, the conference foundered because of two controversies. The first was that the states of the South, and the African states in particular, wanted the former colonial powers and rich industrialized countries to recognize the conference as a historic **chance to apologize for the crimes committed by colonialism and slavery** and to provide some form of late reparation for these early human rights violations (primarily by way of financial compensation and debt relief). These demands correspond to the growing importance of the right to legal remedies and reparation for gross and systematic human rights violations (3.2.7.), and have been compared to the compensation payments made to victims of National Socialism more than half a century after the Holocaust. Although their claims raise a number of complex legal issues there is certainly some historical justification in them. Yet the industrialized countries were quite inflexible and unwilling to accept such arguments, and it proved impossible to establish as much as a voluntary fund for reparation of past crimes and support of victims of present-day racism. The second controversy arose as the conference on racism in South Africa was held at the very time the **conflict between Israel and the Palestinians** was escalating once again. The conference was heavily politicized from all corners and eventually both Israel and the United States withdrew.

4.6. MAIN WORLD CONFERENCES

The fact that in the end, the other states managed to agree on a joint Durban Declaration and Programme of Action, came as quite a surprise to many observers. In substance, however, both documents contain little more than the general statements we have come to know from conventions and declarations made by the United Nations and regional organizations in the past.

4. UNITED NATIONS

LITBOX 4

LITERATURE

Alfredsson, Gudmundur and *Eide*, Asbjorn (Eds.) 1999, The Universal Declaration of Human Rights – A Common Standard of Achievement, The Hague

Alston, Phillip (Ed.) 1992, The United Nations and Human Rights: A Critical Appraisal, Oxford

Alston, Philip and *Crawford*, James (Eds.) 2000, The Future of UN Human Rights Treaty Monitoring, Cambridge

Arambulo, Kitty 1999, Strengthening the Supervision of the International Convenant on Economic, Social and Cultural Rights: Theoretical and Procedural Aspects, Antwerp

Askin, Kelly and *Koenig*, Dorean 2000, Women and International Human Rights Law, 3 volumes, New York

Banton, Michael 2000, Combating Racial Discrimination: The UN and its Member States, London

Bartolomei de la Cruz, Héctor et al. (Eds.) 1996, The International Labor Organization, Westview

Bayefsky, Anne (Ed.) 2000, The UN Human Rights Treaty System in the 21st Century, The Hague/London/Boston

Bayefsky, Anne F. 2001, How to Complain to the UN Human Rights Treaty System, The Hague

Baehr, Peter, *Bayefsky*, Anne, *Flinterman*, Cees and *Senders*, Mignon (Eds.) 1999, Innovation and Inspiration: Fifty Years of the Universal Declaration of Human Rights, Amsterdam

Boerefijin, Ineke 1999, The Reporting Procedure under the International Covenant on Civil and Political Rights, Antwerp

Boulesbaa, Ahcene 1999, The UN Convention on Torture and the Prospects for Enforcement, The Hague

Burgers, J. Herman and *Danelius*, Hans 1988, The United Nations Convention against Torture: A Handbook on the Convention against Torture and Other Cruel, Inhuman or Degrading Treatment or Punishment, Dordrecht

Cook, Rebecca J. (Ed.) 1994, Human Rights of Women: National and International Perspectives, Philadelphia

Craven, Matthew 1995, The International Covenant on Economic, Social and Cultural Rights: A Perspective on Its Development, Oxford

Dunér, Bertil 2002, The Global Human Rights Regime, Lund

4.6. MAIN WORLD CONFERENCES

Eide, Asbjörn, *Alfredsson*, Gudmundur, *Melander*, Göran, *Rehof*, Lars Adam and *Rosas*, Allan (Eds.) 1992, The Universal Declaration of Human Rights: A Commentary, Oslo

Eide, Asbjörn, *Krause*, Catarina and *Rosas*, Allan (Eds.) 2001, Economic, Social and Cultural Rights - A Textbook, 2nd edition, Dordrecht/Boston/London

Fottrell, Deirdre (Ed.) 2001, Revisiting Children's Rights – 10 years of the UN Convention on the Rights of the Child, Leiden

Hanski, Raija and *Scheinin*, Martin (Eds.) 2003, Leading Cases of the Human Rights Committee, Åbo

Heyns, Christof and *Viljoen*, Frans 2002, The Impact of the United Nations Human Rights Treaties on the Domestic Level, The Hague

Hodgkin, Rachel and *Newell*, Peter/UNICEF 1998, Implementation Handbook for the Convention on the Rights of the Child, New York

Humphrey, John 1984, Human Rights and the United Nations: A Great Adventure, New York

ILO 1998, International Labor Standards – A Worker's Manual, 4th ed., Geneva

ILO (Ed.) 2001, The World Employment Report 2001: Life at work in the information economy, Geneva

Joseph, Sarah, *Schultz*, Jennifer, and *Castan*, Melissa 2000, The International Covenant on Civil and Political Rights – Cases, Materials and Commentary, Oxford

Lempinen, Miko 2000, Challenges Facing the System of Special Procedures of the United Nations Commission on Human Rights, Turku

Loescher, Gil 2001, The United Nations High Commissioner for Refugees – A Perilous Path

McGoldrick, Dominic 1991, The Human Rights Committee: Its Role in the Development of the International Covenant on Civil and Political Rights, Oxford

Nowak, Manfred 1993, UN Covenant on Civil and Political Rights - CCPR Commentary, Kehl/Strasbourg/Arlington

Nowak, Manfred (Ed.) 1994, World Conference on Human Rights, Vienna

O'Flaherty, Michael 2002, Human Rights and the United Nations: Practice before the Treaty Bodies, The Hague

Ramcharan, Bertrand 2002, The United Nations High Commissioner for Human Rights: The Challenges of International Protection, The Hague

Simma, Bruno (Ed.) 2002, The Charter of the United Nations: A Commentary, 2 volumes, 2nd ed., Oxford

Symonides, Janusz and *Volodin*, Vladimir/UNESCO (Eds.) 1999, UNESCO and Human Rights: standard-setting

UNESCO 1997, Manual on Human Rights Education, Paris

UNDP (Ed.) 2002, Human Development Report 2002: Deepening democracy in a fragmented world, New York/Oxford

Van Genugten, Willem J.M. (Ed.) 1999, Human Rights Reference Handbook, Netherlands Ministry of Foreign Affairs, The Hague

World Bank (Ed.) 2000/2002, Voices of the Poor, 3 volumes, Oxford

INTERNET

www.un.org - United Nations

www.unhchr.ch - UN High Commissioner for Human Rights

www.unhchr.ch/html/menu2/convmech.htm - UN Treaty Monitoring Bodies

www.unhchr.ch/html/menu2/2/chr.htm - UN Commission on Human Rights

www.un.org/womenwatch/daw - UN Division for the Advancement of Women

www.unhcr.org - UN High Commissioner for Refugees

www.ilo.org - International Labour Organization

www.undp.org - UN Development Programme

www.unesco.org - UN Educational, Scientific and Cultural Organization

www.unicef.org - UN Children's Fund

www.who.org - World Health Organization

www.worldbank.org - World Bank

www.imf.org - International Monetary Fund

www.wto.org - World Trade Organization

www.bayefsky.com - United Nations Treaties Database

5. COUNCIL OF EUROPE (CoE)

5.1. The Three Pillars of the Council of Europe: Democracy, Rule of Law and Human Rights – Theory and Practice

There are three intergovernmental organizations in Europe that deal intensively with protection of human rights: the European Union, the Council of Europe and the Organization for Security and Cooperation in Europe (OSCE). The 15 Western European states that currently comprise the **European Union** (EU) originally organized as a tool for economic integration only. Over the years, the EU gradually developed into a political union where human rights are becoming increasingly important for domestic and foreign relations. In 2004, the EU will be enlarged to 25 European States (9.).

TEXTBOX 73

EUROPEAN ORGANIZATIONS AND THEIR MEMBER STATES

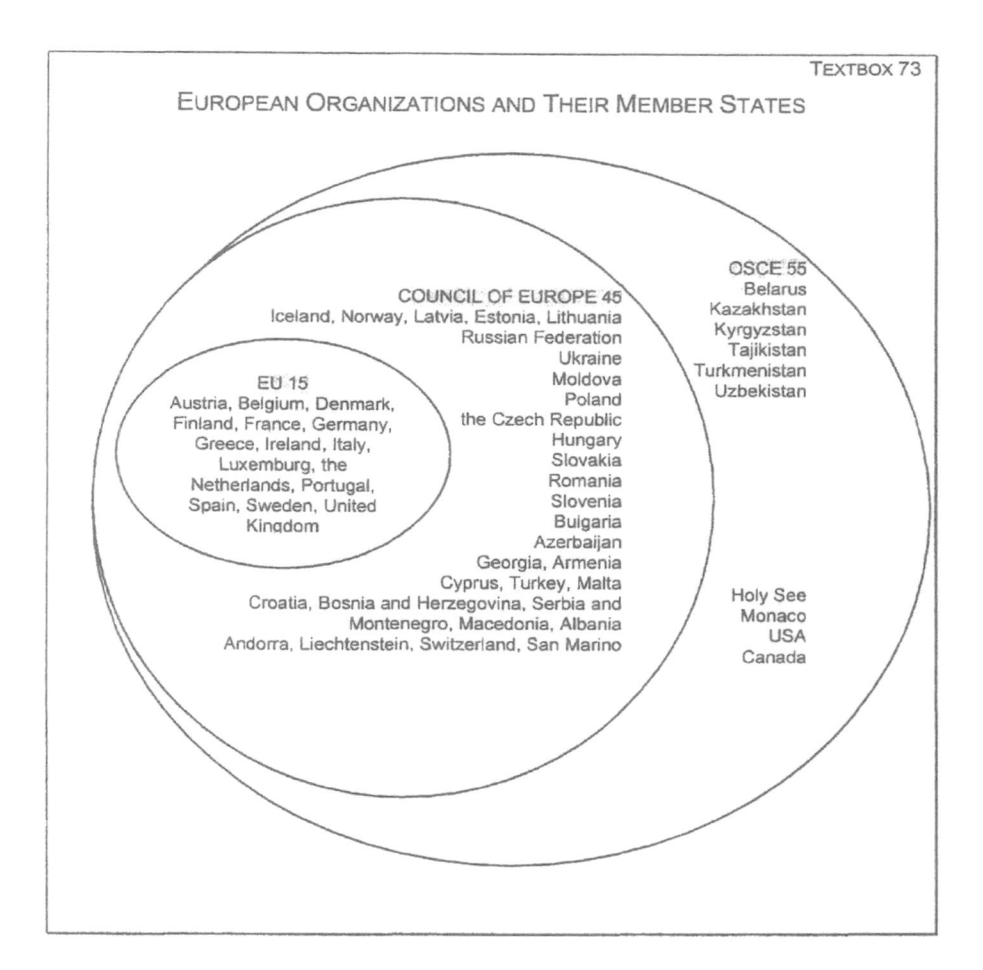

OSCE 55
Belarus
Kazakhstan
Kyrgyzstan
Tajikistan
Turkmenistan
Uzbekistan

COUNCIL OF EUROPE 45
Iceland, Norway, Latvia, Estonia, Lithuania
Russian Federation
Ukraine
Moldova
Poland
the Czech Republic
Hungary
Slovakia
Romania
Slovenia
Bulgaria
Azerbaijan
Georgia, Armenia
Cyprus, Turkey, Malta
Croatia, Bosnia and Herzegovina, Serbia and Montenegro, Macedonia, Albania
Andorra, Liechtenstein, Switzerland, San Marino

EU 15
Austria, Belgium, Denmark, Finland, France, Germany, Greece, Ireland, Italy, Luxemburg, the Netherlands, Portugal, Spain, Sweden, United Kingdom

Holy See
Monaco
USA
Canada

5. COUNCIL OF EUROPE (CoE)

At the other end of the spectrum, there is the **OSCE** with 55 member states, which includes all sovereign European states and some non-European countries, i.e. the United States, Canada and five Central-Asian successor states of the former Soviet Union. The OSCE is first and foremost a security organization, but human rights have always played an important role in the comprehensive security concept of the CSCE and later OSCE, both during and after the Cold War (8.).

TEXTBOX 74

STATUTE OF THE COUNCIL OF EUROPE

Preamble: 'Reaffirming their devotion to the spiritual and moral values which are the common heritage of their peoples and the true source of individual freedom, political liberty and the rule of law, principles which form the basis of all genuine democracy,'

Article 1(b): 'This aim shall be pursued through the organs of the Council by discussion of questions of common concern and by agreements and common action in economic, social, cultural, scientific, legal and administrative matters and in the maintenance and further realisation of human rights and fundamental freedoms.'

Article 3: 'Every member of the Council of Europe must accept the principles of the rule of law and of the enjoyment by all persons within its jurisdiction of human rights and fundamental freedoms,'

Article 8: 'Any member of the Council of Europe which has seriously violated Article 3 may be suspended from its rights of representation and requested by the Committee of Ministers to withdraw under Article 7. If such member does not comply with this request, the Committee may decide that it has ceased to be a member of the Council as from such date as the Committee may determine.'

The third and oldest organization is the **Council of Europe**, with currently 45 member states. Within the Council of Europe, human rights have always been and to this day, continue to be the main priority. It was founded in 1949 by 11 Western European states to promote **human rights**, the **rule of law** and **pluralistic democracy**, all of which are fundamental values for present-day Europe. These three pillars were on the one hand, aimed at combating fascism of the kind practiced in Spain and Portugal for some time after the Second World War and which temporarily flared up in Greece after the military coup in the 1960s. On the other hand, these fundamental values were meant to distinguish Western Europe from the communist states in Central and Eastern Europe.

Only those states that recognize and practice these three fundamental values may become members of the Council of Europe. According to article 8 of the Statute, states may even be expelled from the Council if they are found to act in serious violation of these values, as was in fact the case with the military regime in Greece, which ceased to be a member of the Council between 1970 and 1974 after the European Commission of Human Rights had found particularly gross and systematic human rights violations.

5.1. THE THREE PILLARS OF THE CoE: DEMOCRACY, RULE OF LAW AND HUMAN RIGHTS

Within this community of values defined by common historical and cultural roots, within a limited amount of time, a highly effective human rights protection system was established under the **European Convention for the Protection of Human Rights and Fundamental Freedoms** (ECHR). It was subsequently used as a model for other regional and universal systems. With the end of the Cold War, the Council of Europe to some extent changed its policies by giving priority to a **speedy admission of Central and Eastern European countries** in transition, irrespective of their state of development concerning democracy, the rule of law and human rights. Typical examples of a rushed acceptance – measured by the political situation at the time – are Albania, Croatia, the Ukraine and the Russian Ferderation in 1995 and 1996, and more recently Georgia, Armenia, Azerbaijan, Bosnia and Herzegovina, as well as Serbia and Montenegro.

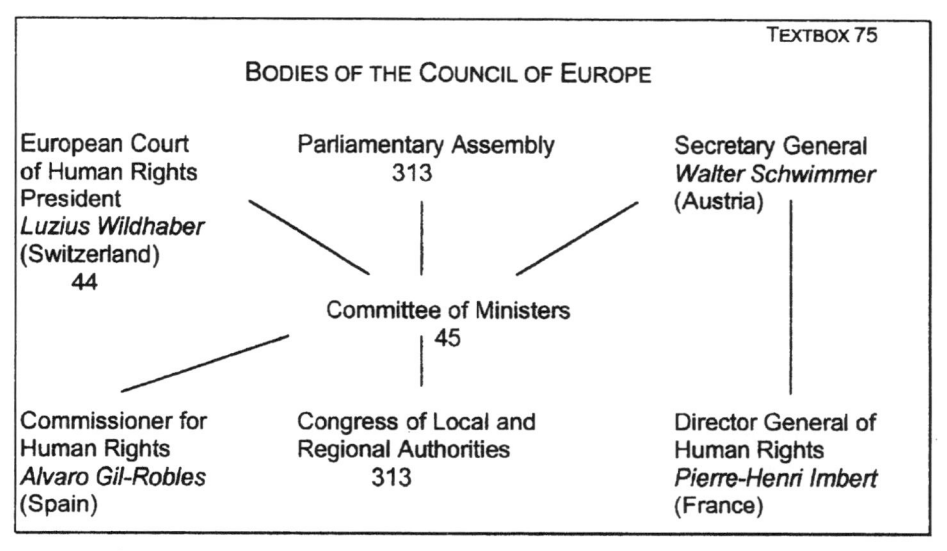

TEXTBOX 75

BODIES OF THE COUNCIL OF EUROPE

European Court of Human Rights
President
Luzius Wildhaber
(Switzerland)
44

Parliamentary Assembly
313

Secretary General
Walter Schwimmer
(Austria)

Committee of Ministers
45

Commissioner for Human Rights
Alvaro Gil-Robles
(Spain)

Congress of Local and Regional Authorities
313

Director General of Human Rights
Pierre-Henri Imbert
(France)

Because of this enlargement policy, many states with a less than satisfactory perception of the rule of law have ratified the ECHR. As a result the European Court of Human Rights is flooded with complaints from states without effective remedies at the national level (as in Russia) and is practically forced to use double standards to prevent the lowering of standards of human rights in the older member states.

In addition, the EU no longer relies on the Council of Europe as a screening institution with respect to human rights and the rule of law, but instead since 1993, along with the traditional economic accession criteria, is using its own (stricter) political and human rights criteria. The Council of Europe has been criticized for having watered down its high standards for the sake of speedy enlargement. On the other hand, this policy has contributed tremendously to European integration as a whole.

5. COUNCIL OF EUROPE (CoE)

> TEXTBOX 76
> **MEMBER STATES OF THE COUNCIL OF EUROPE**
> Chronological order the Statutes of the Council of Europe were ratified in (as of 2002, 44 member states)
> 1949: Belgium, Denmark, France, Greece, Ireland, Italy, Luxemburg, the Netherlands, Norway, Sweden, Turkey, the United Kingdom (founding members)
> 1950 – 1988: Austria, Cyprus, Germany, Iceland, Liechtenstein, Malta, Portugal, San Marino, Spain, Switzerland, Turkey
> 1989: Finland
> 1990: Hungary
> 1991: Poland
> 1992: Bulgaria
> 1993: Czech Republic, Estonia, Lithuania, Romania, Slovakia, Slovenia
> 1994: Andorra
> 1995: Albania, Latvia, Macedonia ('FYROM'), Moldova, Ukraine
> 1996: Croatia, Russian Federation
> 1999: Georgia
> 2001: Armenia, Azerbaijan
> 2002: Bosnia and Herzegovina
> 2003: Serbia and Montenegro

5.2. European Convention on Human Rights (ECHR)

5.2.1. The Traditional Concept of Civil and Political Rights

The Council of Europe as a classical Western European organization has adopted the typically liberal view of giving priority to civil and political rights. While these rights are legally protected by the ECHR in a clear and exemplary way, economic, social and cultural rights are ensured in a far less effective manner by the European Social Charter (5.3.).

As far as **civil and political rights** are concerned, however, the Council of Europe has assumed a pioneering role. It was the first organization to establish a human rights court back in the 1950s, and to introduce a **judicial individual complaints procedure** similar to the protection of fundamental rights before domestic courts. This procedure reflects the basic idea of human rights as legal rights, meaning that the substantive rights to life, liberty, integrity, etc., also require that these rights be enforced procedurally by a national or international court.

The ECHR legal remedies system, especially after the far-reaching reforms of 1998 (5.2.2.), may be considered the first effective attempt to transfer national systems of human rights protection to the international level. Many years later, the OAS and the OAU followed the example of the Council of Europe by setting up their own regional courts of human rights (6.5.3., 7.4.3.). Only the United Nations, more than ten years after the end of the Cold War, continues to adhere to quasi-

5.2. EUROPEAN CONVENTION ON HUMAN RIGHTS

judicial treaty monitoring bodies (4.3.8.), since the establishment of an international court of human rights is still not even seriously discussed (13.).

TEXTBOX 77

EUROPEAN CONVENTION FOR THE PROTECTION OF HUMAN RIGHTS AND FUNDAMENTAL FREEDOMS (ECHR)

Opened for signature in Rome (ETS No. 5): 4 November 1950
Entry into force: 3 September 1953
44 states parties

1954: establishment of the European Commission of Human Rights (up until October 1999, 11th Additional Protocol)

1959: establishment of the European Court of Human Rights

11 November 1998: entry into force of the 11th Additional Protocol; establishment of a single and permanent European Court of Human Rights

---

5.2.2. Gradual Development of the Strasbourg Mechanism

Even in the Council of Europe, the right of victims of human rights violations to have access to a European Court of Human Rights could only be achieved step by step, as this was regarded by most governments as excessive interference with their national sovereignty. Consequently the ECHR originally contained numerous political compromises. The only **mandatory** procedure the states committed themselves to by ratifying the ECHR, was the **inter-state complaints** procedure (5.2.3.) before the **European Commission of Human Rights** and the **Committee of Ministers**, the highest political body in the Council of Europe. The **individual complaints procedure** and the jurisdiction of the **European Court of Human Rights** were **optional**, i.e. the states parties had the option of recognizing them through additional voluntary declarations, usually only for a limited period. Many states, notably Turkey, took decades to recognize these optional procedures.

However even in those cases where states had made the required declarations, it did not mean that applicants could turn to the Court directly. Even if they mastered the screening process before the Commission – which few succeeded in (an average five per cent of all complaints were declared admissible) – they were still not allowed to bring their case before the Court. Instead, they had to rely on the goodwill of their own government (the party against which the complaint is directed), or that of the Commission. Failing this, the Committee of Ministers would decide on the complaint with a two-thirds majority. In other words, even if the majority of state representatives on the Committee believed that a human rights violation had been committed, the complaint had to be dismissed unless a two-thirds majority found against the state concerned. In the event that the complaint was brought before the Court (e.g. by the Commission) the applicants were not allowed to represent themselves, but were represented by the Commission instead.

5. COUNCIL OF EUROPE (CoE)

> **TEXTBOX 78**
>
> ## CONTENTS OF THE ECHR AND THE ADDITIONAL PROTOCOLS
>
> **ECHR 1950/53**: ETS No. 5, 44 states parties
>
> Article 2 Right to life
> Article 3 Prohibition of torture and inhuman or degrading treatment
> Article 4 Prohibition of slavery and forced or compulsory labour
> Article 5 Right to liberty and security of person
> Article 6 Right to a fair and public trial within a reasonable time
> Article 7 Prohibition of retroactive criminal laws (*nulla poena sine lege*)
> Article 8 Right to respect for private and family life, home and correspondence
> Article 9 Freedom of thought, conscience and religion
> Article 10 Freedom of expression
> Article 11 Freedom of assembly and association
> Article 12 Right to marry and found a family
> Article 13 Right to an effective remedy
> Article 14 Accessory prohibition of discrimination
>
> **1st AP 1952/54**: ETS No. 9, 42 states parties
>
> Article 1 Right to peaceful enjoyment of possessions
> Article 2 Right to education and free choice of education
> Article 3 Right to free elections by secret ballot
>
> **4th AP 1963/68**: ETS No. 46, 37 states parties
>
> Article 1 Prohibition of detention for debt
> Article 2 Freedom of movement
> Article 3 Prohibition of expulsion of nationals
> Article 4 Prohibition of collective expulsion of aliens
>
> **6th AP 1983/85**: ETS No. 114, 41 states parties
>
> Article 1 Abolition of the death penalty in times of peace
>
> **7th AP 1984/88**: ETS No. 117, 35 states parties
>
> Article 1 Procedural safeguards relating to expulsion of aliens
> Article 2 Right of appeal in criminal matters
> Article 3 Compensation for miscarriage of justice
> Article 4 Right not to be tried (*ne bis in idem*) or punished twice
> Article 5 Equality between spouses
>
> **12th AP 2000/not in force yet**: ETS No. 177, 4 states parties
>
> Prohibition of discrimination
>
> **13th AP 2002/2003**: ETS No. 187, 14 states parties
>
> Article 1 General abolition of the death penalty in all circumstances

5.2. European Convention on Human Rights

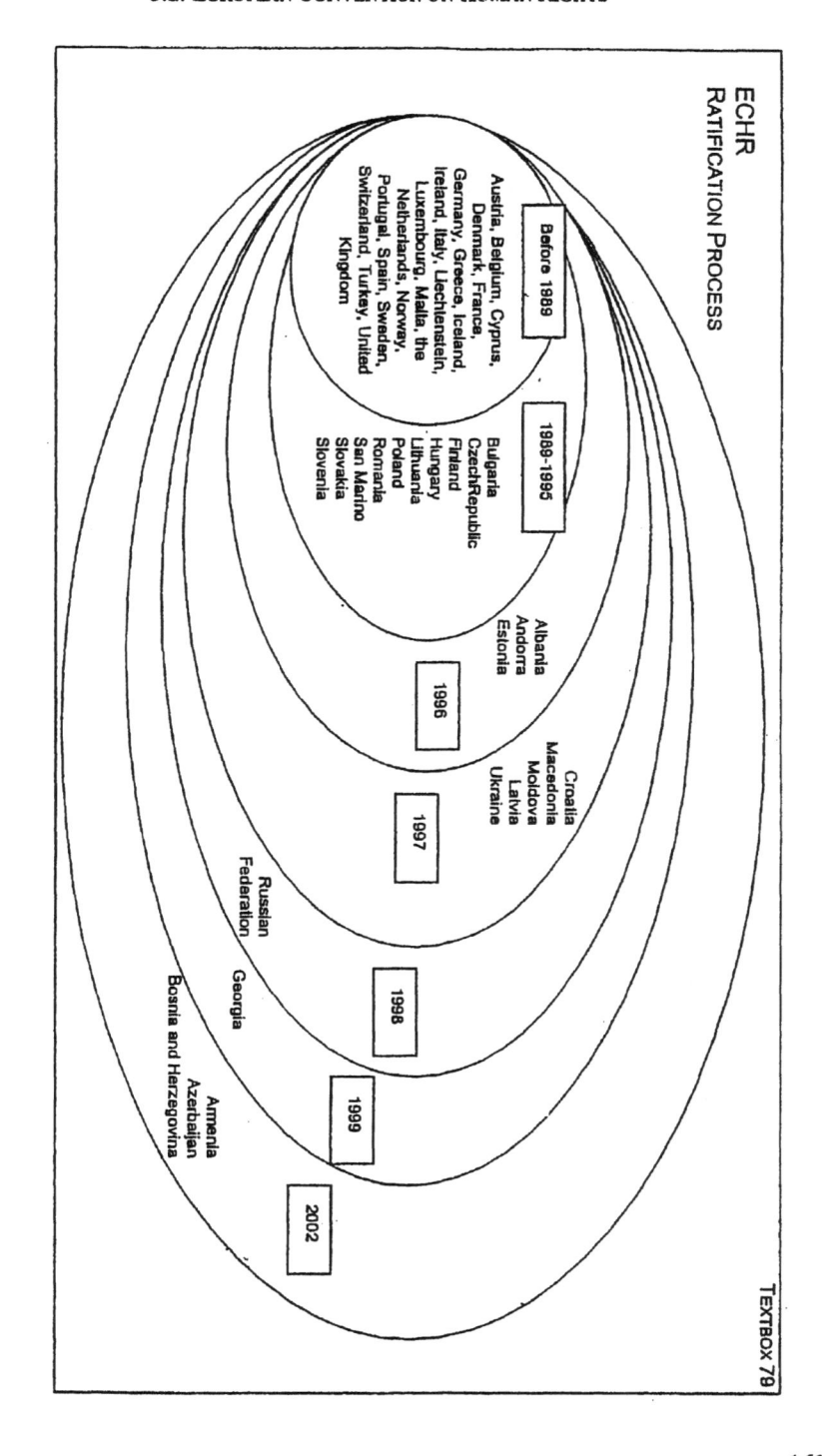

ECHR RATIFICATION PROCESS

Before 1989: Austria, Belgium, Cyprus, Denmark, France, Germany, Greece, Iceland, Ireland, Italy, Liechtenstein, Luxembourg, Malta, the Netherlands, Norway, Portugal, Spain, Sweden, Switzerland, Turkey, United Kingdom

1989-1995: Bulgaria, Czech Republic, Finland, Hungary, Lithuania, Poland, Romania, San Marino, Slovakia, Slovenia

1996: Albania, Andorra, Estonia

1997: Croatia, Macedonia, Moldova, Latvia, Ukraine

1998: Russian Federation, Georgia

1999: Armenia, Azerbaijan

2002: Bosnia and Herzegovina

TEXTBOX 79

This procedure may seem absurd by today's standards, however, it shows that even in the recent past of Western European states, individual complaints against alleged human rights violations to an international court were considered an unacceptable interference with domestic affairs.

It took a long time before legal remedies for individuals were extended by appropriate amendments to the rules of procedure, as well as by adoption of the 9th and 10th Additional Protocols to the ECHR in the early 1990s. The first radical changes to the Strasbourg mechanism were achieved by the adoption of the 11th **Additional Protocol,** which entered into force on 1 November 1998. The members of the Commission and the Court, which until then had been working on a voluntary and part-time basis, were replaced by full-time professional judges of a newly established **single and permanent European Court of Human Rights**. Furthermore, the optional clauses were deleted, which meant that individual complaints and inter-state complaints procedures before an independent court were now compulsory for all states parties. The Committee of Ministers was eliminated from the decision-making procedure and its role reduced to supervising the execution of the judgments of the Court at the national level. Thus, the entire procedure has not only been streamlined and accelerated, but also divested of any political influence. The court remains as the only body to decide on both the admissibility and merits of individual and inter-state complaints. Furthermore, the Court as a permanent body divided into chambers is finally in a position to deal with a much larger number of complaints than its predecessor, which like the Commission did not meet for more than 12 weeks a year. On the other hand, the growing number of states parties and the amount of publicity the Strasbourg procedure is being awarded has also led to a sharp **increase in the number of individual complaints,** which even the permanent Court can no longer possibly deal with. A mere glance at the statistics of individual complaints gives ample proof of this. The number of applications lodged in the five years since 1998 (roughly 135,000) is higher than the total of all the applications submitted during the more than forty years before. Until 1980, the Court delivered on average only one judgment a year, while in the year 2001 it pronounced 889 judgments. Yet despite this enormous output since the 11th Additional Protocol entered into force, the backlog of unsettled cases has not diminished, the rate of *in merito* settled cases has dropped again to less than five per cent and proceedings still take far too long (4 years in some cases). These weaknesses of the Strasbourg system are only partly attributable to the fact that the Court is the victim of its own success. The above mentioned enlargement politics of the Council meant that states with comparatively low levels of human rights protection and insufficient domestic legal remedies were included in the system far too early and without proper preparations. Cases originating from new member states have created much of the Court's enormous workload. In 2002, more than half of all applications (roughly 17,000) were lodged against Central and Eastern European states, with Poland and Russia (more than 4,000 cases each) being at the top. In reaction to the growing caseload, the Committee of Ministers' Steering Committee for Human Rights (CDDH) has again

5.2. European Convention on Human Rights

come up with **far-reaching reform proposals**, which include a new power for the Court to decline to examine in detail those applications that do not raise any 'substantial' issues under the ECHR.

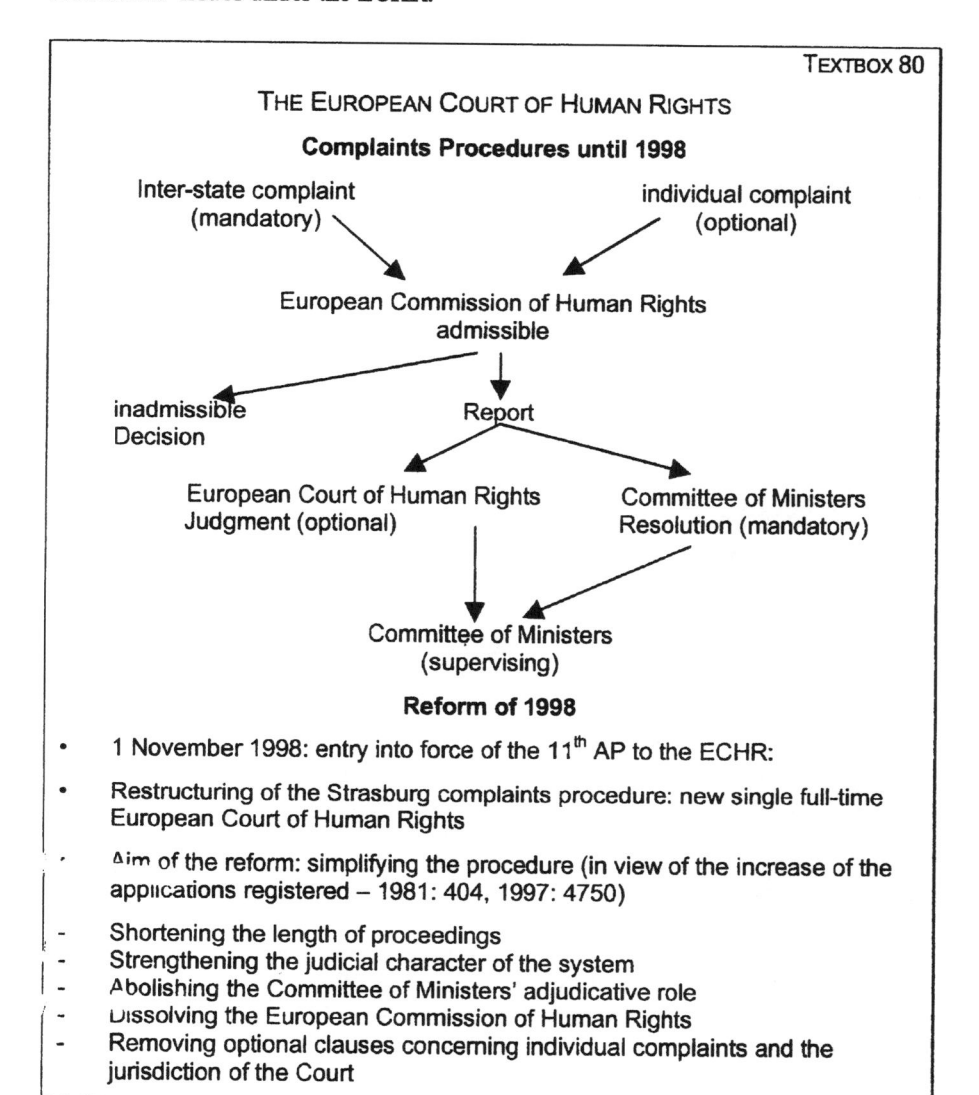

TEXTBOX 80

THE EUROPEAN COURT OF HUMAN RIGHTS
Complaints Procedures until 1998

Inter-state complaint (mandatory) → European Commission of Human Rights ← individual complaint (optional)

European Commission of Human Rights admissible

→ inadmissible Decision

→ Report → European Court of Human Rights Judgment (optional) / Committee of Ministers Resolution (mandatory)

→ Committee of Ministers (supervising)

Reform of 1998

- 1 November 1998: entry into force of the 11th AP to the ECHR:
- Restructuring of the Strasburg complaints procedure: new single full-time European Court of Human Rights
- Aim of the reform: simplifying the procedure (in view of the increase of the applications registered – 1981: 404, 1997: 4750)
  - Shortening the length of proceedings
  - Strengthening the judicial character of the system
  - Abolishing the Committee of Ministers' adjudicative role
  - Dissolving the European Commission of Human Rights
  - Removing optional clauses concerning individual complaints and the jurisdiction of the Court

---

5.2.3. Inter-State Complaints Procedure

Although the inter-state complaints procedure has been **mandatory** since the establishment of the ECHR, few governments have so far availed themselves of the option of taking legal action against other states for violations of human rights.

5. COUNCIL OF EUROPE (CoE)

According to statistics, a mere **12 inter-state complaints** have been filed in the 50 years of the ECHR's existence. Most of them involved bilateral conflicts: the strive for independence in Cyprus (two complaints from Greece against the United Kingdom), the South Tyrol conflict (one complaint from Austria against Italy), the conflict in Northern Ireland (one complaint from Ireland against the United Kingdom), the Turkish invasion of Cyprus (four complaints) and the violations of a Danish citizen's human rights by Turkey (one complaint). As a result, only three complaints were in accordance with the procedure's original intention, which was for unconcerned states to commit themselves, without any bilateral interests whatsoever, to the human rights of persons in other states, and to intervene in the event of gross and systematic violations by making inter-state complaints in the name of a common European *ordre publique*. This was in fact the case with the two complaints against Greece during its military dictatorship in the late 1960s, as well as with the one complaint against the Turkish military regime in the early 1980s. The applicant states in all three cases were the Scandinavian states Denmark, Norway and Sweden, as well as the Netherlands, all of them known for a comparatively high national level of human rights protection and their pro-active human rights politics in foreign and development affairs. They were joined by France in the complaint against Turkey.

Since most of the states accused by the inter-state complaints had not recognized the competence of the Court, and on top of that showed little interest to subject themselves to its jurisdiction in an *ad hoc* fashion, their cases were decided by the Committee of Ministers and some of them were terminated by a friendly settlement. Only **two cases were brought before the Court**. In the case of **Northern Ireland,** the Court concluded that the five combined deep interrogation techniques applied by British security forces against IRA suspects amounted to a practice of inhuman and degrading treatment in violation of article 3 ECHR.

In the **Fourth case of Cyprus against Turkey,** the Court ascertained systematic human rights violations committed by the Turkish occupying forces. Yet by far, the most significant inter-state complaint was the one against the **Greek military junta**. The **European Commission of Human Rights** had been on extensive fact-finding missions to investigate gross and systematic violations of almost all rights under the Convention and the Committee of Ministers was about to exclude Greece from the Council, i.e. to impose the most serious of all sanctions, when the Greek government 'of its own accord' decided to leave the organization. The political and economic pressure of this move, as well as the publicity it caused, were ultimately instrumental in bringing down the military junta in 1974 and replacing it by a democratic government (upon which Greece was immediately welcomed back to the Council). The human rights violations committed under the **Turkish military government** in the early 1980s were hardly less serious than those committed in Greece, yet the Commission's decision in this case differed. In fact, a **friendly settlement** was reached that spurred a shift towards democracy in the country and also brought Turkey closer to the human rights system of the

5.2. EUROPEAN CONVENTION ON HUMAN RIGHTS

Council of Europe, meaning that it finally recognized the jurisdiction of the Court and the individual complaints procedure.

TEXTBOX 81

INTER-STATE COMPLAINTS

States	Date of Admissibility Decision of Commission	Application No	Final Decision
Greece v. United Kingdom I	2.6.1956	176/56	Friendly settlement CM Resolution (59) 12 of 20.4.1959
Greece v. United Kingdom II	12.10.1957	299/57	Friendly settlement CM Resolution (59) 32 of 14.12.1959
Austria v. Italy	11.1.1961	788/60	CM Resolution (63) DH 3 of 23.10.1963
Denmark, Norway, Sweden and the Netherlands v. Greece I	24.1.1968, 31.5.1968	3321/67 – 3323/67, 3344/67	CM Resolution DH (70) 1 of 15.4.1970 CM Resolution DH (74) 2 of 26.11.1974
Denmark, Norway, Sweden and the Netherlands v. Greece II	16.7.1970	4448/70	Struck from the register as proceedings were suspended due to concurring party applications, report of the Commission of 4.10.1976
Ireland v. United Kingdom	1.10.1972	5310/71	Court Judgment of 18.1.1978
Cyprus v. Turkey I	26.5.1975	6780/74	CM Resolution DH (79) 1 of 20.1.1979
Cyprus v. Turkey II	26.5.1975	6950/75	CM Resolution DH (79) 1 of 20.1.1979
Cyprus v. Turkey III	10.7.1978	8007/77	CM Resolution DH (92) 12 of 2.4.1992
France, Norway, Denmark, Sweden and the Netherlands v. Turkey	6.12.1983	9940-9944/82	Friendly settlement: Report of Commission of 7.12.1985
Cyprus v. Turkey IV	28.6.1996	25781/94	Court Judgment of 10.5.2001
Denmark v. Turkey	8.6.1999	34382/97	Friendly settlement: Court Judgment of 5.4.2000 (struck out of the list)

The vast number of human rights violations committed by the Turkish security forces (especially against the Kurds in the Southeast of the country) that the Court has established in recent years due to individual complaints, have clearly shown that

167

the human rights situation in Turkey still leaves much to be desired. Although non-governmental human rights organizations had been asking the international community for years to take a stricter line with regard to the Turkish government, not a single state had endorsed the expulsion of Turkey, as was the case with Greece.

On the whole, governments make very few inter-state complaints under the ECHR, and when they do it is usually in their own **bilateral interest**. There are many reasons for this. At the outset, bringing an inter-state complaint is considered a highly unfriendly act from a diplomatic point of view, which governments are extremely hesitant to engage for the protection of human beings in other states 'alone', i.e. without any interests of their own being involved. Secondly, at the political and the diplomatic level, there are less formal ways of showing one's concerns at human rights violations in other states, e.g. through the UN Commission on Human Rights (4.4.1.), with the OSCE (8.4.), or simply in the context of EU foreign relations (9.4.) or via bilateral foreign and development policies.

Finally, the inter-state complaints procedure before the European Court is a long and complex one. Those governments that have decided to intervene in another country for the protection of human rights generally prefer to do so directly or through international political bodies rather than via the European Court of Human Rights considering that they must avail themselves of political bodies again to enforce the judgments of the latter.

As regards the actual procedure, details are found in the following section on individual complaints procedures (5.2.4.).

5.2.4. Individual Complaints Procedure

The real strength and undisputable success of the Council of Europe regarding the protection of human rights is the **individual complaints procedure before an independent international court,** which decides by a final and binding judgment, whether a state has acted in violation of one or more of the civil and political rights guaranteed by the ECHR. Following a slow start in its first decades, the procedure has really taken off since the 1980s, and even more so since the 1990s. The entry into force of the 11th AP in November 1998 and the creation of a permanent full-time European Court of Human Rights were major turning points towards making the procedure more professional, more efficient and less political (5.2.2.). In total, more than **260,000 individual complaints** have been submitted and more than 100,000 applications have been allocated to a decision body (registered) since the procedure was introduced. The Court has rendered **judgments in more than 3,400 cases**. These figures include all states parties and all rights under the Convention, although a fair share of complaints were made in reference to the right to fair trial proceedings in accordance with article 6 of the ECHR.

5.2. EUROPEAN CONVENTION ON HUMAN RIGHTS

TEXTBOX 82

INDIVIDUAL COMPLAINTS
1955 – 2002

	Applications lodged	Applications allocated (registered)	Applications inadmissible or struck out	Applications admissible	Court Judgments
1955 - 1987	39953	13457	11726	523	154
1988	4246	1009	602	52	26
1989	4923	1445	1243	95	25
1990	5279	1657	1065	151	30
1991	6104	1648	1441	217	72
1992	6456	1861	1515	189	81
1993	9759	2037	1547	218	60
1994	10335	2944	1789	582	50
1995	11236	3481	2182	807	56
1996	12704	4758	2776	624	72
1997	14166	4750	3073	703	106
1998	18164	5981	3658	762	105
1999	22617	8400	3520	731	177
2000	30069	10482	6776	1086	695
2001	33052	13858	8989	739	889
2002	30828	28255	17915	577	844
Total	259891	106023	69817	8056	3442

The **procedure** was revised completely by the 11th AP. The Court is composed of as many judges as there are states parties, i.e. each state is entitled to nominate three candidates. The Parliamentary Assembly elects one judge per state party for a period of six years. The members of the Court are full-time judges that may be re-elected. Applications are addressed to the Court in Strasbourg and many of them are filed after a first correspondence between Registry and the applicants (e.g. if misunderstandings have been put out of the way). Those that are not, have been registered (as from 2002: 'allocated to a decision body') and are examined by the judges in their capacity as rapporteurs. Applications may be declared inadmissible or struck out on procedural grounds by unanimous decision of a **Committee of three**

judges. Complaints are mostly dismissed if domestic remedies have not been fully exhausted, if the six-month period has not been adhered to, if alleged human rights violations are insufficiently established ('manifestly ill-founded') or if the complaints are incompatible with the ECHR (*ratione materiae, temporis, personae* or *loci*).

TEXTBOX 83

INDIVIDUAL COMPLAINTS PROCEDURE

Conditions of Admissibility (article 35 ECHR)

- Exhaustion of domestic remedies
- Application lodged within six months after the final national decision
- No anonymous applications
- No application that is substantially the same as a matter that has already been examined by the Court or that has been submitted to a comparable international procedure
- No application that is incompatible with the provisions of the Convention, manifestly ill-founded or an abuse of the right of application
- The alleged violation must be to the applicant's personal detriment (victim requirement, no *actio popularis*)
- The event must have occurred after the Convention's entry into force for the state concerned

---

The admissibility and merits of inter-state complaints and individual complaints, which have not been dismissed by a Committee of three judges, are decided on by **Chambers composed of seven judges**. In the event that the parties wish to secure a friendly settlement, the Chamber may also decide to agree provided the settlement is justified from the human rights point of view. At this stage again a large portion of the cases are declared inadmissible by the Chamber. The admissibility of complaints is decided either by a separate admissibility decision or together with a judgment on the merits, as is increasingly the case. Cases of major importance (e.g. if existing case law is revised or a serious question affecting the interpretation of the ECHR is raised) may be referred to the Grand Chamber composed of 17 judges.

In principle, the procedure before the Court has been reduced by the 11th AP to **one instance**: The Chamber decides conclusively on the admissibility and/or merits of a case (i.e. whether rights under the Convention have been violated). In exceptional cases, the losing party may **appeal to the Grand Chamber,** however, appeals are rarely accepted (rare examples include important issues in law of general significance, change in precedent, etc.). Thus, the Grand Chamber decides on cases that have been referred to it by a Chamber, or in cases of appeal. The plenary of the

5.2. EUROPEAN CONVENTION ON HUMAN RIGHTS

Court convenes only to decide on organizational issues, but is not vested to decide on complaints.

In the event the Court finds a violation of human rights under the Convention, it has limited competence to commit the state party concerned to **reparation** by means of financial compensation for damages and procedural costs. It does not have any other means of awarding legal redress to the victims of human rights violations, such as by a binding order to take measures of restitution (e.g. releasing prisoners or returning property), measures of rehabilitation, repealing of laws or judgments, criminal prosecution of the persons responsible, etc. (3.2.7.).

This is indeed one of the weaknesses of the ECHR's legal remedy system, which not even the 11th AP was able to repair. The only decisions the Court takes are on alleged violations, while actual implementation of such decisions is within the competence or national sovereignty of the state party alone. It is essentially up to the authorities of that state, for example, to hold torturers criminally responsible for violation of the prohibition of torture, to grant appropriate and free-of-charge medical and psychological rehabilitation to the victims of torture, or to take legal and administrative steps to avoid recurrence.

Monitoring of enforcement of the Court's internationally binding judgments at the national level is incumbent upon the highest political body of the Council of Europe, i.e. the **Committee of Ministers.** The Committee of Ministers is composed of the foreign ministers of the Council's member states (or their permanent representatives in Strasbourg). Because of the limited competence of the Court to order effective reparation measures, monitoring by the Committee of Ministers is generally limited to determining whether victims have received the appropriate compensation for damages.

Still, the importance of the Court's judgements for the states concerned, and to some degree also for the other states parties, must not be underestimated. While victims in many cases are not granted real reparation, simply because reparation is no longer possible, as in the case of torture, the Court's judgments are precedents that often trigger far-reaching national reforms.

Austria, for example, amended its code of criminal procedure several times (e.g. by reducing the maximum duration of detention on remand), it radically reformed its entire legal remedy system concerning administrative acts by introducing independent administrative tribunals (especially in the context of administrative penalties and acts of direct police power), and lifted the public broadcasting monopoly on the grounds that the Court had repeatedly established violations of the Convention.

The individual complaints procedure before the European Court of Human Rights is exemplary at the international level not so much because of the individual legal remedies (which are still primarily within the competence of national authorities), but rather because due to the binding jurisdiction and interpretation of ECHR rights by an independent court, it has created a set of common European minimum standards for civil and political rights.

5. COUNCIL OF EUROPE (CoE)

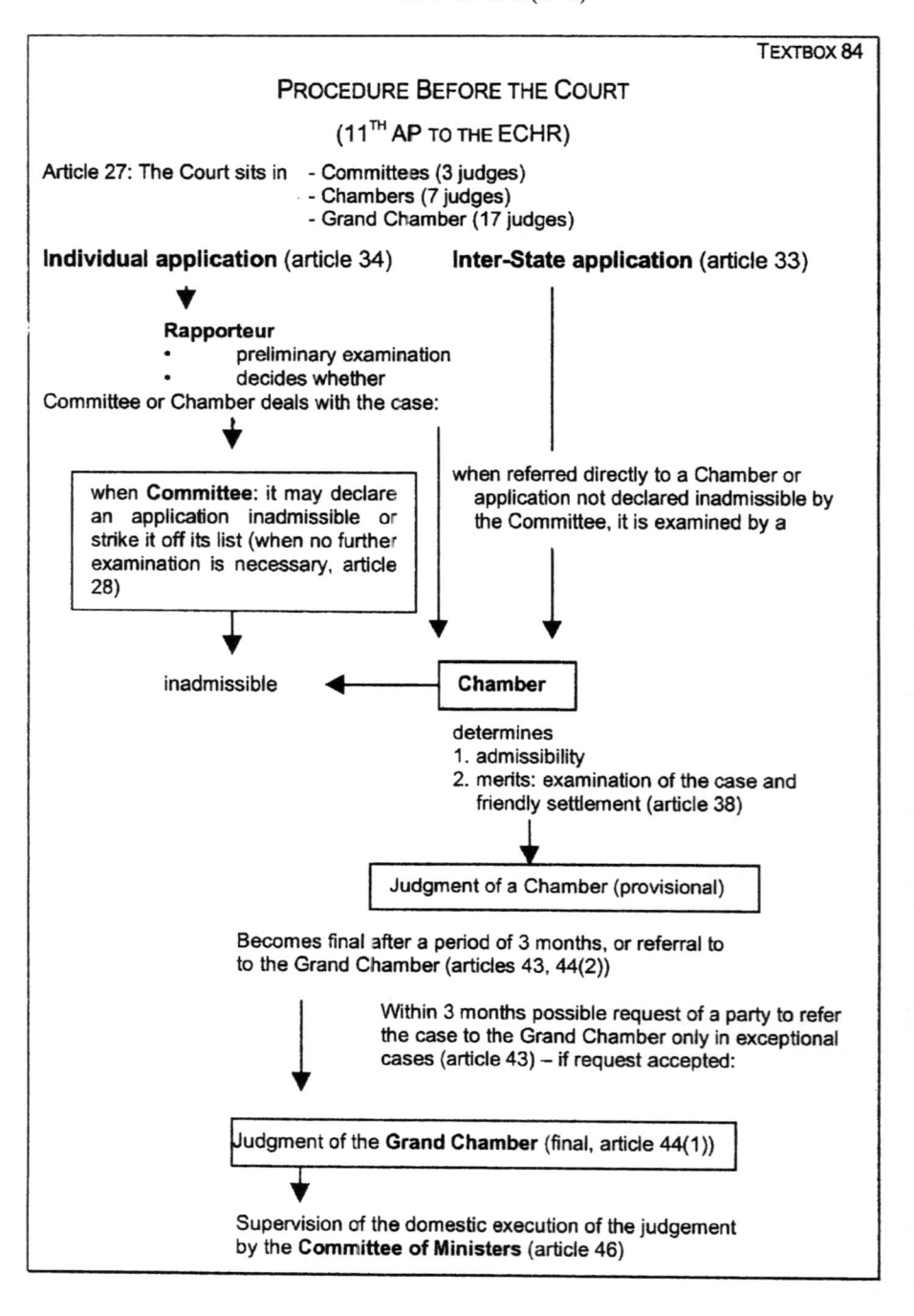

TEXTBOX 84

PROCEDURE BEFORE THE COURT
(11TH AP TO THE ECHR)

Article 27: The Court sits in
- Committees (3 judges)
- Chambers (7 judges)
- Grand Chamber (17 judges)

Individual application (article 34)   **Inter-State application** (article 33)

▼

Rapporteur
- preliminary examination
- decides whether Committee or Chamber deals with the case:

▼

when **Committee**: it may declare an application inadmissible or strike it off its list (when no further examination is necessary, article 28)

when referred directly to a Chamber or application not declared inadmissible by the Committee, it is examined by a

▼ inadmissible ◄—— **Chamber**

determines
1. admissibility
2. merits: examination of the case and friendly settlement (article 38)

▼

Judgment of a Chamber (provisional)

Becomes final after a period of 3 months, or referral to to the Grand Chamber (articles 43, 44(2))

Within 3 months possible request of a party to refer the case to the Grand Chamber only in exceptional cases (article 43) – if request accepted:

▼

Judgment of the Grand Chamber (final, article 44(1))

▼

Supervision of the domestic execution of the judgement by the **Committee of Ministers** (article 46)

172

5.3. European Social Charter (ESC)

The European Social Charter (ESC) adopted in Turin in 1961 is often referred to as the 'little sister' of the better known ECHR. This is due to the fact that the so-called second generation of **economic, social and cultural rights** has not been awarded much significance in the legal perception and legal framework of most European states (5.2.1.). While they have paid lip service to the indivisibility and interdependence of all human rights (2.7.), they have done little to change the apparent inequality.

> TEXTBOX 85
>
> EUROPEAN SOCIAL CHARTER (ESC)
>
> Opened for signature in Turin (ETS No. 35): 18 October 1961
> Entry into force: 26 February 1965
> 26 states parties (+7 states parties to the RevESC only) = 33 states parties
>
> - **Additional Protocol 1988/92**: ETS No. 128, 11 states parties
> - **Amending Protocol 1991**: ETS No. 142, 19 states parties
> - **Additional Protocol** providing for a system of **collective complaints 1995/98**: ETS No. 158, 10 states parties
>
> **Revised European Social Charter (RevESC)**
>
> Opened for signature (ETS No. 163): 3 May 1996
> Entry into force: 1 July 1999
> 15 states parties (including 7 states which only ratified the RevESC)
>
> Combines in a single document:
>
> - rights covered by the Charter in their amended form
> - rights contained in the Additional Protocol
> - new rights
> - improved state reporting procedure
>
> **Monitoring**
>
> - European Committee of Social Rights (previously Committee of Experts): examines reports and collective complaints
> - Governmental Committee: prepares decisions for the Committee of Ministers
> - Committee of Ministers: adopts a resolution and addresses recommendations to those states not honouring their obligations under the Charter

The only fundamental rights recognized by most European constitutions are civil and political rights, while economic, social and cultural rights are often still considered 'non-justiciable' even at the international level. Consequently, the legal remedy system of the ESC is different from that of the ECHR in many ways. Firstly, the rights set out in the ESC and the resulting obligations for states parties are far less stringent than those laid down in the ECHR. Secondly, states parties, in accordance with article 20 of the ESC, save for five out of seven core articles, selectively ratify which rights they prefer to consider as binding (**opting in system, 'à la carte' ratification**), whereas with the ECHR system they may only limit their obligations by making specific reservations.

TEXTBOX 86

EUROPEAN SOCIAL CHARTER

Contents
(selection)

European Social Charter 1961/65: 19 substantive articles including the following 7 core articles (RevESC: 8)

- Right to work
- Right to organize
- Right to bargain collectively
- Right of children and young persons to protection (core article as of 1996)
- Right to social security
- Right to social and medical assistance
- Right of the family to social, legal and economic protection
- Right of migrant workers and their families to protection and assistance

Additional Protocol 1988/92:

- Right to equal opportunities and equal treatment of men and women in employment (core article since 1996)
- Rights to information and participation for workers
- Right of elderly persons to social protection

Revised European Social Charter 1996/99:

- Right to dignity at work
- Rights of workers to protection in cases of termination of employment, insolvency, collective redundancies, etc.
- Right of workers with family responsibilities to equal opportunities
- Right to protection against poverty and social exclusion
- Right to housing

This notwithstanding, less than two-thirds of all Council member states have so far ratified the ESC or the revised ESC, whereas ratification of the ECHR is considered a prerequisite for acceding to the Council of Europe. Furthermore, international monitoring is not incumbent upon an independent court, but upon the **Committee of Ministers** as the highest political body. Before the reforms in the late 1980s, the monitoring of treaty compliance was limited to a **state reporting procedure**. State parties submitted reports at two-yearly intervals, which were first examined by a Committee of Experts. In a second step, the conclusions of these independent experts were screened by a Governmental Committee and by the Parliamentary Assembly. Finally, on the basis of their opinions, the Committee of

5.3. EUROPEAN SOCIAL CHARTER (ESC)

Ministers, by a majority of two-thirds, could make 'necessary recommendations' to the state party concerned.

Considering that the system remained practically **ineffective** (up until 1993 not a single recommendation was made by the Committee of Ministers) and European states were quite rightly accused of using double standards in the field of human rights, the first **modest reforms** were introduced in the late 1980s.

The **Additional Protocol of 1988,** which was ratified by only a few member states, introduced several additional rights to the Charter. The **Amending Protocol of 1991** was to improve and strengthen the reporting procedure by establishing a Committee of Independent Experts elected by the Parliamentary Assembly, and limiting the role of the Parliamentary Assembly in the reporting procedure. However, as this Amending Protocol has to be ratified by all member states, it has not yet entered into force and has in fact been superseded by the **Revised European Social Charter of 1996,** which entered into force in 1999.

TEXTBOX 87
DOUBLE STANDARDS OF THE COUNCIL OF EUROPE

ECHR	(Revised) ESC
- Entry into force 1953	- entry into force 1965 (RevESC 1999)
- 44 states parties	- 33 states parties (ESC + Rev ESC)
- Civil and political rights	- Economic, social and cultural rights
- Must be accepted as a whole	- States may accept rights and obligations selectively ('à la carte')
- Individual and inter-state complaints procedure before a full-time independent court	- Collective complaints system, within final competence of the Committee of Ministers (main political body of the Council of Europe) deciding by a two-thirds majority

---

The revised ESC, along with its original rights and those of the Additional Protocol of 1988, guarantees several other important rights, such as a comprehensive prohibition of discrimination and the right to protection against poverty. The reporting procedure was revised and improved by the introduction of an independent **European Committee of Social Rights** (former Committee of Independent Experts) with presently 12 members (elected for six years each), which has been awarded the main responsibility for assessing from a legal standpoint the compliance of national law and practice with the obligations arising from the (revised) ESC. Relevant conclusions of this body of experts have still to be submitted to a Council of Europe Government Committee, and the final recommendations to the member states to effect specific improvements in their national systems must still be accepted by the Committee of Ministers by a two-thirds majority vote. More than 30 recommendations have been made since 1993, especially to Italy, Greece, Austria, Turkey and France, the main points of criticism being: job security, factual equality of men and women, rights of workers' representatives, the right to strike, issues concerning restructuring of social security systems, guaranteeing social security as an enforceable right, discrimination on the grounds of age or nationality, access to social housing, family reunification for children up to the age of 21, insufficient measures against racism and xenophobia. The revised ESC has so far only been ratified by 15 of the 45 Council member states, with the other states parties adhering to the original Charter of 1961.

The most important reform to the ESC occurred in **1995** with the adoption of an **Additional Protocol**, entering into force in 1998, which for the first time provided for a complaints system. At the time, however, member states were unable to decide on an individual complaints procedure similar to the ECHR, but instead compromised on a **collective complaints system** for certain NGOs (which had to be accepted first), as well as for management and labour organizations. Even though the Committee of Ministers (rather than an independent court) is the final decision-making body (again by a majority of two-thirds!), the first twelve cases dealt with so far have been a positive experience inasmuch as the procedure has been instrumental in establishing a European case law for economic, social and cultural rights. As of May 2003, however, only ten states have recognized the procedure.

The efforts of the Council of Europe to improve protection of economic, social and cultural rights have no doubt added to the value of the ESC, and especially the European Committee of Social Rights as a body of independent experts. On the other hand, these half-hearted and step-by-step reforms have succeeded in creating a fairly incomprehensible and **fragmented system** whose efficiency in the context of the collective complaints system has yet to be proved.

5.4. European Convention for the Prevention of Torture (ECPT)

While the prohibition of torture is laid down in many human rights treaties and represents a peremptory norm of international law (*ius cogens*), many states still systematically practice torture to extract confessions and information on third parties under duress, or simply to intimidate persons. This is why, apart from a mere prohibition and regular treaty monitoring procedures, special mechanisms had to be introduced for protection against and prevention of torture. The United Nations, in their **1984 Convention against Torture** (CAT, 4.3.5.), placed special emphasis on criminal prosecution of torturers and universal jurisdiction. In addition, a Special Rapporteur on Torture was appointed in 1985 and a fund was established to finance projects in aid of victims of torture.

What is more urgently needed, however, is an effective system to prevent torture. The proposal made by the Swiss philanthropist and banker *Jean-Jacques Gauthier*, to introduce a **preventive system of visits to places of detention** to the CAT similar to that of the International Committee of the Red Cross (ICRC), was supported by many NGOs. In 1980, Costa Rica formally submitted a draft optional protocol to CAT to the UN Human Rights Commission, however, the matter was not pursued further until a much later date. The Council of Europe subsequently took up

5.4. European Convention for the Prevention of Torture (ECPT)

the idea and in 1987 adopted the European Convention for the Prevention of Torture and Inhuman or Degrading Treatment or Punishment (ECPT). Seeing the obvious success of this procedure, the UN Human Rights Commission decided to reconsider the original proposal, and in December 2002 the General Assembly adopted an Optional Protocol to CAT for the creation of a universal and preventive system of visits to places of detention (4.3.5.).

The ECPT is based on the simple assumption that the greatest risk of being tortured is during detention, especially in the first few hours or days of having been arrested. In other words, torture and ill-treatment typically occurs during interrogation by the police or other law enforcement agencies, before a person is brought before a judge. Therefore, if an independent body is given the competence to visit and inspect any given place of state detention without prior warning, that visit in itself would have a preventive effect.

TEXTBOX 88

EUROPEAN CONVENTION FOR THE PREVENTION OF TORTURE (ECPT)

Opened for signature (ETS No. 126): 26 November 1987
Entry into force: 1 February 1989
44 states parties

Text amended by 2 Protocols (ETS Nos. 151, 152) 1993/ 2002

No 1: widens the geographical scope ('open convention' for non-member states)
No 2: changes as to the elections of the members of the CPT

Contents:

Protection of persons deprived of their liberty from torture and from inhuman or degrading treatment or punishment

Monitoring:

European Committee for the Prevention of Torture (CPT)
- Preventive system of visits

With this basic idea in mind, the **European Committee for the Prevention of Torture and Inhuman or Degrading Treatment or Punishment** (CPT) was established in 1989, following the entry into force of the Convention. Representatives of the Committee are allowed to visit any place where persons are deprived of their personal liberty by a public authority, in other words prisons as well as places of detention set up by the police or military, psychiatric institutions, etc. The CPT is comprised of one expert per each state party from the fields of law, medicine, psychology, prison administration and others. During the visit, the representatives may inspect all relevant documents, enter each prison cell and speak with prisoners in private. Since 1990, the CPT has carried out regular as well as ad hoc visits to various places of detention in all member states of the Council of

Europe. It has drafted a number of reports on these visits and made recommendations to the governments concerned.

TEXTBOX 89

THREE DIFFERENT APPROACHES TO COMBAT TORTURE

European Convention on Human Rights (ECHR)	European Convention for the Prevention of Torture (ECPT)
Judicial system of complaints	Non-judicial machinery
European Court of Human Rights	European Committee for the Prevention of Torture
Reactive ↓	Preventive ↓
Investigation of past violations	Visits to prevent future violations

UN Convention Against Torture (CAT)

Quasi-judicial mechanisms: reporting, communications, inquiry

UN Committee against Torture

Holding torturers accountable under criminal law

(domestic and universal jurisdiction)

Although the **reports** are confidential in principle, it has become common practice to publish them together with relevant statements from the governments concerned. The CPT may only publish a report without the consent of the government concerned if that government fails to cooperate or refuses to improve the situation in the light of the recommendations of the CPT.

Past experience has shown that these preventive visits from the CPT have reduced the risk of torture and other acts of ill-treatment in places of detention in many European states. Furthermore, the CPT's recommendations have been instrumental in establishing common European **minimum standards for conditions of detention,** which in turn have led to appropriate measures and improvements in many states. As the CPT does not have the capacity to visit all places of detention, especially in larger states, it has requested from states parties to establish similar independent commissions for preventive visits at the national level. Austria followed this recommendation at the police level in 2000 by setting up six visiting commissions, which are subordinate to the human rights advisory council at the ministry of the interior (14.5.). The recently adopted Additional Protocol to CAT also obliges states parties to establish independent national preventive mechanisms to examine the treatment of persons deprived of their liberty and to make recommendations to the relevant authorities.

5.5. European Framework Convention for the Protection of National Minorities

As the socialist regimes collapsed in Central and Eastern Europe a feeling of ideological insecurity began to spread among people in the region, making them highly receptive to nationalist and racist tendencies in particular. Many formerly communist politicians discovered that nationalism lent itself perfectly to promise the people security in their ethnic, linguistic, religious or national identities. The result was a dangerous surge of racism, intolerance, discrimination and conflicts with minorities, as well as secession and creation of 'ethnically clean' national states. Within less than a few years these tendencies created a **new political map of Europe**, inciting the disintegration of Yugoslavia, the Soviet Union and Czechoslovakia, and prompting German reunification, all in the name of the right of peoples to self-determination. While the disintegration of Czechoslovakia was peaceful, and the fall of the Soviet Union happened without major violent conflicts, the nationality conflicts in former Yugoslavia marked the beginning of systematic 'ethnic cleansing' and human rights violations of the worst kind, which culminated in the genocide against Bosnian Muslims and Kosovo Albanians.

TEXTBOX 90

EUROPEAN FRAMEWORK CONVENTION FOR THE PROTECTION OF NATIONAL MINORITIES

Opened for signature (ETS No. 157): 1 February 1995
Entry into force: 1 February 1998
35 states parties

'Open convention': open for signature by any other state invited by the Committee of Ministers (article 27)

Contents

Article 4: right to equality and prohibition of discrimination
Article 5: right to maintain and develop their own culture
Articles 7 to 9: freedom of conscience, religion, expression, assembly and association
Articles 10, 11, 14: right to use freely and learn his or her minority language
Articles 12, 13: right to education and research to foster knowledge of the culture and history of minorities

Monitoring

State reporting procedure before the Committee of Ministers and its Advisory Committee

---

In other states, nationalist politics and minority conflicts reached a dangerous level, such as witnessed in Slovakia or in the Baltic states. To make matters worse, the fall of the Iron Curtain and the resulting immigration flow to Western Europe led to a revival of racism, xenophobia and neo-nazi violence in this part of Europe as well.

5. COUNCIL OF EUROPE (CoE)

Faced with this scenario, many states and international organizations tried to diffuse minority conflicts through preventive and reactive measures against racism and intolerance and by **strengthening the classical protection of minorities** as developed after the First World War in the wake of disintegration of the Ottoman empire and the Austro-Hungarian monarchy (2.4.).

TEXTBOX 91

EUROPEAN CHARTER FOR REGIONAL OR MINORITY LANGUAGES

Opened for signature (ETS No. 148): 5 November 1992
Entry into force: 1 March 1998
17 states parties

'Open convention': open for signature to non-member states of the Council of Europe invited to accede (article 20)

Contents

First 'hard law' instrument within the Council of Europe in the field of minority protection; structured on obligations by states rather than on individual rights.

Principles:
- Linguistic diversity is an important element of the European cultural heritage
- Respect for diversity does not imply linguistic segregation – knowledge of official language is also necessary
- Protection of minority languages is carried out within the framework of the national unity and territorial integrity of European states

Obligations:
- To take measures for the promotion of the use of regional or minority languages in public life, such as in the fields of education, before judicial and administrative authorities, by the media, with regard to cultural activities, in economic and social life

Monitoring

State reporting procedure before the Committee of Ministers and its Committee of Experts

---

Examples of prevention of racism are the Commission against Racism and Intolerance of the Council of Europe (ECRI, 5.9.) or the EU Monitoring Centre on Racism and Xenophobia (EUMC, 9.3.5.). Examples of active minority protection are the adoption of the Concluding Document of the Copenhagen Meeting of the Conference on the Human Dimension of the CSCE in June 1990 (8.3.), the appointment of a High Commissioner on National Minorities by the CSCE in 1992 (8.9.), the adoption of the UN Declaration on the Rights of Persons Belonging to National or Ethnic, Religious and Linguistic Minorities in 1992, as well as the creation of the two Council of Europe conventions discussed below.

5.6. EUROPEAN CHARTER FOR REGIONAL AND MINORITY LANGUAGES

The European Framework Convention for the Protection of National Minorities was established to find a **compromise** between states adhering to traditional protection of minorities, obliging them to take specific positive measures to protect their minorities (e.g. Austria which was in favour of an additional protocol to the ECHR), and states such as France which do not recognize minorities as such and instead would rather see a strict prohibition of discrimination implemented. Not surprisingly, the state obligations and the monitoring mechanism of the Convention are rather weak. Firstly, the Convention is a 'framework agreement' only, whose provisions are quite vague, not even the term 'national minorities' being defined. Secondly, there may be rights for minorities set out in the Convention, yet there are practically no state obligations to protect minorities against the majority through positive measures. Thirdly, the monitoring system does not draw on the judicial legal remedies of the ECHR but on the reporting system of the ESC, which is weak by comparison and which has the Committee of Ministers acting as the final political decision-making body. Despite these restrictions the **Advisory Committee** has so far tried to take an independent and critical position on various state reports and has actually succeeded in making the system modestly efficient. Another positive sign is the fact that most European states, including non-members of the Council of Europe, have ratified the Framework Convention.

5.6. European Charter for Regional and Minority Languages

The European Charter for Regional or Minority Languages of 1992 has met with far less acceptance from the states and thus entered into force as late as 1998. Its aim is to protect **linguistic diversity** as an essential element of the European cultural heritage based on a set of (rather weakly formulated) state obligations. Only 17 of the 45 member states of the Council have so far ratified the Charter. Its international monitoring system, as in the Framework Convention (5.5.), is limited to a simple reporting procedure before the Committee of Ministers, again assisted by a special Committee of Experts.

5.7. European Convention on Human Rights and Biomedicine

New developments in biotechnology and biomedicine are no doubt the biggest challenges for human rights today. Although many classical human rights, such as the right to life, the right to personal integrity or the right to privacy, have set distinct limits for excessive interventions of modern medicine in the dignity of human beings. Several **borderline issues in the field of law and medicine** have yet to be solved. Legislative measures are required in the field of medical law, some of which must touch upon the most central of human rights. It has to be said though that it is not states which primarily threaten the dignity of human beings, but mostly private persons (in science, economy or private health care). Thus, the question for states and international organizations is not so much to what extent state interventions are to be prohibited, but whether in fact the positive state obligation to

5. COUNCIL OF EUROPE (CoE)

protect and ensure life, dignity and privacy of human beings today and in the future is sufficient protection against interventions on the part of **science and economy**.

TEXTBOX 92

EUROPEAN CONVENTION ON HUMAN RIGHTS AND BIOMEDICINE

Opened for signature (ETS No. 164): 4 April 1997
Entry into force: 1 December 1999
16 states parties

'Open convention': open for signature also to non-member states of the CoE

Contents

- Article 1: Protection of human dignity, identity ad integrity.
- Article 2: The interests and welfare of the human being shall prevail over the sole interest of society or science.
- Article 5: Principle of free and informed consent to health intervention.
- Article 11: Prohibition of discrimination on grounds of genetic heritage.
- Article 13: Prohibition of modification in the genome of descendants.
- Article 19: Permission of transplantation of organs or tissues solely for the therapeutic benefit of the recipient and where there is no suitable organ or tissue available from a deceased person and no other alternative therapeutic method of comparable effectiveness.
- Article 21: The human body and its parts shall not, as such, give rise to financial gain.

Monitoring

No specific treaty monitoring body
Advisory opinions of the European Court of Human Rights
State reports on request of the Secretary General of the Council of Europe

Additional Protocol on the Prohibition of **Cloning** Human Beings
Opened for signature (ETS No. 168): 12 January 1998
Entry into force: 1 March 2001
13 states parties

Additional Protocol on **Transplantation** of Organs and Tissues of Human Beings
Opened for signature (ETS No. 186): 24 January 2002
Not entered into force yet
1 state party

The Council of Europe in adopting the European Convention on Human Rights and Biomedicine in 1997, once again proved its pioneering role in the development of human rights protection. Looking at the draft and the final version of the Convention, however, shows how difficult it is to find a sustainable compromise between the legitimate concerns for future development in the field of medical and biological science for the well-being of humankind on the one hand, and the prevention of risks to human rights such concerns necessarily entail, on the other.

Many principles and central provisions of the Convention, such as the principle of voluntary and informed consent of patients to medical interventions, are nothing more than new formulations of principles already inherent in human rights, and especially the right to privacy.

Two of the main principles, both of which are closely connected to ethic standards and the protection of human dignity, are the principle that the human body and its parts must not be used for financial gain, as well as the prohibition of cloning of human beings as contained in the 1998 Additional Protocol. So far though, the Convention and its Additional Protocols have few ratifications by European states. Incidentally, the international monitoring system of this Convention is particularly weak.

5.8. European Commissioner for Human Rights

In addition to the UN High Commissioner for Human Rights established in 1993, as a result of the Vienna World Conference on Human Rights (4.4.8.2.), and the OSCE High Commissioner on National Minorities founded in 1992 (8.9.), the Council of Europe in 1999 established its own Commissioner for Human Rights. The mandate of this independent, non-judicial institution is to promote education in and awareness of human rights, to identify shortcomings in the law and practice of member states, and to address recommendations and opinions to governments. Its competence is best compared to that of a national ombuds-institution for the protection of human rights.

TEXTBOX 93

COUNCIL OF EUROPE COMMISSIONER FOR HUMAN RIGHTS

Resolution 99 (50) of the Committee of Ministers on the Council of Europe Commissioner for Human Rights, 7 May 1999

- Independent non-judicial institution to promote and ensure human rights
- Commissioner elected by the Parliamentary Assembly from a list of three candidates drawn up by the Committee of Ministers, term of office: six years

First Commissioner (elected in 1999): *Alvaro Gil-Robles* (Spain)

Alvaro Gil-Robles, the former Spanish ombudsman, has been elected in 1999 by the Parliamentary Assembly as the first Council of Europe Commissioner for Human Rights. In view of the dominant role of the European Court of Human Rights and other traditional human rights mechanisms of the Council of Europe, and in view of the fact that his office, unlike that of the UN High Commissioner for Human Rights, is separate from the main Council's human rights bureaucracy (the Director General of Human Rights, in particular), it is not an easy task for the Commissioner to develop a similar public profile. His main activities so far have been on-site visits, organizing of seminars and publishing recommendations on certain human rights issues, such as the situation of detained persons during the conflict in Chechnya.

5.9. European Commission against Racism and Intolerance (ECRI)

TEXTBOX 94

EUROPEAN COMMISSION AGAINST RACISM AND INTOLERANCE (ECRI)

45 experts designated by their governments

Tasks

Combat racism, xenophobia, anti-semitism and intolerance at the level of greater Europe

Taking all necessary measures to combat violence, discrimination and prejudice, notably on grounds of race, colour, language, religion, nationality and national or ethnic origin

Activities

- *Country-by-country approach*
  - ECRI examines racism in each of the member states of the Council of Europe, organizes contact visits and draws up reports with recommendations
  - Country reports are made public unless the government in question is expressly against it

- *Work on general themes*
  - Between 1996 and 2003 seven general policy recommendations addressed to the governments of the member states of the Council of Europe were adopted (e.g. combating racism against Roma/Gypsies, racism and xenophobia on the Internet, discrimination against Muslims, national legislation)
  - Collection and dissemination of examples of good practices
  - Awareness raising with civil society
  - Following a proposal made by ECRI, the Committee of Ministers adopted the 12th AP to the ECHR containing a general prohibition of discrimination
  - ECRI was actively involved in organizing the European Conference against Racism in Strasbourg (October 2000), in preparation of the World Conference against Racism in Durban (August/September 2001)

Cooperation with EUMC

Agreement between the European Community and the Council of Europe of 10 February 1999 to establish a close cooperation between the European Monitoring Centre on Racism and Xenophobia (EUMC) and ECRI

Since the end of the Cold War **nationalism, minority conflicts, xenophobia and racist violence** have become the biggest human rights concern in Europe, not only for Central and Eastern European countries in transition, but for traditional

5.10. OTHER RELEVANT TREATIES AND MECHANISMS

Western democracies too. European organizations have reacted in many different ways. In 1992, the then CSCE appointed a High Commissioner on National Minorities to identify minority conflicts at an early stage and to help de-escalate them through silent diplomacy (8.9.). In 1997, the EU created the European Monitoring Centre on Racism and Xenophobia, which is to collect and evaluate comprehensive empirical data on these two phenomena in the 15 member states with the help of an information network set up for that purpose (9.3.5.). The Council of Europe established its own **European Commission against Racism and Intolerance** (ECRI) along with two rather weak conventions and apposite treaty monitoring bodies on protection of minorities.

ECRI did not come about by way of a special convention, but was set up following a decision of the 1st CoE Summit of Heads of State and Government, held in Vienna in October 1993. It consists of one independent expert per member state designated by the respective governments. In June 2002, the Committee of Ministers adopted a new Statute for ECRI, strengthening its role as an independent human rights monitoring body on issues relating to racism and racial discrimination.

The ECRI works on general issues such as preparing a specifically European contribution to the UN World Conference against Racism in 2001 (4.6.4.), and adopts general policy recommendations on issues affecting all member states, such as discrimination against Roma. In addition, it observes the situation in individual member states and publishes country-specific reports and apposite recommendations to the governments. The Commission, in its **country reports** to date, has dealt with these sensitive issues in a highly professional and independent way. As the competences of ECRI and the EU Monitoring Centre on Racism and Xenophobia in the 15 member states tend to overlap, both organizations decided in 1999 to cooperate closely.

5.10. Other Relevant Treaties and Mechanisms

Although the Council of Europe is usually associated with human rights it has also been instrumental in creating common European norms and minimum standards in other areas such as cultural cooperation and environmental protection. Human rights by their very nature affect many areas of life and are increasingly perceived as a cross-cutting issue. Thus, many other treaties of the Council of Europe also contain norms and mechanisms with direct or indirect reference to human rights as shown in Textbox 95.

5. COUNCIL OF EUROPE (CoE)

TEXTBOX 95

OTHER RELEVANT TREATIES OF THE COUNCIL OF EUROPE

Children

- European Convention on the Exercise of Children's Rights 1996/2000
- Convention on Contract concerning Children 2003

Criminal Law

- European Convention on Extradition 1957/60 and two APs 1975/79, 1978/83
- European Convention on the Non-Applicability of Statutory Limitation to Crimes against Humanity and War Crimes 1974/2003
- European Convention on the Suppression of Terrorism 1977/78 and Protocol 2003
- European Convention on the Compensation of Victims of Violent Crimes 1983/88
- Convention on Cybercrime 2001 and AP 2003

Data Protection

- Convention for the Protection of Individuals with regard to Automatic Processing of Personal Data 1981/85 and AP 2001

Migrant Workers

- European Convention on the Legal Status of Migrant Workers 1977/83

Refugees

- European Agreement on the Abolition of Visas for Refugees 1959/60
- European Agreement on Transfer of Responsibility for Refugees 1980/80

Social matters

- European Convention on Social Security 1972/77 and Protocol 1994
- European Code of Social Security 1990

5.10. OTHER RELEVANT TREATIES AND MECHANISMS

> LITBOX 5
> LITERATURE
>
> *Cameron*, Iain 2002, An Introduction to the European Convention on Human Rights, 4th ed., Uppsala
>
> Council of Europe Publishing 2000, European Social Charter - Short guide, Strasbourg
>
> Council of Europe Publishing 2002, European Social Charter – Collected texts, 3rd ed., Strasbourg
>
> *van Dijk*, Pieter and *van Hoof*, Fried 1998, Theory and Practice of the European Convention on Human Rights, 3rd ed., The Hague
>
> *Drzewicki*, Krzysztof, *Krause*, Catarina and *Rosas*, Allan 1994, Social Rights as Human Rights – a European Challenge, Turku
>
> *European Centre for Minority Issues* 1999, Implementing the Framework Convention for the Protection of National Minorities, Flensburg
>
> *Evans*, Malcolm 1998, Preventing Torture – A Study of the European Convention for the Prevention of Torture and Inhuman or Degrading Treatment or Punishment, Oxford
>
> *Frowein*, Jochen and *Peukert*, Wolfgang 1996, Europäische Menschenrechtskonvention, EMRK Kommentar, 2nd ed., Strasbourg
>
> *Gomien*, Donna / *Council of Europe Publishing* 1998, Short guide to the European Convention on Human Rights, 2nd ed., Strasbourg
>
> *Harris*, David and *Darcy*, John 2001, The European Social Charter, 2nd ed., New York
>
> *Harris*, David, *O'Boyle*, Michael and *Warbrick*, Colin 1995, Law of the European Convention on Human Rights, London
>
> *Janis*, Mark, *Kay*, Richard, and *Bradley*, Anthony 2000, European Human Rights Law, Text and Materials, 2nd ed., Oxford
>
> *Kriebaum*, Ursula 2000, Folterprävention in Europa - Die Europäische Konvention zur Verhütung von Folter und unmenschlicher oder erniedrigender Behandlung oder Bestrafung, Study Series of the Ludwig Boltzmann Institute of Human Rights, Vol. 3, Vienna
>
> *Leach*, Philip 2001, Taking a Case to the European Court of Human Rights, Blackstone's Human Rights Series, London

5. COUNCIL OF EUROPE (CoE)

Merrills, John and *Robertson,* Authur 2001, Human Rights in Europe, a study of the European Convention on Human Rights, 4th ed., Manchester

Morgan, Rod and *Evans,* Malcolm 1999, Protecting Prisoners – the Standards of the European Committee for the Prevention of Torture in Context, Oxford

Nowak, Manfred (Ed.) 1994, Europarat und Menschenrechte, Wien

Ovy, Clare and *White,* Robin 2002, Jacobs & White - The European Convention on Human Rights, 3rd ed., Oxford

Starmer, Kier 1999, European Human Rights Law, London

Thornberry, Patrick and *Estebanez,* Maria 1994, The Council of Europe and Minorities, Strasbourg

INTERNET

www.coe.int - Council of Europe

www.conventions.coe.int - Council of Europe Conventions

www.echr.coe.int - European Court of Human Rights

www.coe.int/T/E/Human_Rights/Esc - European Social Charter

www.hudoc.echr.coe.int/hudoc - Case-law of the European Convention on Human Rights

www.hudoc.esc.coe.int/search - Case-law of the European Social Charter

6. ORGANIZATION OF AMERICAN STATES (OAS)

The human rights system of the Organization of American States (OAS) is frequently compared to that of the Council of Europe (5.), mainly in relation to the European Convention on Human Rights (5.2.). The comparison seems obvious because of several common factors: both are regional organizations that allegedly represent all the states of a politically and culturally homogenous region of the world; human rights play a fairly significant role; and human rights protection is based on a regional convention (ECHR and ACHR respectively) that essentially is limited to civil and political rights and enforced by individual and inter-state complaints before a regional human rights commission (which was abolished in Europe in 1999) and a regional court of human rights.

TEXTBOX 96

6.1. FROM THE PAN-AMERICAN UNION TO THE OAS

1889/90: First International Conference of American States (Washington, D.C.), which creates

- The International Union of American Republics – for rapid collection and distribution of commercial information
- The Commercial Bureau of the American Republics – secretariat to the Union

1910: Fourth International Conference of American States (Buenos Aires) establishes the Pan American Union

1948: Ninth International Conference of American States (Bogotá) adopts

- the OAS Charter
- the American Declaration of the Rights and Duties of Man (OAS Resolution XXX)
- the Inter-American Charter of Social Guarantees (OAS Resolution XXIX)

Article 5 of the 1948 OAS Charter (article 3(I) of the current version):

- 'The American States proclaim the fundamental rights of the individual without distinction as to race, nationality, creed, or sex,'

A second glance shows, however, that the two regions, organizations and human rights protection systems are comparable only marginally. While it is true that the Council of Europe lost some of its homogeneity because of the rapid enlargement to the East, it includes or at least claims to include only those states that have achieved a minimum standard of pluralistic democracy, rule of law and human rights, and consequently a minimum economic structure. During the Cold War, only those Western European industrialized countries that did not commit any gross and systematic human rights violations (with some exceptions) were allowed members of the Council of Europe. For the Central and Eastern European countries in transition, a culture of democracy, rule of law and human rights is of vital importance. The Council of Europe's monitoring procedure, before and after accession, plays a significant role in this. The OAS by comparison is composed of a **wide range of states** including both the richest industrialized countries (United States and Canada) and the **poorest countries** of the world (e.g. Haiti), as well as democracies and **military dictatorships** that covered a good part of the entire hemisphere in the 1970s. Consequently, the human rights bodies of the OAS have always had to deal with far more than Europe's 'luxury problems', such as the excessive duration of legal proceedings in Italy. Historically, and presently, OAS human rights bodies are challenged by widespread poverty, systematic torture and assassination of political dissidents, enforced disappearances and much more.

TEXTBOX 97

6.2. PURPOSES AND STRUCTURES OF THE OAS

Regional intergovernmental organization
35 members (all sovereign states of the Americas)
50 permanent observers (49 states plus the EU)
Headquarters in Washington D.C.

Purposes (article 2 of the OAS Charter)

- To strengthen peace and security of the continent;
- To promote and consolidate representative democracy, with due respect for the principle of non-intervention;
- To prevent possible causes of difficulties and to ensure the pacific settlement of disputes;
- To provide for common action on the part of those States in the event of aggression;
- To seek the solution of political, juridical, and economic problems that may arise among them;
- To promote, by cooperative action, their economic, social, and cultural development;
- To eradicate extreme poverty; and
- To achieve an effective limitation of conventional weapons that will make it possible to devote the largest amount of resources to the economic and social development of the member states.

Main organs

- General Assembly
- Permanent Council
- Meeting of Consultation of Foreign Ministers
- General Secretariat, headed by: *César Gaviria* (former President of Colombia)

Finally, it should be noted that the **United States** has always played a particular role. The United States dominated, from an economic, political and a military point of view, the **Pan-American Union,** and after 1948, also the OAS. The United States

6.3. AMERICAN DECLARATION OF THE RIGHTS AND DUTIES OF MAN

has always considered Latin America part of its 'sphere of influence' using the OAS to push through its policies, and above all, has always been sceptical of international and regional human rights protection. The United States position is reflected by the fact that it (and Canada) has still not ratified the American Convention on Human Rights, but also by supporting a number of Latin American military dictatorships that were gross violators of human rights. Notwithstanding the past and present situation, the complex and historically grown system of human rights protection of the OAS is best illustrated by comparing it to that of the ECHR. The following observations are an attempt to set out the main characteristics of the system by way of introduction and at the same time, by way of 13 textboxes, to provide a systematic overview of individual bodies and mechanisms.

TEXTBOX 98

6.3. AMERICAN DECLARATION OF THE RIGHTS AND DUTIES OF MAN

OAS Resolution XXX of 2 May 1948, adopted by the Ninth International Conference of American States in Bogotá

- First international human rights instrument of a general nature, though not binding
- Catalogue of 27 civil, political, economic, social and cultural rights and 10 duties
- Change in the legal status: today the Declaration is considered the main normative instrument giving authoritative interpretation of the 'fundamental rights of the individual' in article 3(I) of the current OAS Charter
- International protection of the 'rights of man' should be the principle guide of an evolving American law, as set out in the preamble.

The American system is driven by the **Inter-American Commission on Human Rights,** composed of seven independent members, which was established as an autonomous body in 1962, and in 1967 became one of the principal organs of the OAS. It is vested with competences concerning all 35 member states as set out in the OAS Charter, and in substance is based on the civil, political, economic, social and cultural rights laid down in the **American Declaration of the Rights and Duties of Man of 2 May 1948** (issued before the Universal Declaration of Human Rights by the United Nations of 10 December 1948). In addition, it also acts as a body of the **1969 American Convention on Human Rights (ACHR),** which entered into force in 1978 and is currently binding for 24 states parties in Latin America and the Caribbean. The Commission deals with numerous **individual petitions** under the two Inter-American legal systems, taking into consideration that NGOs are also entitled to file complaints.

Complaints against OAS member states, which are not states parties of the ACHR, e.g. the United States, may only be filed under the **OAS Charter**. The petition system introduced in 1965 originally referred only to civil and political rights. It was expanded in 1979 and now comprises all human rights set out in the American Declaration of 1948, including economic, social and cultural rights. However, as the Inter-American Court of Human Rights has no jurisdiction in this procedure, it usually ends with a non-binding decision and relevant recommendations from the Commission.

TEXTBOX 99

6.4. CHARTER BASED MECHANISMS

OAS Charter of 30 April 1948 adopted by the Ninth International Conference of American States in Bogotá (OASTS 1-D)

Entry into force: 13 December 1951

Charter-based system of protection is legally binding on **all 35 member states** of the OAS; together with the mechanisms based on the American Convention on Human Rights, it constitutes the Inter-American System for the Protection of Human Rights.

The Charter proclaims and reaffirms the 'fundamental rights of the individual without distinction as to race, nationality, creed, or sex' as one of its principles; however, it does not define these rights, nor does it provide any explicit mechanisms for the promotion and protection of human rights.

Four amendments to the Charter: Protocols of Buenos Aires (1967), Cartagena (1985), Washington (1992) and Managua (1993).

Protocol of Buenos Aires 1967/1970: important changes concerning human rights, strengthening of the system, transformation of the **Inter-American Commission on Human Rights** into an OAS Charter organ

---

Individual complaints procedures against states parties of the ACHR, on the other hand, are based on the ECHR procedure used until 1998 (5.2.2.). In the first stage the Commission decides on the admissibility of a petition. If it cannot reach a friendly settlement, it adopts a report setting forth the facts and its conclusions on the merits. This report, which contains proposals and recommendations of the Commission, is transmitted to the state party concerned and is usually published. Within a period of three months from the date of transmission, the state concerned or the Commission may submit the case to the Inter-American Court of Human Rights if the government in question has accepted the Court's contentious jurisdiction. The petitioner has no standing before the Court. However, petitioners, as of 1 May 2001, are entitled to request the Commission to submit the case to the Court. If the Commission found a violation of the ACHR, it shall, in principle, comply with this request. This rule should drastically raise the number of cases submitted to the Court.

The **Inter-American Court of Human Rights** established in 1979 in San José (Costa Rica) is also composed of seven members. It has the optional competence to decide, by means of a binding and final judgment, on those **individual complaints**,

6.4. CHARTER BASED MECHANISMS

which have been referred to it by the governments concerned or by the Commission. Although 22 of the 24 states parties of the ACHR have recognized the **contentious jurisdiction** of the Court, only very few cases have been submitted. In fact, during its 24 years of existence, the Court has rendered only 34 judgments on the merits.

TEXTBOX 100

6.4.1. INTER-AMERICAN COMMISSION ON HUMAN RIGHTS

Legal basis: article 106 of the OAS Charter and article 33 of the ACHR
Seven independent members elected by OAS General Assembly

Functions

- Develop awareness
- Make recommendations, prepare studies and reports
- Request reports
- Respond to enquiries by member states
- Take action on petitions, handle individual cases with respect to all OAS member states
- Participate in the handling of cases before the Inter-American Court of Human Rights
- Conduct on-site investigations (with consent of the government)

Evolution of the Commission

- *1960: Commission Statute*: refers to an 'autonomous entity' of the OAS with the function to 'promote respect for human rights' (article 1); human rights defined as 'those set forth in the American Declaration on the Rights and Duties of Man' (article 2)
- *1965*: Second Special Inter-American Conference gave additional functions and powers, including limited *individual petition system*
- *1967*: Protocol of Buenos Aires (entry into force in 1970), amending the 1948 OAS Charter, gave the Commission a new status as a *principal organ of the OAS*
- *1969: American Convention on Human Rights* (entry into force in 1978)

  Article 33: 'the following organs shall have competence with respect to ... this Convention:
  a) the Inter-American Commission on Human Rights
  b) the Inter-American Court of Human Rights'

- *1979*: after the entry into force of the ACHR a *Statute for the reconstituted Commission* was adopted in October 1979: according to article 1(2) human rights are understood to be:
  a) the rights set forth in the American Convention on Human Rights, in relation to the States Parties thereto
  b) the rights set forth in the American Declaration of the Rights and Duties of Man, in relation to the other member states

---

193

6. ORGANIZATION OF AMERICAN STATES (OAS)

Of these 34 cases (6.5.3.), most are concerned with gross and systematic human rights violations committed in Central and South American states, including amongst others, enforced disappearances (ever since the now famous judgment in the case *Velásquez Rodríguez v. Honduras* in 1988), arbitrary extra-judicial executions as in the case of *Aloeboetoe v. Surinam*, or torture.

TEXTBOX 101

6.4.2. INDIVIDUAL COMPLAINTS SYSTEM
(based on OAS Charter)

- Individual complaints prior to ACHR:
  In 1965 the Commission was given permission to examine individual petitions in relation to human rights violations. It only made recommendations on the basis of petitions alleging violations of certain civil and political rights of the American Declaration (right to life, equality before the law, freedom of religion, freedom of expression, freedom from arbitrary arrest and due process)

- Since entry into force of the amended Statute of 1979 the Commission may act on petitions alleging a violation of any of the rights enumerated in the American Declaration (including economic, social and cultural rights)

- Complaints procedure with respect to OAS member states not party to ACHR: concludes with the final decision, containing the Commission's findings, conclusions and recommendations to the State; in case of non-compliance the Commission may publish its decision; some decisions are further contained in its annual report to the OAS General Assembly

- Lack of enforcement
  - Inter-American Court has no involvement in Charter-based complaints – derives its jurisdiction from ACHR
  - No legally binding judicial decision
  - General Assembly shows little interest in dealing with individual petitions
  - Non-compliance by states has few consequences

In accordance with article 63 of the ACHR, the Court may issue **provisional measures** and in the case of a conviction may also rule that comprehensive **reparations** be made. Its competence in this respect is far greater than the compensation competence of the European Court of Human Rights. The Inter-American Court of Human Rights has already availed itself of that competence in several cases and, by that, has contributed to the development of the right to reparation under international human rights law (3.2.7.). The ACHR also provides for an optional **inter-state complaints** procedure, which, however, has not been activated once and has only been recognized by 10 states.

Apart from rendering judgments on individual complaints, the Inter-American Court on Human Rights has adopted and published several groundbreaking **advisory opinions** in accordance with article 64 of the ACHR. This advisory competence is not limited to the ACHR, but also applies to other OAS or UN human rights

6.4. CHARTER BASED MECHANISMS

conventions relevant to OAS member states (as ascertained in a well-known advisory opinion of 1982 concerning 'other treaties'). A number of these expert opinions were compiled upon the request of the Inter-American Commission on Human Rights. OAS member states may also ask the Court to provide opinions on the compatibility of their domestic laws with international human rights treaties.

Along with the individual complaints procedure it has been common practice of the **Commission** since the early 1960s to initiate country studies ex-officio and to publish **country reports**, which usually contain a comprehensive and critical analysis of the human rights situation in a given OAS member state. The Commission also conducts on-site examinations with the consent of the state concerned, which, however, are not required for drafting country reports. Country reports are an important monitoring function of the Commission, and its extensive activities have played a **pioneering role in human rights fact-finding activities of intergovernmental organizations** in general, such as the country-specific rapporteurs of the UN Human Rights Commission (4.4.1.4.), expert missions of the OSCE human dimension mechanism (8.4.), or ECRI Reports (5.9.).

TEXTBOX 102

6.4.3. COUNTRY REPORTS

Practice initiated by the Commission
First country studies in the early 1960s: Cuba, Haiti, Dominican Republic
First on-site investigation: Dominican Republic

Preparation of country reports
1. Draft report: Examination of the human rights situation in a country
2. Submission of the draft report to the country's government
3. Analysis of the government's response by the Commission
4. Decision whether to publish the report
5. The Commission may in addition transmit the report to the OAS General Assembly
6. Discussions in the General Assembly can be followed by a resolution – not legally binding

---

The Inter-American system of human rights has been gradually expanded with the creation of a number of **additional protocols to the ACHR** and other human rights treaties since the mid 1980s. Unlike the ECHR, which to this day includes only civil and political rights, the ACHR, in a separate Additional Protocol of 1988 ('Protocol of San Salvador'), has embraced the most important **economic, social and cultural rights** set out already in the 1948 American Declaration on the Rights and Duties of Man.

For the monitoring of states' compliance with these rights, the Protocol of San Salvador introduced a **state reporting procedure** based on the model of the UN (4.3.9.) and the European Social Charter (5.3). So far only 12 states parties have ratified this Protocol. The **individual petitions** procedure before the Commission and the Court has been declared applicable, in terms of economic, social and cultural

6. ORGANIZATION OF AMERICAN STATES (OAS)

rights, only to trade union rights and the right to education, in accordance with article 19(6) of the Protocol.

TEXTBOX 103

6.5. AMERICAN CONVENTION ON HUMAN RIGHTS (ACHR)

Adopted on 22 November 1969 in San José, Costa Rica – 'Pact of San José' (OASTS No. 36)
Entry into force: 18 July 1978
24 states parties (not ratified by Canada, the United States and several states in the Caribbean, including Trinidad and Tobago after denunciation in 1998)

Contents

- Codifies approximately 25 different, mainly civil and political rights, influenced by the ECHR, yet contains several more far-reaching provisions (e.g. right to juridical personality, nationality, equal protection, right to participate in government, minimum economic, social and cultural rights)
- *Additional Protocol in the Area of Economic, Social and Cultural Rights* (Protocol of San Salvador)
  Adopted in San Salvador on 17 November 1988
  Entry into force: 16 November 1999
  12 states parties (Brazil, Colombia, Costa Rica, Ecuador, El Salvador, Guatemala, Mexico, Panama, Paraguay, Peru, Surinam, Uruguay)
- *Protocol to Abolish the Death Penalty* adopted in Asunción on 8 June 1990, Entry into force: 28 August 1991
  8 states parties (Brazil, Costa Rica, Ecuador, Nicaragua, Panama, Paraguay, Uruguay, Venezuela)

Organs (article 33 ACHR)

- Inter-American Commission on Human Rights (also provided for in the OAS Charter): composed of seven experts elected by the General Assembly to represent all OAS members
- Inter-American Court of Human Rights: seven judges elected by an absolute majority vote of the states parties to the Convention in the General Assembly (article 53)

As with the 6th Additional Protocol to the ECHR and the 2nd Optional Protocol to the CCPR, the OAS also adopted a separate Protocol to the ACHR to abolish the **death penalty**. Although only 8 states have so far ratified this Protocol, Latin American states, unlike the United States and most states of the Caribbean, are among the main proponents of a universal ban on the death penalty, along with European states.

As early as 1985, the OAS adopted a regional **Convention to Prevent and Punish Torture** modelled on the 1984 UN Convention against Torture (4.3.5.), which is of eminent importance given that many Latin American states practiced systematic torture during the times of military dictatorships (especially in the 1970s).

6.5. AMERICAN CONVENTION ON HUMAN RIGHTS (ACHR)

TEXTBOX 104

6.5.1. INDIVIDUAL COMPLAINTS PROCEDURE
(according to the ACHR)

'Any person or group of persons, or any nongovernmental entity legally recognized in one or more member states of the Organization, may lodge petitions with the Commission containing denunciations or complaints of violation of this Convention by a State Party' (article 44 ACHR; mandatory)

Examination of the admissibility of the petition (by the **Commission**):

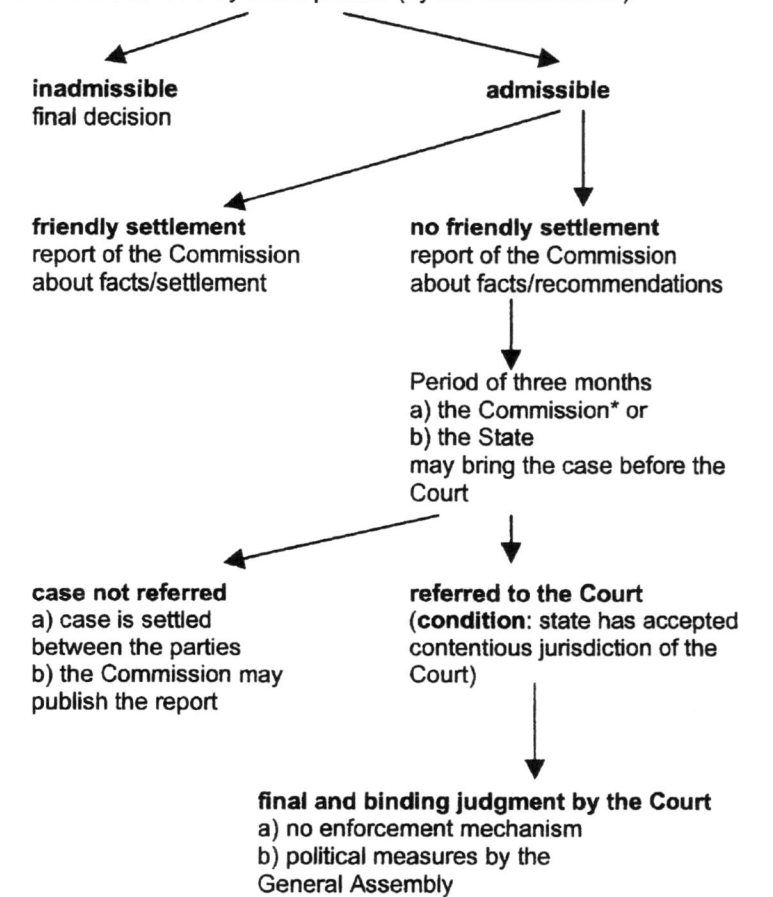

inadmissible
final decision

admissible

friendly settlement
report of the Commission
about facts/settlement

no friendly settlement
report of the Commission
about facts/recommendations

Period of three months
a) the Commission* or
b) the State
may bring the case before the Court

case not referred
a) case is settled between the parties
b) the Commission may publish the report

referred to the Court
(**condition**: state has accepted contentious jurisdiction of the Court)

final and binding judgment by the Court
a) no enforcement mechanism
b) political measures by the General Assembly

*According to the new Rules of Procedure (articles 43 and 44), which took effect on 1 May 2001, the Commission shall in principle ('unless there is a reasoned decision by an absolute majority of the members of the Commission to the contrary'), refer cases to the Court if it has found a violation, the state in question has not complied with the Commission's recommendation, and the petitioner 'is interested in the submission of the case'.

6. ORGANIZATION OF AMERICAN STATES (OAS)

As enforced disappearances were also a product of these military dictatorships (especially in Argentina, Brazil, Chile, Colombia, El Salvador, Guatemala and Peru) and were practiced systematically against political dissidents, the OAS adopted a separate **Convention on the Forced Disappearance of Persons** in 1994. It is the only convention of its kind and similar to the conventions on the prohibition of torture, it is based primarily on prevention and enforcement of national criminal law including the principle of universal jurisdiction (15.1., 15.2.). The United Nations adopted a separate declaration on this phenomenon in 1992 and is currently preparing a convention on the same issue. As early as 1994, the OAS embraced the 1993 UN Declaration on the Elimination of Violence against Women by establishing a regional and internationally binding **Convention on the Prevention, Punishment and Eradication of Violence against Women** ('Convention of *Belem do Para*'), which has since been ratified by as many as 31 member states.

TEXTBOX 105

6.5.2. INTER-STATE COMPLAINTS PROCEDURE

'Any State Party may, when it deposits its instrument of ratification of or adherence to this Convention, or at any later time, declare that it recognizes the competence of the Commission to receive and examine communications in which a State Party alleges that another State Party has committed a violation of a human right set forth in this Convention.' (article 45 ACHR; optional clause)

A declaration concerning recognition of competence may be made to be valid for an indefinite period of time, for a specific period, or for a specific case. So far **10 declarations** have been made under article 45 (Argentina, Bolivia, Chile, Colombia, Costa Rica, Ecuador, Jamaica, Peru, Uruguay, Venezuela)

Admissibility requirements and procedures are the same as those for individual petitions.

No inter-state communications have been lodged to date.

Despite these significant developments, the **OAS human rights protection system leaves a lot to be desired**. In Europe, practically everyone claiming to have had their civil and political rights infringed upon is entitled to go before the European Court in Strasbourg after all domestic remedies have been exhausted, and in fact the Court currently deals with approximately 10,000 individual complaints a year (5.2.4.). In the Americas, however, this judicial system of international human rights monitoring has hardly been put into effect even though it is now more than 30 years since the adoption of the American Convention on Human Rights and more than 20 years since the appointment of the Inter-American Court of Human Rights. For one thing, only 24 of the 35 OAS member states have ratified the ACHR, and some of the larger states like the United States and Canada avoid international supervision under the Convention's system.

6.5. AMERICAN CONVENTION ON HUMAN RIGHTS (ACHR)

> TEXTBOX 106
>
> ### 6.5.3. INTER-AMERICAN COURT OF HUMAN RIGHTS COMPETENCE
>
> Legal basis: article 33 of the ACHR
> Seven judges, nationals of any OAS member state elected in the General Assembly by the states parties of the ACHR
>
> **Advisory jurisdiction** (mandatory)
>
> OAS member states and OAS organs (including the Commission) may under article 64(1) consult the Court regarding the interpretation of the Convention and other human rights treaties.
>
> The Court may upon the request of an OAS member state give an opinion on the compatibility of provisions of that state's domestic laws with human rights (article 64(2) ACHR)
>
> The advisory opinions of the Court in both cases are legally non-binding
>
> **Contentious jurisdiction** (optional):
>
> 'A State Party may, upon depositing its instrument of ratification or adherence to this Convention, or at any subsequent time, declare that it recognizes as binding, *ipso facto*, and not requiring special agreement, the jurisdiction of the Court on all matters relating to the interpretation or application of this Convention.' (optional declaration under article 62 ACHR); applies to individual and inter-state complaints
>
> 22 of the 24 states parties to the Convention accept the jurisdiction of the Court under article 62(1) ACHR (Peru had its declaration withdrawn during the term of office of President *Fujimori*, 1999 – 2001)
>
> Only states parties and the Commission have the right to submit a case to the Court (article 61(1)), not individual petitioners (but as of 1 May 2001, the Commission shall, in principle, refer cases with established violations to the Court)
>
> The Court's judgement is final and not subject to appeal (article 67)
>
> No specific enforcement mechanisms; the OAS General Assembly may take political measures.

Furthermore, only 22 states parties of the ACHR have recognized the contentious jurisdiction of the Court, and Peru even temporarily (1999-2001) withdrew its optional declaration in accordance with article 62 ACHR because of the growing number of judgments issued against it by the Court (6.5.4.). Thirdly, only the states affected by individual petitions and the Commission are entitled to refer a case to the Court. Fourthly, the ACHR, unlike the ECHR, which has conferred to the Committee of Ministers of the Council of Europe the supervision of the domestic implementation of the Court's judgment, does not provide for a separate political enforcement mechanism, a fact which has done little for the efficiency of the system as a whole. For all of these reasons, the **Inter-American human rights protection**

6. ORGANIZATION OF AMERICAN STATES (OAS)

system needs to be strengthened as was the case with the Council of Europe before it adopted the 11th Additional Protocol to the ECHR and established a permanent European Court of Human Rights composed of full-time judges in 1998 (5.2.2.).

TEXTBOX 107

6.5.4. INTER-AMERICAN COURT OF HUMAN RIGHTS JUDGEMENTS ON INDIVIDUAL COMPLAINTS

State	Case	Date	Inter-Am CHR (Ser C) No.
Argentina	Garrido and Baigorria	02.02.96	26 (1996)
Argentina	Cantos	28.11.02	97 (2002)
Bolivia	Trujillo Oroza	26.01.00	64 (2000)
Chile	Olmedo Bustos et al ('Last Temptation of Christ')	05.02.01	72 (2001)
Colombia	Caballero Delgado and Santana	08.12.95	22 (1995)
Colombia	Las Palmeras	06.12.01	90 (2001)
Ecuador	Suárez Rosero	12.11.97	35 (1997)
Ecuador	Benavides Cevallos	19.06.98	38 (1998)
Guatemala	Paniagua Morales et al ('Panel Blanca')	08.03.98	37 (1998)
Guatemala	Blake	24.01.98	36 (1998)
Guatemala	Bárnaca Velásquez	25.11.00	70 (2000)
Guatemala	Villagrán Morales et al ('Street Children')	19.11.01	63 (1999)
Honduras	Velásquez Rodriguez	29.07.88	4 (1988)
Honduras	Godinez Cruz	20.01.89	5 (1989)
Honduras	Fairén Garbi and Solis Corrales	15.03.89	6 (1989)
Nicaragua	Genie Lacayo	29.01.97	30 (1997)
Nicaragua	Mayagna (Sumo) Awas Tingni Community	31.08.01	79 (2001)
Panama	Baena Ricardo et al	02.02.01	72 (2001)
Peru	Cayara	03.02.93	14 (1993)
Peru	Neira Alegria et al	19.01.95	20 (1995)
Peru	Loayza Tamayo	17.09.97	33 (1997)
Peru	Castillo Páez	03.11.97	34 (1997)
Peru	Castillo Petruzzi et al	30.05.99	52 (1999)
Peru	Cesti Hurtado	29.09.99	56 (1999)
Peru	Durand and Ugarte	16.08.00	68 (2000)
Peru	Cantoral Benavides	18.08.00	69 (1998)
Peru	Aguirre Roca et al ('Constitutional Court')	31.01.01	71 (2001)
Peru	Ivcher Bronstein	06.02.01	74 (2001)
Peru	Chumbipuma Aguirre et al ('Barrios Altos')	14.03.01	75 (2001)
Surinam	Aloeboetoe et al	04.12.91	11 (1991)
Surinam	Gangaram Panday	21.01.94	16 (1994)
Trinidad and Tobago	Hilaire, Constantine and Benjamin et al	21.06.01	94 (2001)
Venezuela	El Amparo	18.01.95	19 (1995)
Venezuela	Del Caracazo	11.11.99	58 (1999)

6.6. OTHER RELEVANT TREATIES AND MECHANISMS

All OAS member states would have to show the political will to recognize the ACHR as binding and accept the jurisdiction of the Inter-American Court of Human Rights if such reforms are to have any effect at all. If Canada and the United States are not prepared to do so, then at least those Latin American states and peoples who have suffered most from serious human rights violations in the recent past could introduce the necessary reforms.

After all, Europe only managed to establish a full-time Court of Human Rights after the end of the Cold War due to the support of those states and peoples who had suffered most from the systematic human rights violations committed by communist regimes. Within the OAS, a first small step in that direction was the **adoption of new Rules of Procedure by the Inter-American Commission,** which entered into force on 1 May 2001. With the new procedure petitioners are now entitled to request the Commission to refer cases, on their behalf, to the Court if it has found a violation. The Commission is obliged, in principle, to comply with such a request unless a majority of its members decides against it with good reason.

TEXTBOX 108

6.6. OTHER RELEVANT TREATIES AND MECHANISMS

- Inter-American Convention to Prevent and Punish *Torture*
  Adopted at Cartagena de Indias, Colombia, on 9 December 1985
  Entry into force: 28 February 1987
  16 states parties

- Inter-American Convention on the Forced *Disappearance* of Persons
  Adopted at Belém do Pará, Brazil on 9 June 1994
  Entry into force: 28 March 1996
  10 states parties

- Inter-American Convention on the Prevention, Punishment and Eradication of *Violence against Women* – '*Convention of Belém do Pará*'
  Adopted at Belém do Pará, Brazil, on 9 June 1994
  Entry into force: 5 March 1995
  31 states parties

The reform may not be so grand an advance, yet it does bare resemblance to some of the smaller reforms to the ECHR such as the 9th Additional Protocol adopted in 1990. That additional protocol never entered into force because it was ultimately overrun by the much larger reform of the 11th Additional Protocol. Hopefully, this timid attempt at reforming the ACHR protection system will meet a similar fate.

6. ORGANIZATION OF AMERICAN STATES (OAS)

> LITBOX 6
>
> ### LITERATURE
>
> *Buergenthal*, Thomas and *Shelton*, Dinah, 1995, Protecting Human Rights in the Americas: Cases and Materials, 4th ed., Kehl/Strasbourg/Arlington
>
> *Davidson*, Scott 1997, The Inter-American Human Rights System, Dartmouth
>
> *Harris*, David and *Livingstone*, Stephen (Eds.) 1998, The Inter-American System of Human Rights, Oxford
>
> Inter-American Commission on Human Rights and Inter-American Court of Human Rights (1985-present), Inter-American Yearbook of Human Rights, Dordrecht
>
> Inter-American Commission on Human Rights 2001, Basic Documents pertaining to Human Rights in the Inter-American System, Washington D.C.
>
> *Kokott*, Juliane 1986, Das interamerikanische System zum Schutz der Menschenrechte, Berlin
>
> *Medina Quiroga*, Cecilia 1988, The Battle of Human Rights: Gross, Systematic Violations and the Inter-American System, Dordrecht
>
> *Shelton*, Dinah HRLJ 2001, 169, New Rules of Procedure for the Inter-American Commission on Human Rights
>
> *Thomas*, Christopher R. 1998, The Organization of American States in its 50th year - overview of a regional commitment, Washington D.C.
>
> *Thomas*, Christopher R. and *Magloire*, Juliana T. 2000, Regionalism versus Multilateralism: the Organization of American States in a global changing environment, Boston
>
> ### INTERNET
>
> www.oas.org - Organization of American States (OAS)
>
> www.cidh.oas.org/DefaultE.htm - Inter-American Commission for Human Rights
>
> www.corteidh.or.cr/index-ingles.html - Inter-American Court for Human Rights
>
> www.corteidh.or.cr/seriecing/index.html - *case law* of the Inter-American Court for Human Rights
>
> www.oas.org/cim/default.htm - Inter-American Commission of Women
>
> www.oas.org/EN/FINFO - Inter-American Indigenous Institute
>
> www.padf.org - the Pan-American Development Foundation

7. ORGANIZATION OF AFRICAN UNITY (OAU)/AFRICAN UNION (AU)

Establishment of the Pan-American Union and its successor organization, the OAS (6.), with headquarters in Washington D.C., was mainly controlled by the interests of the United States. The Organization of African Unity (OAU) and its successor organization, the African Union, on the other hand, is very much a **post-colonial organization**. It was founded in 1963 to support pan-African unity and strive towards complete abolition of colonialism. Its members include all African states with the exception of the Kingdom of Morocco, which was excluded because of the conflict in the Western Sahara.

TEXTBOX 109

7.1. ORGANIZATION OF AFRICAN UNITY (OAU)

Regional intergovernmental organization
Founded on 25 May 1963 in Addis Ababa, Ethiopia
53 members (all African states except Morocco)

OAU Structure and Purposes

OAU organs: General Secretariat, Council of Ministers, Assembly of Heads of State and Government

OAU purposes (article 2 OAU Charter): promotion of unity and solidarity of African states, defence of sovereignty, territorial integrity and independence of its members, abolition of all forms of colonialism from Africa.

To achieve these purposes: coordination and harmonization of diplomatic, economic, educational, health, scientific and defence policies of the member states.

Upon the initiative of Libya the OAU was recently changed to the **African Union** on the model of the European Union to achieve more unity and solidarity among the African states and peoples. This economically and politically motivated reform, however, has done little to improve the rather modest human rights protection system in the region.

Although the OAU, at the time it was founded, placed special **emphasis on fighting colonialism, racism and apartheid**, its Charter makes no mention whatsoever of human rights. In those days, political decision-makers in Africa were quite concerned that their peoples be granted the right to self-determination from the European colonial powers; however, they were not inclined to take this right further than political independence. They did not grant their own peoples the right to self-determination vis-à-vis the new African states (as the Biafra war in Nigeria showed in all brutality), nor did they allow African people any individual rights within these new states that might be enforced by regional monitoring bodies.

7. ORGANIZATION OF AFRICAN UNITY (OAU)/AFRICAN UNION (AU)

Instead, they seemed to be of the opinion that by abolishing colonialism and apartheid they would automatically guarantee individual human rights as well. Sadly enough, the most serious and systematic violations of human rights, such as those committed by the atrocious regimes of *Idi Amin* in Uganda and 'Emperor' *Bokassa* in Central Africa, had to occur to convince African leaders that these assumptions had been wrong.

TEXTBOX 110

7.2. AFRICAN UNION

History

3 June 1991: *Abuja Treaty* establishing the African Economic Community (entry into force: 12 May 1994)

9 September 1999: Fourth Extraordinary Session of the Assembly of Heads of State and Government in Libya (*Sirte Declaration*) – establishment of the African Union is decided on Libyan initiative

10-12 July 2000: 36th ordinary session of the Assembly of Heads of State and Government (Lomé): formal adoption of the *constitutive act*

26 May 2001: the constitutive act enters into force

9 July 2002: *Inaugural summit of the African Union* as successor organization to the OAU in Durban (South Africa), first presidency: South Africa

Purposes of the African Union

The Sirte Declaration decides to replace the OAU and 'strengthen the continental organisation', to make it more effective and keep pace with the political, economic and social developments taking place in Africa and outside.

According to the constitutive act, greater unity and solidarity is to be achieved among the African countries and peoples, while peace, stability and security are to be promoted.

Human and peoples' rights are to be promoted and protected in accordance with the African Charter on Human and Peoples' Rights and other relevant human rights instruments (article 3(h) of the constitutive act)

All institutions provided for in the Abuja Treaty, i.e. the African Central Bank, the African Monetary Union, the African Court of Justice and in particular the Pan-African Parliament shall be established without delay.

NEPAD (New Partnership for Africa's Development), established to promote economic development in Africa with the support of the industrialized world, is also involved in the new political order on the African continent.

In other African states too, such as in *Mobuto's* Zaire, Guinea, Equatorial Guinea, Mauritania and Chad, human rights were violated systematically for many decades. Upon the initiative of several legendary heads of state, such as *Julius*

Nyerere (Tanzania) or *Leopold Senghor* (Senegal), the **African Charter on Human and Peoples' Rights** was adopted in Banjul in 1981. The **Banjul Charter** entered into force in 1986 and was soon ratified by all OAU member states.

> TEXTBOX 111
>
> 7.3. HUMAN RIGHTS AND COLONIALISM
>
> Colonialism was responsible for the most egregious and systematic human rights violations in Africa.
>
> Drawing on the *right of peoples to self-determination* all former British, French, Portuguese and Spanish colonies in Africa gained political independence (except for the Western Sahara). Two major issues closely connected to colonialism were resolved after years of international pressure as Namibia was granted independence in 1990 and the white apartheid regime in South Africa came to an end in 1993.
>
> Nevertheless, while colonialism has been overcome, Africa is still faced with enormous challenges concerning human rights (poverty, lack of economic self-determination, dependence on the North, ethnic/religious conflicts, brutal one-party and suppressive regimes), some of which have even increased.
>
> The African states did not succeed in making good their claim at the Third UN *World Conference against Racism in Durban* (2001, 4.6.4.) for the former colonial powers and other industrialized states to pay reparation for the human rights violations committed through colonialism and slavery.

Although the catalogue of duties listed in articles 27 to 29, including those of the individual not to compromise the security of the state and to preserve the integrity of the country, is of course, susceptible to being misused by governments, it does award a kind of priority to the community over the individual, which is characteristic of African societies in general and to the African perception of human rights in particular.

As its name implies, it contains individual civil, political, economic, social and cultural rights, but also contains a number of **collective rights of peoples** such as the right to equality, self-determination, development, peace and a satisfactory environment, in other words 'solidarity rights' of the so-called 'third generation' (2.6.). With the exception of the right to self-determination of peoples, which is also included in article 1 of the two UN Covenants, the Banjul Charter is the only international treaty to have embraced these solidarity rights of peoples. In addition the Charter, like the American Declaration of the Rights and Duties of Man (6.3.), includes a number of **duties of the individual** towards the community as well as typically **African values** like solidarity and respect for the family and for other communities ('extended family', clan, tribe), the duties to work, to pay taxes, to preserve and strengthen 'positive African cultural values in his relations with other members of the society, in the spirit of tolerance, dialogue and consultation'.

7. Organization of African Unity (OAU)/African Union (AU)

> TEXTBOX 112
>
> ### 7.4. African Charter on Human and Peoples' Rights
> #### (Banjul-Charter)
>
> Adopted on 27 June 1981 in Banjul (Gambia)
> Entry into force: 21 October 1986
> Ratified by all 53 OAU member states
>
> #### Contents
>
> Civil, political, economic, social and cultural rights, collective rights of peoples (all three 'human rights generations') as well as duties of the individual.
>
> Influenced by UN human rights instruments and African tradition
>
> Draft Protocol to the Charter on the Rights of Women in Africa (2000): protection against discrimination and far-reaching measures for the promotion of gender equality at the legal, economic and social level
>
> #### Monitoring
>
> - African Commission on Human and Peoples' Rights (11 members)
> - Mechanisms (all mandatory):
>   - state reporting procedure
>   - individual complaints procedure
>   - inter-state complaints procedure
> - The Additional Protocol to the Charter adopted on 9 June 1997 to establish an African Court of Human and Peoples' Rights has not entered into force to date.

In addition to the above, a comprehensive **draft protocol to the Charter on the Rights of Women in Africa** was submitted in September 2000 following several years of consultations, which, amongst others, provides for measures against discrimination and violence against women, against harmful practices, as well as for equal rights concerning political participation, property, right to inheritance, marriage, divorce, and the rights of women in the context of family planning and reproductive health.

The international **monitoring procedures** are far less innovative than the substance of the Banjul Charter, and reveals the stark scepticism African politicians have towards a human rights protection system that infringes upon their sovereignty.

7.4. AFRICAN CHARTER ON HUMAN AND PEOPLES' RIGHTS

TEXTBOX 113

7.4.1. THE AFRICAN CONCEPT OF INDIVIDUAL AND COLLECTIVE RIGHTS AND DUTIES

Individual rights:
Less important and far more limited than with the ECHR or the ACHR

Rights of peoples:
Include the right of peoples to self-determination, full sovereignty over their national resources, the rights to development, peace and security, as well as the right to a 'generally satisfactory environment favourable to their development' (article 24)

Duties:
Each individual has duties 'towards his family and society, the State and other legally recognized communities and the international community' (article 27(1))

Enjoyment of rights is restricted by the duty to exercise them 'with due regard to the rights of others, collective security, morality and common interest' (article 27(2)). The catalogue of duties is highly susceptible to being misused by governments

---

While the **African Commission on Human and Peoples' Rights** with headquarters in Banjul (Gambia) is vested with a fair range of competences, the apposite monitoring procedures, i.e. the reporting, inter-state and individual complaints procedures are considerably less efficient than those of other comparable conventions at the international and the regional levels.

TEXTBOX 114

7.4.2. AFRICAN COMMISSION ON HUMAN AND PEOPLES' RIGHTS

Established on the basis of article 30 of the African Charter on Human and Peoples' Rights

11 members, elected by the OAU Assembly of Heads of State and Government (articles 31 and 33)

Meets twice a year for two week sessions

Important role of NGOs (with observer status) in the work of the Commission

Functions (article 45):

- promoting human and peoples' rights through studies, seminars, awareness raising, et.
- protecting these rights (reporting and complaints procedures)
- interpreting the Charter
- performing other tasks which may be entrusted to it by the Assembly of Heads of State and Government

7. ORGANIZATION OF AFRICAN UNITY (OAU)/AFRICAN UNION (AU)

This is most evident with the **individual communications procedure** pursuant to article 55, which seems more like the 1503 procedure before the UN Human Rights Commission (4.4.1.3.) than a treaty monitoring procedure.

TEXTBOX 115

7.4.3. AFRICAN COURT ON HUMAN AND PEOPLES' RIGHTS (TO BE ESTABLISHED)

Additional protocol to the Banjul Charter, adopted on 9 June 1998 (not in force yet)

Jurisdiction

- Advisory opinions

On any legal matter relating to the Charter or any other relevant human rights instruments

- Issues of interpretation

- Concerning interpretation and application of the Charter, the protocol or other relevant human rights instruments; as well as concerning its own jurisdiction (article 3)
- Judgements are final and not subject to appeal (article 28)
- Judgements are binding: the states concerned undertake to comply with the judgement and to guarantee its execution (article 30); Council of Ministers monitors execution (article 29)

- Complaints procedure

Submittal of cases to the Court (articles 5, 6) by:
a) the Commission
b) the state party which has lodged a complaint to the Commission
c) the state party against which the complaint has been lodged at the Commission

In exceptional cases individuals, groups and NGOs may also institute complaints before the Court

---

Not only victims, but NGOs and other persons or groups are entitled to file communications, making the procedure a real *actio popularis*. Such communications, however, are only dealt with if the majority in the Commission decides so, which means that victims have no procedural right that their claim be considered by the Commission.

However, even if a communication has been recognized and declared admissible it has to be part of a **systematic pattern of gross human rights violations** to be considered any further. Isolated individual cases, no matter how serious, are therefore never examined.

7.4. AFRICAN CHARTER ON HUMAN AND PEOPLES' RIGHTS

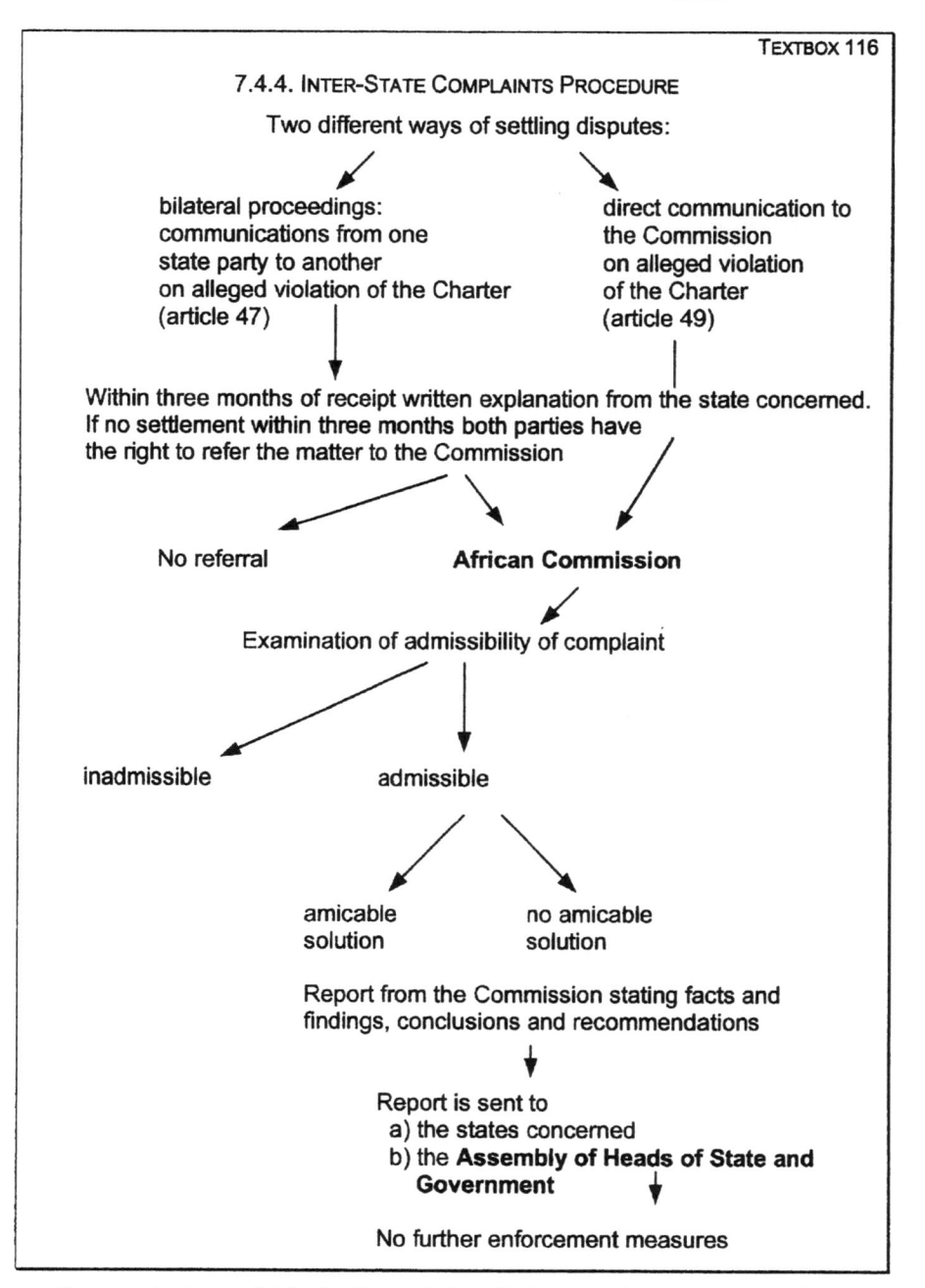

> **TEXTBOX 116**
>
> ### 7.4.4. INTER-STATE COMPLAINTS PROCEDURE
>
> Two different ways of settling disputes:
>
> - **bilateral proceedings:** communications from one state party to another on alleged violation of the Charter (article 47)
> - **direct communication to the Commission** on alleged violation of the Charter (article 49)
>
> Within three months of receipt written explanation from the state concerned. If no settlement within three months both parties have the right to refer the matter to the Commission
>
> → No referral
> → **African Commission**
>
> Examination of admissibility of complaint
>
> - inadmissible
> - admissible
>   - amicable solution
>   - no amicable solution
>
> Report from the Commission stating facts and findings, conclusions and recommendations
>
> Report is sent to
> a) the states concerned
> b) the **Assembly of Heads of State and Government**
>
> No further enforcement measures

Communications which the Commission finds 'reveal the existence of a series of serious or massive violations of human and peoples' rights' (article 58(1)), have to be brought before the Assembly of Heads of State and Government, a purely political body.

TEXTBOX 117

7.4.5. INDIVIDUAL COMPLAINTS PROCEDURE

Communications from others than states parties, in accordance with the rules of procedure of the Commission: individuals and NGOs (*actio popularis*) – the Commission only considers a communication if a simple majority of its members so decide (article 55)

Examination of the admissibility of a communication by the **Commission** (article 56):
- not anonymous
- exhaustion of local remedies, unless it is obvious that this procedure is unduly prolonged
- not based exclusively on news disseminated by the mass media
- submitted within a 'reasonable period' from the time local remedies are exhausted

↙   ↘

admissible   inadmissible

↓

Communication transmitted to the state concerned
Examination by the Commission of whether communication relates to cases of 'a series of serious or massive violations of human and peoples' rights' as defined in article 58(1)

↙   ↘

affirmative   negative

↓

Assembly of Heads of State and Government may request the Commission under article 58(2) to undertake an in-depth study and make a factual report including its findings and recommendations

↓

The report is only published by the Commission upon the decision of the Assembly of Heads of State and Government (article 59(2))

The Commission is only entitled to undertake an **in-depth study** of these cases and to prepare a fact-finding report with recommendations if so requested by the highest political body of the African Union (article 58(2)). Finally, the entire procedure is strictly confidential, and even the publication of a report of the

7.5. OTHER RELEVANT TREATIES AND MECHANISMS

Commission depends on a respective decision of the Assembly of Heads of State and Government.

In practice, the Commission gives priority to securing a friendly settlement. Under the pressure from NGOs, which have lodged most complaints under article 55, the Commission in recent years has increased its efforts to examine individual cases, to identify those that reveal the existence of a series of massive human rights violations, and to draw the attention of the Assembly of Heads of State and Government to these systematic patterns, as in cases against Nigeria (Ogoni people case), Malawi, and the Democratic Republic of Congo (Zaire).

TEXTBOX 118

7.5. OTHER RELEVANT TREATIES AND MECHANISMS

- OAU Convention Governing Specific Aspects of *Refugee* Problems

Adopted in Addis Ababa on 10 September 1969
Entry into force: 20 June 1974
44 states parties

Disputes between states parties are to be referred to the Commission for Mediation, Conciliation and Arbitration of the African Union (article 9)

- African Charter on the Rights and Welfare of the *Child*

Adopted in Addis Ababa on 11 July 1990
Entry into force: 29 November 1999
29 states parties

Comprehensive catalogue of rights of the child, many of them similar to those of the CRC, but also 'responsibilities of the child' (towards family and society) (article 31)

Establishment (2002) of an expert Committee on the Rights and Welfare of the Child as a monitoring body (article 32) in charge of a reporting procedure and an individual complaints procedure

---

In light of the African tradition of dialogue, consultation and mediation, it is not surprising that both the individual and **inter-state complaints procedures** are primarily designed at securing a **friendly settlement** rather than at judicial investigation and decision. Article 46 of the Banjul Charter even encourages the settlement of an inter-state human rights dispute between two parties without any involvement of the Commission. According to article 49, any state party may, however, also decide to refer an inter-state complaint directly to the Commission. Unlike the UN and Inter-American procedures, which have never been resorted to, the Democratic Republic of Congo has lodged a complaint against Rwanda, Burundi and Uganda, which is presently pending before the Commission.

In addition to the complaints procedures, the Commission has been concentrating on activities of a more general nature, such as organizing seminars and conferences and promoting cooperation with NGOs and national human rights commissions, as well as on **examining state reports**. Article 62 of the Banjul Charter requires states parties to submit every two years, a report on legislative and other measures taken with a view to giving effect to the rights and freedoms recognized and guaranteed by the Charter.

It is hoped that monitoring of the treaty will improve substantially once the **African Court on Human and Peoples' Rights,** provided for in the 1997 Additional Protocol to the Banjul Charter, is established and working. For this to happen, however, the states parties, the African Union, and the international community will have to give far more financial support than in previous years.

Aside from the Banjul Charter, two additional conventions are worth mentioning in this context. One is the **1969 OAU Convention Governing the Specific Aspects of Refugee Problems in Africa,** which encompasses a wider scope of application to the definition of 'refugee' than the UN Refugee Convention's restrictive limitations (3.1.4., 4.4.8.5.) that were included to satisfy European refugee politics. In addition to persons persecuted individually, the African Convention extends its protection also to persons who have had to leave their country because of wars, civil wars and other armed conflicts or unrests. The 1990 **African Charter on the Rights and Welfare of the Child,** ratified by 29 African states to date, contains a comprehensive catalogue of rights of children, which in many parts is also far more extensive than that of the UN Convention on the Rights of the Child (4.3.6.).

7.5. OTHER RELEVANT TREATIES AND MECHANISMS

> LITBOX 7
> LITERATURE
>
> Amnesty International 1991, A Guide to the African Charter on Human and Peoples' Rights, London
>
> *An-Na'im,* Abdullahi and *Deng,* Francis (Eds.) 1990, Human Rights in Africa: Cross Cultural Perspectives, Washington D.C.
>
> *An-Na'im,* Abdullahi A. 2002, Cultural Transformation and Human Rights in Africa, New York
>
> *Ankumah,* Evelyn 1996, The African Commission on Human and Peoples' Rights: Practice and Procedures, The Hague
>
> *Danielsen,* Astrid 1994, The State Reporting Procedure under the African Charter, Copenhagen
>
> *Heyns,* Christof 2002, Human Rights Law in Africa 1996-2000, 4 volumes, The Hague
>
> *M'Baye,* Keba 1992, Les droits de l'homme en Afrique, Paris
>
> *Maluwa,* Tiyanjana 1999, International law in post-colonial Africa, The Hague
>
> *Matsheza,* Philliat and *Zulu,* Leonard 2001, Human Rights Enforcment and Implementation Mechanisms: A Practical Guide to the United Nations and the Organization of African Unity Human Rights Protection Mechanisms, Harare
>
> *Murray,* Rachel 2000, The African Commission on Human and Peoples' Rights and International Law, Oxford
>
> *Nmehielle,* Vincent O. Orlu 2001, The African Human Rights System: Its Laws, Practice and Institutions, The Hague
>
> *Ouguergouz,* Fatsah 2003, The African Charter on Human and Peoples' Rights: A Comprehensive Agenda for Human Dignity and Sustainable Democracy in Africa, The Hague
>
> *Österdahl,* Inger 2002, Implementing Human Rights in Africa: the African Commission on Human and Peoples' Rights and Individual Communications, Uppsala
>
> *Tonndorf,* Uwe 1997, Menschenrechte in Afrika - Konzeption, Verletzung und Rechtsschutz im Rahmen der OAU, Freiburg i. Br.
>
> *Umozurike,* Oji 1997, The African Charter on Human and Peoples' Rights, The Hague

7. ORGANIZATION OF AFRICAN UNITY (OAU)/AFRICAN UNION (AU)

Wohlgemuth, Lennart, *Ewald,* Jonas and *Yates,* Bill (Eds.) 1998, Three Human Rights Organisations based in Banjul, Africa: The African Commission on Human and Peoples' Rights, The African Centre for Democracy and Human Rights Studies, The African Society of International and Comparative Law, Stockholm

INTERNET

www.africa-union.org – African Union

www.achpr.org - African Commission for Human and Peoples' Rights

www1.umn.edu/humanrts/africa/ - University of Minnesota/Human Rights Library: African Human Rights Resource Center

www.up.ac.za/chr/ahrdb/ahrdb.html - University of Pretoria/African Human Rights Database

8. Organization for Security and Cooperation in Europe (OSCE)

The **Conference on Security and Cooperation in Europe** (CSCE) has gradually developed during the Cold War and ultimately served as a catalyst for the fall of the socialist regimes in Central and Eastern Europe. The Soviet Union and its allies in the Warsaw Pact were interested in this institutionalized form of cooperation with the West mainly for two reasons: one was to keep the arms race with NATO at bay; and the other was to have the *de facto* political order in post-war Europe accepted both politically and by international law (i.e. the borders drawn to divide Europe into West and East, which in fact had not been laid down formally in any peace treaty). The United States and its European allies in NATO for their part, were keen for the communist states to be accommodating on cooperation in various fields, including human rights and humanitarian aspects (family reunification, exchange programmes for young people, cultural contacts, etc.) in return for conceding to disarmament politics and factual recognition of the status quo in Europe. The neutral and non-aligned countries contributed their fair share to the process of mutual recognition and détente. Because of its close relationship with China, Albania was the only sovereign European state not to be included in the CSCE process, while the United States and Canada formed the non-European part of the process.

The historic **Helsinki Final Act** of August 1975 provided the foundation for recommendations, commonly referred to as the **three 'baskets'** of the Helsinki process. Human rights were among the ten fundamental principles of the CSCE and also formed the core of the third (humanitarian) basket. Based on this basket, virtually all Central and Eastern European states began to establish 'Helsinki Committees' and comparable non-governmental institutions after 1975 (e.g. 'Charta 77' in Czechoslovakia or '*Solidarność*' in Poland). They called for observance of the CSCE obligations with regard to human rights and soon became the **nucleus of a civil society** that ultimately triggered the **'velvet revolutions'** of 1989. The CSCE was a catalyst in this historic process inasmuch as it legitimized the demands for observance of human rights and actively supported the organizations in civil society concerned with human rights.

In the beginning, the CSCE was little more than a loosely arranged conference, which produced a final document with all states agreeing to the mere minimum of where and when to convene the next follow-up meeting. Given the enormous tensions caused by the Soviet invasion of Afghanistan, the military regime in Poland and NATO's armament politics, however, little progress was made in the first years, and the second follow-up meeting in Madrid (1980 to 1983) threatened to fail several times.

The first real change came about when *Michail Gorbachev*, the then Soviet president, introduced his '*glasnost*' and '*perestroika*', and the socialist camp was split into three at the Third CSCE Follow-Up Meeting in Vienna (1986 to 1989). The result was a split between a group of reform states (Poland, Hungary, the USSR and to some extent Yugoslavia as a non-aligned state), and a group of states

8. ORGANIZATION FOR SECURITY AND COOPERATION IN EUROPE (OSCE)

unwilling to reform (German Democratic Republic (GDR), Czechoslovakia, Bulgaria), and Romania which under *Ceauscescu's* regime had become a tail ender and outsider that threatened to topple consensus in Vienna several times. Despite this rift in the communist bloc, or perhaps because of it, the states in the West succeeded in turning the **Vienna Concluding Document** of 15 January 1989 into a milestone of diplomacy. The Vienna Concluding Document already harboured the seeds of future revolutions, especially in the GDR, Czechoslovakia, Bulgaria and Romania, which would finally bring down 'real socialism' in Europe, cause the collapse of the Iron Curtain and put an end to the Cold War.

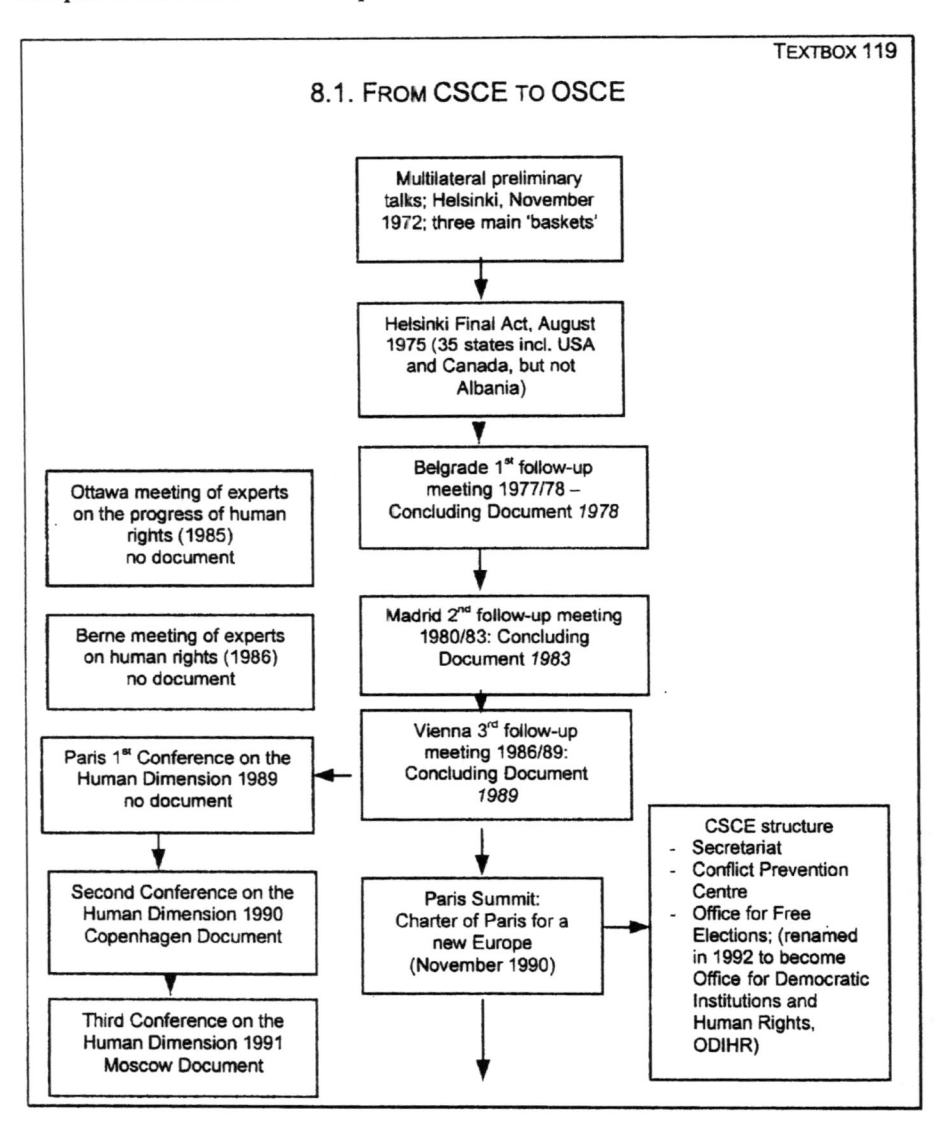

TEXTBOX 119

8.1. FROM CSCE TO OSCE

- Multilateral preliminary talks; Helsinki, November 1972; three main 'baskets'
- Helsinki Final Act, August 1975 (35 states incl. USA and Canada, but not Albania)
- Belgrade 1st follow-up meeting 1977/78 – Concluding Document *1978*
- Ottawa meeting of experts on the progress of human rights (1985) no document
- Madrid 2nd follow-up meeting 1980/83: Concluding Document *1983*
- Berne meeting of experts on human rights (1986) no document
- Vienna 3rd follow-up meeting 1986/89: Concluding Document *1989*
- Paris 1st Conference on the Human Dimension 1989 no document
- Second Conference on the Human Dimension 1990 Copenhagen Document
- Paris Summit: Charter of Paris for a new Europe (November 1990)
- Third Conference on the Human Dimension 1991 Moscow Document

CSCE structure
- Secretariat
- Conflict Prevention Centre
- Office for Free Elections; (renamed in 1992 to become Office for Democratic Institutions and Human Rights, ODIHR)

8.1. FROM CSCE TO OSCE

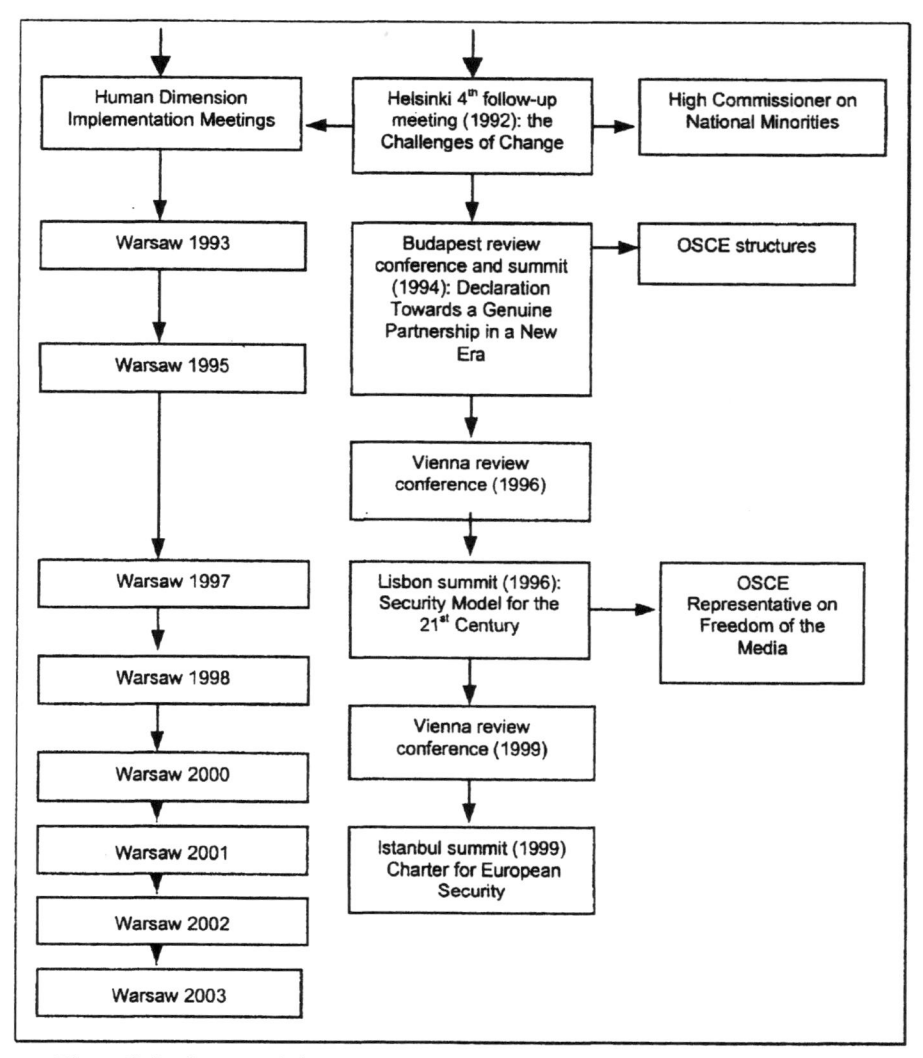

```
┌─────────────────────┐   ┌─────────────────────┐   ┌─────────────────────┐
│ Human Dimension     │◄──│ Helsinki 4th follow-up│──►│ High Commissioner on│
│ Implementation      │   │ meeting (1992): the  │   │ National Minorities │
│ Meetings            │   │ Challenges of Change │   │                     │
└─────────────────────┘   └─────────────────────┘   └─────────────────────┘
         │                          │
         ▼                          ▼
┌─────────────────────┐   ┌─────────────────────┐   ┌─────────────────────┐
│    Warsaw 1993      │   │  Budapest review    │──►│   OSCE structures   │
└─────────────────────┘   │ conference and summit│   └─────────────────────┘
         │                │ (1994): Declaration │
         ▼                │ Towards a Genuine   │
┌─────────────────────┐   │ Partnership in a New│
│    Warsaw 1995      │   │        Era          │
└─────────────────────┘   └─────────────────────┘
         │                          │
         │                          ▼
         │                ┌─────────────────────┐
         │                │   Vienna review     │
         │                │ conference (1996)   │
         │                └─────────────────────┘
         │                          │
         ▼                          ▼
┌─────────────────────┐   ┌─────────────────────┐   ┌─────────────────────┐
│    Warsaw 1997      │   │ Lisbon summit (1996):│──►│        OSCE         │
└─────────────────────┘   │ Security Model for the│   │ Representative on   │
         │                │    21st Century     │   │  Freedom of the     │
         ▼                │                     │   │       Media         │
┌─────────────────────┐   └─────────────────────┘   └─────────────────────┘
│    Warsaw 1998      │             │
└─────────────────────┘             ▼
         │                ┌─────────────────────┐
         ▼                │   Vienna review     │
┌─────────────────────┐   │ conference (1999)   │
│    Warsaw 2000      │   └─────────────────────┘
└─────────────────────┘             │
         │                          ▼
         ▼                ┌─────────────────────┐
┌─────────────────────┐   │ Istanbul summit (1999)│
│    Warsaw 2001      │   │ Charter for European │
└─────────────────────┘   │      Security       │
         │                └─────────────────────┘
         ▼
┌─────────────────────┐
│    Warsaw 2002      │
└─────────────────────┘
         │
         ▼
┌─────────────────────┐
│    Warsaw 2003      │
└─────────────────────┘
```

The call for human rights was essential to this 'velvet revolutions' and many of its figureheads like *Lech Wałęsa* in Poland and *Vaclav Havel* in Czechoslovakia were leading exponents in the 'Helsinki movement'.

8. Organization for Security and Cooperation in Europe (OSCE)

TEXTBOX 120

8.2. The CSCE during the Cold War

'Helsinki Process'

- Appointed to overcome the East-West conflict
- New comprehensive approach to European security
- Preliminary talks in Helsinki 1972

Helsinki Final Act, 1 August 1975

- Participating states defined principles and commitments concerning relations between states as well as between states and their citizens
- 35 participating states including Canada and the United States, but not Albania
- Decisions are taken unanimously (principle of consensus)
- Politically binding, but not legally binding

Three 'baskets' of Recommendations

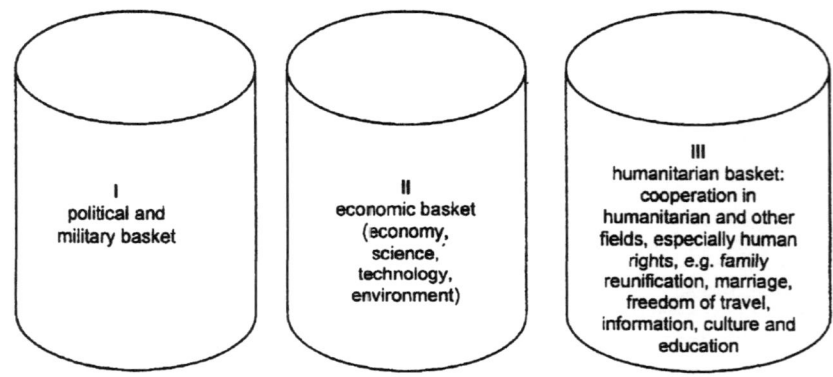

I political and military basket

II economic basket (economy, science, technology, environment)

III humanitarian basket: cooperation in humanitarian and other fields, especially human rights, e.g. family reunification, marriage, freedom of travel, information, culture and education

Ten Principles Guiding Relations between Participating States

1. Sovereign equality, respect for the rights inherent in sovereignty
2. Refraining from the threat or use of force
3. Inviolability of frontiers
4. Territorial integrity of states
5. Peaceful settlement of disputes
6. Non-intervention in internal affairs
7. Respect for human rights and fundamental freedoms, including the freedom of thought, conscience, religion or belief
8. Equal rights and self-determination of peoples
9. Cooperation among states
10. Fulfilment in good faith of obligations under international law

8.3. HUMAN DIMENSION

> **TEXTBOX 121**
>
> ### 8.3. HUMAN DIMENSION
>
> Human dimension = (political) obligation within the OSCE to ensure human rights and fundamental freedoms, rule of law and principles of democracy
>
> These obligations apply to all participating states alike
>
> Legal basis:
> - Vienna Concluding Document 1989
> - Vienna and Moscow Mechanisms 1989/91
>
> #### Conference on the Human Dimension
>
> - **Paris** (May – June 1989): no concluding document
> - Revolutions of 1989: political changes in Central and Eastern Europe; end of the Cold War; fall of the Iron Curtain
>
> - **Copenhagen** (June 1990): Document of the Copenhagen Meeting
> - Important source of obligations within the human dimension; recognition of the protection and promotion of human rights as one of the fundamental purposes of government; comprehensive catalogue of human rights; protection of national minorities
>
> - **Moscow** (September-October 1991): Document of the Moscow Meeting
> - ascertains that the obligations within the human dimension are of imminent importance to all participating states
> - 'Moscow Mechanism' to appoint emergency missions in the event of serious human rights violations
> - some new obligations: e.g. supporting a lawfully elected government in the event of an overthrow; protection of human rights during public emergency
>
> #### Follow-Up
>
> - Two-week Human Dimension Implementation Meetings in Warsaw (in years with no OSCE summits): 1993, 1995, 1997, 1998, 2000, 2001, 2002, 2003
> - Review conferences (prior to summits) held regularly in Vienna

The **Human Dimension Mechanism and Conference** was established in the Vienna Concluding Document. It was the first time in the history of the CSCE that a formal mechanism for dealing with concrete human rights violations, an **inter-state complaints procedure**, was created by the participating states. One of the first cases dealt with by the **'Vienna Mechanism'** was that of the Czech human rights activist *Vaclav Havel* and his detention. The Vienna Mechanism also provided for missions of experts as fact-finding tools, which were to become characteristic of the Human Dimension as such. Concrete human rights issues that were not resolved bilaterally or with the help of a mission of experts, were referred to one of the three Human Dimension Conferences (Paris 1989, Copenhagen 1990 and Moscow 1991) decided on in Vienna. The Iron Curtain fell between the conference in Paris and the one in Copenhagen, which is why in retrospect, the **Copenhagen Document** and its

8. ORGANIZATION FOR SECURITY AND COOPERATION IN EUROPE (OSCE)

comprehensive provisions on human rights and minorities are of such eminent importance in the history of the CSCE. The attempted coup against President *Gorbachev* at the time of the Moscow Human Dimension Conference from 10 September to 4 October 1991 was no less significant. At that conference, the '**Moscow Mechanism**' was finally agreed upon, which provides for the deployment of emergency missions (compulsory) of up to three rapporteurs in the event of serious human rights violations (8.4.). The first of these missions, which may be sent to a country upon the initiative of 10 CSCE states without that country's consent, was sent to former Yugoslavia shortly after the Moscow mechanism was installed. In December 2002, the Moscow Mechanism was re-activated by 10 Western states in relation to Turkmenistan. Since Turkmenistan refused to appoint a rapporteur, the mission was only carried out by one Rapporteur who submitted his report in March 2003.

The legitimacy and continued existence of the CSCE was first challenged when the Iron Curtain fell. It was considered a typical Cold War institution and as such – at least from the Western point of view – had achieved far more than its founders had ever hoped. In fact, instead of mere détente and disarmament it had brought about the dissolution of the Warsaw Pact, and instead of gradual improvement of human rights and economic and cultural cooperation, it had achieved the collapse of repressive regimes and the end of a Europe split into two. The CSCE Heads of State and Government, in the **Charter of Paris for a New Europe,** solemnly declared the end of the Cold War on 21 November 1990 (8.5.). They promised a 'new era of democracy, peace and unity' in Europe supported by the three pillars of a (Western) European value system as embraced by the Council of Europe, i.e. democracy, rule of law and human rights (5.1.).

The first 'transition states' in Central and Eastern Europe had already joined the Council of Europe and the ECHR, others were about to follow and subjected themselves to the now obligatory mechanisms of inter-state and individual complaints before the European Court of Human Rights. Hence, the question was raised whether it still made sense to keep up a political version of the inter-state complaints procedure in the framework of the CSCE Human Dimension, which in itself was conceived in the spirit of confrontation during the Cold War.

The question of continued legitimacy of the CSCE was soon overtaken by the **political reality in the unified Europe**. Peoples' right to self-determination had not only been instrumental in reunifying Germany and in peacefully dividing Czechoslovakia, it had also incited a new wave of **nationalism** in Yugoslavia and the Soviet Union and with it, had triggered a process of dissolution of these two multinational states dominated by ethnic and religious conflicts that culminated in civil war and in the case of the Balkans, even genocide.

In other Central and Eastern European countries too, the sudden collapse of 'real socialism' had left an ideological void and fear amongst the population, both of which were conducive to nationalist and racist tendencies, causing violent minority conflicts in many areas. To make matters worse, the fall of the Iron Curtain and the dire economic situation in Central and Eastern Europe prompted a new wave of

8.4. HUMAN DIMENSION MECHANISMS

migrants that was met with **xenophobic fears and racism** in most Western European countries. Instead of embarking on the new era of peace and unity promised by the Charter of Paris, Europe was about to drop back into an era of nationalism, racism and bloody minority conflicts.

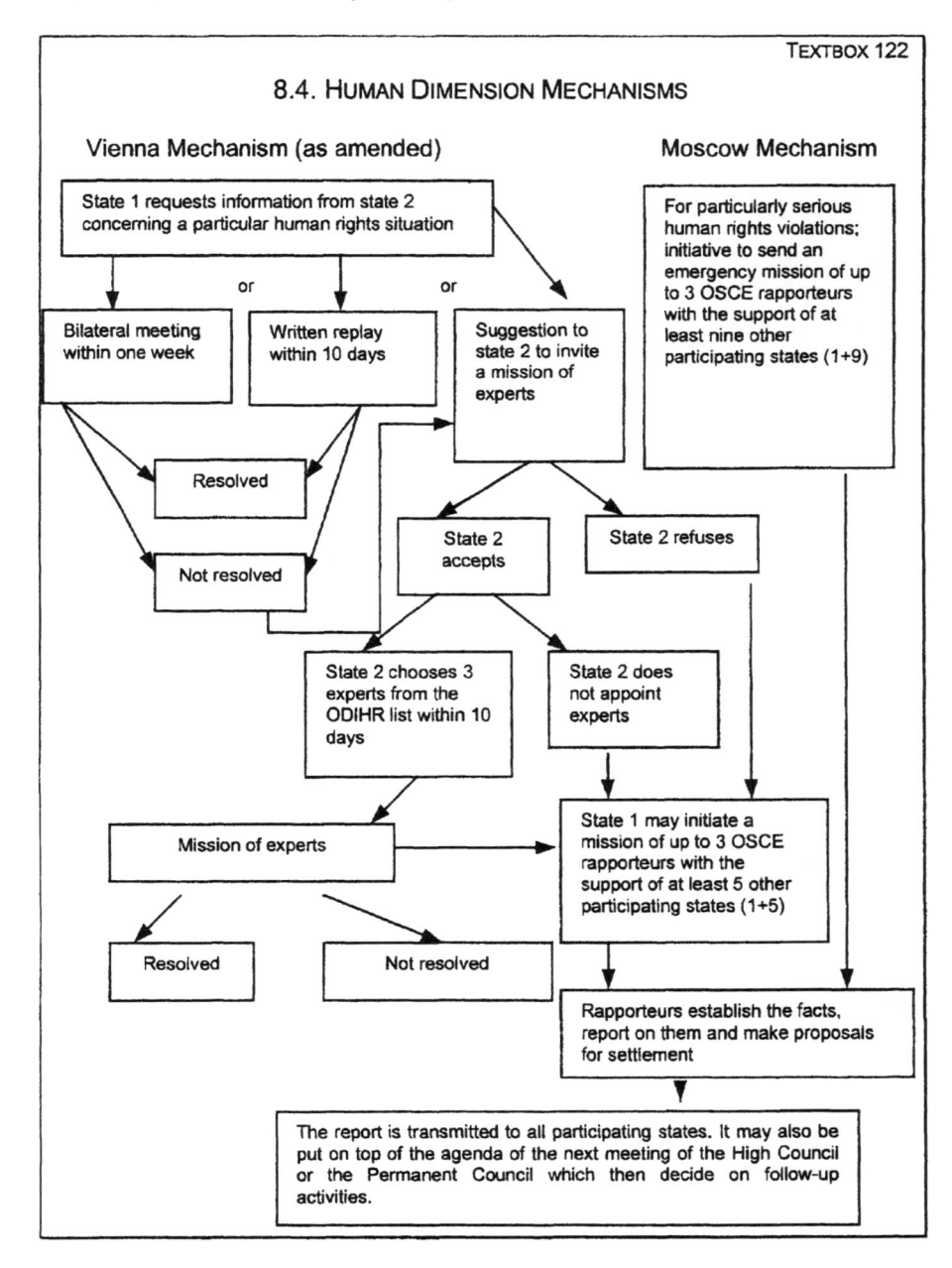

TEXTBOX 122

8.4. HUMAN DIMENSION MECHANISMS

Vienna Mechanism (as amended)

- State 1 requests information from state 2 concerning a particular human rights situation
  - or → Bilateral meeting within one week
  - or → Written replay within 10 days
  - or → Suggestion to state 2 to invite a mission of experts

- Bilateral meeting / Written replay → Resolved / Not resolved
- Not resolved → Suggestion to state 2 to invite a mission of experts

- Suggestion → State 2 accepts / State 2 refuses
- State 2 accepts → State 2 chooses 3 experts from the ODIHR list within 10 days / State 2 does not appoint experts
- State 2 chooses 3 experts → Mission of experts → Resolved / Not resolved
- State 2 does not appoint experts → State 1 may initiate a mission of up to 3 OSCE rapporteurs with the support of at least 5 other participating states (1+5)
- State 2 refuses → State 1 may initiate a mission of up to 3 OSCE rapporteurs with the support of at least 5 other participating states (1+5)

Moscow Mechanism

For particularly serious human rights violations; initiative to send an emergency mission of up to 3 OSCE rapporteurs with the support of at least nine other participating states (1+9)

↓

Rapporteurs establish the facts, report on them and make proposals for settlement

↓

The report is transmitted to all participating states. It may also be put on top of the agenda of the next meeting of the High Council or the Permanent Council which then decide on follow-up activities.

8. Organization for Security and Cooperation in Europe (OSCE)

The CSCE met these challenges by reorienting itself from the roots, using the **concept of comprehensive security** as a substantive basis. On the formal side, it sped up the process of institutionalization while on the operational side it began to implement a number of long-term missions.

TEXTBOX 123

8.5. Charter of Paris for a New Europe

Signed on 21 November 1990

'Europe is liberating itself from the legacy of the past' and declares the Cold War formally over.

'A new era of democracy, peace and unity' as an expression of the new political climate in Europe after 1989

Common commitment towards human rights, democracy and the rule of law, the Charter re-affirms major human rights, above all civil and political rights

'Full respect for these precepts is the bedrock on which we will seek to construct the new Europe'

First attempts at institutionalising the CSCE:

- Summits of Heads of State or Government, every 2 years
- Council of Ministers of Foreign Affairs
- Committee of Senior Officials
- Secretariat (Prague)
- Conflict Prevention Centre (Vienna)
- Office for Free Elections (Warsaw) – turned into Office for Democratic Institutions and Human Rights (ODIHR) in 1992
- Support for creation of a parliamentary assembly

At the **Budapest Summit in 1994**, the Heads of State or Government decided to develop a common and comprehensive security model for Europe for the 21st century as a foundation for the OSCE. Along with the military, political and diplomatic components of conflict prevention, promotion and protection of human rights, democracy and rule of law are considered essential elements of comprehensive security as seen by the OSCE. Its tasks in this new generation of complex international peace keeping operations, as in Bosnia and Herzegovina or in Kosovo, (8.12., 16.9. and 16.14.), are to build democracy and human rights by organizing and monitoring elections, monitoring human rights or strengthening independent media and an independent judiciary.

The **process of institutionalization** began in 1990 with the Charter of Paris and the establishment of the first permanent Secretariat in Prague, the Conflict Prevention Centre in Vienna, and the Office for Free Elections in Warsaw. Political

8.6. THE CSCE IN SEARCH OF A NEW IDENTITY

bodies were instituted to provide the structure for the future organization. In 1992, the CSCE defined itself as a 'regional arrangement in the sense of Chapter VIII of the Charter of the United Nations' and established the Office of the Secretary General. Finally, at the Budapest Summit in 1994, the Heads of State or Government decided to transform the CSCE to become the **Organization for Security and Cooperation in Europe (OSCE)** with its own **permanent structures**.

TEXTBOX 124

8.6. THE CSCE IN SEARCH OF A NEW IDENTITY

Growing nationalism and intolerance, minority conflicts for ethnic and religious reasons

The CSCE reacted by
- forging the concept of comprehensive security
- speeding up institutionalization
- establishing long-term missions

Helsinki Summit 1992: 'The Challenges of Change'
- the CSCE considers itself a 'regional agreement in the sense of Chapter VIII of the Charter of the United Nations' and establishes:
    - The High Commissioner on National Minorities
    - CSCE Forum for Security Cooperation
    - Economic Forum
- suspends membership of Federal Republic of Yugoslavia (July 1992)

Meeting of the Council of Ministers, Stockholm 1992
- establishes the post of Secretary General

Budapest Summit 1994
- 'a common and comprehensive security model for Europe for the 21st century'
- decision to rename CSCE as OSCE
- new name effective as of 1 January 1995
- permanent OSCE structures

Its principal organs since then – apart from the summits of Heads of State or Government – have been the Ministerial Council, the Senior Council and the Permanent Council of currently 55 participating states that convenes weekly in Vienna. The 'Chairman-in-Office' is selected each year from among the CSCE foreign ministers and is supported by the Ministerial Troika, i.e. the preceding and succeeding chairpersons.

The OSCE Secretariat in Vienna is headed by the Secretary General, while the main department of the Secretariat concerned with human rights, the **Office for Democratic Institutions and Human Rights** (ODIHR), is located in Warsaw. This new structure bears strong resemblance to that of an inter-governmental

8. Organization for Security and Cooperation in Europe (OSCE)

organization, formally, however, the OSCE has not yet been constituted as an organization in the legal sense, but continues to operate as a loose association (conference) of 55 participating states.

The post of the **High Commissioner on National Minorities** established in 1992 is a perfect example of how human rights have been incorporated into the CSCE's comprehensive security concept. The express purpose of the post was to act as an instrument of conflict prevention, in other words to give off warning signals during the early stages of minority conflicts and use silent diplomacy as a way of mediation (14.3.). Nevertheless, the activities of the High Commissioner are of course of eminent importance to human rights inasmuch as they include comprehensive implementation of the human rights of persons belonging to minorities, as laid down in the 1990 Copenhagen Document on the Human Dimension.

TEXTBOX 125

8.7. THE OSCE: STRUCTURES AND INSTITUTIONS

55 participating states (Yugoslavia readmitted on 27 November 2000)

Decisions are taken by consensus

Decisions are politically but not legally binding

Summits: meetings of Heads of State or Government of participating states to set priorities and provide orientation at the highest political level:

- Helsinki 1975
- Paris 1990
- Helsinki 1992
- Budapest 1994
- Lisbon 1996
- Istanbul 1999

Review conferences in Vienna in preparation of the summits; implementation meetings in Warsaw on the Human Dimension (in years without a summit)

Principal Organs

- **Ministerial Council** (foreign ministers of participating states)

Is convened in those years when no summit takes place:

New York (1990), Berlin, Moscow (1991), Prague, Helsinki, Stockholm (1992), Rome (1993), Budapest (1995), Copenhagen (1997), Oslo (1998), Vienna (2000), Bucharest (2001), Porto (2002), Maastricht (2003)

8.7. THE OSCE: STRUCTURES AND INSTITUTIONS

- **Senior Council** (successor to the Committee of Senior Officials)

Monitors, controls and coordinates OSCE activities and convenes once a year as the Economic Forum (Prague), additional meetings or emergency meetings optional (3 meetings 1991-1994 concerning the former Yugoslavia)

- **Permanent Council** (successor to the Permanent Committee)

Composed of permanent representatives of participating states, it is one of the two OSCE bodies for political consultation and decision-making, convenes weekly in Vienna (see Forum for Security Cooperation)

- **Chairman-in-Office**

Bears overall responsibility for executive action and coordination of OSCE activities; selected each year from among the foreign ministers of the participating states, is assisted by the Ministerial Troika, i.e. the preceding and succeeding chairpersons

- 2002: Chairman-in-Office *Jakob Gijsbert Jaap de Hoop Scheffer* (Netherlands), and Troika: Portugal, Netherlands, Bulgaria

- **Secretary General** (Secretariat)

Provides operational support to the Organization's activities

Ján Kubis (Slovak Republic) 1999 to 2003

Giancarlo Aragona (Italy) 1996 to 1999

Wilhelm Höynck (Germany) 1993 to 1996

- **Forum for Security Cooperation** (FSC)

Meets weekly in Vienna to discuss concrete security and stability measures (arms control, confidence- and security-building, etc.)

- **Parliamentary Assembly**

More than 300 parliamentarians from participating states

Aim: promoting inter-parliamentary dialogue and cooperation

Parliamentarians appointed for cooperation with ODIHR during OSCE missions, '*democratic assistance program*' (former Soviet Union)

- **Court of Conciliation and Arbitration** (Geneva), established in 1992

Thanks to the excellent pioneering work of *Max van der Stoel*, the former Dutch foreign minister, the post is now established as a highly effective instrument in the OSCE's comprehensive security concept. In 2001, the Swedish diplomat, *Rolf Ekéus* took up this important function.

In 1997, the post of **OSCE Representative for Freedom of Media** was established on the model of the post of High Commissioner. It also contains elements of human rights protection and conflict prevention, and through the commitment of *Freimut Duve*, the German media expert, has become yet another efficient instrument in this context.

The Conference on the Human Dimension opened in Vienna in 1989 and was completed in principle with the third conference in Moscow in 1991. Since then regular implementation meetings on the human dimension have been held in Warsaw under the guidance of the ODIHR, which, however, are more reminiscent of seminars than of operational monitoring procedures for human rights.

The **Vienna and the Moscow Mechanisms** (8.4.) provide the main procedural basis for complaints about human rights violations that occur in one of the participating states. They provide an exception to the principle of consensus and allow for the compulsory deployment of **missions of up to three OSCE rapporteurs** upon the initiative of a certain number of participating states (1 state +5 or 1 state +9). Although these fact-finding missions in theory are a human rights investigation instrument comparable to the Special Rapporteurs of the UN Human Rights Commission (4.4.1.4.), in practice they have turned out to be a relict from Cold War times. There has not been a single case of a Western state taking an initiative against another Western state (e.g. Turkey), and since the Cold War both sides of the former Iron Curtain have become increasingly reluctant to activate this mechanism.

TEXTBOX 126

8.8. HUMAN RIGHTS AS PART OF A COMPREHENSIVE SECURITY CONCEPT

Lisbon Summit 1996: Security Model for the 21st Century

The OSCE's comprehensive approach to security requires improvement in the implementation of all commitments in the human dimension, in particular with respect to human rights and fundamental freedoms. ... Among the acute problems within the human dimension the continuing violations of human rights...continue to endanger stability in the OSCE region' (article 9)

Istanbul Summit 1999: Charter for European Security

- 'Peace and security in our region are best guaranteed by the willingness and ability of each participating state to uphold democracy, the rule of law and respect for human rights' (Art. 14)
- Established 'REACT' - Rapid Expert Assistance and Cooperation Teams
- Set up an 'Operation Centre' at the Conflict Prevention Centre to plan and deploy field operations – adoption of the 'Platform for cooperative security' to strengthen cooperation between OSCE and other international organizations and institutions
- Extended the OSCE's peace-keeping role
- Extended commitments in the human dimension: nationalism, racism, chauvinism, xenophobia and anti-Semitism; Roma and Sinti
- Introduced the human dimension to field operations

In the early days, the Moscow Mechanism was used to investigate the human rights situation in the former Yugoslavia, but because of its limited competences

8.9. HIGH COMMISSIONER ON NATIONAL MINORITIES (HCNM)

during armed conflicts and gross and systematic human rights violations, it has proved as ineffective as other comparable mechanisms of traditional human rights protection.

TEXTBOX 127

8.9. HIGH COMMISSIONER ON NATIONAL MINORITIES (HCNM)

Created in 1992 (Helsinki Document, Chapter II)

Rolf Ekéus (Sweden): 2001 – 2004

Max van der Stoel (Netherlands): 1993 – 2001

Office in The Hague

Mandate

'Instrument of conflict prevention at the earliest possible stage'

- He/she 'will provide 'early warning' and, as appropriate, 'early action' at the earliest possible stage in regard to tensions involving national minority issues which have not developed yet beyond an early warning stage, but, in the judgement of the High Commissioner, have the potential to develop into a conflict within the CSCE area, affecting peace, stability or relations between participating States, requiring the attention of and action by the Council or the CSO'.
- Is not an 'ombuds-person for minorities' or investigating officer for individual human rights violations (note: *commissioner 'on'*, not *'for' national minorities*)
- No definition of 'national minorities' in the mandate
- Conducts on-site missions, using preventive, silent diplomacy
- May draw up reports and recommendations to be communicated to governments
- Interventions do not require the consent of OSCE organs or participating states

'Within the mandate...the High Commissioner will work in confidence and will act independently of all parties involved directly in the tensions'

High Commissioner does not consider:

- National minority issues in situations involving organized acts of terrorism
- Violations of OSCE commitments with regard to an individual personbelonging to a national minority

Activities to date:

- Mediating in minority issues such as Albania, Croatia, Estonia, Hungary, Kazakhstan, Kyrgyzstan, Latvia, Lithuania, Macedonia, Romania, the Slovak Republic, the Ukraine, etc.
- Special study on the situation of Roma and Sinti in the OSCE area

8. Organization for Security and Cooperation in Europe (OSCE)

Only recently, there have been certain initiatives to re-activate this mechanism (e.g. the initiative of Western states in relation to Turkmenistan at the end of 2002).

TEXTBOX 128

8.10. OSCE Representative on Freedom of Media

Established in 1997 by decision No. 193 of the Permanent Council and confirmed by the Copenhagen Ministerial Council

Freimut Duve (Germany): 1997 – 2003

Office in Vienna

Mandate

- 'He or she will address serious problems caused by, inter alia, obstruction of media activities and unfavourable working conditions for journalists'
- Will observe media developments and provide an early warning system with regard to freedom of expression and freedom of media
- Will support full compliance with OSCE principles and commitments in all participating states concerning freedom of expression and freedom of media, including 'hate speech'
- 'Rapid response' in case of serious non-compliance
- 4 areas: governments, parliaments, media and NGOs
- Close cooperation with the Permanent Council, ODIHR and HCNM

Activities to date

- Interventions with issues of freedom of expression, e.g. in Azerbaijan, Belarus, Bosnia and Herzegovina, Croatia, Georgia, Kazakhstan, Kyrgyzstan, Macedonia, Moldova, Romania, Russian Federation, Slovak Republic, Tajikistan, Turkmenistan, Turkey, Uzbekistan, Yugoslavia
- Emphasis on 'structural censorship', persecution of journalists, defamation sentences, closing down of newspaper editing houses

---

The missions of experts and rapporteurs of the early 1990s were subsequently replaced by **long-term missions** established by the OSCE in the crisis regions of the Balkans, Caucasus, the Baltics and in Central Asia. These field missions were conducted by the OSCE on its own or in cooperation with the United Nations and other organizations and their complex peacekeeping operations. The biggest missions to date were those in former Yugoslavia (Bosnia and Herzegovina, Croatia and Kosovo), where the OSCE was primarily responsible for promoting and monitoring human rights, democracy and the rule of law (8.12., 16.4. and 16.9.). In practice, however, the OSCE has been hampered in its activities by the fact that, unlike the United Nations and other organizations operating in the field, it still acts as a loose association of participating states.

8.11. OFFICE FOR DEMOCRATIC INSTITUTIONS AND HUMAN RIGHTS (ODIHR)

Thus, the OSCE primarily relies on staff seconded by the various governments, which means that larger states in particular are in a position to exert far more **bilateral influence** than with field operations conducted by staff recruited directly through the United Nations, the UNHCR, and others like them. This may also be the reason why countries like the United States, in the Dayton Peace Agreement for Bosnia and Herzegovina in 1995 or when establishing the UN Mission in Kosovo following the NATO air raids, were so keen to have the UN replaced by 'North Atlantic' organizations like NATO and the OSCE, as far as possible. This strategy, of course, is not conducive to the coherence and efficiency of any field operation. It has in fact been the cause of much **politicization** and has made coordination and cooperation very difficult.

TEXTBOX 129

8.11. OFFICE FOR DEMOCRATIC INSTITUTIONS AND HUMAN RIGHTS (ODIHR)

Main OSCE body for the human dimension

Originally the 'Office for Free Elections' established by the Charter of Paris in 1990

1992 Ministerial Council Meeting Prague: mandate extended and office renamed

Office in Warsaw

Director: *Christian Strohal* (Austria) since 2003

Mandate

- Promoting demoscrati elections through observation and development of national election and human rights institutions
- Providing technical support for national legal institutions
- Supporting field missions in their activities concerning the human dimension
- Promoting the development of NGOs and civil society
- Monitoring the observance of participating states' commitments towards the human dimension
- Contact point for Roma and Sinti issues

If the OSCE is to extend its function as 'a regional arrangement' in the sense of Chapter VIII of the UN Charter on maintenance of peace in Europe, it would seem better to do so as an inter-governmental organization and by gradually diminishing the bilateral influence of its (powerful) participating states. By way of conclusion it has to be said that the CSCE/OSCE, because of its flexible political structure unrestrained by international treaties, in the 1990s was able to meet the challenges in Europe in a relatively short time. It shed its role as a Cold War institution to become an organization capable of presenting a **strategy to prevent conflicts** and strengthen democracy and the rule of law in Europe.

8. ORGANIZATION FOR SECURITY AND COOPERATION IN EUROPE (OSCE)

> TEXTBOX 130
>
> ### 8.12. OSCE FIELD MISSIONS AND ACTIVITIES
>
> - emphasis on human rights, democracy and the rule of law
> - usually deployed by the Permanent Council with the consent of the host country
> - different sizes, ranging from four (liaison office in Central Asia) to several hundred persons (Kosovo, Croatia, Bosnia and Herzegovina)
>
> - **South Eastern Europe:**
>
> Kosovo, Bosnia and Herzegovina, Croatia, Serbia and Montenegro (the main OSCE missions), OSCE presence in Albania, as well as a 'spill-over' monitor mission in Skopje
>
> Example *Kosovo*:
>
> - First missions of long duration in Kosovo, Sandjak and Vojvodina in autumn 1992; closed in 1993 when the Federal Republic of Yugoslavia refused to have the 'memoranda of understanding' continued
> - October 1998 – March 1999: Kosovo verification mission (KVM) deployed to monitor armistice and movement of troops and to promote development of human rights and democracy (the Federal Republic of Yugoslavia's adherence to UN SC Res. 1160 and 1199)
> - Current mission in Kosovo, deployed in 1999 (Decision of the Permanent Council no. 305 of 1 July 1999, in reference to the UN SC Res. 1244 of 10 June 1999) as a separate component of the UN transition administration mission in Kosovo (UNMIK): responsible for training police force and judges, supporting civil society and independent media, organising and monitoring elections, monitoring, protecting and promoting human rights
>
> - **The Baltics and Eastern Europe:**
>
> OSCE advisory and monitoring group in Belarus; missions in Estonia, Latvia, Moldova, project coordination in the Ukraine
>
> - **Caucasus:**
>
> Office in Baku (Azerbaijan), assistance group to Chechnya, mission in Georgia, 'Personal Representative of the Chairman-in-Office on the Conflict Dealt with by the Minsk Conference '(Nagorno Karabakh conflict), office in Yerevan (Armenia)
>
> - **Central Asia:**
>
> Centres in Almaty (Kazakhstan), Ashgabad (Turkmenistan), Bishkek (Kyrgyzstan), Dushanbe (Tajikistan), Tashkent (Uzbekistan)

Promoting and protecting human rights has become an integral part of the **comprehensive OSCE security concept,** be it through the preventive activities of the High Commissioner on National Minorities, or the Representative for Freedom of Media, the organization and monitoring of elections, appointment of human rights

8.12. OSCE FIELD MISSIONS AND ACTIVITIES

monitors during field missions, or the development of human rights structures and the promotion of civil society institutions in the context of long-term field missions.

8. ORGANIZATION FOR SECURITY AND COOPERATION IN EUROPE (OSCE)

LITBOX 8
LITERATURE

Binder, Johannes 2001, The Human Dimension of the OSCE: From Recommendation to Implementation, Study Series of the Ludwig Boltzmann Institute of Human Rights, Vol. 10, Vienna

Bloed, Arie (Ed.) 1993, The Conference on Security and Co-operation in Europe, Analysis and Basic Documents, 1972-1993, Dordrecht

Bloed, Arie and *van Dijk*, Pieter (Eds.) 1991, The Human Dimension of the Helsinki Process - The Vienna Follow-up Meeting and its Aftermath, Dordrecht

Bothe, Michael, *Ronzitti*, Natalino and *Rosas*, Allan (Eds.) 1997, The OSCE in the Maintenance of Peace and Security: Conflict Prevention, Crisis Management, and Peaceful Settlement of Disputes, The Hague

Höynck, Wilhelm 1996, From CSCE to OSCE, Vienna

Institut für Friedensforschung und Sicherheitspolitik an der Universität Hamburg / IFSH (Ed.), OSZE-Jahrbuch, Baden-Baden

International Helsinki Federation for Human Rights (IHF), Helsinki Monitor, Quarterly on Security and Cooperation in Europe, The Hague

International Helsinki Federation for Human Rights (IHF) 1999, OSCE Review Conference: Human Dimension Issues, Vienna

Kemp, Walter A. (Ed.) 2001, Quiet Diplomacy in Action: the OSCE High Commissioner on National Minorities, The Hague

Lutz, Dieter S. and *Tudyka*, Kurt P. (Eds.) 2000, Perspektiven und Defizite der OSZE, Baden-Baden

Maier, Dieter A. 1996, Die Entwicklung des Menschenrechtsregimes der KSZE/OSZE von Helsinki bis Budapest, Vienna

Nooy, Gert de (Ed.) 1996, Cooperation security, the OSCE, and its Code of Conduct, The Hague

ODIHR 1998, OSCE Combating Torture and other Cruel, Inhuman or Degrading Treatment or Punishment: the Role of the OSCE, Warsaw

ODIHR 2001, OSCE Human Dimension Commitments - A Reference Guide, Warsaw

OSCE 2001, Freedom of Expression, Free Flow of Information, Freedom of Media: The Representative on the Freedom of the Media, The Hague

OSCE 2002, OSCE Handbook, 3rd ed., Vienna

Sabahi, Farian and *Warner*, Daniel (Eds.) 2003, The OSCE and the Multiple Challenges of Transition: the Caucasus and Central Asia, Burlington

Simonsen, Sven Gunnar (Ed.) 1997, Conflicts in the OSCE Area, Oslo

Stoel, Max van der 1999, Peace and Stability through Human and Minority Rights: Speeches by the OSCE High Commissioner on National Minorities, Baden-Baden

Zaagman, Rob 1999, International Ethnic Conflict Prevention: Estonia and Latvia and the role of the OSCE High Commissioner on National Minorities, Flensburg

INTERNET

www.osce.org - Organization for Security and Cooperation in Europe (OSCE)

www.osce.org/odihr - Office for Democratic Institutions and Human Rights (ODIHR)

www.osce.org/hcnm - OSCE High Commissioner on National Minorities

www.osce.org/fom - OSCE Representative of Freedom of Media

9. EUROPEAN UNION (EU)

The process of European integration can be illustrated by three concentric circles (5.1.): from the OSCE (originally 35, currently 55 members), via the Council of Europe (originally 11, currently 45 members), to the European Union (originally 6, currently 15 as of 2004 25 members). The OSCE (formerly CSCE) was founded in 1975 as an instrument of détente between East and West during the Cold War. Its aim was to include all European states (except Albania in the beginning), as well as Canada and the United States (8.). Membership in the other two (originally exclusively Western European) organizations was reserved for those states whose constitution and legal system was founded on **common European fundamental values (rule of law, democracy and human rights)**. Thus, membership with the Council of Europe constitutes an important first step on the road map to Europe for Central and Eastern European states in transition, inasmuch as the Council, ever since its foundation in 1949, has considered and monitored observance of these values as a prerequisite for accession (albeit less rigidly in the recent past, 5.1.).

Yet what these states are ultimately aiming for, is full economic and political **integration into the European unification process**, i.e. accession to the European Union. Membership in the Council of Europe is in fact an indispensable prerequisite for admission to the EU, which since 1993, along with the traditional economic criteria, has also been examining actual adherence to the political requirements. With the acceptance of Serbia and Montenegro on 3 April 2003, the Council of Europe now includes all European OSCE states with the exception of Belarus, Monaco and the Holy See.

Of the 30 Council of Europe states not yet members of the EU, ten (Cyprus, the Czech Republic, Estonia, Hungary, Latvia, Lithuania, Malta, Poland, Slovakia, and Slovenia) will be admitted in 2004, bringing the number of EU states to 25. The three European Communities (EEC, ECSC, Euratom) originally aimed primarily at establishing a common European economic space where human rights did not feature prominently and hence were not entrenched in the foundation treaties of 1951 and 1957. It was not until the creation of the EU in the Treaty of Maastricht in 1992 that political integration of Europe was declared an overriding goal.

In its **external relations**, particularly its development cooperation and more recently its Common Foreign and Security Policy, the EU has pursued, however, for many years an **active human rights policy** criticizing their partner countries for non-compliance with minimum international human rights standards. Considering the lack of a common EU bill of rights and of an equally critical human rights policy towards its member states, the EU was increasingly criticized for applying **double standards**.

9. European Union (EU)

> **Textbox 131**
>
> ## 9.1. The Significance of Human Rights in the Process of European Integration
>
> Human rights were not explicitly included in the 1951 Treaty of Paris (ECSC) or the 1957 Treaties of **Rome** (EEC and Euratom) yet there were beginnings:
>
> - Principle of equal pay for male and female workers, article 141 (ex article 119) EC Treaty
> - Prohibition of discrimination on grounds of nationality, article 12 (ex article 6) EC Treaty
> - Freedom of movement for workers, article 39 (ex article 48) EC Treaty
>
> 1977: joint declaration on the respect of fundamental rights (European Parliament, Council and the Commission)
>
> 1986: preamble of the Single European Act refers to democracy and human rights
>
> 1989: the European Parliament adopts the Declaration on the Fundamental Rights and Freedoms
>
> 1989: Charter of fundamental social rights of workers is adopted
>
> - 1992 (1993): **Maastricht** Treaty on the European Union (EU Treaty)
>
>   - Preamble EU Treaty: makes reference to freedom, democracy, human rights, fundamental freedoms and rule of law
>   - Article 6(2) (ex article F(2)) EU Treaty: 'the Union shall respect fundamental rights, as guaranteed by the European Convention for the Protection of Human Rights and Fundamental Freedoms and as they result from the constitutional traditions common to the member states, as general principles of community law '
>   - Article 17 (ex article 8) ff EC Treaty: citizenship of the Union, freedom of movement, right to vote at municipal elections, right to petition the European Parliament
>   - Article 177 (ex article 130u) ff EC Treaty: development cooperation
>   - Article 11 (ex article J.1) EU Treaty: objectives of the common foreign and security policy
>
> 1996: opinion 2/94 of the European Court of Justice: Community legally prevented from acceding to the ECHR
>
> - 1997 (1999): Treaty of **Amsterdam**
>
> contains fundamental EU provisions on protection of human rights

9.1. THE SIGNIFICANCE OF HUMAN RIGHTS IN THE PROCESS OF EUROPEAN INTEGRATION

a) EU Treaty

- Article 6(1) (ex article F) EU Treaty, new paragraph 1: 'The union is founded on the principles of liberty, democracy, respect for human rights and fundamental freedoms, and the rule of law, principles which are common to the Member States'
- Article 7 EU Treaty (new), see also article 309 EC Treaty, article 96 ECSC Treaty and article 204 Euratom Treaty: possibility to suspend certain of the rights of a member state in the event of a serious and persistent breach of the principles laid down in article 6(1)
- Article 49 (ex article O) EU Treaty: new passage: only a European state, 'which respects the principles set out in Article 6(1)', may apply to become a member of the Union

b) EC Treaty

- Articles 2 and 3 EC Treaty: list of tasks now also includes 'equality between men and women'; new paragraph in article 3: '[t]he community shall aim to eliminate inequalities and to promote equality between men and women'
- Article 13 EC Treaty (new): supplements article 12 (ex article 6): prohibition of discrimination based on nationality, but also based on sex, racial or ethnic origin, religion or belief, disability, age or sexual orientation
- Article 63 EC Treaty (ex article 73 k): asylum and immigration policy
- Article 136 (ex article 117) EC Treaty: social policy
- Article 286 EC Treaty (new): better protection of individuals with regard to processing of personal data

1998: Vienna Declaration to commemorate the 50th anniversary of the Universal Declaration of Human Rights

1999: First Annual Report on Human Rights published by the Council of the European Union

- 2000: Treaty of **Nice**:
- Institutional reforms in view of the envisaged EU enlargement
- Amendment of article 7 EU Treaty (possibility of suspending certain rights in order to prevent serious human rights violations in the future): the Council, acting by a majority of four-fifths of its members, may determine that there is a clear risk of a serious breach by a member state of fundamental rights and submit apposite recommendations to the member state concerned.
- Adoption of the **EU Charter of Fundamental Rights** on 7 December 2000 as a non-binding bill of rights for the European Union; intention of incorporating the Charter into EC/EU Treaties.

If the EU, in its policy towards African, Caribbean, and Pacific (ACP) states (9.4.3.), the United States, and other third countries, calls for observance of human rights and wants to be taken seriously as a real 'global player' instead of a mere 'global payer', it must leave no doubt as to its commitment to human rights by the way it deals with problems, such as racism, xenophobia, or the treatment of refugees and migrants within its own borders.

TEXTBOX 132

9.2. HUMAN RIGHTS AS ADMISSION CRITERIA

- Article 49 EU Treaty: Any European state, 'which respects the principles set out in Article 6(1)', may apply to become a member of the Union
- Article 6(1) EU Treaty: 'The union is founded on the principles of liberty, democracy, respect for human rights and fundamental freedoms, and the rule of law, principles which are common to the Member States'
- Article 46 EU Treaty: competence of the European Court of Justice includes article 49
- Principles set out in art 6(1) are not within the competence of the European Court of Justice, however, it may examine decisions in accordance with article 49, as regards adherence to these principles by a candidate country
- According to the political criteria set out in Copenhagen in 1993 candidate countries must have in place stable institutions guaranteeing democracy, rule of law, human rights and respect for as well as protection of minorities.
- As of 2004, admission of 10 new member states: Cyprus, the Czech Republic, Estonia, Hungary, Latvia, Lithuania, Malta, Poland, Slovakia and Slovenia

---

It must not content itself with pointing to the European Court of Justice in Luxembourg as the one watching over the observance of human rights guaranteed in the ECHR (9.3.2.), if at the same time it is not prepared to have its measures examined by international human rights protection bodies such as the European Court of Human Rights in Strasbourg. This is why the EU has recently decided on a number of measures to strengthen **protection of human rights within its borders**. According to article 49 of the EU Treaty, respect for human rights, as one of the principles of the EU (article 6 EU Treaty) has become an express **prerequisite for admission**.

TEXTBOX 133

9.3. HUMAN RIGHTS WITHIN THE EU

- Importance of the European Convention on Human Rights
- Jurisdiction of the European Court of Justice
- Asylum and migration policy
- Protection against discrimination
- European Monitoring Centre on Racism and Xenophobia (EUMC)

9.3. HUMAN RIGHTS WITHIN THE EU

Observance of these prerequisites is examined by the Commission, Parliament and the Council during the admission procedure, and in some cases, as with the Slovak Republic (during the *Meciar* government), has resulted in negative positions on the part of the Commission.

TEXTBOX 134

9.3.1. THE SIGNIFICANCE AND STATUS OF THE EUROPEAN CONVENTION ON HUMAN RIGHTS (ECHR)

- Despite many attempts the EC has not acceded to the ECHR to date; Opinion of the ECJ of 28 March 1996: given the state of Community law at the time the Community was unable to accede; 1977 Treaty of Amsterdam has not provided the necessary changes to the Treaty
- With the proclamation of the EU Charter of Fundamental Rights on 7 December 2000, accession has become even more unlikely
- In practice, however, the European Court of Justice already applies the ECHR
- The ECHR is explicitly referred to under article 6(2) EU Treaty

---

Any serious and persistent breach of human rights by a state, as defined in article 7 of the EU Treaty, may invoke **sanctions** such as suspension of the right to vote even after that state has been admitted to the EU.

TEXTBOX 135

9.3.2. JURISPRUDENCE OF THE EUROPEAN COURT OF JUSTICE (ECJ) IN LUXEMBOURG

The founding treaties initially contained no specific provisions on human rights, yet the ECJ gradually began to take into account human rights in its judgments (e.g. cases Stauder, Internationale Handelsgesellschaft, Nold, Solange II, Wachauf, Cinéthèque, Demirel, ERT, Kremzow), thereby establishing the case law of human rights as general principles of Community law based on constitutional traditions common to the member states as well as international treaties (above all the ECHR)

Specific human rights recognized by the Court of Justice so far include:
Human dignity, equality, non-discrimination, freedom of association, freedom of religion, privacy, property, respect for family life

---

In the Treaty of Nice of December 2000, measures and recommendations set out in article 7 were extended to include **prevention** of human rights violations in member states. This was the Union's reaction to the measures imposed against Austria by the other 14 EU states following that country's acceptance of a right-wing populist party (FPÖ) in its new government in February 2000 (which by the way could not be considered sanctions in the sense of article 7).

9. EUROPEAN UNION (EU)

The European Court of Justice, in its Opinion of 1996, declared the Community not legally capable to accede to the ECHR, and the 1997 Treaty of Amsterdam had not created the necessary legal requirements for such an accession.

Faced with such odds, the German EU presidency in 1999 initiated a successful drafting process of a common EU bill of rights by a 'Convention' consisting of high level politicians and parliamentarians, which soon resulted in the EU's solemn adoption of the **EU Charter of Fundamental Rights** in December 2000 (9.5.4.).

This first comprehensive catalogue of human rights for the EU, which along with the civil and political rights coined in the ECHR also includes economic, social and cultural rights, as well as other EU-specific human rights and programmatic provisions, is, however, not legally binding.

TEXTBOX 136

9.3.3. ASYLUM AND MIGRATION POLICY

- Schengen Agreement 1985/Schengen Implementation Agreement 1990 for more freedom of movement among the Schengen states (all 15 EU member states with the exception of the United Kingdom and Ireland), but more security along the EU's external borders ('fortress Europe')

- Dublin Convention 1990 (basis for a common European asylum policy)

- Maastricht Treaty 1992: immigration and asylum under the third pillar of the EU (Justice and Home Affairs)

- Amsterdam Treaty 1997: asylum and migration moved from third to first pillar (Title IV TEC - 'Towards an Area of Freedom, Security and Justice'); five year transitional period followed by decisions with a qualified majority; limited competence of the ECJ

- European Council in Tampere 1999: steps towards a common asylum and migration policy

- Topics of current discussion and harmonization through Regulations and Directives:

- Controlling migration
- Developing a common European asylum law
- Treating citizens from third countries
- Temporary protection of refugees
- Burden sharing
- Combating trafficking in human beings

A second high level 'European Convention', convened by the Laeken European Council in December 2001, was called to deal with the future EU constitution, but also to discuss ways of strengthening the legal status of the EU Charter of Fundamental Rights and incorporating it into primary EC law.

So far, no agreement has been found to establish a permanent institution for monitoring the human rights situation in member states, notwithstanding the

9.3. HUMAN RIGHTS WITHIN THE EU

recommendation of the *Comité des Sages* in 1998 to establish an EU Human Rights Monitoring Agency (9.5.1.). But the European Parliament is publishing its reports on the situation as regards fundamental rights in the EU, and in 2002 the Parliament initiated the creation of an **EU network of independent experts on fundamental rights** to assist it in this monitoring task. In May 2003, the first report of this network on the situation of fundamental rights in the EU and its member states in 2002 has been published. Already in 1997, an independent **European Monitoring Centre on Racism and Xenophobia** was created, with headquarters in Vienna, to deal with one of the most serious and widespread human rights issues in Europe (9.3.5.).

Furthermore, **article 13** was inserted in the **EC Treaty in 1997** as a major provision for the first pillar, and in 2000, was implemented by two directives obligating member states to take suitable measures against **racial discrimination** in all areas (e.g. the labour and housing market), as well as for **equal treatment** in employment and occupation of groups hitherto discriminated against (e.g., persons with disabilities and homosexuals) (9.3.4.).

TEXTBOX 137

9.3.4. PROTECTION AGAINST DISCRIMINATION IN THE EUROPEAN UNION

Article 13 EC Treaty:
'Without prejudice to the other provisions of this Treaty and within the limits of the power conferred by it upon the Community, the Council, acting unanimously on a proposal from the Commission and after consulting the European Parliament, may take appropriate action to combat discrimination based on sex, racial or ethnic origin, religion or belief, disability, age or sexual orientation.'

Two Council Directives for article 13 EC Treaty:

- COD 2000/43 of 29 June 2000
Implementing the principle of equal treatment between persons irrespective of racial and ethnic origin
- COD 2000/78 of 27 November 2000
Establishing a general framework for equal treatment in employment and occupation

In both cases: burden of proof will be shifted to the person who has been accused of discrimination, provided the alleged victim can establish a *prima facie* case of discrimination

Community Action Programme to Combat Discrimination (2001 to 2006)

Asylum and migration law is another highly sensitive area of human rights. Current efforts in this context are aimed at harmonization existing national standards to create a common **European asylum and migration policy**. The EU Annual Report on Human Rights has been instrumental in making EU human rights policies and measures within the EU more transparent. Despite this progress, it is too early to

9. EUROPEAN UNION (EU)

say whether the EU is capable of protecting human rights against violations committed by member states in any way comparable to other international organizations such as the Council of Europe.

TEXTBOX 138

9.3.5. EUROPEAN MONITORING CENTRE ON RACISM AND XENOPHOBIA (EUMC)

Established in 1997 as an independent body (Council Regulation 1035/97)
Office in Vienna
Tasks:
- Reviewing the extent and development of racism and xenophobia in the European Union
- Collecting objective, reliable and comparable information
- Analyzing reasons
- Establishing best practices
- Proposing measures
- Drafting annual reports
- Cooperating with the Council of Europe (ECRI), the UN and other international organizations
- Setting up RAXEN (European Racism and Xenophobia Information Network): 15 national focal points
- Organizing round table discussions

To begin with it would have to incorporate the Charter of Fundamental Rights into the Treaties of the EU and establish a judicial or quasi-judicial instance to monitor member states' actual observance of the rights laid down in the Charter. In the event of a violation, this **monitoring body** should have the power to order the necessary measures to be taken by member states or at least make the necessary recommendations to the political bodies of the EU.

TEXTBOX 139

9.4. HUMAN RIGHTS AND EU EXTERNAL RELATIONS

- Common Foreign and Security Policy (CFSP)
- Human rights and development cooperation
- Lomé Conventions and Cotonou Agreement
- Human rights clauses in bilateral EU treaties

Given the supranational character of the European Union, an independent authority within the EU (such as the European Court of Justice or a separate human rights monitoring agency) or outside the EU (e.g. the European Court of Human Rights) would also have to be entrusted to monitor the compliance of measures taken by EU bodies (Council, Commission, Parliament) with European human rights standards.

The EU has been actively pursuing **human rights policies** in its **external relations** for many years. The Lomé Conventions were agreed upon back in the

9.4. HUMAN RIGHTS AND EU EXTERNAL RELATIONS

1980s to regulate **development cooperation** with those African, Caribbean and Pacific (ACP) states that the EU, because of the global distribution of influence (the United States in Latin America, Japan in Asia), felt primarily responsible for. In these multilateral treaties, the EU gradually introduced provisions establishing a policy of human rights conditionality.

As of 1995, all bilateral trade agreements and other treaties between the EU and third countries are required to include separate **human rights clauses**. Such clauses are, in fact, an essential element of these treaties and may cause their unilateral dissolution or suspension on the part of the EU in the event of systematic human rights violations (9.4.4.). For that very reason, Australia refused to sign a respective bilateral agreement with the EU. However, most transition and developing countries are economically dependent on cooperation with the EU and are, therefore, prepared to accept human rights clauses, albeit reluctantly.

TEXTBOX 140

9.4.1. COMMON FOREIGN AND SECURITY POLICY (CFSP)

Objectives (article 11 EU Treaty)

- To preserve peace and strengthen international security, in accordance with the principles of the UN Charter as well as the principles of the Helsinki Final Act and the objectives of the Paris Charter.
- To develop and consolidate democracy and the rule of law, and respect for human rights and fundamental freedoms

Organs

- Council
- Secretary General of the Council as High Representative for the CFSP (1999 – 2004: *Javier Solana Madariaga*, Spain)
- Commission
- European Parliament

Instruments and initiatives

- Common strategies (e.g. on Russia/Chechnya, Ukraine, the Mediterranean region)
- Common positions on various states (especially in Africa and Asia) and topics (ICC)
- Joint actions (e.g. the EU Police Mission in Bosnia and Herzegovina)
- Demarches/declarations
- Political dialogue (e.g. with China, Iran and the USA)
- Election observation and assistance
- Human rights monitoring in the field
- Coordinated EU action in multilateral fora, e.g. UN, OSCE, Council of Europe

---

A typical example in this context is article 9(2) of the **Cotonou Agreement** signed by 77 ACP states, the EC and its fifteen member states in June 2000 (9.4.3.).

9. European Union (EU)

While article 96, in the event of a serious human rights violation, provides for a consultation procedure with the member state concerned, the EU may, upon the failure of such negotiations, initiate unilateral measures, and in the worst case even suspend development cooperation. **Conditionality of human rights,** as applied to human rights clauses amongst others, may in some cases lend itself very effectively to the implementation of human rights, yet because of the actual inequality of contracting partners is still highly controversial (3.1.6.).

TEXTBOX 141

9.4.2. Human Rights and Development Cooperation

Article 177 EC Treaty:

1. Community policy in the sphere of development cooperation, which shall be complementary to the policies pursued by the member states, shall foster:

   - The sustainable economic and social development of the developing countries, and more particularly the most disadvantaged among them;
   - The smooth and gradual integration of the developing countries into the world economy;
   - The campaign against poverty in the developing countries.

2. Community policy in this area shall contribute to the general objective of developing and consolidating democracy and the rule of law, and to that of respecting human rights and fundamental freedoms.

3. The Community and the member states shall comply with the commitments and take account of the objectives they have approved in the context of the United Nations and other competent international organizations.

Council Regulations of 29 April 1999 constitute legal basis for a wide range of projects in the field of human rights and democratization:
- EC 975/99
- EC 976/99

European Initiative for Democracy and Human Rights (EIDHR), Chapter B 7-70 of the EU budget

---

More important than human rights conditionality is, therefore, the active policy of implementing human rights in the framework of specific **development cooperation projects.** In the framework of bilateral and multilateral treaties, such as the Lomé Conventions and Cotonou Agreement, the EU has pursued various human rights goals, such as the strengthening of constitutional, democratic and human rights structures, implementation of political rights and freedoms (right to vote, freedom of media, the right to establish and join a political party, freedom of association and assembly), promotion of an independent judiciary, efficient police and prison administration, and of basic services in the fields of health and education.

In its first pillar (article 177 EC Treaty) the EU has also pledged itself to fighting poverty, consolidating democracy and the rule of law, and pursuing

9.4. HUMAN RIGHTS AND EU EXTERNAL RELATIONS

development cooperation under the banner of human rights (9.4.2.). To provide a legal basis for all measures under Chapter B7-70 of the EU budget concerning human rights and democratization (**European Initiative for Democracy and Human Rights**) the Council adopted two regulations in 1999 (on the general objective of developing and consolidating democracy, rule of law, and respecting human rights and fundamental freedoms through implementation of development cooperation and Community operations).

TEXTBOX 142

9.4.3. LOMÉ CONVENTIONS AND COTONOU AGREEMENT

Origins of development cooperation in 1958
Relevance of human rights for development cooperation first recognized in the 1980s
Today the EU and its members account for more than 50 per cent of all offical development aid (USA: 20 per cent, Japan: 18 per cent)

- Lomé Conventions III, IV, IV/2 (articles 5 and 366a of Lomé IV, 1989)
- Cotonou Agreement, signed on 23 June 2000
  States parties: 77 ACP states, the EC and all 15 EU member states

Contents of the Cotonou Agreement

Article 9(2): 'The Parties refer to their international obligations and commitments concerning respect for human rights. They reiterate their deep attachment to human dignity and human rights, which are legitimate aspirations of individuals and peoples. Human rights are universal, indivisible and inter-related. The Parties undertake to promote and protect all fundamental freedoms and human rights, be they civil and political, or economic, social and cultural. In this context, the Parties reaffirm the equality of men and women.'

Article 96 sets out a new consultation procedure for the event of a violation of one of the convention's essential characteristics; the Cotonou Agreement places greater emphasis on individual states' responsibility than the Lomé Conventions; in cases of 'special urgency' (i.e. a particularly serious and flagrant violation of one of the essential elements referred to in article 9(2)), appropriate measures shall be taken without delay.

Every year more than EUR 100 million are made available for human rights projects under this initiative, which aim to counter racism and xenophobia, protect the rights of children, minorities and indigenous peoples, abolish the death penalty, strengthen political rights, monitor elections, spread human rights education, and to support the International Criminal Court, among others.

Development and consolidation of democracy, the rule of law and human rights is also one of the main objectives of the **Common Foreign and Security Policy (CFSP)**, which represents the second pillar of the EU (article 11, EU Treaty, 9.4.1.).

Common strategies, positions and joint actions are its main legal instruments. **Common strategies** are defined at the level of the European Council (of heads of

9. EUROPEAN UNION (EU)

state or government) with the aim to improve overall coherence of the EU's international activities.

> **TEXTBOX 143**
>
> **9.4.4. HUMAN RIGHTS CLAUSES IN BILATERAL TREATIES OF THE EU**
>
> - A growing trend of including human rights clauses in EU's external trade and cooperation relations, ranging from simple bilateral trade agreements to elaborate association agreements
> - Council decision of May 1995 on basic modalities of the human rights clause in agreements with third countries
> - Respect for human rights as 'essential element' of the agreement
> - Rights of the Community to suspend or terminate an agreement because of systematic human rights violations

In 1999, one such common strategy was developed to provide Russia with a new framework for political and security-policy dialogue, which also covered the Chechnya conflict. **Joint actions** as defined for the Western Balkans or Palestine, generally refer to concrete measures with financial repercussions, such as appointments of EU monitoring missions or the establishment of the first EU police mission in Bosnia and Herzegovina as of January 2003.

> **TEXTBOX 144**
>
> **9.5. RECENT DEVELOPMENTS**
>
> - A 'Human Rights Agenda' for the Year 2000
> - EU Vienna Declaration of 10 December 1998
> - EU Annual Report on Human Rights
> - EU Charter of Fundamental Rights

The **common positions** define the approach of the EU to specific human rights issues, which must be implemented by concrete measures of individual member states. The majority of common positions were established in relation to specific regions or states in Africa (Angola, the Democratic Republic of Congo, Liberia, Nigeria, Rwanda, Sierra Leone or Zimbabwe) or Asia (e.g. Afghanistan or Myanmar). In June 2001, the EU decided in a common thematic position to support the International Criminal Court (15.6.).

Apart from the above instruments, the CFSP has developed several other ways to achieve its objectives. These include mechanisms for **political dialogue** (e.g. the EU human rights dialogue with China established in 1997, the recently established dialogue with Iran or the dialogue with the United States on disputed issues, such as the ICC and the abolition of the death penalty), demarches, or concerted action at the level of international bodies such as the UN Human Rights Commission and General Assembly (4.4.1., 4.4.6.), the Council of Ministers of the Council of Europe or the OSCE's human dimension (8.3., 8.4.). In 1999, the former Secretary General of

9.5. Recent Developments

NATO, *Javier Solana Madariaga* (Spain), was appointed High Representative of the European Union's Common Foreign and Security Policy ('Monsieur PESC').

TEXTBOX 145

9.5.1. 'Leading by Example':
A 'Human Rights Agenda' for the European Union for the Year 2000

- Agenda and Final Report of a research project by the European University Institute in Florence presented in Vienna in October 1998
- *Comité des Sages* consisting of *Antonio Cassese, Catherine Lalumière, Peter Leuprecht* and *Mary Robinson*

Main recommendations:

- To appoint an EU Commissioner for Human Rights
- To establish a Human Rights Office of the Council related to the High Representative for the CFSP
- To establish an EU Human Rights Monitoring Agency
- To develop global human rights reports
- To accede to the ECHR and the ESC
- To prepare an EU Code of Conduct for Businesses
- To develop procedures for the suspension of external agreements and EU membership in case of serious human rights violations
- To give priority to human rights education

The **EU Annual Report on Human Rights**, which has been published by the Council since 1999, provides a solid overview of the Union's foreign policy and the broad range of actions taken in the field of human rights (9.5.3.). It does, however, not assess the factual human rights situation in other countries, as e.g. the annual human rights reports of the United States Department of State.

There is no question that the EU is now well established as a **'global payer'** as far as human rights are concerned. Average expenses on the part of the EU and its 15 member states for specific projects and measures of human rights protection are more than double that of the United States. Yet it remains to be seen whether that has also made it a **'global player'** in this scenario. Looking at today's major human rights issues and challenges, such as the Balkans, the Middle East, Iraq or Afghanistan, it becomes clear that the United States is increasingly taking major decisions on its own, including those on humanitarian interventions, while the EU is primarily concerned with financing economic and political reconstruction. By the same token, there are significant differences in the way Europe and the United States deal with fundamental human rights issues, concerning the death penalty or the International Criminal Court, for example. It is to be hoped that the EU will develop its own profile with regard to these issues and make it a prominent and convincing part of its external relations.

9. EUROPEAN UNION (EU)

TEXTBOX 146

9.5.2. VIENNA DECLARATION OF 10 DECEMBER 1998

Adopted by the European Council on the occasion of the 50th anniversary of the Universal Declaration of Human Rights

Measures envisaged:

- To publish an annual EU human rights report
- To develop human rights education, in particular through the continuation of the European Master's Degree in Human Rights and Democratization (EMA) in Venice
- To convene a periodic human rights discussion forum with the participation of EU institutions, academic institutions and NGOs
- To establish a common roster of European human rights and democracy experts
- To foster democracy, rule of law and human rights in third countries by means of Council Regulations
- To strengthen relevant EU structures

In 1998 – the Human Rights Year – a *comité des sages* comprising well-known European personalities presented a '**Human Rights Agenda for the European Union for the Year 2000**' that included far-reaching recommendations on how to improve human rights protection in the EU, e.g. by appointing a separate EU Commissioner for Human Rights and establishing an EU Human Rights Monitoring Agency on the model of the European Monitoring Centre on Racism and Xenophobia (9.5.1.). Of these recommendations, however, only a few were integrated into the **Vienna Declaration** endorsed by the European Council on 12 December 1998 (9.5.2.).

TEXTBOX 147

9.5.3. EU ANNUAL REPORT ON HUMAN RIGHTS

Four annual reports to date (1998/99, 1999/2000, 2000/2001, 2001/2002) adopted by the Council (with the consent of all 15 member states)

Annual survey of EU activities related to human rights, both within the EU and in its international affairs

The Annual Report of the Council is not a global survey of the human rights situation in the world, as, e.g., the annual human rights reports of the United States Department of State or Amnesty International

---

Development of human rights in the European Union took a far more promising turn with the German presidency's initiative in 1999 to organize a 'Convention' to draft the **EU Charter of Fundamental Rights**. Within less than a year, the Convention comprised of representatives of governments, the Commission, Parliament and national parliaments, was able to draw up a bill of rights for the

9.5. RECENT DEVELOPMENTS

Union, which though not legally binding, was highly innovative in substance and far more comprehensive than the catalogue of civil and political rights contained the ECHR. If the current 'European Convention' succeeds in entrenching the Charter of Fundamental Rights in primary law, it will have accomplished a major step towards a common European constitution.

TEXTBOX 148

9.5.4. EU CHARTER OF FUNDAMENTAL RIGHTS OF 7 DECEMBER 2000

Development

- European Council of Cologne June 1999: Decided that the 'fundamental rights applicable at the Union level should be consolidated in a Charter and thereby made more evident'
- European Council of Tampere October 1999: Composition of the 'body to elaborate a draft EU Charter of Fundamental Rights' ('Convention')
- Adoption and Proclamation of the Charter as a non-binding declaration in Nice on 7 December 2000

Contents

- Seven chapters: dignity, freedoms, equality, solidarity, citizens' rights, justice and general provisions (e.g. with regard to the scope of guaranteed rights)
- Contains 'civil and political rights' as well as 'economic, social and cultural rights', yet no longer divides the two categories as with the generations model (2.6.)
- The 'Convention' did not incorporate the rights as set out in the ECHR and the ESC in the new Charter, but defined its own bill of rights – leads to different European standards and problems of interpretation, especially as rights are formulated in a less detailed way than in the ECHR or the ESC, contains some new elements, such as environmental protection in article 37 and the right to good administration in article 41
- Article 52(1): general limitation clause for all rights and freedoms of the Charter
- Article 52(3): unclear relationship between the EU Charter and the ECHR
- Non-binding instrument – the 'European Convention', which is currently preparing a constitution for the EU, has been asked to consider the various modalities for and consequences of incorporating the Charter into the Treaties of the EC/EU.

9. European Union (EU)

LITBOX 9

Literature

Alston, Philip (Ed.) 1999, The EU and Human Rights

Aschenbrenner, Jo Beatrix 2000, Menschenrechte in den Außenbeziehungen der Europäischen Union - Gemeinschaftspolitik versus GASP, Frankfurt/Main, Berlin, Wien

Bell, Mark 2002, Anti-Discrimination Law and the European Union, Oxford

Betten, Lammy and *Grief,* Nicholas 1998, EU Law and Human Rights, London

Comité des Sages 1998, Leading by Example: A Human Rights Agenda for the European Union for the Year 2000, Florence

Council of the European Union, 2000-2003 Annual Reports on Human Rights, Brussels

Council of the European Union 2001, Charter of Fundamental Rights of the European Union: Explanations Relating to the Complete Text of the Charter, Brussels

Eriksen, Erik Oddvar, *Fossum* John Erik and *Menéndez,* Agustín José (Eds.) 2003, The Chartering of Europe. The European Charter of Fundamental Rights and its Constitutional Implications, Baden-Baden

Feus, Kim (Ed.) 2000, The EU Charter of Fundamental Rights – Text and Commentaries, London

Fierro, Elena 2003, The EU's Approach to Human Rights Conditionality in Practice, New York

Hoffmeister, Frank 1998, Menschenrechts- und Demokratieklauseln in den vertraglichen Außenbeziehungen der Europäischen Gemeinschaft, Berlin/Heidelberg

Meyer, Jürgen (Ed.) 2003, Kommentar zur Charta der Grundrechte der Europäischen Union, Baden-Baden

Neuwahl, Nanette A. and *Rosas,* Allan (Eds.) 1995, The European Union and Human Rights, The Hague

Nowak, Manfred and *Chunying,* Xin 2000, EU - China Human Rights Dialogue, Study Series of the Ludwig Boltzmann Institute of Human Rights, Vol. 4, Vienna

Internet

www.europa.eu.int - European Union

ue.eu.int/df/default.asp?lang=en - Charter of Fundamental Rights of the European Union

www.ue.eu.int/pesc/human_rights/hr.asp?lang=en - EU Annual Reports on Human Rights

9.5. RECENT DEVELOPMENTS

www.europa.eu.int/comm/external_relations/human_rights/intro - The EU Human Rights and Democratization Policy

www.europa.eu.int/eur-lex/de/index.html - EUR-Lex

10. EFFORTS OF OTHER REGIONAL ORGANIZATIONS TO PROTECT HUMAN RIGHTS

Thus far, regional human rights protection only exists in Europe, America (including the Caribbean) and Africa, and in fact all of the states on these three continents, with the exception of Morocco, are subject to some of the relevant procedures and are monitored by them. In **Asia and the Pacific area**, on the other hand, there is no single regional organization, which might cover the entire continent, nor are there any mechanisms to monitor human rights. This has a great deal to do with the heterogeneity of Asia, which is far more pronounced than in other regions, including countries as diverse and powerful as India, China, Russia, Japan and Indonesia, and regions as diverse as the Middle East, the Central Asian Republics, South East Asia or the Pacific Area, which extends as far as Australia and New Zealand. By the same token, Asia is home to a significant number of states that have been committing gross and systematic human rights violations and continue to do so (including, amongst others, Afghanistan, Cambodia, China, Indonesia, Iran, Iraq, Myanmar, North Korea, Saudi Arabia, Syria, Vietnam or the Palestinian territories occupied by Israel). Furthermore, it is regions like this that are seriously questioning the universality of human rights (2.7.), and thus the legitimacy of international human rights protection by putting forward arguments such as '**Asian values**' or the priority of **Islamic law** (Sharia) over international law. Not by chance, ratification of the UN's human rights treaties in this region has been far less forthcoming than elsewhere. Despite a number of interesting initiatives by NGOs (preparation of an 'Asian Human Rights Charter' by more than 200 NGOs), at the sub-regional level (ASEAN – Association of Southeast Asian Nations, SAARC – South Asian Association for Regional Cooperation) and by creating a network of national human rights institutions (Asia-Pacific Forum of National Human Rights Institutions), the Asian region, nevertheless, represents the biggest challenge as far as efficient monitoring of human rights is concerned.

Meanwhile, however, European human rights protection has been extended to include large parts of Asia. The **Council of Europe** and the competences of the European Court of Human Rights includes the Asian part of Turkey and Cyprus, as well as more recently Russia and many other successor states to the Soviet Union, including the Caucasus region. Many human rights treaties established by the Council of Europe, such as the Conventions on minorities or biomedicine (5.5. to 5.7.) were deliberately conceived as open conventions, implying that they may also be ratified by states that are not members of the Council of Europe. Of course, Asian states may also avail themselves of this option. The **OSCE** and its human rights mechanisms also cover the Central Asian Republics. Given the serious minority conflicts in these states, the High Commissioner on National Minorities in particular has been displaying great activity in the region. The OSCE established a number of long-term missions and centres as well as a liaison office in Central Asia and seems to be willing to re-activate the Moscow mechanism of the human dimension for those Central Asian Republics with the most serious human rights problems (8.).

Finally, the **Commonwealth of Independent States** (CIS), which presently comprises twelve of the former Soviet republics, in 1995 adopted a Convention on Human Rights and Fundamental Freedoms based on the standards of the UN, the OSCE and the Council of Europe, and the ECHR in particular. The CIS even created in 1993 a Human Rights Commission in Minsk (Belarus) with the mandate of considering inter-state and individual communications. The present activities of the OSCE seem, however, more promising to develop a human rights culture in those successor states of the Soviet Union that are not subject to the monitoring procedures of the Council of Europe.

TEXTBOX 149

10.1. ORGANIZATION OF THE ISLAMIC CONFERENCE (OIC)

Established on 25 September 1969 in Rabat (Morocco)
56 member states

Objectives (as set out in the Charter of 1972)

- To promote Islamic solidarity among member states
- To consolidate cooperation among them
- To eliminate racial discrimination and colonialism
- To support international peace and security
- To safeguard the dignity of all Muslims, their independence and national rights
- To promote cooperation and understanding among member states and other countries

Islamic documents on human rights

- Universal Islamic Declaration of Human Rights, 19 September 1981: issued by the Islamic European Council (a private institution, seated in London)
- The Cairo Declaration on Human Rights in Islam, 5 August 1990: issued by the OIC

First attempts at sub-regional human rights protection have made themselves felt in the **Arab-Islamic area** and the documents to that effect may well be regarded as a contribution to the ongoing debate on universalism or rather a reaction to the claim of universality of human rights. Back in 1981, the Islamic European Council – a private institution seated in London – adopted a Universal Islamic Declaration of Human Rights, based on which the Organization of the Islamic Conference in 1990 passed the first intergovernmental, albeit non-binding **Declaration on Human Rights in Islam** in Cairo. It contains all of the civil, political, economic, social and cultural rights included in the Universal Declaration of Human Rights of 1948 and the relevant UN treaties. In addition, it includes several collective rights of peoples (the right to self-determination against colonial repression, the right to a clean environment), as well as principles of humanitarian law. All of the above rights and

10.2. LEAGUE OF ARAB STATES

freedoms, however, are subordinate to Islamic Sharia, which incidentally also serves as the only source of interpretation for these rights.

The same is true for the **Arab Charter on Human Rights** adopted by the Council of the **Arab League** in 1994. It was intended as a treaty under international law, but for lack of any ratifications it has yet to enter into force.

TEXTBOX 150

10.2. LEAGUE OF ARAB STATES

Established on 22 March 1945
22 member states

Aims (as set out in the 1945 Charter)

- Draw closer the relations between member states and coordinate their political activities with the aim of realizing a close collaboration between them
- Safeguard the independence and sovereignty of the member states
- Consider in a general way the affairs and interests of the Arab countries

The Arab League is the partner of the European Union within the Euro-Arab Dialogue

Organs

- Council of the Arab League
- Joint Arab Defence Council
- Arab Economic and Social Council
- Specialized Ministerial Councils (10)
- Permanent Committees (16)
- General Secretariat

Arab Charter on Human Rights

Adopted on 15 September 1994 by the Council of the League of Arab States (Resolution 5437), not ratified by any states, therefore not yet in force

Resembles very much the Universal Declaration of Human Rights and the two UN Covenants, contains various civil, political, economic, social and cultural rights as well as the rights to self determination and protection of minorities

Monitoring

Committee of Experts on Human Rights (7 members)
- State reporting procedure (article 41)

This explains why a regional monitoring mechanism – a committee of seven experts for the examination of inter-state reports – has thus far not been established. The wording of the Arab Charter is far less original than that of the African Charter of Human and Peoples' Rights (7.4.), except for its reference to Arab nationalism, which is a little surprising for a human rights document. Given the fact that the Arab Charter was adopted in close proximity to the Vienna World Conference on Human

10. EFFORTS OF OTHER REGIONAL ORGANIZATIONS TO PROTECT HUMAN RIGHTS

Rights (4.6.1.), and seeing the obvious lack of willingness of the 22 member states of the Arab League to subject themselves to an inter-Arab state reporting procedure, it is hard to imagine that it was intended as anything more than a political reaction to the universality of human rights set out in the Vienna Declaration. It was hardly a serious attempt at improving the human rights situation in the Arab world.

LITBOX 10

LITERATURE

Harvard Law School Human Rights Program / Center for the Study of Developing Countries at Cairo University 2000, International Aspects of the Arab Human Rights Movement - An Interdisciplinary Discussion Held in Cairo in March 1998, Cambridge

Amarsaikhan, Uyanga 2003, Human Rights Protection and Asian Values: Prospects for a Regional Human Rights Mechanism in Asia, Vienna

An-Naim, Abdallah 1990, Toward an Islamic Reformation: Civil Liberties, Human Rights, and International Law, Syracuse

An-Naim, Abdullah 1992, Human Rights in Cross-Cultural Perspectives, Philadelphia

Akasha Izeldien Khalil 1992, Human Rights in the Arab World, Budapest

Dalacoura, Katerina 2003, Islam, Liberalism and Human Rights: Implications for International Relations, 2nd ed., London

Mayer, Ann Elizabeth 1999, Islam and Human Rights: Tradition and Politics, 3rd ed., Boulder

Moussalli, Ahmad 2001, The Islamic Quest for Democracy, Pluralism, and Human Rights, Gainesville

Tibi Bassam 1999, Im Schatten Allahs - der Islam und die Menschenrechte, 2nd ed., München u.a.

INTERNET

www.arableagueonline.org/arableague/index.jsp - Arab League

www.oic-oci.org - Organization of the Islamic Conference

11. NON-GOVERNMENTAL ORGANIZATIONS (NGOS)

It is safe to say that non-governmental organizations have become the universal **conscience of human rights**. Thousands of local, national, regional and international human rights groups and organizations and millions of human rights defenders have formed a global network to scrutinize the human rights situation in all countries of the world, to conduct fact finding missions, react to human rights violations quickly and without bureaucracy, to publicly report on such violations, and to force governments to act thereupon ('mobilization of shame').

TEXTBOX 151

11.1. NGOs AS PART OF CIVIL SOCIETY

Common characteristics of NGOs:

- Non-profit-making
- Voluntary
- Independent, in particular from governments
- Non-self-serving in aims and related values

Variety of NGOs

- There is no clear borderline between human rights NGOs and NGOs working in related fields, such as humanitarian law, refugee policy, peace, development cooperation, environmental protection, etc.
- International, regional, national and local NGOs
- 1,529 NGOs were registered at the 1993 Vienna World Conference on Human Rights, more than 3,600 were registered at the World Summit for Children in May 2002

Interdependence of human rights and civil society:

- The promotion and protection of human rights is one of the aims and objectives of civil society (by means of NGOs)
- The protection of human rights (e.g. freedom of speech, assembly and association) is a precondition for the development of civil society

---

Intergovernmental human rights protection would be unthinkable today without NGOs, seeing as governments, despite their lip services to the contrary, are not genuinely interested in human rights violations committed in other countries. It is thanks to the moral and political pressure imposed by NGOs, the media and other key players in **global civil society** that governments are pressured to draft, sign and ratify international treaties of human rights protection, and voluntarily subject themselves to international human rights monitoring bodies and procedures.

However, few of these bodies are composed of truly independent experts, as in the case of human rights courts or quasi-judicial bodies of experts, who are interested in finding the truth and improving specific situations even without pressure from NGOs. Many human rights bodies (such as the UN Human Rights

Commission or the various OSCE bodies) are made up of state representatives and, unless they are motivated by mutual political interests, are only effective because NGOs take an active interest in them or conduct lobbying.

Most organizations, in order to become an active part in human rights bodies, need to be formally recognized, e.g. as having consultative status awarded by the Economic and Social Council of the United Nations or the Council of Europe's Committee of Ministers. NGOs that have **consultative status** are entitled to speak at the UN Human Rights Commission (4.4.1.) or other ECOSOC sub-organizations (4.4.4.) in almost the same way as state representatives, to publish written contributions as official UN documents, to publicly criticize governments for human rights violations, and to participate in drafting the Commission's resolutions. In the Council of Europe, NGOs with consultative status play a significant role in filing collective complaints to the European Social Committee (5.3.) or in contributing to the preparation of visits by the European Committee for the Prevention of Torture (5.4.). An extremely fruitful cooperation has been developed between NGOs and the African Commission on Human and Peoples' Rights, which has granted observed status to many international, regional and national NGOs (7.4.2.). They enjoy the right of active participation in many of the Commission's activities and also assist the Commission financially and by means of organizing seminars, training programs, human rights documentation and information work.

TEXTBOX 152

11.2. FACT FINDING AND 'MOBILIZATION OF SHAME'

Main functions of human rights NGOs

- Fact-finding: collection of information from all relevant sources, missions to countries on human rights fact-finding, election monitoring, trial monitoring, etc.
- Distribution of reliable information on human rights violations by all available means
- Lobbying with governments, IGOs, the media, etc.
- Promotion of human rights through human rights education, conferences, publications and other means of awareness raising
- Participation in the drafting of new international instruments
- Assistance to victims of human rights violations through legal representation, psychological, medical, financial and other means of support
- Active contribution to IGO human rights activities

A formal recognition of NGOs (consultative or observer status) is only in some cases (e.g. UN Human Rights Commission) a precondition for active participation. For most monitoring procedures, NGOs are welcome to contribute without any specific status: They can lodge individual complaints (*actio popularis* before the

11.3. CONTRIBUTION OF NGOs TO THE WORK OF IGOs

Inter-American and African Commission, legal representation of victims in all procedures), initiate inquiry procedures (CAT, CEDAW), submit information to state reporting procedures, etc.

Although there is no universally recognized **legal definition of NGOs**, a number of criteria are common to most human rights NGOs. They are private non-profit organizations (associations, foundations, etc.) with voluntary (i.e. non-compulsory) membership, work for the promotion and protection of human rights in a broad sense and enjoy a fairly high degree of independence from governments. Some NGOs act at a global level, others in certain regions, most NGOs only act at the national or sub-national level.

TEXTBOX 153

11.3. CONTRIBUTION OF NGOs TO THE WORK OF IGOs

- **United Nations:**
- Consultative status with ECOSOC: right to attend, speak and provide written information to the Commission on Human Rights, its Sub-Commission and other functional commissions of ECOSOC
- 1235 and 1503 procedures
- Treaty bodies: participation in the state reporting procedure (CESCR, CRC), initiation of inquiry procedure (CAT, CEDAW), collective complaints (CEDAW)
- ILO: tripartite structure

- **Council of Europe:**
- Consultative status
- ESC: collective complaints
- ECPT: NGOs essential for preparation of visits
- ECHR: support of NGOs when lodging individual complaints (e.g. against Turkey)

- **OSCE:**
- Human dimension implementation meetings
- High Commissioner on National Minorities

- **OAS:**
- Right to lodge petitions under article 44 ACHR
- Country reports of Inter-American Commission

- **OAU:**
- Observer status with the African Commission on Human and Peoples' Rights
- Right to submit communications under article 55, African Charter on Human and Peoples' Rights

---

Few NGOs deal with all human rights, as most of them are either concerned with **civil and political rights**, or with one human right in particular (e.g. SOS Torture, or Article 19 for freedom of expression). Some NGOs limit their focus to groups of persons, such as children, women, minorities or workers, or regions, e.g.

the International Helsinki Federation for Human Rights or the Asia Human Rights Commission.

TEXTBOX 154

11.4. UN DECLARATION ON HUMAN RIGHTS DEFENDERS

'Declaration on the right and responsibility of individuals, groups and organs of society to promote and protect universally recognized human rights and fundamental freedoms', GA Res. 53/144 of 9 December 1998

Commonly known as the UN Declaration on Human Rights Defenders

Tensions between governments and human rights NGOs exist in all countries

Contents

- Right to meet or assemble peacefully and to form associations (article 5)
- Right to seek, obtain, receive and hold, to impart or disseminate information on all human rights (article 6)
- Right to have effective access, on a non-discriminatory basis, to participation in the government and in the conduct of public affairs and the right to submit criticism and proposals for improving their functioning (article 8)
- In the exercise of human rights and fundamental freedoms, including the promotion and protection of human rights as referred to in the present Declaration, everyone has the right to benefit from an effective remedy and to be protected in the event of violation of those rights; to this end everyone whose rights are allegedly violated has the right to complain before an independent, impartial and competent judicial or other authority established by law (including the right to a public hearing, due redress and compensation and enforcement) (article 9)
- The state shall conduct a prompt and impartial investigation whenever there is reasonable ground to believe that a violation of human rights has occurred (article 9)
- The state shall protect everyone against violence, threats, or discrimination as a consequence of his or her legitimate exercise of the rights referred to in the present Declaration (article 12)
- The state has the responsibility to promote the understanding by all persons under its jurisdiction of their rights and to facilitate the teaching of human rights (articles 14 and 15)

More recently, NGOs also have been formed for the sole purpose of dealing with one or more **economic, social or cultural rights**, such as the right to food (FIAN), or housing (Centre on Housing Rights and Evictions). Given the overlapping interests of refugee, peace, environment and development movements, it is no longer possible to keep NGOs working in these fields distinct from those mentioned above. While some human rights NGOs, like humanitarian or development organizations, do carry out concrete projects in the field and offer assistance to victims of human rights violations (e.g. rehabilitation of torture victims), fact finding, monitoring, reporting and lobbying still remains the main focus for most human rights NGOs.

What makes NGOs distinct from governmental organizations is their **independence**. However, in practice this very characteristic takes on different shapes, which is largely to do with the different political systems prevailing. In the liberal democracies of the West it does not take much to steer clear of and take a critical stance towards governments and other power holders, such as political parties, religious communities or ethnic groups.

But even in the West, many NGOs are dependent, in one way or another, on public funding. Only a few NGOs with large memberships (such as Amnesty International) or based in countries with a long tradition of rich private donors and foundations (e.g. Switzerland or the United States) can afford to do without any public subsidies. In many countries of the South, with no liberal political structures nor numerous private foundations, it is much more difficult for NGOs to establish and finance efficient networks independent of their governments, and for NGOs to criticize these governments for gross and systematic human rights violations. Many human rights activists suffered torture, enforced disappearance and even lost their lives for their actions and their courage to stand up for other people's rights. Many of these NGOs can only work underground or in exile, and most are dependent on the financial support from the North, which is often linked to public development cooperation (e.g. from Sweden, Norway, Denmark, the Netherlands or Canada).

TEXTBOX 155

11.5. WELL-KNOWN INTERNATIONAL HUMAN RIGHTS NGOS

- African Center for Democracy and Human Rights Studies, Banjul
- Amnesty International, London
- Andean Commission of Justice, Lima
- Anti Slavery International, London
- Article 19, London
- Asia Human Rights Commission, Hong Kong
- Association for the Prevention of Torture, Geneva
- Care International, Atlanta
- Center on Housing Rights and Evictions, Utrecht
- Coalition for the International Criminal Court, New York
- Defence for Children International, Geneva
- *Fédération International des Ligues des Droits de l'Homme*, Paris
- Food First Informations & Aktions Netzwerk (FIAN), Heidelberg
- Human Rights Watch, New York
- International Commission of Jurists, Geneva
- International Helsinki Federation for Human Rights, Vienna
- International Planned Parenthood Federation, New York/London
- International Save the Children Alliance, London
- International Service for Human Rights, Geneva
- International Work Group for Indigenous Affairs, Copenhagen
- Minority Rights Group International, London
- Oxfam International, London

11. Non-governmental Organizations (NGOs)

To protect human rights NGOs and human rights activists from persecution by governments or other sources of power, the United Nations adopted a **Declaration on Human Rights Defenders** in 1998. It took the Human Rights Commission 13 years to draft this Declaration, with NGOs as the driving force behind it. Once again the length of the process shows how many governments still vehemently resisted the development of a global human rights oriented civil society. Endless compromises had to be made to find an agreement – some of them painful. Nevertheless, the Declaration contains a number of principles, which though not legally binding, help expand the range of activities of human rights NGOs and will improve protection of individual activists. In 2000, the UN Human Rights Commission appointed a thematic Special Rapporteur to monitor adherence to the Declaration (4.4.1.5.).

LITBOX 11

Literature

Badelt, Christoph 2002, Handbuch der Nonprofit Organisation - Strukturen und Management, 3rd ed., Stuttgart

Bennett, Jon 1995, Meeting Needs: NGO coordination in practice, London

Brett, Rachel 1995, The Role and Limits of Human Rights NGOs at the United Nations, Political Studies, volume 43

Korey, Williams 1998, NGOs and the Universal Declaration of Human Rights: A Curious Grapevine, New York

Lindblom, Anna-Karin 2001, The Legal Status of Non-governmental Organisations in International Law, Uppsala

Nowak, Manfred (Ed.) 1994, World Conference on Human Rights - The Contribution of NGOs, Reports and Documents, Vienna

Ölz, Martin 2002, Die NGOs im Recht des internationalen Menschenrechtsschutzes, Study Series of the Ludwig Boltzmann Institute of Human Rights, Vol. 5, Vienna

Steiner, Henry J. 1991: Non-Governmental Organizations in the Human Rights Movement, Cambridge

Welch, Claude E. 2001, NGOs and Human Rights - promise and performance, Philadelphia

Wiseberg, Laurie 1991, Protecting Human Rights Activities and NGOs: What More Can Be Done?, Human Rights Quarterly, volume 13

Internet

www.acdhrs.org - African Center for Democracy and Human Rights Studies

www.amnesty.org - Amnesty International

www.cajpe.org.pe - Andean Commission of Jurists

11.5. Well-Known International Human Rights NGOs

www.antislavery.org - Anti-Slavery International

www.article19.org - Article 19

www.ahrchk.net - Asia Human Rights Commission

www.apt.ch - Association for the Prevention of Torture

www.care.org - Care International

www.cohre.org - Center on Housing Rights and Evictions

www.defence-for-children.org - Defence for Children International

www.fidh.org - Fédération International des Ligues des Droits de l'Homme

www.fian.org - FoodFirst Informations- & Aktions-Netzwerk

www.hri.ca - Human Rights Internet

www.hrw.org - Human Rights Watch

www.icj.org - International Commission of Jurists

www.ihf-hr.org - International Helsinki Federation for Human Rights

www.plannedparenthood.org/global - International Planned Parenthood Federation

www.savethechildren.net - International Save the Children Alliance

www.ishr.ch - International Service for Human Rights

www.iwgia.org - International Work Group for Indigenous Affairs

www.minorityrights.org - Minority Rights Group International

www.oxfam.org.uk - Oxfam International

12. TRADITIONAL PROCEDURES AND MECHANISMS FOR THE INTERNATIONAL PROTECTION OF HUMAN RIGHTS

Looking at the different procedures and mechanisms of human rights protection described so far, one can easily see the wide range of options, some less effective than others, but also how they all complement and reinforce one another. To attempt a general assessment, however, one has to bear in mind that this system is not the result of a well-planned, coordinated and structured initiative, but rather that it grew haphazardly in reaction to concrete international or regional threats, problems and challenges of the past fifty years. Its measures and mechanisms were wrenched out during long-winded political negotiations in accordance with the political and historical conditions of the respective international and regional organizations. It is in fact surprising that so many international and regional human rights treaties have been finally adopted notwithstanding the dogma of state sovereignty and non-interference in national affairs and the sustained resistance from most governments.

TEXTBOX 156

12.1. STATE REPORTING PROCEDURE

Legal basis:

Provided for in the respective treaties
Mandatory
Types of reports: initial report, periodic/follow-up reports, emergency reports

- UN: provided for in all seven core UN human rights treaties
- ILO: direct reporting obligation derived from the ILO Charter (article 35)
- Council of Europe: European Social Charter, European Framework Convention on the Protection of National Minorities, European Charter for Regional and Minority Languages
- OAU/AU: African Charter on Human and Peoples' Rights (Banjul Charter)

Functions of reporting:

- Supervision of domestic implementation of international obligations at the national and international level
- Regular evaluation of law and practice at the domestic level
- Identification of problems
- Formulation of human rights policy
- Public scrutiny at the international level
- Exchange of information – ongoing dialogue

The **state reporting procedure** is the main treaty-monitoring tool for the United Nations, but is also employed by other organizations such as the ILO, the OAU and the Council of Europe. In principle, it is considered far less effective than the complaints or investigation procedures, which is why states frequently agree to use it as the lowest common denominator. Despite its limited capacity, the reporting procedure can easily contribute to improving the human rights situation in the member states concerned. To achieve this, governments have to be seriously interested in having adherence to their obligations under international law objectively evaluated and, furthermore, must be willing to engage in a constructive and critical dialogue with all the parties concerned. Such a dialogue has to begin not during the examination, but much earlier when the state report is being drafted. Relevant government and administrative bodies, as well as other domestic organs, such as courts, parliaments, ombuds institutions, national human rights commissions, etc., not to mention representatives of civil society, NGOs, academic experts and the media, should all be actively involved from the very beginning.

TEXTBOX 157

12.2. INTER-STATE COMPLAINTS PROCEDURE

Legal basis:

Council of Europe:	ECHR (mandatory)	few cases
OAS	ACHR (optional)	no cases
OAU/AU	African Charter (mandatory)	one case
OSCE	Human Dimension	few cases
ILO:	Article 26 ILO Charter (mandatory)	few cases
UN:	CERD (mandatory)	no cases
	CCPR (optional)	no cases
	CAT (optional)	no cases

Reasons for inefficiency:

Weak legal provisions (e.g. UN treaties)
Reluctance of states to criticize other states in formal proceedings without own interests

---

An open and transparent process like this could result in either a balanced and objective state report accepted by everyone concerned, or a government report that includes other opinions on controversial issues. For the procedure to be successful, it would also have to include an open and constructive dialogue with the treaty monitoring body concerned, showing governments' willingness to take its recommendations seriously. Finally, the bodies in charge of drafting the report and those responsible for examining it would have to be provided with the necessary staff and financial support, taking into account that follow-up may be required.

State reporting procedures were developed to give a comprehensive overview of contracting states' obligations under international law, including the way these are put into practice at the national level. Complaints and investigation procedures, on the other hand, were intended for **individual cases** and situations of alleged human rights violations.

We distinguish between **inter-state complaints**, which in accordance with traditional international law rely on other governments to initiate investigations on concrete issues, **individual complaints** designed for victims of specific human rights violations, **collective complaints** and *actio popularis*, which are essentially a tool for NGOs, as well as **inquiry procedures** and other **fact-finding mechanisms**. The latter were established to be initiated by the respective treaty monitoring bodies themselves or by certain political bodies, such as the UN Human Rights Commission, the UN Security Council, the OSCE Permanent Council or the Committee of Ministers with the Council of Europe.

TEXTBOX 158

12.3. INDIVIDUAL COMPLAINTS PROCEDURE

Legal basis:

Council of Europe:	ECHR (mandatory)
OAS	ACHR (mandatory before the Inter-American Commission)
OAU/AU	African Charter on Human and Peoples' Rights (mandatory)
UN	OP to CCPR and CEDAW
	CERD (optional)
	CAT (optional)
	1503 procedure (mandatory)

Functions:

- Relief to individual victims of human rights violations
- Interpretation of the normative content of human rights provisions through the development of case law
- Changes of national law and practice
- Preventive effect at the national level

Admissibility criteria:

- Exhaustion of domestic remedies
- Victim requirement
- Compatibility *ratione materiae, personae, temporis, loci*
- Minimum substantiation
- No anonymous application, abuse of right of application
- No submission to other international bodies

Legal effects:

Legally binding (ECHR, ACHR) – non legally binding (UN, OAU/AU)

Supervision of implementation/follow-up:

By political bodies (ECHR, ACHR) or treaty monitoring bodies (UN)

All these procedures aim at investigating a **concrete individual human rights violation** or a concrete **situation of gross and systematic human rights violations**. These investigations may result in a report of a Special Rapporteur or a commission of experts, a decision of a quasi-judicial treaty monitoring body, a resolution of a political body or a judgment of a human rights court.

12. TRADITIONAL PROCEDURES AND MECHANISMS FOR THE PROTECTION OF HUMAN RIGHTS

Frequently there will be mediations during these procedures between the investigation bodies and the governments concerned, which are aimed at arriving at a **friendly settlement**. Should the investigative bodies find that a human rights violation has been committed, this may have political consequences (e.g. a resolution from the UN Human Rights Commission or the General Assembly), or even consequences binding under international law, such as the obligation to restitution, compensation, rehabilitation or other forms of **reparation** (3.2.7.), provided the bodies have sufficient competencies (such as courts in particular). Generally, however, complaints and inquiry procedures do not necessarily achieve reparation for the victims. The actual significance of these procedures, therefore, is not so much that of being legal remedies to the victim, but, ironically, rather that of being fact-finding tools to expose human rights violations, to unmask those responsible and to prevent future human rights violations. The complaints procedure has also been instrumental in clarifying the normative contents of human rights provisions by means of interpretation and developing case law.

TEXTBOX 159

12.4. INQUIRY PROCEDURE

Legal basis:

UN	CAT (mandatory, opting out) 7 cases
	CEDAW (OP, mandatory, opting out) 1 case pending
OAS	Country reports of the Inter-American Human Rights Commission (mandatory, opting out) 83 on-site visits (1961-2003)

Functions:
Ex officio proceedings in case of well founded information of gross and systematic violations (not dependent on complaints)

Weaknesses:
Confidentiality
On-site visits dependent on state permission
Long and complicated proceedings

On a completely different level, there is the **system of preventive visits** developed on the experiences of the International Committee of the Red Cross (ICRC), and introduced for torture prevention as part of the European Convention for the Prevention of Torture in 1989. The United Nations actually discussed the same procedure for more than 20 years before the General Assembly finally adopted it as an Optional Protocol to the UN Convention against Torture in December 2002.

The procedure is not about investigating violations that have already happened, but about **preventing torture and ill-treatment** during detention. This is to be achieved by having independent expert bodies making preventive and unannounced visits to all places of detention on the territory of states parties. While an international system of visits like this cannot reach all corners, it does have a

12.5. OTHER FORMS OF FACT-FINDING, INVESTIGATION AND REPORTING

deterrent effect and the reports and recommendations of the CPT have in fact contributed substantially to improving prison conditions in Europe. Governments' resistance to this system is best explained by the fact that unannounced on-site visits by international expert bodies can take place without any further permission of the government concerned apart from the ratification of the treaty. Such a system, as laid down in the ECPT, in fact represents a fairly far-reaching interference with the traditional understanding of state sovereignty.

TEXTBOX 160

12.5. OTHER FORMS OF FACT-FINDING, INVESTIGATION AND REPORTING

UN:

ECOSOC Resolution 1235: Special Rapporteurs, Working Groups, etc.
SC: Commissions of Experts, Ad hoc Tribunals

OSCE:

Missions of Experts and Rapporteurs
High Commissioner on National Minorities
OSCE Representative on Freedom of the Media

Council of Europe:

Missions of Experts
Human Rights Commissioner
European Commission against Racism and Intolerance (ECRI)

European Union:

European Monitoring Centre on Racism and Xenophobia (EUMC)

NGO activities

Human rights field monitoring:

UN: peacekeeping and peace-building operations
UN High Commissioner for Human Rights: field offices
UN Civilian Police Missions
OSCE Missions of Long Duration
EU Monitoring and Police Missions
Complex Field Operations (e.g. Bosnia and Herzegovina, Kosovo) involving UN, OSCE, NATO, UNHCR, EU and other organizations

---

At the United Nations, governments finally agreed on the following compromise: After the entry into force of the OP to CAT, states parties will elect a Subcommittee (of the CAT Committee) on Prevention with the power to carry out on-site visits. Most visits, will, however be conducted by independent domestic visiting bodies (so-called national preventive mechanisms), which must be set up by states parties and which will be assisted (and to some extent coordinated) by the Subcommittee on Prevention.

12. Traditional Procedures and Mechanisms for the Protection of Human Rights

A similar division of labour between international and domestic visiting bodies has been frequently recommended by the CPT in order to allow for regular visits to all places of detention, even in states parties as huge as the Russian Federation.

TEXTBOX 161

12.6. System of Visits

System of preventive visits to places of detention for the prevention of gross human rights violations such as torture, enforced disappearance, etc.:

ECPT (regular visits and ad-hoc visits)

CAT (OP 2002)

ICRC: visits to prisoners of war as part of monitoring of humanitarian law

---

12.6. SYSTEM OF VISITS

> LITBOX 12
> ### LITERATURE
>
> *Alfredsson*, Gudmundur, *Grimheden*, Jonas, *Ramcharan*, Bertram G. and *de Zayas*, Alfred 2001, International Human Rights Monitoring Mechanisms - Essays in Honour of Jakob Th. Möller, The Hague
>
> *Alston*, Philip 1997, Effective Functioning of Bodies Established Pursuant to United Nations Human Rights Instruments – Final Report on Enhancing the Long-term Effectiveness of the United Nations Human Rights Treaty System, UN Doc.E/CN.4/1997/74
>
> *Alston*, Philip and *Crawford*, James (Eds.) 2000, The Future of UN Human Rights Treaty Monitoring, Cambridge
>
> *Baxi*, Upendra 2002, The Future of Human Rights, Delhi
>
> *Bayefsky*, Anne F. (Ed.) 2000, The UN Human Rights Treaty System in the 21st Century, The Hague
>
> *Bayefsky*, Anne F. (Ed.) 2001, The UN Human Rights Treaty System: Universality at the Crossroads, New York
>
> *Chandler*, David (Ed.) 2002, Rethinking Human Rights: Critical Approaches to International Politics, New York
>
> *Harris*, David J. and *Livingstone*, Stephen 1998, The Inter-American System of Human Rights, Oxford
>
> *Oberleitner*, Gerd 1998, Menschenrechtsschutz durch Staatenberichte, Frankfurt am Main/Wien
>
> *Weston*, Burns H. and *Marks*, Stephan 1999, The Future of International Human Rights, New York
>
> ### INTERNET
>
> www.echr.coe.int/Hudoc.htm - *case law* of the European Court of Human Rights
>
> www.cpt.coe.int/en/visits.htm - Visits by the European Committee for the Prevention of Torture
>
> www.corteidh.or.cr/seriecing/index.html - *case law* of the Inter-American Court of Human Rights
>
> www.unhchr.ch/html/menu2/convmech.htm - UN Treaty Monitoring Bodies
>
> www.ilo.org/public/english/standards/norm/enforced/index.htm - ILO-International Labour Standards

13. SHORTCOMINGS OF TRADITIONAL PROCEDURES AND NEW TRENDS IN THE INTERNATIONAL HUMAN RIGHTS REGIME

The procedures and mechanisms of international and regional human rights protection described in chapters 4 to 11, and analyzed in a comparative manner in chapter 12, gradually developed within the framework of intergovernmental organizations during the second half of the 20th century **in reaction to specific threats**. They do not represent a structured and harmonized system of international human rights protection. The urgent need for the protection of human rights became evident after the Nazi holocaust. This also explains why the first binding human rights treaty equipped with an efficient monitoring system (ECHR) was established in Europe. The apartheid policy of Southern Africa and *Pinochet's* coup in Chile in 1973 were largely responsible for changing the UN's 'no power to take action' doctrine. Massive international criticism of the 'national security' doctrines of the Chilean and other Latin American dictatorships contributed to strengthening the Inter-American human rights system and the role of the Inter-American Human Rights Commission in particular. At the same time, the African Charter on Human and Peoples' Rights was drafted in the light of the gross and systematic human rights violations committed in Uganda under *Idi Amin*. The CSCE and its human rights component (above all: Helsinki Committees), which was instrumental in bringing down the Communist regimes in Central and Eastern Europe, were also established in the 1970s to create détente between East and West. After the end of the Cold War, it was the genocide in Bosnia and Herzegovina that caused another leap in the development of international human rights protection. In its wake, the OSCE prepared its comprehensive security concept including the field missions of long duration. A new generation of peace-keeping and peace-building operations was established because of the apparent need to join together human rights and maintenance of peace. Last but not least, ad hoc international criminal tribunals were created by the UN Security Council for the former Yugoslavia and Rwanda, which provided the basis for the recent establishment of a permanent International Criminal Court.

This brief overview of some of the milestones of human rights development in the past 50 years not only shows the dynamics and the revolutionary power of the human rights idea, but also draws attention to the weaknesses of **reactive and event-driven human rights policies**. Most traditional mechanisms of international human rights protection were developed during the Cold War and today are considered as bowing too much to the doctrine of state sovereignty. Seeing as regional human rights courts in Europe, Latin America and in Africa (soon to be) are in a position to deliver final and binding judgments on **individual complaints**, it is difficult to understand the reluctance of states to establish a permanent International Court of Human Rights. While the European Court of Human Rights today hands down almost 1,000 judgments and many thousands of further decisions per year in relation to a total of 44 states parties to the ECHR, the three quasi-judicial expert committees of the United Nations in charge of individual 'communications' have together issued some 500 non-binding decisions ('views') in relation to more than 100 states parties in a quarter century! Since the number of individual complaints decided on by the Inter-American Court of Human Rights is marginal too (35 in more than 20 years), it is safe to say that in practice the individual complaints procedure is only effective in Europe, albeit with some weaknesses as well. Such weaknesses are, amongst others, the long duration of proceedings before the European Court of Human Rights, lack of competence on the part of the Court to award real reparation to victims instead of financial compensation only, and the flood of minor cases brought before the Court (e.g. the long duration of proceedings before Italian civil courts). At the same time, many of the big human rights issues in Europe, such as growing racism and xenophobia or treatment of migrants and refugees, are not playing a major role in the Court's jurisprudence.

The **inter-state complaints procedure** is generally considered outdated as most governments today have a host of other, quicker and less formalistic mechanisms at their disposal to vent their concern over gross and systematic human rights violations committed in other countries. The inter-state complaints procedure was developed on the basis of the traditional concept of international law, according to which only states (and not the actual victims of human rights violations) were entitled to file complaints against other states before an international court or a quasi-judicial authority. Today, the understanding of individual victims as subjects of international law is no longer questioned and the majority of states have accepted that their people are entitled to file individual complaints against their 'own' government. Whenever a government accuses another state of a human rights violation, it either does so as part of its bilateral relations with that state (e.g. in the context of development cooperation), or with the relevant intergovernmental political institutions, such as the OSCE's Permanent Council or the UN Human Rights Commission.

In theory, the **state reporting procedure** constitutes an important instrument to make governments sufficiently aware of their obligations under international law, of problems and shortcomings at the level of domestic implementation and the need for improvement. The truth, however, is that the vast number of state reporting obligations and procedures in the past (within the ILO, the UN, the Council of Europe or the OAU) has made this mechanism practically ineffective. Most governments complain about the number of reports they are obligated to draft periodically, and which they often do with much delay if at all, while the relevant expert bodies complain about the lack of discipline among governments and the limited time they are given to examine the numerous reports. Furthermore, evaluation studies conducted by the United Nations have shown that even in theory, and given the current resources available, the system is doomed to fail. Hypothetically, if all governments were to present their outstanding reports by 'tomorrow', the treaty monitoring bodies would take approximately ten years to examine them, by which time thousands of new reports would have become due.

Thus, for this system to be effective at least within the United Nations, it would have to be fundamentally **reformed**, as repeatedly pointed out by experts. Rather

13. Shortcomings of Traditional Procedures and New Trends

than drafting many different, yet frequently overlapping, state reports and appointing examination bodies, states ought to be obligated to preparing one **comprehensive report** (every five years) concerning the implementation of all human rights obligations resulting from the UN human rights treaties they have ratified, as well as potential problems and difficulties they might encounter during the implementation. These reports should then be discussed by a **single permanent examination body** composed of a sufficient number of full-time experts. The body should be authorized to call for and examine emergency reports, as the case may require. Parallel to this, a permanent **international court of human rights,** composed of full-time judges, ought to be established on the model of the European Court of Human Rights in Strasbourg to deal with current and future complaints and inquiry procedures. With both institutions in place, the seven treaty monitoring bodies conceived during the Cold War could be dissolved in the long run. Sadly though, all initiatives to introduce such a **structural reform,** which would make monitoring of human rights treaties more efficient without an undue rise in costs, have so far had little political support.

This structural reform and others like it could markedly improve the efficiency of existing procedures and mechanisms of international and regional human rights protection, provided governments show the political will to support it. Furthermore, the developments in the 1990s and the new problems and challenges for human rights that have become apparent with the **disintegration of the bipolar world order** and **globalization** now call for answers, ideas and concepts well beyond those of traditional human rights protection as conceived in reaction to the Nazi holocaust. By and large, these **new problems** could be summarized as follows:

- Growing gap between normative framework and reality of human rights
- New causes for systematic human rights violations, such as the rise in racism, religious intolerance, minority problems, organized crime, terrorism and internal armed conflicts;
- Collapse of state structures ('failed states');
- Diminishing role of the state caused by privatization, deregulation and other aspects of neo-liberalism;
- Increasing human rights violations committed by non-state actors (e.g. transnational corporations, organized crime, terrorism, paramilitary organizations) who are globally networked and avail themselves of global structures, e.g. the Internet; and
- Increasing human rights violations committed by intergovernmental organizations (international financial institutions, UN transition administrations, peace-keeping, peace-building and peace-making operations, etc.).

13. Shortcomings of Traditional Procedures and New Trends

While no clear answers have been found to these new problems and challenges as yet there is some indication as to how the international community is reacting to them. It has recognized:

- The need to move from protection to prevention of human rights violations, taking into account that traditional procedures of human rights protection are essentially reactive, in other words they are applied in reaction to human rights violations already committed;
- The need to fight human rights violations not on the surface but at their root causes (poverty, ethnic and religious conflicts, globalization driven by neo-liberalism, etc.);
- The need not only to hold states accountable for human rights violations, but also non-state actors and intergovernmental organizations (both as organizations and individually);
- The need to combat impunity by further developing international criminal law (ICC, universal jurisdiction);
- The need for effective measures of conflict prevention, conflict resolution, mediation, reparation and reconciliation (e.g. Truth and Reconciliation Commissions);
- The need to understand human rights as an essential element of securing peace and sustainable development (elimination of poverty); and
- The need to impose measures of constraint of a political, economic and military nature as a means of protection and prevention of human rights violations.

Chapters 14 to 16 will look at some of these new trends in international human rights protection, presenting selected case studies in support.

14. MECHANISMS FOR THE PREVENTION OF HUMAN RIGHTS VIOLATIONS

Mary Robinson, the second UN High Commissioner for Human Rights, referred to the 21st century as the century of prevention. As the human rights system was developed after the Second World War, **promotion** of human rights was its main priority. To that end, a number of universal and regional standards were drawn up in the form of declarations, conventions and implementation mechanisms (2.8.). Intergovernmental organizations were equipped with a wide range of monitoring bodies, procedures and mechanisms based on these standards. Their task was to provide international **protection** to victims against concrete human rights violations committed by governments (12.). To ensure that this kind of protection is really effective, the decisions taken by the relevant international organs must be enforced through appropriate measures in the states concerned. The lack of effective implementation and enforcement of the decisions taken by international human rights bodies is one of the biggest shortcomings of the current human rights system, and the uncanny difference between high normative standards on the one hand, and the sad state of human rights in most countries on the other, is threatening to undermine the authority and legitimacy of the system. One of the greatest challenges for the 21st century must surely be to achieve better implementation, either by making individual perpetrators responsible under criminal law (15.) or by setting measures of constraint at the political, the economic or the military level, including humanitarian interventions (16.). Yet more important even than the political will for effective implementation is the **prevention** of human rights violations, and any mechanisms developed to that end must set in at the root causes of such violations.

'An ounce of prevention is worth a pound of cure' is an old truism, which, needless to say, applies to the prevention of human rights violations as well. What is better and cheaper by far than having to call the fire brigade to fight a fire is to prevent it in the first place. Similarly, **early warning systems** and action plans designed to fight and remove the causes of human rights violations (e.g. nationalism and intolerance, which are the cause of ethnic and religious tensions) are better and cheaper than having to end gross and systematic human rights violations already committed (from 'ethnic cleansing' to genocide), and then having to embark on the long and thorny road towards reconciliation, peace, reconstruction, justice and reparation for the victims. As the examples of National Socialism, Cambodia, Rwanda or Bosnia and Herzegovina clearly illustrate, even the best reactive protection systems cannot 'repair' any of the gross and systematic human rights violations committed, such as genocide, torture, rape, enforced disappearances, or arbitrary executions.

Once artificially cultivated hate between peoples or religious groups has reached the level of 'ethnic cleansing' or even genocide, the international community, in its reactive role of fire brigade can do little more than attempt to stem and quench the wildfire. It then has to set off on long-term peacekeeping and peace-building operations to help rebuild from scratch the economy, rule of law, democracy and human rights in the countries concerned and support the people on their way towards reconciliation and peace.

14. Mechanisms for the Prevention of Human Rights Violations

CASEBOX 3

14.1. UN Preventive Deployment Force in Macedonia (UNPREDEP)

First UN peacekeeping mission with preventive mandate
Composition (February 1999): 1049 troops, 35 military observers, 26 civilian police, 203 international and local civilian staff

Context and history

- Armed conflict in Croatia and Bosnia and Herzegovina destabilizes the region and threatens to provoke conflict in Macedonia
- UNPROFOR's Macedonia Command (UN Protection Force in Former Yugoslavia, originally in Croatia only) established in February 1992 (SC Res. 795 (1992), following request by President *Gligorov* of Macedonia
- March 1995: UNPREDEP established (UN Preventive Deployment Force in Macedonia) by SC Res. 983 (1995)
- UNPREDEP terminated in February 1999, after extension of the mandate vetoed by China in the SC

Mandate and activities

- To monitor and report any developments in the border area (with Albania and the Federal Republic of Yugoslavia) which could undermine confidence and stability in Macedonia and threaten its territory
- To monitor the flow of illicit arms following SC Res. 1160 (1998)
- To facilitate dialogue among political parties
- To liase with armed forces in Macedonia and neighbouring countries
- To patrol operations and observation posts on the border, community patrols and civilian police monitors
- To monitor human rights and inter-ethnic relations
- To mediate in border encounters
- To participate in projects for development and the strengthening of civil society
- To assist in coordination of international agencies, e.g. OSCE 'spill-over' mission in Skopje

Comments

- UNPREDEP was highly successful in preventing the spill over of external conflicts to Macedonia – yet lost support from Macedonian government once it turned its attention to internal sources of instability
- The situation became increasingly unstable after the termination of the UNPREDEP mission – an internal conflict evolved between the Macedonian government and the Albanian rebels during the year of 2001, which was only settled through NATO mediation.

14.1 UN PREVENTIVE DEPLOYMENT FORCE IN MACEDONIA (UNPREDEP)

As convincing as the advantages of and the need for measures of preventive human rights protection may seem in theory, it is still extremely difficult to put them into practice. Admittedly, it was impossible to predict the actual scale of the **genocide committed in Rwanda or Bosnia and Herzegovina**, however by the same token, nobody can claim that there were no early warnings. The UN Special Rapporteur on Arbitrary Executions in his report to the UN Human Rights Commission in 1993, already made a point of the escalating conflict between the Hutu and the Tutsi in Rwanda, and the risk of violence this entailed. At that time, peacekeeping troops had already been deployed to Rwanda and surely it would not have been impossible to extend their mandate and better equip them so as to avoid genocide. Sadly though, the international community showed no political will to intervene against the will of the Hutu dominated government in Rwanda by an act of prevention. The same is true for Bosnia and Herzegovina, and even more so for Kosovo, where first signs of an impending escalation were detected as early as 1989. For preventive measures to be effective they would have had to be imposed against the will of the *Milosevic* regime in Yugoslavia, but no state was willing to send ground troops to Kosovo to prevent possible human rights violations. When, in March 1999, following the unsuccessful peace negotiations of Rambouillet, NATO was finally prepared to start a humanitarian intervention (16.14.), the conflict between Serbia and the Kosovo-Albanian Liberation Army (KLA) had escalated to an extent where effective prevention was no longer possible.

On the other hand, the UN did manage, with the help of the United Nations Preventive Deployment Force (UNPREDEP) requested by the Macedonian government, to stop the armed ethnic conflict between Serbs and Albanians in Kosovo from spreading to **Macedonia** (14.1.). Because of China's veto in the Security Council – after Macedonia had just recognized Taiwan – the UNPREDEP troops were forced to withdraw, and in early 2001 the situation in Macedonia took a dangerous turn for the worse. The international community, and NATO in particular, had to intervene once more to calm the waters. The OSCE with its spill-over mission established in 1992 also contributed to preventing ethnic violence in Kosovo from spreading to Macedonia.

The **UN Office of the High Commissioner for Human Rights** embarked on a first and comparatively large-scale field operation in reaction to the genocide in Rwanda (16.7.). In 1994, it also deployed a small group of preventive human rights field monitors to Burundi with the mandate to prevent a similar genocide (14.2.). As with all preventive measures, it is difficult to measure its success since one can only speculate as to what would have happened without the preventive mission. It is safe to say though that although a number of ethnically motivated acts of violence and massacres were committed in Burundi they never did reach the level of the genocide committed in Rwanda, where the death toll was approximately 800,000. Deployment of military and/or human rights field staff is only one, and usually the last resort in a series of options for the prevention of human rights violations.

14. Mechanisms for the Prevention of Human Rights Violations

CASEBOX 4

14.2. Burundi Field Mission of the UN High Commissioner for Human Rights (UNHCHR)

Context and history

- Attempted *coup d'etat* in Burundi on 21 October 1993; estimated 50,000 massacred followed by rising levels of inter-ethnic violence, subsequent ongoing civil war
- April 1994: genocide in Rwanda, estimated 800,000 people killed, fears that war in Burundi will escalate to the proportion of the Rwandan genocide
- September 1994: UNHCHR and government of Burundi sign agreement of cooperation for technical assistance programme
- March 1995: Commission on Human Rights expresses the need to further increase preventive action in Burundi, in particular through the presence of human rights experts and observers throughout the country and the appointment of a special rapporteur (Res. 1995/90)
- June 1995: government agrees to deployment of 35 field monitors, deployment delayed due to funding constraints; UNHCHR issues an appeal to Commission on Human Rights; in April 1996, five monitors were deployed after funding provided by EU
- July 1996: Hutu government ousted in Tutsi *coup d'etat*, UN sanctions follow
- August 1996: human rights observers down to four after security situation deteriorates, by mid 1997 15 observers deployed once again, 1998: memorandum of understanding with UN Office for Project Services (UNOPS)

Mandate and activities

Three components to the mission:
- Technical cooperation activities
- Mission of observations
- Legal assistance programme

Examples of preventive activities:
- Visits to main detention centres with a focus on individual and private interviews and regular assessment of detention conditions
- Field visits to regroupment camps
- Training of military, police, gendarmerie and judiciary
- Capacity building and support to civil society
- Confidence building measures

Comments

- No clear assessment of preventive impact of the mission
- Viability of prevention mandate even in situation of armed conflict
- Lack of coordinated integrated approach until 1999, dependence on voluntary contributions – continuous funding problems

14.2. Burundi Field Mission of the UN High Commissioner for Human Rights

In Central and Eastern Europe, a number of **minority conflicts** and self-determination movements surged after the end of the Cold War and the ideological vacuum filled with nationalism in its wake. The situation was highly conducive to armed conflicts and human rights violations of the kind experienced in former Yugoslavia: One need only consider the collapse of Czechoslovakia or the Soviet Union, the nationalism levelled at the Hungarian minority in the Slovak Republic during *Meciar's* time, the politics of Baltic states to refuse the Russian minority citizenship, the suppression of the Greek minority in Albania, the discrimination against Roma in many countries or the enormous ethnic and religious tensions and conflicts in the Caucasus (e.g. Chechnya, Georgia), in Nagorno Karabach (between Armenia and Azerbaijan) and in the Central Asian Republics.

While the Council of Europe reacted to these minority issues by drafting and adopting two fairly weak minority conventions to be monitored by the state reporting method (5.5., 5.6.), the OSCE with its comprehensive security concept was already a step ahead in 1992. It had established the post of the **High Commissioner on National Minorities,** which proved a new conflict prevention mechanism (8.9.). *Max van der Stoel*, the former Dutch foreign minister, was able to scale down the minority conflicts and prevent human rights violations using silent diplomacy, mediation and his own persistence. He was supported in his efforts by the Permanent Council and other OSCE bodies, as well as by the Council of Europe and the EU, who understood that they might well have to reconsider membership of candidate countries in view of the minority conflicts he was warning about. The two case studies on the Slovak Republic and Albania (14.3.) would seem to support the above thesis, although again it is difficult to prove beyond reasonable doubt that the conflicts would have escalated without the interventions of the OSCE High Commissioner.

Effective prevention of human rights violations must address their root causes. If **armed conflicts** lie at the root of human rights violations, it follows that such conflicts must be scaled down and prevented. Naturally, human rights protection and **securing peace** go hand in hand (3.1.5.). If **poverty** and **chronic underdevelopment** are found to be the main cause for systematic violations of economic, social, cultural, civil and political rights, preventive human rights protection must seek to eradicate the two. This is where human rights and development are indelibly linked to each other (3.1.6.).

Many of the gross human rights violations, such as torture, arbitrary executions or enforced disappearances are only made possible because the police, the military or other law enforcement bodies are actively supported or at least given tacit permission by their governments to use extensive force without being held accountable. Again, preventive human rights protection must be tackled at the root of the problem, i.e. **the weaknesses of political systems** and the lack of constitutional or democratic guarantees. Thus, measures for the furtherance of the **rule of law, democracy and good governance** (3.1.7.) are a major contribution towards prevention of human rights violations.

14. Mechanisms for the Prevention of Human Rights Violations

> CASEBOX 5
>
> ### 14.3. OSCE High Commissioner on National Minorities (HCNM) – Case Studies
>
> #### Albania (1993 – 1996)
>
> - Repressive communist regime until 1991; relationship between government and Greek minority (and Greece) deteriorates
> - First set of recommendations from the HCNM (8.9.) in September 1993 (following two visits): strengthening democratic institutions, establishing government office for minority issues, incorporating constitutional safeguards for minorities into legislation, legislation for minority education, restitution/compensation for church property confiscated under communist regime
> - Summer/autumn 1994: arrest and trial of five Greek activists in Albania; in June 1994, the HCNM visits detainees in jail and districts populated by Greek minority.
> - October 1994: HCNM visits with two experts to make a study of inter-ethnic relations; main emerging issue: provision of Greek language education
> - Recommendations: changes in educational system, installation of procedures to deal with ethnic discrimination, rebuilding of religious communities, human rights training for police
>
> *Results*
>
> Release of Greek activists, private minority schools established, Treaty of Friendship, Cooperation, Good Neighbourliness and Security between Greece and Albania (1996); Greek language education expanded within existing Albanian schools
>
> #### Slovakia and Hungary (1993 – 2000)
>
> - Internal tensions and complaints from both states about the treatment of their minority in the other's country
> - Team of experts (1993 – 1996) appointed by the HCNM, regular visits
> - Recommendations: on minority legislation, minority representation in Parliament, minority ombudsman, minority self-government, Slovak language education in Hungary, Slovak language law, choice of educational facility, state funding of Hungarian cultural events, law on local elections in Slovakia
>
> *Results*
>
> Due to the insistence of the HCNM to deal with the conflicts in both states (especially the situation of the Hungarian minority in Slovakia), most recommendations were implemented and the conflict abates

TEXTBOX 162

14.4. UN DECLARATION AND UN WORKING GROUP ON ENFORCED DISAPPEARANCES

UN Declaration on the Protection of All Persons from Enforced Disappearance

GA Res. 47/133 of 18 December 1992

What is enforced or involuntary disappearance?

- Persons are arrested, detained or abducted against their will or otherwise deprived of their liberty
- By government officials or by organized groups of private individuals acting on behalf of, or with the support, direct or indirect, consent or acquiescence of the government
- Followed by a refusal to acknowledge the deprivation of liberty, thereby placing such persons outside the protection of the law

Preventive safeguards

- Every detainee to be held in an officially recognized place of detention and to be brought promptly before a judicial authority
- Accurate information on details of detention to be made available to family members, counsel and those with legitimate interest
- Official, up-to-date register of all detainees to be maintained in every place of detention, to be available to all those with legitimate interest
- Release of detainees to be documented and verifiable
- National law to specify under what conditions deprivation of liberty can be authorized, and by whom
- Orders and instructions do not justify enforced disappearance; every person who receives such orders or instructions has the right and the duty to disobey; this duty is to be given special emphasis during training
- Right to complaint before an independent state authority
- Prohibition under criminal law (enforced disappearance as a continuous offence under criminal law punishable by according penalties)

UN Working Group on Enforced or Involuntary Disappearances

- Established in 1980 as first thematic mechanism of the UN Commission on Human Rights
- Consists of five independent experts
- Preventive role: transmission of cases of immediate concern to governments with a view to clarifying the fate and whereabouts of disappeared persons; urgent action procedure for transmission of cases where victims have only recently disappeared (often leads to clarification and release); many preventive measures contained in the UN Declaration are based on recommendations and practice of the working group

The same holds true for holding perpetrators individually accountable under domestic and/or international criminal law, as **impunity** for gross and systematic violations of human rights is one of its major root causes. Many of the worst human rights violations are committed while victims are detained, as this is where they are most openly exposed to law enforcement bodies. Establishing guarantees for the **right of personal liberty** not only ensures protection of this important human right, but also constitutes a major prerequisite for preventing other human rights violations.

Thus, there are guarantees pertaining to the very ground for detention. According to article 5 of the ECHR, individuals may only be arrested or detained in such cases as listed therein (detention after conviction, detention on remand, detention for the prevention of the spreading of infectious diseases, detention with a view to deportation, etc.). All other forms of deprivation of personal liberty, in particular the preventive administrative detention of potentially dangerous persons (as imposed on suspected terrorists by the United States in Guantanamo Bay on Cuba) are prohibited. Every person arrested has the right to be informed promptly of the reasons for their arrest, and to call for a person of their trust (relatives, friends), a lawyer, or a doctor, or, if they are foreigners to the country, the consulate of their home country.

Based on the old Anglo-Saxon principle of **'habeas corpus'** every person arrested also has the right to have an independent court decide speedily on the lawfulness of his or her detention. Detention must be kept as short as possible and may not be extended beyond fulfilling its purpose (e.g. pre-trial detention because of the risk of escape, the risk of suppression of evidence or danger of recurrence). Incommunicado detention, (i.e. detention without informing the outside world of the facts and the place of detention), as practiced regularly by many dictatorships, is prohibited in any event. Respecting all the guarantees of the right of personal liberty significantly reduces the risk of torture, enforced disappearances and similar human rights violations.

The **UN Convention against Torture** (CAT, 4.3.5.), the **UN Declaration on the Protection of All Persons from Enforced Disappearance** (14.4.), and similar instruments at the regional level, especially in Latin America, provide a series of additional measures for the prevention of these human rights violations. Such measures include, amongst others, the prohibition of secret places of detention; introduction of local and central detention registers to keep track of when and where people were arrested, detained and released; precise identification of law enforcement agents entitled to deprive a person of their personal liberty; statutory obligation not to comply with superiors' orders to torture; and appropriate human rights training for law enforcement bodies. Given the fact that police interrogators frequently resort to torture just after a person has been arrested to obtain a confession by coercion or to extract information on third parties, monitoring measures during the interrogation, such as video or audio tapes, might also help to prevent the practice of torture or ill-treatment. Furthermore, compulsory medical examinations immediately after the arrest ought to be considered as yet another way

14.4. UN Declaration and UN Working Group on Enforced Disappearances

of reducing the risk of torture. Past experience with torture, enforced disappearances and arbitrary execution shows that urgent actions on the part of NGOs, such as Amnesty International or SOS Torture, or the respective thematic mechanisms established by the UN Human Rights Commission, such as the Special Rapporteur on Torture or the Working Group on Disappearances (4.4.1.5., 14.4.), have a preventive effect on authorities and thus help to protect victims from further human rights violations.

In 1987, the Council of Europe passed the **European Convention for the Prevention of Torture** (ECPT, 5.4.), which has proved another major mechanism for the prevention of human rights violations. It provides for regular, unannounced visits to all of those places in states parties where persons are deprived of their personal liberty (prisons, military and police jails, psychiatric institutions, educational institutions for adolescents, etc.). The European Committee for the Prevention of Torture (CPT), consisting of independent experts, has been appointed to conduct these visits. As the case study on Austria shows (14.5.), the three visits to Austria carried out by the CPT to date (1990, 1994 and 1999) have markedly reduced the risk of being ill-treated while in police custody. At the same time, the CPT's recommendations triggered a series of legislative measures and helped to improve detention conditions in general. In 1999, acting upon a recommendation from the CPT and following the tragic death of a young Nigerian during forced deportation, the Austrian Minister of the Interior established a human rights advisory council and six visiting commissions. Their task is to conduct regular and unannounced visits to all places of police detention, to monitor the exercise of police power in general, e.g. during police raids, demonstrations and arrests and to submit respective recommendations via the human rights advisory council to the Minister. In December 2002, the UN General Assembly adopted an OP to CAT, which is modelled on the ECPT, but which at the same time obliges states parties to establish independent domestic bodies for preventive visits of places of detention, similar to the Austrian visiting commissions described above.

It is clear from the above examples and case studies that some mechanisms for the prevention of human rights violations have already been put into place and are actually proving fairly efficient. However, this is hardly enough. Future efforts would have to focus on developing mechanisms for the prevention of human rights violations in many other fields. NGOs in particular are called upon to make the necessary proposals. Needless to say, each tool for the protection of human rights is preventive by its very nature. Thus, if a human rights court ascertains a concrete violation, its judgment in the case ought to be incentive enough for the country concerned (and others in a similar situation) to establish legal and other measures to prevent similar violations in the future. The same holds true for judgments of domestic or international criminal courts by which individual perpetrators of major human rights violations are convicted and sentenced to appropriate penalties.

> CASEBOX 6
>
> ## 14.5. AUSTRIA AND THE EUROPEAN COMMITTEE FOR THE PREVENTION OF TORTURE (CPT)
>
> ### Context
>
> 1980: reports of Austrian ombudsman mention problems of ill-treatment in Austria, issue raised in parliament
> 1987: torture in Austria mentioned for the first time in Amnesty International annual report
> 1990: Amnesty International publishes report 'Austria: Torture and Ill Treatment'
>
> ### Activities of the CPT
>
> Three visits to date (May 1990, September 1994, September 1999); the first two reports primarily criticized that detainees in police custody were in serious risk of being ill treated; furthermore, general conditions of detention (especially in police jails) were below standard. The third report (published in June 2001) acknowledged some of the improvements in police custody, yet criticized enforcement of deportations.
>
> Response of Austrian authorities: at the beginning reserved, later more open and willing to cooperate
>
> Selected *recommendations of the CPT* regarding police detention:
>
> - to promptly inform detainees of their rights (to notify a person of their own choice and/or counsel, to be examined by a doctor)
> - to allow legal counsel to be present during police interrogation
> - to introduce electronic recording of police interrogation
> - to improve the recruitment and training of law enforcement personnel
> - to enact standard rules for police interrogation
> - to prepare comprehensive documentation on every individual case of detention
> - to establish an independent authority to regularly visit police jails
>
> Legal and other *measures of the Austrian Government* in reaction to CPT reports:
>
> - enactment of extensive legislation on police powers (Security Police Act 1991, internal regulations, etc.), amendments to the judicial and administrative codes on criminal procedure, enactment of general Rules on Police Detention 1999 with comprehensive rights of detainees, etc.
> - introduction of a comprehensive system of information and documentation in police jails
> - improvement of the human rights training of law enforcement personnel
> - establishment of a Human Rights Advisory Council at the Ministry of Interior and six fairly independent commissions with the task of regularly inspecting all police detention places, of controlling the exercise of police powers in general, and preparing recommendations to the Minister of Interior

14.5. AUSTRIA AND THE EUROPEAN COMMITTEE FOR THE PREVENTION OF TORTURE

Comments

Although many CPT recommendations have not been implemented yet, the visits and reports of the CPT certainly had a major impact on the recognition of many structural problems in the Austrian system of police detention; brought the issue to public attention through reports in the media; governments generally have a more effective and constructive way of reacting to reports from international bodies than to 'mere' NGO reports; NGO fact finding has a major impact on the efficiency of IGO bodies like the CPT; overall the CPT's preventive activities have done more to improve police detention conditions in Austria than reactive control mechanisms such as the European Court of Human Rights or the Austrian Constitutional Court

LITBOX 14

LITERATURE

Association for the Prevention of Torture 1999, The Prevention of Torture at the Dawn of a New Millenium: Some reflections for the 10th Anniversary of the European Committee for the Prevention of Torture and Inhuman or Degrading Treatment or Punishment (CPT), Strasbourg

Dunér, Bertil, (Ed.) 1998, An End to Torture: Strategies for its Eradication, London/New York

Kemp, Walter A. (Ed.) 2001, Quiet Diplomacy in Action: The OSCE High Commissioner on National Minorities, The Hague/London/Boston

Kriebaum, Ursula 2000, Folterprävention in Europa, Study Series of the Ludwig Boltzmann Institute of Human Rights, Vol. 3, Vienna

Morgan, Rod/*Evans*, Malcolm 2001, Combating torture in Europe - The work and standards of the European Committee for the Prevention of Torture, Strasbourg

Nowak, Manfred 1996, Monitoring Disappearances: The Difficult Path From Clarifying Past Cases to Effectively Preventing Future Ones, European Human Rights Law Review

Nowak, Manfred 2002, Verhütung von Menschenrechtsverletzungen durch preventives Besuchssystem: Controlling der Sicherheitsexekutive in Österreich, in: Festschrift für Stefan Trechsel zum 65. Geburtstag, Zürich, 55-78

Vankovska-Cvetkovska, Biljana 1999, UNPREDEP in Macedonia: Achievements and Limits of Preventive Diplomacy, Online Journal of Peace and Conflict Resolution 2.1, (www.uottawa.ca/associations/balkanpeace/bio/vankovska.html)

INTERNET

www.unhchr.ch/html/menu2/7/b/mdiswg.htm - UN Working Group for Enforced or Involuntary Disappearances

www.un.org/depts/dpko - United Nations *peace-keeping operations*

www.unhchr.ch - High Commissioner for Human Rights

www.osce.org/hcnm - High Commissioner on National Minorities

www.cpt.coe.int - European Committee for the Prevention of Torture and Inhuman or Degrading Treatment of Punishment (CPT)

www.menschenrechtsbeirat.at - Menschenrechtsbeirat im österreichischen Bundesministerium für Inneres

15. INDIVIDUAL CRIMINAL RESPONSIBILITY FOR SERIOUS HUMAN RIGHTS VIOLATIONS

International law in principle is a legal framework established between states, which means that, as a rule, only states can be held accountable for violations of human rights guaranteed under international law. Ultimately it is up to states how to practice responsibility at the national level. The fact is that those individuals who commit human rights violations, i.e. law enforcement officers, military staff, politicians, etc., are hardly ever held accountable under criminal, disciplinary or civil law. Quite the opposite: even with the most serious and systematic human rights violations, the powerful ones always found ways of escaping responsibility by way of comprehensive amnesty laws, immunity or belated pardoning. In most countries, while shoplifters, tramps and others accused of petty crimes are prosecuted under criminal law, dictators, heads of juntas and police chiefs, for the longest time, knew they were protected by the overriding principle of impunity even if they had committed the most serious of human rights violations, such as genocide, torture or enforced disappearances. Even an overthrow of their government did not stop the *Idi Amins, Baby Docs, Pol Pots* and other human rights violators from seeking refuge in other countries and living the rest of their lives in safety and luxury.

The principle of **exclusive state responsibility** has proved largely **ineffective** in the context of human rights simply because it has not been an effective deterrent. The only states that take their human rights obligations seriously are those with a highly developed legal culture, while those actually responsible for serious human rights violations tend to ignore human rights protection under international law. Thus, over the years it has become clear that state responsibility ought to be complemented by **perpetrators' individual responsibility under criminal and civil law**. This not only has a deterrent effect on state functionaries, but might also prove a useful way of preventing **human rights violations by non-state actors**, such as transnational corporations, intergovernmental organizations, organized crime, terrorism, guerrilla movements or rebels.

The struggle against **impunity** (*impunidad*) began in the 1970s in Latin America where the military dictatorships that ruled most of the continent, were fighting a ruthless war against left-wing guerrilla groups in the name of 'national security'. Large sections of the population – members of communist and social democratic parties, union leaders, as well as scientists, artists, intellectuals and clergy adhering to a theology of liberation – were terrorized through systematic torture and murder, and thousands of people disappeared. **General *Augusto Pinochet Ugarte's* military coup** of 11 September 1973 against the democratically elected left-wing government of President *Salvador Allende* became a symbol for this kind of repression. Numerous Chile solidarity committees were formed in all parts of the world because *Allende* in particular had raised people's hopes of a 'third way' between communism and capitalism, a way out of poverty, repression and underdevelopment that most people in Latin America and other parts of the so-called 'third world' were afflicted with.

15. INDIVIDUAL CRIMINAL RESPONSIBILITY FOR SERIOUS HUMAN RIGHTS VIOLATIONS

CASEBOX 7

15.1. THE STRUGGLE AGAINST IMPUNITY AT THE NATIONAL LEVEL: THE 'DIRTY WAR' IN ARGENTINA

Background

The 'Dirty War' took place between 1976 and 1983, when a military junta governed Argentina. Human rights groups say that during those years about 30,000 people were killed or disappeared into torture centres. About 15,000 cases have been officially documented.

Problem of impunity for human rights crimes

1983: the new civilian government under president *Raul Alfonsin* appoints the National Commission on the Disappearance of Persons (CONADEP)
1985: the Buenos Aires Federal Appeals Court tried a number of former junta members (*Videla, Viola, Agosti, Massera* and *Lambruschini*) and police chiefs for human rights violations (e.g. illegal detention, torture, homicide) and sentenced them to between four years and life.
1986: the 'Punto Final' Act (Full Stop Law) sets deadlines for courts to complete investigations on human rights violations
1987: the 'Obediencia Debida' Act (Law of Due Obedience) applies the principle of due obedience to all officers below the rank of colonel
1989: Amnesties: President *Carlos Menem* pardons even top junta leaders who were imprisoned for human rights abuses

Reactions

The *UN Human Rights Committee* expresses its concern that 'pardons and general amnesties may promote an atmosphere of impunity for perpetrators of human rights violations' and notes that 'respect for human rights may be weakened by impunity for perpetrators of human rights violations'.

The *Inter-American Commission on Human Rights* states that by passing these laws Argentina has contravened the right to judicial protection and the right to a fair trial of ACHR.

NGOs play an important role in the fight against impunity; e.g. Mothers of the *Plaza de Mayo* (founded in 1976): an organized group of mothers and grandmothers of junta victims met each week demanding to know the fate and whereabouts of their relatives who were detained by the military junta between 1976 and 1983 and then disappeared

1998: the National Congress repeals the Full Stop and Due Obedience Laws. Since then human rights violations committed during the period of military government have been the subject of legal proceedings within Argentina and abroad (Spain, Italy, Germany)

1999: for the first time ever a former junta member (*Emilio Massera*, former leader of the military junta) is ordered by a court to payment of damages for human rights violations

15.2. THE PRINCIPLE OF UNIVERSAL JURISDICTION UNDER THE UN CONVENTION AGAINST TORTURE: THE CASE OF *HISSÈIN HABRÉ* IN SENEGAL

Because of the human rights violations committed by *Pinochet's* regime, Chile soon found itself internationally isolated. The international community, above all the OAS and UN, reacted by developing new mechanisms for international human rights protection (see the UN Human Rights Commission's procedures in particular, 4.4.1.). But it was only in 1998, 25 years after the military coup, that *Pinochet* was finally arrested in London (15.3.).

CASEBOX 8

15.2. THE PRINCIPLE OF UNIVERSAL JURISDICTION UNDER THE UN CONVENTION AGAINST TORTURE (CAT)

THE CASE OF *HISSÈIN HABRÉ* IN SENEGAL

Hissèin Habré took power in Chad in 1982, overthrowing the government of *Goukouni Wedeye*. His one-party regime was marked by widespread abuse and campaigns against the ethnic Sara (1986), Hadjerai (1987) and the Zaghawa (1989). *Habré* was deposed in December 1990 by current President *Idriss Debry* and has lived in exile in Senegal since.

A 1992 Chad truth commission report accused *Habré* and his government of 40,000 political murders, and systematic acts of torture and brutality.

In February 2000, the exiled dictator of Chad was indicted on torture charges in Senegal and placed under house arrest.

In July 2000, the Senegalese Court of Appeal dismissed torture charges against *Habré*. The judges ruled that Senegal had no jurisdiction to pursue charges that *Habré* was guilty of torture, because the crimes were not committed in Senegal. They ignored Senegal's obligation under the CAT (which Senegal had ratified in 1986) to prosecute alleged torturers who enter its territory.

In March 2001, the Senegalese Supreme Court of Appeal again refused to accept jurisdiction.

In September 2001, the president of Senegal, *Abdoulaye Wade*, declared in an interview that he was prepared to have *Habré* extradited to a country capable of organizing a fair trial.

2002: Belgium opens proceedings against *Habré*, an examining magistrate travels to Chad.

April 2003: a vote in the Belgian Parliament to amend Belgium's landmark anti-atrocity law creates political and diplomatic hurdles to the prosecution of many human rights crimes, however, cases which had been brought to a standstill, i.e. that against *Hissèin Habré*, will now move forward.

For many decades *Pinochet* managed to shield himself and his army of torturers from prosecution with the help of a 1978 amnesty law. On the other hand, *Raul Alfonsin*, the democratically elected president of Argentina, was at first able to bring to trial and put into prison the army officers responsible for **Argentina's 'dirty war'** against the left-wing opposition between 1976 and 1983, among them the heads of the junta, Generals *Jorge Videla* and *Eduardo Viola*.

The National Commission on the Disappearance of Persons, together with other investigation commissions appointed by the civil government, the church and human rights groups conducted a thorough investigation and documentation of the human rights violations committed by the military junta. However, because these crimes were investigated so relentlessly, the military increased their pressure and a new military coup seemed almost inevitable. *Alfonsin* and his government were forced to pass two notorious laws in 1986 and 1987 (*'Punto Final'* and *'Obediencia Debida'*), which practically brought the investigations to a halt (15.1.). In 1989, President *Carlos Menem* went so far as to pardon the junta leaders who had already been imprisoned. **Argentina** thus became the epitome of the plight of democratic governments struggling at the **domestic level** alone **against impunity** for systematic human rights violations committed by a former military regime. The victims of these crimes and their relatives (such as the mothers and grandmothers of the *Plaza de Mayo* in Buenos Aires), however, battled on for the truth, for justice and against impunity. In recent years, new civil and penal procedures have been instituted against members of the former military regime, both in Argentina and in several European states. Argentina is a good example of how deep a scar such serious and systematic human rights violations have left and how, even decades later, real reconciliation and peace will not come about as long as the truth is not told and justice is not rendered.

Investigating crimes against human rights and prosecuting the perpetrators is thus important from another point of view as well, which is **to render justice to victims of human rights violations** and thus, to facilitate the democratic reconstruction and peace process that is often necessary in the wake of some of the most serious human rights violations. In some states, such as South Africa and Guatemala, victims were encouraged to take the thorny road of coming to terms with the past with the help of a **truth and reconciliation commission**, but in other cases criminal law seems to be the only tool available to find the truth and to seek justice.

For all of the above reasons, criminal prosecution of human rights violations at the national level is rarely successful, which is why the struggle against impunity had to be raised to the international level. One of the tools developed for that purpose is the principle of **'universal jurisdiction'**. It was originally applied to persons who had committed crimes in territories outside national jurisdiction, such as pirates, slave traders at sea and airline hijackers. The first human rights convention to embody the concept of 'universal jurisdiction' was the **UN Convention against Torture** (4.3.5.) of 1984. The principle of 'universal jurisdiction' entitles, and even obligates, states parties to take into custody and bring before a criminal court persons suspected of torture, irrespective of these countries' traditional competence as derived from the principle of territoriality, as well as the active and passive personality (or nationality) principle, provided extradition to another state having direct jurisdiction is not possible (principle of *'aut dedere aut iudicare'*).

CASEBOX 9
15.3. DIPLOMATIC IMMUNITY VERSUS CRIMINAL RESPONSIBILITY
THE PINOCHET CASE BEFORE THE BRITISH HOUSE OF LORDS

Background

11 September 1973: bloody military coup and overthrow of democratically elected Chilean president *Salvador Allende*

1974: General *Augusto Pinochet Ugarte* declares himself president of the military junta; 1978 amnesty law: no responsibility for crimes committed in Chile between 11 September 1973 and 10 March 1978

1981: Pinochet declares himself president of Chile

1990: Pinochet hands over presidency to civilian president *Aylwin*, but remains commander-in-chief of the army until May 1998

May 1998: Pinochet becomes senator for life

Pinochet before British and Chilean courts

October 1998: Pinochet arrested on 16 October during a visit to UK, based on a Spanish provisional arrest warrant (issued by judge *Balthasar Garzon*) because of the alleged responsibility for the murder of Spanish citizens in Chile during his presidency; second Spanish provisional warrant follows, alleging his responsibility for systematic acts of murder, torture, disappearance, etc. (also the Swiss and the French government filed extradition requests, criminal proceedings against him also begin in Belgium, Italy, Luxembourg, Norway, Sweden and the United States)

November 1998: House of Lords states that a former head of state does not have immunity with respect to crimes against humanity

December 1998: House of Lords sets aside its decision on the ground that one of the judges is linked to Amnesty International which intervened in the hearing – rehearing of the appeal

March 1999: House of Lords: *Pinochet* can be extradited only for the crimes of torture and conspiracy to torture, committed after December 1988 (the date on which CAT became binding on the UK, Spain, and Chile). Law Lords agree on the principle that torture is an international crime

March 2000: British home secretary *Jack Straw* rules that Pinochet will, due to his frail medical condition, not be extradited for trial to Spain (neither to Switzerland, Belgium or France) – on 3 March 2000, he is taken to Chile

August 2000: decision of the Chilean Supreme Court of Justice to strip *Pinochet* of his parliamentary immunity

December 2000: decision by a Chilean judge to arrest and try Pinochet

July 2001: court decides that Pinochet is mentally unfit to be tried at this point in time

July 2002: the Supreme Court and the Santiago Appeals Court upheld the lower court's ruling and found that the mental infirmity of *Pinochet* was serious and irreversible, leading them to exempt him from prosecution for human rights crimes.

15. INDIVIDUAL CRIMINAL RESPONSIBILITY FOR SERIOUS HUMAN RIGHTS VIOLATIONS

The arrest of **General *Augusto Pinochet Ugarte*,** the former Chilean dictator, by British security forces on 16 October 1998 following a Spanish warrant of arrest, made a worldwide stir. However, even without the Spanish warrant British police could (and should) have arrested him. The principle of universal jurisdiction clearly provides that a state party to the UN Convention against Torture, such as the United Kingdom, has the jurisdiction to take into custody and bring before a British court any person having committed torture, regardless of whether they did so in the United Kingdom (principle of territoriality), and whether they are British citizens (active personality or nationality principle) or have tortured British citizens (passive personality or nationality principle). In other words, even Chilean citizens who have tortured Chileans in Chile fall under British jurisdiction by virtue of the principle of universal jurisdiction. Authorities may, in fact, intervene upon the mere suspicion of torture.

Once *Pinochet* had been taken into custody, the British authorities and politicians had to decide whether to indict him in England or extradite him to another country with a more direct jurisdiction. Chile was out of the question, as *Pinochet* himself had introduced a general pardon, however, there was mention of Spain and Italy where, based on the principle of passive personality, he was wanted for acts of torture committed against Spaniards and Italians in Chile. The United States was also interested in extradition, claiming the principle of territoriality. They accused *Pinochet* of having commissioned the murder of Chilean dissidents in the United States, such as the former Foreign Minister *Orlando Letelier*. Extradition from European countries to the United States, however, was generally viewed critically, bearing in mind the principle of non-refoulement and the risk of the death penalty.

In the end *Pinochet* was not extradited to Spain, primarily due to his frail medical condition and to the efforts of Britain's then Home Secretary, *Jack Straw*, to solve the tricky case by mutual consent. There was little speculation at the time that he might one day be tried under criminal law in Chile.

The *Pinochet* case is significant for international law and the principle of universal jurisdiction mainly because, for the first time ever, the British House of Lords decided that **former heads of state accused of torture did not enjoy immunity** (15.3.). At the same time it made clear that the UN Convention against Torture could not be applied retroactively.

The example of *Hissèin Habré*, **the exiled dictator of Chad** (15.2.), also shows how difficult it is politically to exercise the principle of universal jurisdiction in cases involving prominent politicians. In other, less prominent cases, such as two nuns from Rwanda, who because of their participation in the genocide in Rwanda were convicted by the Belgian courts, the principle has successfully been applied.

Nevertheless, most states, including those strongly committed to democracy, human rights and the rule of law, hesitate to apply the principle of universal jurisdiction, which is largely due to the fact that assuming a subsidiary competence is generally considered an unfriendly act against other states. Most governments are only inclined to take such a step for bilateral reasons, as in the case of Belgium and

15.4. INTERNATIONAL CRIMINAL TRIBUNAL FOR THE FORMER YUGOSLAVIA (ICTY)

its former colony Rwanda. This may also explain why Spain has taken such a keen interest in solving crimes against human rights in Latin America. Ultimately, of course, there is always the risk that the principle of universal jurisdiction may be abused for political interests.

TEXTBOX 163

15.4. INTERNATIONAL CRIMINAL TRIBUNAL FOR THE FORMER YUGOSLAVIA (ICTY)

Established by the SC under Chapter VII of the UN Charter: Res. 827 of 25 May 1993
Seat: The Hague, Netherlands

Organs

- Three trial chambers and one appeals chamber (shared with ICTR), 16 permanent judges and 9 *ad litem* judges
- President: *Theodor Meron* (United States of America): since 2003
- Chief Prosecutor (shared with ICTR): *Carla Del Ponte* (Switzerland): since 1999
- Registry (head: *Hans Holthius*, Netherlands): services the chambers and the prosecutor

Jurisdiction

- *Ratione materiae* (articles 2-5 of the Statute): grave breaches of the 1949 Geneva Conventions, violations of the laws or customs of war, genocide, crimes against humanity (the latter '*when committed in armed conflict...and directed against any civilian population*', crimes listed are similar to those in the ICC Statute)
- *Ratione personae* (articles 6 and 7): every (natural) person, who planned, instigated, ordered, committed or otherwise aided and abetted in the planning, preparation or execution of a crime referred to in articles 2 to 5
- *Ratione loci*: (article 8): 'territory of the former Socialist Federal Republic of Yugoslavia...'
- *Ratione temporis* (article 8): period beginning on 1 January 1991

The ICTY reports annually to the General Assembly and the Security Council.

Problem of arresting indicted persons (such as Bosnian Serb leaders *Radovan Karadzic* and *Ratko Mladic*) in Bosnia and Herzegovina, Croatia and in Serbia and Montenegro (economic pressure from the United States, arrests by SFOR)

As of May 2003:

76 accused, of whom 24 at large
50 accused currently in custody (including *Slobodan Milosevic* and *Momcilo Krajisnik*), 19 accused have been transferred/provisionally released
37 sentences, 20 of which final (including those concerning *Tihomir Blaskic* and *Dario Kordic*), 5 acquittals, 12 appeals ongoing

Consequently, the second alternative of jurisdiction would seem more effective in the long run. In this case, it is no longer individual states, which in the interest of humanitarian law and human rights bring to trial politicians of other states, but an **independent international criminal court**. First attempts at establishing international criminal tribunals were undertaken after the First World War, where the German Emperor *Wilhelm* was to be held responsible for crimes, as well as after the Second World War with the **international war crimes tribunals of Nuremberg and Tokyo**. The convictions of several high-ranking war criminals in Germany and Japan were considered important precedents, but to this day these ad hoc criminal tribunals appointed by the Allied Forces bear the stamp of 'victors' justice'.

To deter future genocide, article VI of the 1948 **UN Convention against Genocide** held out the prospect of a permanent 'international penal tribunal'. However, it was not until 1998, precisely half a century later, that the international community agreed in Rome to adopt the Statute of the International Criminal Court. In the meantime, many serious and systematic human rights violations were committed and never atoned for, amongst them, those committed by the Khmer Rouge in Cambodia. The genocide on Bosnian Muslims, the first committed in Europe after the Nazi holocaust, sadly became the necessary motivation for the UN Security Council to finally decide, upon the initiative of the United States, to establish the **International Criminal Tribunal for the Former Yugoslavia** (ICTY, 15.4.) on the basis of a Chapter VII Resolution adopted in May 1993. Its jurisdiction comprises war crimes, genocide and crimes against humanity committed on the territory of the former Yugoslavia since 1991. In preparation for this Tribunal, the Security Council had in October 1992 appointed an expert commission (later known as the **'Bassiouni Commission'**), which thoroughly investigated these crimes and handed a 3,000 page report to the public prosecutor in 1994. A second **ad-hoc International Criminal Tribunal for Rwanda** (ICTR, 15.5.) was established in Arusha in November 1994, upon the initiative of the new government in Rwanda. Its task is to prosecute those responsible for the genocide in Rwanda. On the explicit request of the UN Security Council (Res. 1315 of 14 August 2000), the UN in January 2002, on the basis of an agreement with the Government of Sierra Leone, established a **Special Court for Sierra Leone** to prosecute persons who bear the greatest responsibility for serious violations of international humanitarian law and Sierra Leonen law committed in the territory of Sierra Leone since 30 November 1996. A similar treaty-based *sui generis* criminal court of mixed jurisdiction and composition will soon be established to try those responsible for the genocide committed by the Khmer Rouge in **Cambodia** from 1975 to 1979 (16.8.).

The ad-hoc tribunals for the former Yugoslavia and Rwanda began with enormous political, bureaucratic, financial and practical problems. Although resolutions of the Security Council, in accordance with Chapter VII of the UN Charter, are binding under international law, there were many doubts as to the Security Council's legitimacy to establish criminal tribunals. Besides, the same former Yugoslav politicians that the international community negotiated with were those held responsible for having committed the crimes, and some of them had

15.5. INTERNATIONAL CRIMINAL TRIBUNAL FOR RWANDA (ICTR)

actually been charged when the peace negotiations were still ongoing. Since the NATO led International Implementation (later: Stabilization) Force (IFOR, SFOR), established under the Dayton Peace Agreement of 1995 (16.4.), turned out to be very reluctant to arrest indicted war criminals, it proved difficult to transfer those persons from Serbia and the 'Republika Srpská' (one entity of Bosnia and Herzegovina) to the ICTY in The Hague.

TEXTBOX 164

15.5. INTERNATIONAL CRIMINAL TRIBUNAL FOR RWANDA (ICTR)

Established by the SC under Chapter VII of the UN Charter: Res. 955 of 8 November 1994
Seat: Arusha, Tanzania

Organs

- Three trial chambers and one appeals chamber (shared with ICTY), 14 judges
- President: *Erik Mose* (Norway), since 2003
- Chief Prosecutor (shared with ICTY): *Carla del Ponte* (Switzerland), since 1999
- Registry (head: *Adama Dieng*, Senegal): services the chambers and the prosecutor

Jurisdiction

- *Ratione materiae* (articles 2 to 4 of the Statute): genocide, crimes against humanity (similar to the term in the statute of the ICC), violations of common article 3 of the Geneva Conventions and of Additional Protocol II
- *Ratione personae* (articles 5 and 6): every (natural) person, who planned, instigated, ordered, committed or otherwise aided and abetted in the planning, preparation or execution of a crime referred to in articles 2 to 4
- *Ratione loci* (article 7): 'territory of Rwanda...as well as to the territory of neighbouring states in respect of serious violations of international humanitarian law committed by Rwandan citizens'
- *Ratione temporis*: (article 7): 1 January 1994 to 31 December 1994

The ICTR reports annually to the General Assembly and the Security Council

Problem of different standards of ICTR and Rwandan national courts (death penalty, conditions of detention, fair trial, etc.)

As of May 2003:

55 accused currently in custody in Arusha (of whom 12 ministers of the 1994 transitional government)
10 final sentences, of which seven guilty verdicts (among them prime minister *Jean Kambanda*, the first head of government ever sentenced for genocide), 3 acquittals, 3 ongoing appeals,
20 ongoing proceedings in the first instance

In Rwanda, the situation is aggravated by the fact that a great many people actively participated in the genocide of 1994.

TEXTBOX 165

15.6. THE LONG AND WINDING ROAD TO THE ADOPTION OF THE ROME STATUTE FOR AN INTERNATIONAL CRIMINAL COURT (ICC)

- **Military tribunals of Nuremberg (1945) and Tokyo (1946)**

In Resolution 260 of 9 December 1948 adopting the Genocide Convention, the UN General Assembly (GA) invited the International Law Commission (ILC) 'to study the desirability and possibility of establishing an international judicial organ for the trial of persons charged with genocide'. The Commission concluded that it was both desirable and possible. The GA then established a committee, which prepared a draft statute in 1951 and a revised draft statute in 1953. Consideration of both was postponed pending the adoption of a definition of 'aggression'.

The question of an ICC has been considered periodically since then. In December 1989, the GA asked the ILC to resume work on an ICC with jurisdiction to include drug trafficking.

- **Establishment of the ad hoc International Criminal Tribunals for the Former Yugoslavia (ICTY) in 1993, and for Rwanda (ICTR) in 1994**

In 1994, the ILC submitted the completed draft statute for an ICC to the GA. The ad hoc committee and the preparatory committee (1995 – 1998) prepared a draft text and the GA then convened the UN Diplomatic Conference of Plenipotentiaries on the Establishment of an ICC, held in Rome from 15 June to 17 July 1998 (160 states participated, a large number of NGOs contributed). Its task was to finalize a draft statute which was adopted with 120: 7 votes (China, Iraq, Israel, Libya, Qatar, USA, Yemen) and 21 abstentions.

- **The Rome Statute of the International Criminal Court entered into force on 1 July 2002, having been ratified by 60 states.**

The United States signed in December 2000, yet withdrew their signature on 6 May 2002, claiming that it had no intention to become party to the Statute. Furthermore, the UN Security Council passed Resolution 1422 (2002) (with much pressure from the United States) to ensure that the ICC would not become active against members of UN authorized operations who were not citizens of a state party to the Statute. Other US efforts to obstruct the functioning of the ICC include bilateral agreements with states parties aimed at exempting US citizens from being extradited to The Hague.

As of May 2003, 139 states have signed and 90 have ratified the Statute.

While the main criminals ('big fish') are prosecuted by the ICTR in Arusha, with all the guarantees of a fair trial and no fear of a death penalty, the host of 'smaller fish' have been imprisoned in Rwanda under inhuman conditions while awaiting trials

15.7. INTERNATIONAL CRIMINAL COURT ICC

that often do not meet the international standards of a fair trial, and in some cases end with a death sentence.

TEXTBOX 166

15.7. INTERNATIONAL CRIMINAL COURT (ICC)

Rome Statute of the ICC, adopted on 17 July 1998
Entry into force: 1 July 2002
90 states parties
Seat: The Hague, Netherlands

Aims

- To end impunity
- To deter future war and human rights criminals
- To help end conflicts
- To compensate for the shortcomings of ad hoc tribunals (ICTY, ICTR)

Organs

- Pre-Trial, Trial and Appeals Division, 18 judges
- President: *Philippe Kirsch* (Canada)
- Chief Prosecutor: *Luis Moreno Ocampo* (Argentina)

Jurisdiction

- *Ratione materiae* (article 5)
- Genocide
- Crimes against humanity (15.8.)
- War crimes
- Crime of aggression (once a definition for such a crime has been determined and accepted)

- *Ratione personae* (article 25)
  Every (natural) person, who is a national of a state party or who commits a crime within the jurisdiction of the ICC on the territory of a state party, shall be criminally responsible if that person:
- Commits such a crime (whether as an individual, jointly or through another person)
- Order, solicits or induces the commission of such a crime
- Aids, abets or otherwise assists in the commission or attempted commission of such a crime
- In any other way contributes to the commission or attempted commission of such a crime by a group of persons acting with a common purpose
- In respect of the crime of genocide, directly or publicly incited others to commit genocide

- *Ratione temporis* (article 11)
  Jurisdiction applies only with respect to crimes committed after the entry into force of the Statute (1 July 2002).

- *Principle of complementary jurisdiction* (articles 1 and 17)
- The ICC acts only when national courts are unable or unwilling

Notwithstanding the above problems, the ad-hoc tribunals are no doubt a major step ahead in the struggle against impunity. In the former Yugoslavia, the international community exerted so much political, diplomatic and economic pressure that most of the key players in the war crimes, genocide and crimes against humanity committed in Croatia, Bosnia and Herzegovina and Kosovo between 1991 and 1999, among them *Slobodan Milosevic,* the former president of the Federal Republic of Yugoslavia (Serbia and Montenegro), are now being held accountable in The Hague. The same is true for Rwanda where many of the protagonists of the genocide are kept in custody in Arusha or, like the former Prime Minister *Jean Kambanda*, have already been sentenced. The Special Court for Sierra Leone in May 2003 issued an arrest warrant against the President of Liberia, *Charles Taylor*. While both ad-hoc tribunals have their shortcomings inasmuch as they are employed rather selectively and were established after the crimes had already been committed, they have also been instrumental in bringing about a breakthrough in the protracted negotiations to establish a permanent **International Criminal Court** (ICC). On 17 July 1998, 50 years after the Genocide Convention, the ICC Statute was adopted in Rome with 120 votes against 7 and 21 abstentions.

Sadly the **United States**, whose initiative for the ICTY had actually triggered the whole discussion, then **decided to plot against the ICC**, venturing a number of rather grotesque arguments (see below). In doing so they first succeeded in watering down some of the basic principles of the Rome Statute, and finally nevertheless voted against the ICC together with China, Iraq, Israel, Libya, Qatar, and Yemen. The main advocates of the ICC, the European and Latin American countries, had accepted the United States's various attempts at weakening the Statute in the hope that a compromise would eventually be achieved. By 31 December 2000, the agreed deadline, 139 states had signed. The United States, under the *Clinton* administration, was finally also among the signatory states. In April 2002, however, the *Bush* administration announced several measures to undermine the ICC and even 'withdrew' its signature. At that point, however, the 60 ratifications required had been made and the Rome Statute of the ICC entered into force on 1 July 2002. The judges were sworn-in on 11 March 2003, and with the prosecutor taking office on 16 June 2003, the ICC was actually fully functional to take up its important mission. The United States, nevertheless, continued their hostile attitude by adopting the American Servicemembers' Protection Act of 2002 (ASPA, commonly known as the 'Hague Invasion Act'), by putting heavy pressure on other states to enter into bilateral agreements aimed at exempting United States citizens form being extradited to The Hague, and by even forcing the Security Council to adopt Resolution 1422 (2002), which requests the ICC, for a period of 12 months (extended for another 12 months by SC Res. 1487 of 12 June 2003), not to commence any investigation or prosecution against any official of the United States and other non-state parties having committed international crimes in the context of any 'United Nations established or authorized operation'. It is highly doubtful whether these bilateral agreements and SC Res. 1422 are compatible with the relevant provisions (articles 16 and 98) of the ICC Statute.

15.8. THE CONCEPT OF CRIMES AGAINST HUMANITY

The ICC is responsible for criminal prosecution of international crimes, such as **genocide** (in the sense of the Genocide Convention), **aggression** (not applicable yet as the statutory definition of this offence is pending), **crimes against humanity** (15.8.) and **war crimes** (e.g. grave violations of the 1949 Geneva Conventions), provided these crimes were not committed before 1 July 2002.

TEXTBOX 167

15.8. THE CONCEPT OF CRIMES AGAINST HUMANITY
Article 7 ICC Statute

For the purpose of this Statute, 'crime against humanity' means any of the following acts when committed as part of a widespread or systematic attack directed against any civilian population, with knowledge of the attack:
- Murder
- Extermination
- Enslavement
- Deportation or forcible transfer of population
- Imprisonment or other severe deprivation of physical liberty in violation of fundamental rules of international law
- Torture
- Rape, sexual slavery, enforced prostitution, forced pregnancy, enforced sterilization, or any other form of sexual violence of comparable gravity
- Persecution against any identifiable group or collectivity on political, racial, national, ethnic, cultural, religious, gender or other grounds
- Enforced disappearance of persons
- The crime of apartheid
- Other inhumane acts of similar character intentionally causing great suffering, or serious injury to body or to mental or physical health

All these terms are specified and defined in the statute and in the 'elements of crime'

Once the ICC has charged a person, no amnesty or immunity can protect them from prosecution. Heads of state or government are not excluded from this rule. This competence, however, only applies to territories or nationals of states that have ratified the Statute. Thus, the **main argument by the United States against the ICC**, which is that its citizens (such as members of the armed forces deployed in international peacekeeping operations) must not be brought before a non-independent court against their will, is **hardly convincing**, as the following facts clearly illustrate:
- The ICC, its judges and prosecutors, are independent of all states as illustrated by the ICTY and the ICTR;
- The ICC has competence to deal with crimes committed by United States citizens on United States territory only after the United States has ratified that Rome Statute;

- Even now crimes committed by United States soldiers in other countries are primarily under the jurisdiction of these countries' courts, which in many cases are far less independent than the ICC;
- Unlike the ad-hoc tribunals, which are given preference over national criminal courts, the ICC is subject to the **principle of complementary jurisdiction**, which means it only has competence over those cases where the competent national courts are unable or unwilling to prosecute 'their' war criminals and human rights violators under criminal law;
- The ICC does not have jurisdiction over individual human rights violations, but over genocide, war crimes and crimes against humanity only, for which there has to be proof of a widespread or systematic attack against the civilian population; and
- The UN Security Council may for a period of 12 months suspend the ICC's jurisdiction in exceptional cases, e.g. if it is about to negotiate a truce with potential war criminals.

As with the ad-hoc tribunals, proceedings with the ICC are instituted by an **independent public prosecutor**, who may also act upon referral by states parties or the Security Council. To avoid any political interference, the ultimate decision as to whether the evidence submitted by the public prosecutor, the Security Council or individual governments is sufficient to commence an investigation, and whether the competent national courts of the country on whose territory the crime was committed are able and willing to prosecute, rests with one of the pre-trial chambers of the ICC. Much will depend on how the ICC is going to interpret this limitation of its jurisdiction in practice.

TEXTBOX 168

15.9. CHALLENGES FOR THE ICC

- No consensus in Rome: Can the ICC function without the United States and China? Is it possible to bring the dissenters on board and if so, how?
- Independence of the prosecutor
- Interference by the Security Council (see SC Res. 1422 of 12 July 2002 with respect to members of UN authorized operations)
- Principle of complementarity: on what grounds does the ICC decide that national courts are unable or unwilling to act?
- Narrow definition of crimes against humanity in times of peace
- Arrest/detention of accused criminals on the territory of states that have not ratified the ICC Statute or refuse to cooperate with the ICC

At any rate, states parties must not be given the opportunity to try and protect war criminals and human rights violators from the ICC by simple fictitious action. On the other hand, the principle of complementarity also fulfils a **positive role** in putting national courts under pressure, which are rather sceptical of prosecuting human rights criminals under international law, irrespective of whether their

15.9. CHALLENGES FOR THE ICC

competence is based on the principle of territoriality, personality or universal jurisdiction.

Ultimately, all that matters is to break the taboo of impunity, which in the past has always protected those mainly responsible for war crimes, as well as gross and systematic human rights violations in times of war and peace. Whether or not this kind of criminal prosecution will be assumed primarily by national courts, or by the ICC, is only of secondary importance.

15. INDIVIDUAL CRIMINAL RESPONSIBILITY FOR SERIOUS HUMAN RIGHTS VIOLATIONS

LITBOX 15

LITERATURE

Bassiouni, M. Cherif 1998, The Statute of the International Criminal Court: A documentary History, New York

Cassese, Antonio 2003, International Criminal Law, Oxford

Cassese, Antonio et al. 2002, The Rome Statute for an International Criminal Court – A Commentary, 3 volumes. Oxford

Frey, Linda 1999, The History of Diplomatic Immunity, Columbus

Guest, Iain 1990, Behind the Disappearance: Argentina's Dirty War Against Human Rights and the United Nations, Philadelphia

Humanitarian Law Center (Ed.) 2000, Proceedings Of The International Conference On War-Crimes Trials, in: Spotlight On, Belgrade

Ingelse, Chris 2001, The role of the UN Committee against Torture in the Development of the UN Convention against Torture, The Hague

International Commission of Jurists (Ed.) 2001, Argentina - Amicus Curiae brief on the incompatibility with international law of the full stop and due obedience laws, Geneva

International Commission of Jurists (Ed.) 1999, Crimes Against Humanity - Pinochet Faces Justice, Geneva

International Council on Human Rights Policy (Ed.) 1999, Hard cases: bringing human rights violators to justice abroad - A guide to universal jurisdiction, Geneva

Jones, John R.W.D. 2000, The practice of the International Criminal Tribunals for the former Yugoslavia and Rwanda, New York

Joyner, Christopher C. (Ed.) 1998, Reining in impunity for international crimes and serious violations for fundamental Human Rights: proceedings of the Siracusa Conference, 17-21 September 1998, Toulouse

Politi, Mauro 2001, The Rome Statute of the International Criminal Court: a challenge to impunity, Ashgate

Program in Law and Public Affairs (Ed.) 2001, The Princeton Principles on Universal Jurisdiction, New Jersey

Roth-Arriaza, Naomi 1995, Impunity and human rights in international law and practice, New York

Siedler, Rachel 1995, Impunity in Latin America, London

15.9. CHALLENGES FOR THE ICC

Triffterer, Otto (Ed.) 1999, Commentary on the Rome Statute of the International Criminal Court, Baden-Baden

Woodhouse, Diana (Ed.) 2000, The Pinochet case: a Legal and Constitutional Analysis, Oxford

INTERNET

www.un.org/icty - International Criminal Tribunal for the former Yugoslavia

www.ictr.org - International Tribunal for Rwanda

www.un.org/law/icc/ - Rome Statute for the International Criminal Court

www.iccnow.org/ - Coalition for the International Criminal Court

www.madres.org - Association of Mothers of the Plaza de Mayo

16. Human Rights and the Maintenance of Peace and Security

During the Cold War, international human rights protection and maintenance of peace and security seemed quite distinct from one another. The international community was mainly occupied with collective peace securing, and the UN Security Council was entitled, through the UN Charter, to impose sanctions or authorize military interventions only in the event of a breach of, or threat to international peace.

By the same token, measures for the protection of human rights were considered an inadmissible interference with domestic affairs in the sense of article 2(7) of the UN Charter, the only exception granted being in the case of voluntary ratification of human rights treaties and the apposite international monitoring mechanisms (3.1.1.).

TEXTBOX 169

16.1. Chapter VII UN Charter: Powers of the UN Security Council in the Event of a Threat to the Peace, Breach of the Peace or Act of Aggression

Article 39

'The Security Council shall determine the existence of any threat to the peace, breach of the peace, or act of aggression and shall make recommendations, or decide what measures shall be taken in accordance with Articles 41 and 42 to maintain or restore international peace and security.'

Article 41

'The Security Council may decide what measures not involving the use of armed force are to be employed to give effect to its decisions, and it may call upon the Members of the United Nations to apply such measures. These may include complete or partial interruption of economic relations and of rail, sea, air, postal, telegraphic, radio, and other means of communication, and the severance of diplomatic relations.'

Article 42

'Should the Security Council consider that measures provided for in Article 41 would be inadequate or have proved to be inadequate, it may take such action by air, sea, or land forces as may be necessary to maintain or restore international peace and security. Such action may include demonstrations, blockade, and other operations by air, sea or land forces of Members of the United Nations.'

It was some time before the conviction reached the point that human rights protection and peace securing had more to do with each other than met the eye. Not only are human rights threatened by armed (national and international) conflicts, but systematic violations of these rights also constitutes one of the main causes of ethnic, religious, social and political tensions, which frequently develop into unrest and armed conflicts (3.1.5.). Experience has shown that democratic states with a highly developed human rights culture are unlikely to go to war against each other while dictatorial regimes that systematically violate human rights quite often turn against their own people, or even against other states, all to uphold their own power. Measures for the prevention of armed conflicts must necessarily take into account the human rights situation in the states concerned. A short overview of the states where the UN Security Council imposed sanctions in accordance with article 41 of the UN Charter reveals that all of them have seriously and systematically violated human rights, be it civil, political, economic, social or cultural rights (16.3.).

TEXTBOX 170

16.2 THE SECURITY COUNCIL AND HUMAN RIGHTS

First cases of serious human rights violations (apartheid) to be qualified by the SC as constituting a threat to international peace and security were Southern Rhodesia (1966) and South Africa (1977)

During the 1990s, serious and systematic human rights violations were increasingly considered as threats to international peace and security justifying intervention notwithstanding article 2(7) of the UN Charter (3.1.1.)

Problems:

- Veto of permanent members – no intervention in their 'domestic affairs' (e.g. Tibet/China, Chechnya/Russia)
- Difficulty of targeting economic sanctions to avoid suffering of civilian population
- No permanent UN military capability: UN dependent on willingness of member states to provide troops
- Humanitarian intervention by military force: When is it justified? How to balance the suffering caused by systematic human rights violations with the suffering caused by military interventions?

This new awareness of the **interdependence of human rights protection and peace securing** has also led to a change in the premises under international law. Considering that already in the 1960s and 1970s, the serious and systematic human rights violations committed in connection with apartheid policies in southern Africa were qualified as a threat to international peace and security by the UN Security Council, the argument of national sovereignty laid down in article 2(7) of the UN Charter gradually lost ground as well.

Today, international protection of human rights is not only considered a legitimate task of international law, but an obligation of the international community. In cases of extremely serious and systematic human rights violations, the Security Council is entitled to take the necessary measures under Chapter VII of the UN Charter, including political and diplomatic pressure as well as economic sanctions (article 41, 16.3.) and military interventions (article 42). Typical cases of

military intervention for the protection of human rights on the basis of Security Council resolutions are Iraq and Somalia, the former Yugoslavia, Haiti, Sierra Leone, East Timor and, to some extent, Afghanistan.

However, human rights violations alone are not enough to convince politicians of the need for such drastic measures as imposing economic sanctions or military interventions. Such decisions usually are based on other determining factors such as assaults on neighbouring countries, as in the case of **Iraq** in 1990 (16.11.), open support of terrorist movements, as in the case of **Afghanistan** (16.15.), unsolved issues of self-determination as accrued from colonial times (**East Timor**, 16.10.), enormous streams of refugees as in **Haiti, Iraq** or **former Yugoslavia** (16.9. and 16.14.), or the phenomenon of 'failed states', as in **Sierra Leone** or **Somalia** (16.12.).

Bearing in mind the prohibition to use force as laid down in article 2(4) of the UN Charter, such '**humanitarian interventions**' are only admissible for reasons of self defence (article 51), such as in the case of Afghanistan, or as a measure of **collective security** authorized by the UN Security Council in accordance with Chapter VII of the UN Charter. Since permanent members of the Security Council (China, France, Russia, the United Kingdom, or the United States) have a right to veto important measures on the maintenance of peace and human rights protection, and have actually done so in the past mainly for political reasons, the United States and NATO in recent years have tended to conduct 'humanitarian interventions' even **without** the required **authorization from the Security Council.**

This gradual change in states' practice might be illustrated by two examples. First, the Tanzanian government, despite gross and systematic human rights violations committed by **Uganda** under *Idi Amin* in the 1970s, did not want the massive military invasion and subsequent overthrow of the regime to be considered a 'humanitarian intervention' (16.13, the same is true for other frequently mentioned cases, i.e. 'humanitarian intervention' in Bangladesh or Cambodia). By the same token, NATO, in 1999, felt no qualms about legitimizing their air raids against the **Federal Republic of Yugoslavia** that brought down the *Milosevic* regime, as 'humanitarian intervention' for the protection of the Kosovo Albanians against systematic human rights violations by Serbian security forces (16.14.). Although these interventions were carried out in violation of applicable international law, many commentators and human rights activists welcomed them as *ultima ratio* to enforce human rights and prevent further 'ethnic cleansing' operations. Of course, there is always the risk that continuing such one-sided interventions, as announced by the United States and NATO in the wake of events of 11 September 2001, would seriously undermine the role of the United Nations as the highest authority of maintaining peace and security and protecting human rights. Fundamental reforms of the UN Charter and especially the decision-making procedures in the Security Council are urgently called for in reaction to this spreading unilateralism.

The close link between human rights protection and peace securing is also reflected in the **'comprehensive security' concept developed by the OSCE** (8.8.). Preventive diplomacy as practiced by the High Commissioner on National

Minorities (8.9.), for example, no longer distinguishes between measures of human rights protection and conflict prevention. Similarly, the **'human security'** concept initiated by Canada and other states, combines elements of classical peace maintenance and disarmament with elements of environmental protection and human rights.

The change in this relationship between maintenance of peace and human rights protection over the last ten years, however, is most evident in the context of international peacekeeping and peace building operations. Although the UN Charter does not expressly provide for **peacekeeping operations,** the UN blue helmets have for many years played an important role in monitoring actual adherence to cease-fire agreements. The case study on **Cyprus** (16.5.) graphically illustrates this traditional form of peacekeeping operations. To begin with, an international or national armed conflict is ended temporarily by a cease-fire agreement, usually through mediation by the UN. In a second step, UN soldiers are deployed in a clearly marked buffer zone between the two enemy armies. Their mandate is limited to monitoring adherence to the cease-fire based on three fundamental principles: consent of all conflicting parties, strict neutrality and no use of force on the part of the UN soldiers except in self-defence. For this reason traditional peacekeepers only carry light arms. In the event that one of the conflicting parties no longer agrees to the operation or even threatens to use military force against the blue helmets, peacekeepers are evacuated and the operation is called off as unsuccessful. Quite frequently, however, blue helmets continue their operations for decades (in the case of Cyprus: almost 40 years) and until the conflicting parties have finally entered a peace agreement. In the case of Cyprus the most recent efforts of UN SG *Kofi Annan* were again refused by the Turkish Cypriot leader *Rauf Denktash* in April 2003. Their mandate does not allow traditional UN peacekeeping forces to take any more specific peace-building measures to promote the process of reconciliation and sustainable peace, including human rights.

The above situation is not only very costly, but highly unsatisfactory as well. Thus, a **second generation of peace operations** developed after the end of the Cold War. Along with their peacekeeping function, i.e. monitoring adherence to a cease-fire, these now include a peace-building element and are therefore referred to as peacekeeping and **peace-building operations**. **El Salvador** clearly played a pioneering role in this new development (16.6.). Following a decade-long bloody civil war between the government and the guerrilla organization FMLN, the two parties decided in 1991, with the support of the United Nations and several states in the region, to establish a UN observer mission (ONUSAL) to verify the provisions of provisional peace agreements including the San José Agreement on Human Rights. Although a permanent peace agreement was not signed until 1992, ONUSAL's Human Rights Division immediately began to investigate the human rights situation in El Salvador on the basis of specific complaints and other on-site fact-finding methods in accordance with its mandate under the San José Agreement on Human Rights. For the first time in the history of the United Nations as many as 30 **human rights monitors** were actively involved in a field operation. Furthermore,

16.2 THE SECURITY COUNCIL AND HUMAN RIGHTS

no mention was made about any 'inadmissible' interference into El Salvador's national affairs.

This first step towards human rights field activities was instrumental in redefining peacekeeping's image, and was also to radically change people's understanding of active human rights work. The monitors from the ONUSAL Human Rights Division soon realized that human rights field operations were not to be limited to monitoring only, but had to help build the structures necessary for sustainable protection of human rights. During the institution-building process special emphasis was therefore placed on radically reforming the judiciary, the police, and prison administration. In addition, ONUSAL carried out a series of human rights educational programmes, contributed towards establishing national human rights institutions (National Council for the Defence of Human Rights), strengthened human rights NGOs and helped addressing past human rights violations committed, which was the task of a newly established truth commission. At the same time, a strong election and democratization division helped to prepare and monitor the general elections in 1994. When ONUSAL was withdrawn in 1995 and replaced by smaller UN missions, the human rights situation had improved markedly and the foundations for sustainable peace in El Salvador had been laid.

The UN peace operations in El Salvador were successful for a number of reasons. After decades of civil war, both conflicting parties, as well as the population of this small Central American country, were seriously interested in a sustainable peace and were willing to cooperate with and be supported by the international community. What was also crucial was the fact that monitoring and protection of human rights, democratization and building-up of constitutional structures were considered essential elements in the peace process. Ultimately, however, it was the comprehensive approach that made the human rights operation so successful and, apart from contributing towards monitoring and investigating the current human rights situation objectively, it also helped to create national structures of human rights protection and made sure that human rights violations of the past and their root causes (such as in particular unfair distribution of land) were dealt with.

This **integrative approach** chosen by ONUSAL was subsequently used as a model for equally successful operations like the one in **Guatemala**. The war between the army and the guerrilla organization URNG was still waging when the UN human rights monitoring mission MINUGUA was established in November 1994. MINUGUA continued its activities as a human rights mission only until the final peace agreement was signed in December 1996. It was part of a peace process initiated by the UN, which eventually ended 36 years of a civil war that had cost the lives of 150,000 people. In **Cambodia,** where the UN Transitional Authority (UNTAC) had been instituted by the Paris Peace Agreements of 1991 (16.8.), the human rights monitors and civilian police were vested with far-reaching competences (e.g. the power to arrest).

16. Human Rights and the Maintenance of Peace and Security

> Textbox 171
>
> ## 16. 3. Sanctions of the Security Council under Article 41
>
> ### Examples
>
> - *Afghanistan* (1999 -): flight ban, freeze on Taliban funds (and, as of 2000, those of *Osama Bin Laden*), air and arms embargo (2000)
> - *Angola* (1993 – 2002): oil and arms embargo against UNITA, restrictions on travel of senior officials, flight restrictions, freeze on funds in Angola and abroad, no official contacts, prohibition of imports, of uncontrolled diamonds, mining equipment (as of 1998), etc.
> - *Cambodia* (1992 – 1994): oil embargo and supported moratorium on log exports against PDK-controlled areas of Cambodia
> - *Ethiopia and Eritrea* (2000 – 2001): arms embargo
> - *Former Yugoslavia* (1991 – 1996): 1991 – general and complete embargo on all deliveries of weapons and military equipment, 1992 – full trade embargo, flight ban, prevention of participation in sporting and cultural events, prohibition of unapproved transportation of petroleum, coal, steel, other products, 1994 – Bosnian Serb officials prevented from entering foreign territories, ban on trade with Bosnian Serb territory, except for relief supplies, freeze on Bosnian Serb assets abroad, September 1994 – sanctions partially lifted, 1996 – sanctions lifted
> - *Federal Republic of Yugoslavia/Kosovo* (1998 – 2001): embargo on all military equipment
> - *Haiti* (1993 – 1994): arms and oil embargo, freeze on foreign assets, later on all commodities and products except medical supplies and foodstuffs
> - *Iraq* (1990 – 2003): full trade embargo (except medical supplies, foodstuffs, and other humanitarian items), 1991 – 'oil for food' agreement, 1997 – limited petroleum exports allowed, restrictions on travel of selected Iraqi officials, 1999 – ceiling on Iraqi oil exports removed
> - *Liberia* (1992 -): arms embargo, restrictions on travel, and prohibition of direct or indirect imports of rough diamonds, prohibition of imports of timber from Liberia
> - *Libya* (1992 – suspended 1999): arms and air embargo, reduction in diplomatic staff, freeze on Libyan funds abroad, ban on imports of equipment for oil refining and transportation
> - *Rwanda* (1994 – suspended 1995/96): arms embargo on Rwanda and neighbouring suppliers, restrictions on arms sales to non-government forces for use in Rwanda remain limited
> - *Sierra Leone* (1997 -): arms and oil embargo (except on oil for verified humanitarian purposes), restrictions on travel of military junta; lifted 1998, with exception of arms sales to non-governmental forces, 2000 – prohibition of direct or indirect imports of all rough diamonds from Sierra Leone
> - *Somalia* (1992 -): arms embargo
> - *South Africa* (1977 – 1994): arms embargo
> - *Southern Rhodesia* (1966 – 1979): oil, other commodities
> - *Sudan* (1996 – 2001): limited diplomatic sanctions

16. 3. Sanctions of the Security Council under Article 41

> **Comments**
> - Mandatory economic and other sanctions imposed by the SC are, in principle, an effective tool to put pressure on governments to improve the human rights situation (example: South Africa)
> - At the same time, sanctions often have the most severe and adverse impact on the most vulnerable segments of the population, such as the poor, women and children (example: Iraq)
> - Need to better target sanctions and to provide for humanitarian exemptions
> - Need to develop 'smart sanctions', which seek to pressure regimes rather than peoples, such as freezing financial assets, blocking financial transactions and imposing travel restrictions on the political elites (examples: Liberia and Sierra Leone)

Despite several setbacks and their insufficient numbers, they were able to contribute, at least to some extent, in developing a human rights culture in a country still suffering from the genocide committed by the Khmer Rouge in the 1970s.

Nevertheless, successful human rights peace operations are few. In most cases of serious and systematic human rights violations that have resulted in armed conflicts and even genocide, the international community reacted too late, and with insufficient means – or not at all. **Rwanda** is one such example where operations failed. Despite the fact that the UN Human Rights Commission's Special Rapporteur on Arbitrary Executions in 1993 had already warned the international community of the dangerous developments in the ethnic and social conflict between the Hutu and the Tutsi, the members of the Security Council in 1994, when the genocide against the Tutsi began, were unable to pass a decision to have the existing peace operation in Rwanda (UNAMIR) expanded and equipped accordingly, let alone to strengthen it with a mandate under Chapter VII. On the contrary, only a few days after the genocide that killed 800,000 people began on 6 April 1994, the UN Security Council ordered the withdrawal of most of the UNAMIR forces. Only as late as June 1994, France began its *'Opération Turquoise'* to set up a humanitarian protection zone in the southwestern part of the country, providing refuge to some of the Tutsi. In other parts of the country, the genocide was ended not by international measures, but by a military victory of the Rwandese Patriotic Front (RPF) who have since formed a Tutsi-dominated government. One day after the genocide began in Rwanda, *José Ayala Lasso* took up office as first UN High Commissioner for Human Rights (4.4.8.2.). Pressed by the UN Secretary General and the Security Council's failure, he decided to intervene and visited Rwanda in early May. During an emergency session the same month, the UN Human Rights Commission appointed a Special Rapporteur for Human Rights in Rwanda and sanctioned the first and largest human rights field operation of the Office of the High Commissioner to date (16.7.). The original plan was to appoint one human rights monitor per administrative district, i.e. a total of 147, yet even in 1995, there were never more than 100 persons on the entire operation. Considering the unimaginable dimensions of the humanitarian crisis and the total collapse of all constitutional structures, a human rights operation of that size could hardly be expected to achieve much. Receiving their orders from

Geneva, they also had enormous structural and logistic problems to battle with. The Office of the High Commissioner for Human Rights had virtually no experience with the logistics of field operations, and had to rely on voluntary financial contributions, which made long-term planning impossible. Furthermore, there was a distinct lack of cooperation with UNAMIR, the New York based field operation, which between the summer 1994 and March 1996 had again increased its personnel to approximately 5,000 persons, most of them military or UN police.

Surprisingly, this human rights operation, despite the adverse circumstances, was able to make a small contribution towards establishing rule of law and human rights structures, as with the judiciary. Nevertheless, it is generally and rightly regarded as an example of UN failure during and following serious human rights violations, such as genocide. For field operations to be successful, they need to be comprehensive and well coordinated and must include human rights as an important element alongside other components of a military and non-military nature. Examples of such **complex peace operations** are Bosnia and Herzegovina (after 1995), Kosovo (following the NATO intervention in 1999) and East Timor.

Sadly, the collapse of the **Former Yugoslavia** and especially the genocide in **Bosnia and Herzegovina**, which cost the lives of approximately 250,000 mainly Muslim people between 1992 and 1995, is yet another story of failure on the part of the international community to unite in the face of massive human rights violations. The different European states were unable to set aside old alliances and to agree on concerted actions to end the 'ethnic cleansing' that was being committed by all parties in the various armed conflicts, but especially by the Serb paramilitary units under the protection of the Yugoslav National Army. Half-hearted measures such as setting up 'safe havens' for the distressed Muslim enclaves that were to be protected by UNPROFOR, the UN Protection Force, on the basis of a Chapter VII mandate from the Security Council, proved a disaster, especially highlighted by the massacre of nearly 7,000 Bosnian Muslims in Srebrenica before the very eyes of lightly armed Dutch blue helmets in the summer of 1995. Finally, in reaction to Srebrenica and other systematic human rights violations of the worst kind, the United States finally took up the main responsibility. In November 1995, using massive political pressure, it pushed through the **Dayton Peace Agreement** (16.4.) that was signed by the presidents of the Federal Republic of Yugoslavia (*Sobodan Milosevic*), Croatia (*Franjo Tudman*), and Bosnia and Herzegovina (*Alija Izetbegovic*). The agreement initiated the largest and most complex international peace operation based on a UN Security Council mandate to date (16.9.).

However, the United States did insist that the role of the UN be reduced as far as possible and be replaced by North Atlantic and European organizations. The military component responsible for ensuring internal security was referred to an international Implementation Force (IFOR) of originally 60,000 troops under NATO's supreme command, which later became a **Stabilisation Force (SFOR)**. Control and coordination of the civil component, which normally rests with a Special Representative of the UN Secretary General, in this case was referred to the **High Representative** who is responsible not to the UN, but to the Peace

16.4. STRUCTURE OF THE DAYTON PEACE AGREEMENT FOR BOSNIA AND HERZEGOVINA

Implementation Council (PIC). The PIC was expressly established for the operation to comprise all key players involved in the peace process in Bosnia and Herzegovina, above all the so-called 'Contract Group' (France, Germany, Russia, the United Kingdom, the United States, later also Italy). Human rights and democratization are major elements of the civil component in this peace process, with the **OSCE** assuming the main responsibility for preparing elections, monitoring human rights and creating constitutional and human rights structures. This explains why the OSCE's largest field mission to date is the one deployed to Bosnia and Herzegovina (8.12.).

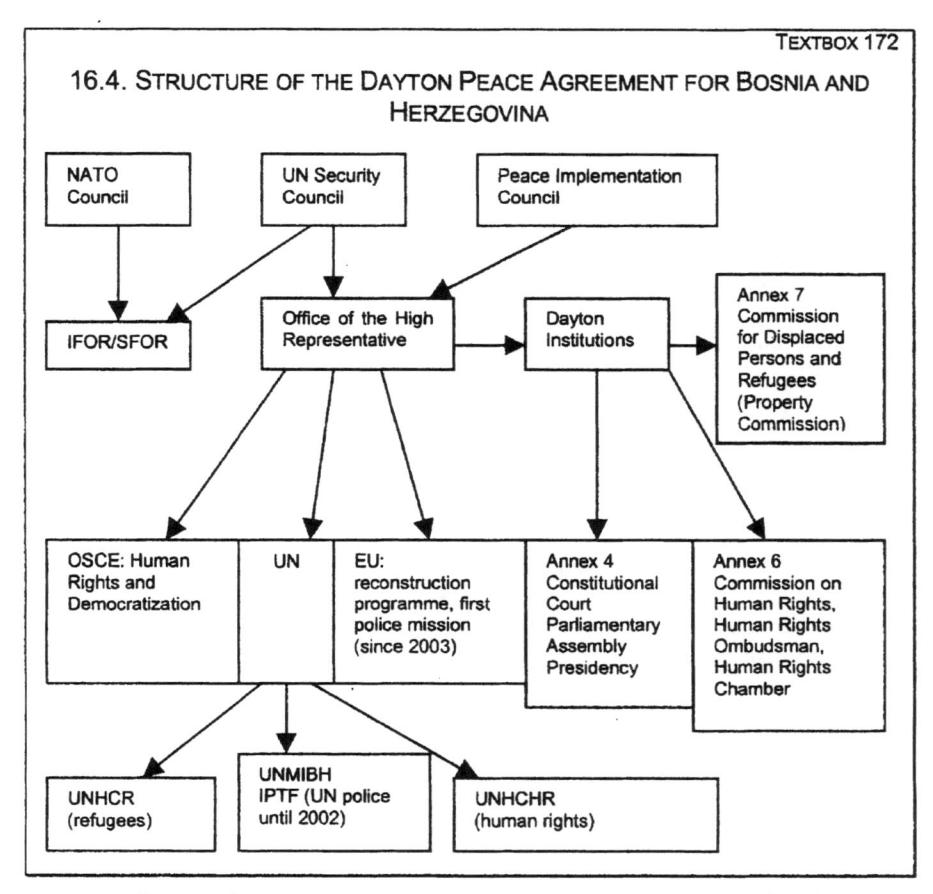

TEXTBOX 172

16.4. STRUCTURE OF THE DAYTON PEACE AGREEMENT FOR BOSNIA AND HERZEGOVINA

- NATO Council
- UN Security Council
- Peace Implementation Council
- IFOR/SFOR
- Office of the High Representative
- Dayton Institutions
- Annex 7 Commission for Displaced Persons and Refugees (Property Commission)
- OSCE: Human Rights and Democratization
- UN
- EU: reconstruction programme, first police mission (since 2003)
- Annex 4 Constitutional Court Parliamentary Assembly Presidency
- Annex 6 Commission on Human Rights, Human Rights Ombudsman, Human Rights Chamber
- UNHCR (refugees)
- UNMIBH IPTF (UN police until 2002)
- UNHCHR (human rights)

According to the Dayton Peace Agreement, which also provides for a new constitution for Bosnia and Herzegovina, the European Convention on Human Rights, together with 15 other international and European human rights treaties, are considered equal to, and in the case of the ECHR, above national law. To facilitate the implementation of human rights, a number of 'Dayton institutions' were created consisting of national as well as international members primarily appointed by bodies of the **Council of Europe**. One of these institutions is the **Human Rights Chamber for Bosnia and Herzegovina** established on the model of the European Court of Human Rights (5.2.) as the highest court rendering final and legally binding judgments on individual complaints alleging violation of human rights under the ECHR or discrimination in the enjoyment of civil, political, economic, social and cultural rights provided for in 15 further human rights treaties.

Given that during the 'ethnic cleansing', approximately half of the Bosnian population were displaced from their homes, special emphasis must be placed on facilitating the return of refugees and internally displaced persons and solving property issues. A separate **Commission for Real Property Claims** was appointed for that very purpose.

UN involvement in this context is essentially limited to a civilian police force (IPTF = International Police Task Force), which has been replaced in 2003 by the European Union Police Mission (EUPM), and the UNHCR (4.4.8.5.) in charge of repatriation of refugees and internally displaced persons. The UNHCR in fact proved the main humanitarian organization already during the war. The International Criminal Tribunal for the Former Yugoslavia (ICTY, 15.4.) is responsible for prosecuting and punishing human rights crimes committed during the war, and the UN Office of the High Commissioner for Human Rights (4.4.8.2.) has also established a small field presence, which, among other tasks, supported the Human Rights Commission's Special Rapporteur (4.4.1.4.). The **European Union**, along with the World Bank, the UNDP and other development organizations is primarily responsible for economic reconstruction.

This much abridged enumeration of main organizations and institutions illustrates the complex nature of the peace operation in Bosnia and Herzegovina (16.9.). Nowhere else in the world has the international community invested so much money and human resources into post conflict peace building. Perhaps, according to many, the enthusiasm and support for peace building in the Balkans stemmed from the shame of earlier inaction that resulted in the first genocide committed on European territory after the Second World War. Virtually all relevant international and European organizations are involved in this peace operation, which is certainly not unwelcome from the point of view of regional subsidiarity, yet on the other hand creates enormous problems with coordination and competition. This is why the PIC, over the years, has extended the powers of the **High Representative** (e.g. to impose laws or remove politicians who are obstructing the peace process), making him the **main political decision maker in Bosnia and Herzegovina** and turning the country into a **quasi-protectorate** of the international community. Nonetheless, while extending its own powers at this stage, the international community definitely wishes to withdraw and is urging Bosnian politicians to assume more 'ownership' and responsibility for their country.

Undoubtedly, much has been achieved in more than seven years of implementing the Dayton Peace Agreement with regard to ending the armed conflict and building economic, democratic, constitutional and human rights structures. It remains to be seen, however, whether this peace process is sustainable enough for

16.4. STRUCTURE OF THE DAYTON PEACE AGREEMENT FOR BOSNIA AND HERZEGOVINA

the international community to withdraw. The truth is that many politicians, parties and structures responsible for the war and the 'ethnic cleansing' are still in power today. Many critics believe that in view of such serious human rights violations it would have been better to establish a genuine international protectorate to foster the building of new structures from the very beginning and then pass these on to a new political elite.

In the case of **Kosovo** some lessons had already been learnt from Bosnia and Herzegovina. After the peace conference at Rambouillet failed, NATO conducted a military intervention between March and June 1999 (16.14.) to avoid yet another genocide on former Yugoslav territory, and prepare the ground for an **international transitional administration**. Of course, some of the structures were simply adapted from Bosnia and Herzegovina, however, by the same token, the international community had learnt not to conduct too complex an operation. While the military component in Kosovo (KFOR) is also under NATO command, the civil component UNMIK has been assigned to a Special Representative of the UN Secretary General. In Kosovo as well, the UN transitional administration is built on **four pillars**. Again the EU has been put in charge of economic reconstruction, the OSCE is responsible for human rights and democratization, and the UNCHR (which was later put outside the UN Mission in Kosovo) has been in charge of the repatriation of refugees and internally displaced persons. UN proper is responsible for establishing new government structures, including the administration, police force, judiciary and legislation, which in the case of a transitional administration is far more difficult than with a monitoring peace operation. The Kosovo transitional administration may well serve as a model in some aspects, but the peace operation as such suffers two fundamental shortcomings: firstly, it does not offer any long-term perspective as to whether Kosovo will become an independent state or be reintegrated into Serbia once the transitional administration is ended. No date has been set for a referendum to that end. Secondly, its cooperation with the Kosovo-Albanian nationalists has been far too close to allow the Serbian population to become actively involved in the peace process.

The UN has also established a transitional administration in **East Timor** (16.10.). On the face of it, the international community decided to intervene because of the continuing serious and systematic human rights violations committed by Indonesia. However, what ultimately legitimized the United Nations involvement was a more deeply rooted problem of **self-determination**, similar to Namibia, Palestine or the Western Sahara. A second reason was the weakness of the Indonesian government following the collapse of the *Suharto* regime. It took several long and drawn-out negotiations before an agreement was reached to hold a **referendum** on the future of East Timor. The two options were extensive autonomy as part of Indonesia, or complete independence. The referendum was organized and monitored by the UN (UNAMET) without any international military protection.

As soon as the word was out of the overwhelming vote for independence, Indonesian militia with the support of the Indonesian military began a massacre of civilians in East Timor in which almost 10,000 people lost their lives. If it had not been for the rapid **humanitarian intervention** of the Australian led strike force INTERFET based on a Chapter VII Security Council resolution, further serious human rights violations would have been committed and the UN mission would surely have failed. East Timor's infrastructure had been largely destroyed by the militia's atrocities and the United Nations felt compelled to install a **transitional administration** (UNTAET) in November 1999 to provide the necessary constitutional, democratic and human rights structures, and to organize the first free elections and prepare the country for its independence. In May 2002, following new elections, the transitional administration was replaced by a scaled-down **peace operation** UNMISET, which is to accompany the post-conflict peace building process offering support in security issues and reconstruction of democracy and the judiciary.

The UN's main difficulty in East Timor was that the Indonesian government refused to have international troops present during the referendum, and instead insisted that the Indonesian military would ensure national security. Thus, the UN was faced with the alternative of entering a security risk or letting the unique chance of self-determination and an end to serious human rights violations in East Timor go by. There is no question that the massacres committed by Indonesian militia were a serious setback for the UN mission, but by and large most people in East Timor today, because of the rapid intervention of INTERFET and the smooth functioning of the transitional administration, consider the operation a success. As far as human rights are concerned, a solid foundation has been laid for preventing further human rights violations and prosecuting those of the past.

16.5. UN Peacekeeping Force in Cyprus (UNFICYP)

CASEBOX 10

16.5. UN Peacekeeping Force in Cyprus (UNFICYP)

Characteristics of traditional peacekeeping operations

- No explicit mention in UN Charter: 'Chapter VI and a half'
- Implementation of a cease-fire across a clearly marked border with agreement of parties; primarily staffed by military personnel
- Consent of all conflicting parties
- Strict neutrality: no interference in internal affairs
- No use of force (except in self-defence)

Context and history

Cyprus gains independence in 1960, series of constitutional crises result in outbreak of violence between Greek Cypriot and Turkish Cypriot forces in December 1963

UNFICYP established by SC Res. 186 (1964); operational in March 1964

July/August 1974: Coup d'état by Greek Cypriots favouring union with Greece: Turkey invades Cyprus, occupies main Turkish Cypriot enclave in the north; de facto cease-fire on 16 August 1974; UNFICYP deployed along a buffer zone between the cease-fire lines of the Cyprus National Guard and the Turkish forces. Mandate repeatedly extended thereafter

April 2003: Failure to settle on a comprehensive UN peace plan for the reunification of the island before admission to the EU in 2004; SC (Res. 1475 of 14 April 2003) criticizes the negative approach of the Turkish Cypriot leader *Rauf Denktash,* fully supported the 'carefully balanced plan' of the SG and asked him to continue to make available his good offices for Cyprus

Strength (31 March 2003): 1,373 total uniformed personnel, including 1,338 troops, 35 civilian police; supported by 44 international and 105 local civilian staff

Mandate and activities

- 'To use its best efforts to prevent a recurrence of fighting and, as necessary, to contribute to the maintenance and restoration of law and order'
- Surveillance from observation points, mobile and standing patrols deployed as necessary
- Humanitarian tasks within the buffer zone, e.g. security coverage for agricultural activities, religious services, assistance in maintenance of water and power supplies, fire-fighting, assistance in provision of medical facilities

Comments

Presence of UNFICYP essential for the maintenance of the cease-fire on the island, yet mandate based on narrow understanding of the term peace (defined as absence of war) – no specific human rights mandate

16. HUMAN RIGHTS AND THE MAINTENANCE OF PEACE AND SECURITY

CASEBOX 11

16.6. UN OBSERVER MISSION IN EL SALVADOR (ONUSAL)

Observadores de las Naciones Unidas en El Salvador

Context and history

Decade long civil war between the Government of El Salvador and the *Frente Farabundo Marti para la Liberación Nacional* (FMLN)

ONUSAL established by SC Res. 693(1991) to verify compliance with the provisions of various agreements, including the *San José Agreement on Human Rights* of 26 July 1990, the first specific human rights settlement concluded in the context of a comprehensive peace agreement; Human Rights Division (1991) – first human rights component instituted during a peace operation, joined by military and police divisions (1992) and electoral division (1993) as mandate is expanded

1995: ONUSAL withdraws after elections for the presidency, the legislative assembly, the mayors and municipal councils in March 1994. Small civilian mission (United Nations Mission in El Salvador, MINUSAL) remains, renamed UN Verification Office (UNOV) in May 1996; UN activities terminated in July 1997

Strength: up to 380 military observers; 8 medical officers; and 631 police observers; provision for 140 civilian international staff and 180 local staff. Of these approximately 30 human rights observers, 36 long term election observers (increased to 900 during the elections)

Mandate and activities (Human Rights Division)

- Active verification of compliance with agreements (above all: San José Agreement on Human Rights) between government and FMLN
- Investigation of specific cases of alleged human rights violations; promoting human rights in the country; making recommendations for the elimination of violations; and reporting to the UN SG, GA, SC
- Establishment of institutions for the protection of human rights, human rights education and dissemination of human rights information

Comments

General consensus on success of mission; the mission operated within a clear framework of agreement between parties, firm legal basis

Crucial importance of inclusion of human rights considerations in political negotiations

Viable cease-fire contributed to the success

Sound basis for development of a judicial system, human rights ombudsman and national civilian police

Problems of coordination with the UN Human Rights Commission's Special Rapporteur

Clear division of labour between ONUSAL (monitoring present human rights situation and institution building) and the Truth Commission (dealing with the past)

16.7. First Field Presence of the UN High Commissioner for Human Rights: UN Field Operation in Rwanda (HRFOR)

CASEBOX 12

16.7. FIRST FIELD PRESENCE OF THE UN HIGH COMMISSIONER FOR HUMAN RIGHTS: UN FIELD OPERATION IN RWANDA (HRFOR)

Context and history

6 April 1994: genocide begins in Rwanda

Despite early warning the international community fails to prevent genocide; approximately 800,000 victims; UN withdraws UNAMIR (United Nations Assistance Mission for Rwanda) peacekeeping troops in face of genocide (later re-deployed)

May 1994: UN High Commissioner for Human Rights (HCHR) visits Rwanda, UN Commission on Human Rights appoints Special Rapporteur and orders field presence in responding to the request of the new government

Target strength for field officers for August 1994: 147, most administrative districts (prefectures) were to have offices by November, yet by February 1995, only 82 observers in the field, more arrived in the following months with EU support

28 July 1998: HRFOR withdraws

Mandate and activities

- To investigate the genocide and other serious human rights violations
- To monitor the ongoing human rights situation
- To implement programmes for technical cooperation – particularly in the area of administration of justice
- To work with others to re-establish mutual confidence and thus to facilitate the return of refugees and displaced persons and the rebuilding of civil society

Comments

Mission much criticised, especially in the early stages

Confusion over the role of the operation in documenting and investigating genocide led to widespread public disillusionment; lack of experience and capacity of UNHCHR; inadequate recruitment and training of human rights field monitors

Lack of logistic support, dependence on voluntary funding

Confusion about competence of HCHR, ICTR (15.5.), Special Rapporteur and still existing Human Rights Centre in Geneva

Insufficient cooperation with other UN organizations operating in Rwanda

Difficult working environment: in the aftermath of the genocide, prisons were overcrowded with people suspected of having participated in the genocide; and the population had little understanding for the monitoring of 'minor' human rights violations of the present instead of only dealing with the genocide (investigative mandate of HRFOR was passed on to ICTR)

CASEBOX 13

16.8. BETWEEN PEACEKEEPING AND PROTECTORATE: UN TRANSITIONAL AUTHORITY IN CAMBODIA (UNTAC)

Context and history

Decade long civil war following Vietnamese invasion (1978) and Khmer Rouge genocide (1975 – 1979)

1991 *Paris Agreements on the Comprehensive Political Settlement of the Cambodia Conflict* (signed by the four Cambodian factions) decided that tragic recent events require specific measures to ensure human rights, and delegated to the UN 'all powers necessary' to ensure the implementation of the Agreements

UN Advance Mission in Cambodia (UNAMIC) established immediately after signing of agreements to help maintain the cease-fire and begin a major training programme in mine clearing and awareness

UNTAC established in February 1992 by SC Res. 745; operational in March 1992; UNAMIC integrated into UNTAC in March 1992

Seven distinct components: human rights, the organization and conduct of free and fair elections, military arrangements, civil administration, the maintenance of law and order (civilian police), repatriation and resettlement of refugees and displaced persons and the rehabilitation of essential infrastructure

Strength: approximately 22,000 military and civilian staff, including initially only 10 human rights officers; later increased to one human rights officer in every province, plus headquarters and training staff

1992: obstruction of disarmament process by Khmer Rouge

1993: boycott of UN supervised elections

UNTAC mandate ends in September 1993 following the promulgation of the Constitution for the Kingdom of Cambodia and the formation of a new government; UNTAC human rights component succeeded by a field office of the UNHCHR, which is responsible to the Special Representative of the UN Secretary General for human rights

1994: marked deterioration of human rights situation, 25,000 flee to Thailand in March, armed conflicts between government and Khmer Rouge resumed

1997: bloody coup, civil war

Mandate and activities

- Wide ranging powers: direct control of all administrative organizations; unrestricted access to all operations and information; supervision of the enforcement and judicial process; power of UN civilian police to arrest, detain and prosecute
- Supervision, monitoring and verification of the withdrawal of foreign forces, disarmament, support for de-mining
- Preparation and supervision of elections
- Assistance in the repatriation of refugees

16.8. BETWEEN PEACEKEEPING AND PROTECTORATE: UN TRANSITIONAL AUTHORITY IN CAMBODIA (UNTAC)

- Human rights (section E of UNTAC mandate): development and implementation of a programme of human rights education; general human rights oversight during the transitional period, e.g. conditions of detention; investigation of human rights complaints and corrective action; reassignment or removal from office of administrative personnel

Comments

Successful in the following objectives:
- Administration handed over to freely elected coalition, efficient repatriation of refugees
- Innovative and successful role in encouraging growth of human rights NGO's
- Extensive educational programmes
- Active support of new legislation, e.g. provisions relating to the judiciary, criminal law and procedure during the transitional administration; government ratified main human rights conventions
- Several hundred political prisoners released; improvement of conditions of detention
- Funding fully integrated into the UNHCHR budget
- Secured support for UN human rights presence beyond peacekeeping mandate

Problems

- Short time frame: elections organized without real chance of lasting democratic consolidation; refugees repatriated without long-term reintegration and protection – civil war broke out once more
- Accusation of top down approach, cultural insensibility
- Human rights component in fact neglected during the operation
- Failure to establish a criminal tribunal for the genocide in Cambodia notwithstanding various initiatives in this respect: Agreement on the establishment of a special court (similar to Sierra Leone:15.) only in 2003.

16. Human Rights and the Maintenance of Peace and Security

CASEBOX 14

16.9. Comprehensive Peace Operation: The International Community's Quasi Protectorate in Bosnia and Herzegovina

Context and history

Disintegration of the former Yugoslavia, war, extensive 'ethnic cleansing' and genocide in Bosnia and Herzegovina (1992 – 1995)

Failure of major decision makers to agree on comprehensive field operation during the armed conflict, culminated in the inability of UN Protection Force Peacekeepers (UNPROFOR) to prevent the fall of the 'safe haven' in Srebrenica in July 1995 – over 7,000 massacred

Dayton Peace Agreement

Initialled on 21 November 1995 at a US military air base in Dayton (Ohio) and signed on 14 December 1995 in Paris by the Presidents of the Federal Republic of Yugoslavia, Croatia and Bosnia and Herzegovina as a result of United States led peace initiative. Endorsed by SC Res. 1031 of 15 December 1995.

- BiH divided into two new entities: the (Bosniak/Croat) Federation of Bosnia and Herzegovina and the Republika Srpska, each with substantial political autonomy,
- Eleven annexes covering military aspects, regional stabilization, delineation of Inter-Entity Boundary Line, holding of democratic elections (supervised by OSCE), BiH constitution (Annex IV), arbitration procedure, human rights (Annex VI), assistance to refugees, civilian implementation of the Peace Agreement and an International Police Task Force
- Deployment of NATO led international Implementation Force (IFOR) authorized by the UN Security Council (later Stabilization Force SFOR), responsible for all military aspects of the peace agreement
- Designation of a High Representative as the final authority regarding civilian aspects of the Peace Agreement, appointed by Peace Implementation Council, endorsed by SC Res. 1031 of 15 December 1995

High Representatives to date:
- *Carl Bildt* (Sweden): December 1995 to June 1997
- *Carlos Westendorp* (Spain): June 1997 to July 1999
- *Wolfgang Petritsch* (Austria): July 1999 to May 2002
- *Paddy Ashdown* (UK): since May 2002

8 – 9 December 1995: Peace Implementation Conference (London) calls on international community to mobilize a new start for the people of BiH – *Peace Implementation Council* (PIC) set up composed of all states, international organizations and agencies at the conference

Total strength: up to 60,000 military and 1,700 police officers plus thousands of civilian personnel seconded to and employed by all the organizations involved

16.9. Comprehensive Peace Operation: The International Community's Quasi Protectorate in Bosnia and Herzegovina

Main international organizations active in human rights in BiH

- *OHR:* Office of the High Representative: coordination and enforcement
- *OSCE*: human rights (investigations, institution building, facilitating refugee returns, judiciary), democratization (civil society activities, media, political parties programme, rule of law programme), elections (organization, supervision, monitoring)
- *UNHCR:* responsible for return and reintegration of more than 2 million displaced persons and refugees, lead agency for humanitarian assistance, reconstruction, protection and advocacy
- *UNMIBH* (United Nations Mission in Bosnia and Herzegovina): International Police Task Force (IPTF), Civil Affairs Unit, Judicial System Assessment Programme, Human Rights Office, Public Affairs Office. UNMIBH was terminated on 31 December 2002 and replaced by European Union Police Mission (EUPM)
- *UNHCHR*: field office of the High Commissioner established already during the war (1993) and working in formal cooperation with UNMIBH; provides human rights expertise and guidance to UN agencies, focusing on gender and anti-trafficking, social and economic rights, police training, support to Special Rapporteur and Expert on Missing Persons
- *Special Rapporteurs* of the UN Human Rights Commission:
  Tadeusz Mazowiecki (Poland): 1992 – 1995
  Elisabeth Rehn (Finland): 1995 – 1998
  Jiri Dienstbier (Czech Republic): 1998 – 2001
  José Cutileiro (Portugal): 2001 – 2003
- UN *Expert on Missing Persons* on the territory of former Yugoslavia:
  Manfred Nowak (Austria): 1994 – 1997
- *EU*: economic reconstruction, funding of human rights programmes and projects, European Union Police Mission (EUPM): first EU police mission, took over from UN Civilian Police (IPTF) on 1 January 2003 in accordance with SC Res. 1423 of 12 July 2002
- *Council of Europe*: training and assistance activities
- Also active: World Bank, UNESCO, WHO, UNDP, UNICEF, WFP, ICRC

Comments

Marked improvement of the human rights situation since 1995, yet Bosnian politicians not ready to take 'ownership', i.e. full responsibility for peace process; High Representative still has to make extensive use of his 'Bonn powers' (granted by the PIC in December 1997) to impose laws, remove politicians and functionaries from office and de facto govern the country

Dayton constitution only transitional solution: too complex; ethnic/religious parities established in political bodies; entities vested with too much power; joint institutions need strengthening

Major problems of cooperation and coordination between different agencies

International community not yet ready for a new initiative to establish a sustainable peace in the entire region ('Dayton 2')

16. HUMAN RIGHTS AND THE MAINTENANCE OF PEACE AND SECURITY

CASEBOX 15

16.10. SELF-DETERMINATION AND UN TRANSITIONAL ADMINISTRATION IN EAST TIMOR (UNTAET)

Context and history

1974: Portuguese revolution: chaotic 'decolonization process', Portuguese in East Timor withdraw from Dili to Atauro (1975)

1975: Fretilin (Revolutionary Front for an Independent East Timor) declares independence on 28 November; Indonesia invades and occupies East Timor on 7 December

1991: Massacre of mourners (more than 100 dead) at Santa Cruz cemetery in Dili (capital of East Timor), filmed and photographed by international journalists

1992: Fretilin leader *Xanana Gusmão* arrested and detained by Indonesians (until 1999)

1996: Nobel peace prize awarded to human rights activist *José Ramos Horta* (present Minister of Foreign Affairs) and Bishop *Carlos Belo*

May 1998: President *Suharto* of Indonesia overthrown, succeeded by President *Habibie* who offers autonomy status to East Timor, later adds option of independence if autonomy is rejected

1999: further massacres in Liquica by militia with Indonesian military support and in Dili

Agreements between Indonesia and Portugal

Signed in New York on 5 May 1999: the two parties entrust the UNSG to organize and conduct a 'popular consultation' in order to ascertain whether the East Timorese people accepted or rejected a special autonomy for East Timor within Indonesia

- **UNAMET (United Nations Mission in East Timor)**, SC Res. 1246 of 11 June 1999

July 1999: registration for referendum, ballot on 30 August (450,000 electorate, but about 60,000 IDPs), approximately 99 per cent voted, 200 voting posts, 150 international observers

4 September 1999: results announced: 78.5 per cent for independence, rejecting autonomy within Indonesia – violence by militia and Indonesian military (TNI) begins, more than 10,000 killed

- **INTERFET (International Force for East Timor)**, SC Res. 1264 of 15 September 1999

Humanitarian intervention by a multinational force to restore peace and security, to protect UNAMET and to facilitate humanitarian assistance

19 September 1999: Indonesian government accepts result of referendum

20 September 1999: INTERFET arrives in East Timor under Australian command, ends massacres and re-establishes security

- **UNTAET (United Nations Transitional Administration for East Timor)**, SC Res. 1272 of 25 October 1999

16.10. SELF-DETERMINATION AND UN TRANSITIONAL ADMINISTRATION IN EAST TIMOR

Maximum strength: approximately 9,000 personnel
31 October 1999: last Indonesian troops leave East Timor
September 2000: killings of UNHCR workers in Atambua, West Timor
August 2001: constituent assembly elections; Fretilin wins largest share
January 2002: special court set up in Indonesia to try human rights abuses by military, truth commission established in East Timor
14 April 2002: presidential elections: *Xanana Gusmão* elected (more than 80 per cent)
20 May 2002: declaration of independence, application for UN membership, UNTAET downscaled to UNMISET
27 September 2002: East Timor admitted as the 191st member of the United Nations

- **UNMISET (UN Mission of Support in East Timor)**, SC Res. 1410 of 17 May 2002
  Provides assistance and contributes to security and human rights
  Strength: 5,000 military, 1,250 police, 100 civilian personnel

Mandate of UNTAET

Full responsibility for the administration of East Timor during its transition to independence (October 1999 to May 2002):
- to provide security, maintain law and order and protect human rights
- to establish an effective administration
- to assist in the development of civil and social services
- to coordinate humanitarian and development assistance
- to support capacity-building for self government

Comments

Despite the massacres after the referendum, the four UN operations can be considered successful in implementing the right to self-determination in this former Portuguese colony, as well as in establishing the necessary governmental and human rights structures

As international military protection was refused by Indonesia for the referendum, the UN was forced to take a certain security risk

Part of the success was due to rapid humanitarian intervention under Australian command as provided by the Security Council

No effective criminal prosecution of perpetrators in the absence of international tribunal; special court set up by Indonesia too weak

16. HUMAN RIGHTS AND THE MAINTENANCE OF PEACE AND SECURITY

CASEBOX 16

16.11. HUMAN RIGHTS PROTECTION BY THE SECURITY COUNCIL AS A DIRECT CONSEQUENCE OF INTERNATIONAL PEACE MAKING: CASE STUDY IRAQ

Context and History

The *Kurdish minority* in Iraq lives mainly in the mountainous region in the north east of the country. Although Iraq has recognized the Kurdish claim to a voice in internal affairs to a greater extent than Turkey or Iran, it has also exerted more direct and brutal repression on them when faced with political opposition. The Iran – Iraq war resulted in brutal attacks on Iraqi Kurd civilians culminating in chemical weapons attacks on Kurdish villages. Many were relocated into government built 'collective towns'. In August and September of 1988, 55,000 Kurds fled from Iraq to Turkey.

The *Shiite Arabs* in the marshlands in the south of the country (Marsh Arabs) were also persecuted in Iraq; during the Iran-Iraq war a number of leading Shiite Muslims were imprisoned and killed in mass executions. As work resumed on the canal project to drain the marshland the entire way of life of the population was threatened; Iraq accused them of giving shelter to political dissidents and entertaining political links with the Shiite leadership in Iran.

Iraqi Invasion of Kuwait and Operation Desert Storm

2 August 1990: The Iraqi military forces of dictator *Saddam Hussein* invade and occupy Kuwait; SC Res. 660 demands immediate withdrawal of Iraqi forces

6 August 1990: SC Res. 661 imposes mandatory wide ranging economic sanctions on Iraq

29 November 1990: SC Res. 678 authorizes the use of all necessary means to restore international peace and security in the area

16 January 1991: US led *Operation Desert Storm* begins with massive air attacks on Iraqi targets

28 February 1991: hostilities suspended, Iraq withdraws (11 April, official cease-fire)

3 April 1991: SC Res. 687 provides for the demarcation of border, PoW releases, compensation payments, and demands that Iraq declare and destroy its chemical, biological and missile capability and submit to inspection; UN Special Commission on Iraq established *(UNSCOM)* to carry out on site weapons inspection with the assistance of the International Atomic Energy Authority (IAEA)

9 April 1991: SC Res. 689 establishes UN Iraq-Kuwait Observer Mission *(UNIKOM)* to monitor the demilitarized zone; withdrawn in March 2003

March/April 1991: uprisings by both Kurds in the north and Shiites in the south crushed: huge refugee flows to the north: an estimated 1.5 million Kurds flee to Turkey and Iran

16.11. Human Rights Protection by the Security Council as a Direct Consequence of International Peace Making: Case Study Iraq

Security Council Protection of Human Rights

- SC Res. 688 of 5 April 1991 condemns the repression of the Iraqi civilian population, the consequences of which (massive refugee flows) threaten international peace and security in the region, and demands that Iraq immediately end repression
- On the basis of SC Res. 688, the SC declares no fly zones for Iraqi aircraft in the north (Operation Northern Watch for the protection of the Kurdish population) and south (Operation Southern Watch for the protection of the Shiite Muslims); as from 1996, the no fly zones covered about one-third of Iraqi territory; enforcement of no fly zones by allied air forces operating primarily from Turkey; increase in retaliatory bombings; international protection of Iraqi civilian population in no fly zones continues until US led invasion of Iraq in spring 2003
- 20 March to 14 April 2003: US and UK led forces, without explicit authorization of the SC, invade Iraq and overthrow the regime of *Saddam Hussein* in reaction to non-cooperation with UN weapons inspectors (UNSCOM) and alleged development of weapons of mass destruction

Comments

Although the regime of *Saddam Hussein* has had one of the worst human rights records worldwide since the early 1980s, and even used chemical weapons against its Kurdish population in 1988, the international community at that time did not react (not even by a resolution in the UN Commission on Human Rights)

Only after the Iraqi invasion of Kuwait in 1990, the UN reacted by all means available under Chapter VII of the UN Charter (military intervention, economic sanctions, deployment of weapons inspectors, etc.) in order to restore international peace and security

In the aftermath of Operation Desert Storm, which led to the international isolation of the *Saddam Hussein* regime, also a number of UN measures for the protection of human rights (e.g. appointment of a Special Rapporteur by the Commission on Human Rights in 1991) have been taken

SC Res. 688 is the first resolution in which the SC explicitly defined the direct consequences of state repression against its own civilian population (i.e. massive refugee flows) as a threat to international peace and security in the sense of article 39 of the UN Charter and, consequently, created 'safe havens' (no fly zones) for the protection of human rights which have been enforced for more than 10 years by military action

The final overthrow of the *Saddam Hussein* regime by an US led military intervention in spring 2003 has many political and economic reasons, but has certainly not been motivated primarily by human rights concerns

CASEBOX 17

16.12. HUMANITARIAN INTERVENTION FOR THE PROTECTION OF HUMAN RIGHTS IN 'FAILED STATES': CASE STUDY SOMALIA

Context and History

In early 1991 the repressive regime of *Mohamed Siad Barre* in Somalia has been overthrown by armed opposition forces. However, no accepted new political leadership emerged. Instead, fighting between different armed groups and 'clans' continued, leading to the collapse of all central government structures. The situation was aggravated by severe famine caused by long draught; in 1992 about half of the country's population (4.5 million people) has been seriously threatened with starvation. In the end an estimated 300,000 people died of malnutrition and related diseases, 2 million people fled the country or were internally displaced. The UN Secretary General called it the 'worst humanitarian crisis in the world'.

1991: after the defeat of President *Siad Barre*, rival opposition groups, in particular General *Mohamed Fahrah Aidid* and *Ali Mahdi*, claim control and authority over Somalia. An independent Somaliland Republic is proclaimed in the north of the country, but is recognized neither by Somali groups nor by the international community. Heavy fighting continues, especially in the capital of Mogadishu and in the north despite famine worsening, making international food relief efforts extremely difficult.

January 1992: SC Res. 733 imposes arms embargo

March 1992: SC Res. 746 urges continuation of humanitarian work; deployment of UN observers to monitor cease-fire

UNOSOM (I):

SC Res. 751 of 24 April 1992 establishes the United Nations Operation in Somalia (UNOSOM I); mandate extended by SC Res. 767 and 775 of July and August 1992

Mandate

- Monitor cease-fire in Mogadishu through 50 military observers
- Provide protection and security for UN personnel, equipment, supplies at seaports and airports in Mogadishu
- Escort deliveries of humanitarian supplies from ports to city distribution centres

UN Secretary General appoints *Mohamed Sahnoun* (Algeria) as Special Representative for Somalia; mandate is expanded to include additional Somali areas for protection and to increase strength to 4,219 troops; first group of security personnel arrives in Mogadishu only on 14 September 1992, almost five months after UNOSOM establishment.

Secretary General proposes a 100 day action programme for accelerated humanitarian assistance, however, disagreement between UN and Somali factions continues, *Sahnoun* resigns.

16.12. Humanitarian Intervention for the Protection of Human Rights in 'Failed States': Case Study Somalia

October/November 1992: General *Aidid* demands withdrawal of the Pakistani UNOSOM battalion; attacks against UNOSOM troops and regular fighting with Somali forces; the security situation deteriorates rapidly, convoys of relief organizations, warehouses, vehicles are looted, relief staff abducted

United Task Force (UNITAF) – 'Operation Restore Hope'

3 December 1992: SC Res. 794 authorizes UN member states to use 'all necessary means' to create a secure environment for the delivery of humanitarian aid

4 December 1992: United States launches Operation Restore Hope: a United Task Force (UNITAF) is established with military forces from various states under US command (not UN);

9 December 1992: First UNITAF (night) landing of US marines confronted by CNN television lights; despite 37,000 UNITAF troops the security situation in Somalia improved only slightly, attacks on UN, relief and NGO personnel still continued; preparations for transition from UNITAF to another UN operation

UNOSOM (II):

SC Res. 814 of 26 March 1993 establishes United Nations Operation in Somalia (UNOSOM II)

Mandate

- Establish a secure environment throughout Somalia by appropriate action, including enforcement measures and disarmament
- Monitor cessation of hostilities
- Prevent resumption of violence, seize unauthorized small arms, clear mines, assist in repatriation of refugees, rebuilding of economy and institutional structures
- Protect personnel and equipment of UN, ICRC, NGOs
- Provide humanitarian and other assistance to the people of Somalia
- Assist the process of national reconciliation

Strength: 28,000 military personnel (supported by 17,700 troops of the US Joint Task Force in Somalia) and 2,800 civilian staff

May 1993: UNITAF hands over powers to UNOSOM (II), much more comprehensive mandate, but not successful in reconciling the Somali factions; instead, the conflict between UN troops and General *Aidid* escalate with UN forces (Pakistan, US) being killed, but also becoming involved in serious human rights violations against civilians

March 1995: UNOSOM (II) is withdrawn from Somalia after 147 of its staff killed and several hundred Somalis died in the conflict

16. HUMAN RIGHTS AND THE MAINTENANCE OF PEACE AND SECURITY

Comments

SC Res. 794 (1992) is the first UN resolution to explicitly authorize military intervention within a country without invitation or consent of government concerned, as no responsible government was in power (failed state/collapsed state)

Gross human rights violations were indirectly used to justify the situation being determined as a 'threat to international peace' (Ch. VII), as the 'human tragedy' in Somalia, including mass refugee movements affected the entire region

UNOSOM failed to establish a secure environment and to promote the process of national reconciliation; nevertheless, UNOSOM was successful in providing and protecting humanitarian assistance to the starving population; an estimated quarter of a million lives were saved

Some lessons learnt from Somalia/UNOSOM:

Importance of comprehensive and realistic mandate – what started as a very limited support operation for humanitarian assistance turned into a full military intervention with the objective to seize General *Aidid*

A clear mandate requires clear responsibilities – in Somalia no consistent policy existed with regard to disarmament of warring factions and arrests

Importance of a strong and realistic political vision on future development of the country as well as clear long-term strategy, including an 'exit strategy'

Question of liability of the UN for violations committed by UN troops, only Canada, Belgium and Germany opened investigations against their own personnel

Question of impartiality of aid delivery in situation of conflict

'The CNN factor': again, as in the Gulf War, the increasing role of the media

Failure of UNOSOM/UNITAF had serious repercussions on responses to future conflicts (Rwanda)

CASEBOX 18

16.13. THE TANZANIAN INTERVENTION IN UGANDA IN 1979: A 'HUMANITARIAN INTERVENTION'?

In spring 1979, the Tanzanian army invaded Uganda from the south supported by exiled Ugandan militia, forcing President *Idi Amin Dada* to flee the country and effectively ending eight years of *Amin's* military dictatorship.

Context and history

1962: Uganda gains independence from the United Kingdom, *Milton Obote* becomes its first Prime Minister; growing tensions between local groups and the central government lead to armed conflict, military expenditure triples over three years.

16.13. THE TANZANIAN INTERVENTION IN UGANDA IN 1979: A 'HUMANITARIAN INTERVENTION'?

1971: while President *Obote* is attending a conference abroad, Colonel *Idi Amin* seizes power; after some initial popular moves (including release of a few political prisoners) and positive reactions from western countries, *Amin* dissolves the National Assembly and rules by decree; comprehensive intelligence and security network; the entire population is brought under jurisdiction of military tribunals; human rights and political activities are suspended.

1972: Nationalization campaign: *Amin* announces that all Ugandan Asians (Indians, etc.), a prosperous community brought to Uganda by the United Kingdom to build the transport system and now dominating the retail trade, have to leave the country within 90 days; in fact tens of thousands of Asians are expelled, leaving behind their shops and enterprises, all United Kingdom companies are nationalized without compensation. *Amin* supported by Libya and some Gulf states; first invasion attempt by pro-*Obote* guerrillas launched from Tanzania fails.

1973-1978: Repression of opposition intensifies, massacres on civilians and students, murder of the Anglican archbishop; several initiatives by non-governmental human rights organizations to make UN act against the *Amin* regime, making *Amin* responsible for killing more than 100,000 people.

1978/79: In October 1978 – presumably to prevent outbreak of a mutiny in the army – Ugandan troops cross borders and devastate Tanzanian villages; the Tanzanian army repulses the attacks and enters Uganda; President *Nyerere* of Tanzania convenes a conference (March 1979) of all major Ugandan opposition groups to agree on a common political agenda against *Amin*. In the meantime Tanzanian troops joined by guerrilla forces of *Yoweri Museveni* (President of Uganda since 1986) and others continue to advance in Uganda.

1979: Despite some last minute support from Libyan mercenaries and oil companies' petrol supplies *Idi Amin's* army has to retreat; in April 1979, Kampala is taken; *Amin* escapes to Libya (later to Saudi Arabia) and *Yusuf Lule*, a scientist, is sworn in as Uganda's new president.

The Organization of African Unity (OAU) condemns Tanzania for violating the principle of non-interference in a state's internal affairs.

Comments

Although the intervention by Tanzania brought to an end one of the most repressive regimes in Africa and is often quoted as a successful humanitarian intervention for the protection of human rights, Tanzania did not rely on humanitarian arguments or human rights violations to justify its action.

The principal justification Tanzania provided was that the invasion was a response to an earlier act of aggression on the part of Uganda against its own territory, and Tanzania only acted in self-defence in conformity with article 51 of the UN Charter.

The invasion by Tanzanian troops was, therefore, not an action provided for within the UN framework of collective security.

The OAU's critical reaction shows that the principle of state sovereignty was then still regarded as almost absolute; Tanzania did not wish to set a case of precedence for other states to copy.

16. HUMAN RIGHTS AND THE MAINTENANCE OF PEACE AND SECURITY

CASEBOX 19

16.14. NATO HUMANITARIAN INTERVENTION FOR THE PROTECTION OF HUMAN RIGHTS: CASE STUDY KOSOVO

NATO intervention in Kosovo has been qualified as 'humanitarian intervention', but it took place without specific authorization from the UN Security Council. There is considerable discrepancy between the legality of this intervention and its legitimacy that poses serious challenges for the development of human rights protection in the 21st century.

Context and history

1974 – 1989: Kosovo enjoys extensive autonomy, which is later revoked after the rise in Serbian nationalism and the coming to power of *Slobodan Milosevic*

1990-1997: Discriminatory policies and human rights abuses in Kosovo result in campaign of passive resistance by Kosovo Albanians. The 1995 Dayton Peace Agreement for Bosnia and Herzegovina does not address the Kosovo crisis.

Late 1997 – 1998: Acts of armed revolt by Kosovo Albanians meet with severe response from Serb security forces. 'Kosovo Liberation Army' (KLA) grows in size and effectiveness. Human rights abuses in Kosovo increase. Self-defence militias form independently in villages.

Spring/summer 1998: Large-scale military operations against KLA result in destruction of Albanian villages; 'ethnic cleansing' operations carried out. Over 250,000 are driven from their homes.

March 1998: SC Res. 1160 imposes an arms embargo on Yugoslavia and calls for autonomy and 'meaningful self-administration' in Kosovo.

June 1998: First public consideration of military intervention by NATO. OSCE border monitors begin to report substantial violence along the Kosovo-Albanian border.

September 1998: SC Res. 1199 defines the situation as 'a threat to peace and security in the region' under Chapter VII, demands a cease-fire and the withdrawal of Yugoslav forces 'used for civilian repression'

October 1998: NATO votes to authorize air strikes if Serbian security forces do not withdraw from Kosovo within 96 hours.

October 1998: United States Special Envoy *Richard Holbrooke* brokers agreement to scale down Serb forces in Kosovo, allow refugees home, allow OSCE *Kosovo Verification Mission* (KVM) into the territory with an envisaged presence of 2000 staff. SC Res. 1203 affirms the agreement. SC Res. 1207 calls for Yugoslav authorities to comply with request of ICTY for cooperation, including arrests.

December 1998/early 1999: sporadic hostilities and apparent preparations for repetition and intensification of 'ethnic cleansing' operations.

February 1999: *Conference of Rambouillet* (Paris) offers set of constitutional agreements for an autonomous Kosovo. Serbia refuses proposals for 'enabling force' of 30,000 NATO troops in Kosovo.

March 1999: OSCE withdraws Kosovo Verification Mission in the light of deteriorating security situation. There are massive preparations for Yugoslav/Serbian military intervention in Kosovo.

16.14. NATO HUMANITARIAN INTERVENTION FOR THE PROTECTION OF HUMAN RIGHTS: CASE STUDY KOSOVO

24 March 1999: *NATO alliance begins air strikes* against strategic targets. President *Clinton* announces intention not to use ground troops. Assumption is that a relatively short campaign will bring *Milosevic* back to the negotiation table.

Instead, coordinated campaign of 'ethnic cleansing' at unprecedented scale begins in major towns and villages. Over 90 per cent of the Kosovo Albanian population displaced. Public opinion in western states supports NATO intervention. Objectives shift to include the return of refugees. Bomb targets now include military-industrial structures.

June 1999: Serb parliament formally approves a peace plan based on G8 principles. On 10 June, NATO suspends air strikes after 78 days. FRY troops withdraw. SC Res. 1244 establishes the framework for *UN civilian interim administration (UNMIK)* and the establishment of an international security presence (KFOR) under NATO command.

Comments

NATO forced FRY to withdraw army and police from Kosovo; stopped the systematic suppression of the Albanian people in Kosovo; established framework for UN transitional administration and overthrow of *Milosevic* regime.

Demonstration of strength and cohesion of NATO military alliance.

Failure of international community to respond to early warning evidence of widespread human rights abuses and political unrest in Kosovo.

Civilian casualties: Though difficult to quantify, there is evidence of around 500 civilian deaths as a result of NATO bombing during the 78 day campaign; high profile bombing of two IDP convoys, a passenger train, and civilian deaths in the bombing of RTS (Serbian radio station); no NATO casualties.

Failure to deal with KLA as perpetrators of human rights abuses in wake of Serbian withdrawal.

Final status of Kosovo remains unresolved even in 2003 (four years after NATO intervention); inter-ethnic relations remain extremely tense during UN transitional administration and up until the present day.

Framework of principles of humanitarian intervention required as *ultima ratio* for enforcement of human rights; principles to be incorporated in UN mechanisms.

Need for comprehensive reform of UN: Changes to the veto right? Expansion of the Security Council?

Arguments for and against intervention

Against

- Only UN Security Council acting under Chapter VII can authorize the use of force; article 53 UN Charter allows regional organizations to engage in enforcement actions provided that they do so on the basis of SC authorization.
- NATO decisions to intervene taken without obtaining or even seeking a SC Resolution;

- No secondary appeal to the General Assembly: under the 'Uniting for Peace' Resolution, GA would have been authorized to act in the event that the SC cannot meet its obligations to address threats to international peace and security unanimously.
- NATO constituting treaty does not provide for defence measures, unless one or more members are exposed to an armed attack. That was not the case in Kosovo.
- Therefore: intervention illegal under present international law.

For

- The moral priority of preventing gross human rights abuses, genocide and crimes against humanity justifies humanitarian intervention even when SC cannot find political consensus. Moral imperative clear: need for action in the face of gross human rights violations
- Intervention without the approval of the SC was necessary: Russia and China made clear that any authorization by the SC to use force would be vetoed. No realistic alternative to NATO action in 1999.
- Implied authorization to use force once a 'threat to international peace and security' has been identified under Chapter VII (difficult to justify at this point in time).
- Customary principles of international law permit interventions in cases of extreme humanitarian necessity.

CASEBOX 20

16.15. HUMAN RIGHTS AND THE FIGHT AGAINST TERRORISM: CASE STUDY AFGHANISTAN

Context and History

8 December 1998: Afghanistan mentioned as terrorist safe haven (SC Res. 1214)

15 October 1999: *Osama Bin Laden* first mentioned as sponsor of terrorism (SC Res. 1267), terrorism – human rights relationship stressed

Prior to 2001: 'Deep concern' of SC over human rights in Afghanistan, especially concerning women and mass executions (on both sides of the civil war); but requirements for a 'humanitarian intervention' not present

30 July 2001: SC Res. 1363 declares situation in Afghanistan threat to international peace and security

11 September 2001: terrorist attacks on New York and Washington (more than 3,000 dead), *Osama Bin Laden's* terrorist organization *Al-Qa'ida* suspected of having pulled the wires

12 September 2001: SC Res. 1368 declares 11 September attacks as grounds for self-defence under article 51 of the UN Charter, thereby enabling future unilateral United States action

NATO for the first time ever declares applicability of article 5 of the Washington Treaty (mutual collective defence)

16.15. Human Rights and the Fight against Terrorism: Case Study Afghanistan

28 September 2001: SC Res. 1373 demands comprehensive cooperation by all states to combat threats to international peace and security caused by terrorist acts; Counter-Terrorism Committee (CTC) established to monitor implementation of the resolution by member states; member states to issue reports on implementation

October 2001: US air strikes are launched against Taliban targets in Afghanistan

November 2001: Northern Alliance enters Kabul after Taliban forces flee the capital; end of Taliban regime; UK and US troops put down a revolt by foreign Taliban prisoners in a military barracks near Mazar-I-Sharif. Amnesty International calls for an inquiry

5 December 2001: Agreement on Provisional Arrangements in Afghanistan pending the re-establishment of permanent government institutions signed in Bonn; contains references to human rights (Human Rights Commission, education, UN power to investigate)

20 December 2001: SC Res. 1386 authorizes the establishment of an International Security Assistance Force (ISAF), which is, however, restricted to maintain security only in Kabul and its surrounding areas

22 December 2001: *Hamid Karzai* sworn in as Prime Minister of the new Interim Afghan Administration, established in Bonn

January 2002: Taliban and *Al-Qa'ida* prisoners are flown to a US naval base in Guantanamo Bay (Cuba); infringement of basic international humanitarian and human rights standards (chains and cages; unlimited preventive detention without access to judicial protection); all prisoners initially denied prisoner of war status under Geneva Conventions 1949 (no 'competent tribunal' under article 5, 3rd Geneva Convention)

April 2002: *Zahir Shah*, former Afghan King, returns to Kabul, convenes the *Loya Jirga* (traditional Afghan assembly) on 10 June 2002, *Karzai* confirmed as prime minister; *Loya Jirga* is to pass a new constitution and call for elections at a later point in time.

Comments

- Terrorism constitutes one of the major contemporary threats to human rights and international security
- Anti-terrorist measures also constitute a major threat to human rights (example: Camp 'X-Ray' at Guantanamo Bay)
- US led 'war against terrorism', including military intervention in Afghanistan, is based on the right to self-defence under article 51 UN Charter rather than on the system of collective security; gross and systematic violations of human rights by the Taliban regime only used as additional argument to justify the overthrow of this regime (main argument was link to terrorism)
- Aims of destroying the *Al-Qa'ida* network of *Osama Bin Laden* in Afghanistan and of removing the Taliban regime achieved; but the efforts of the international community to assist the Afghan people in achieving sustainable peace and development, democracy, rule of law and human rights are very weak ('light footprint approach' of the Special Representative of the UNSG, *Lakhdar Brahimi*)

16. HUMAN RIGHTS AND THE MAINTENANCE OF PEACE AND SECURITY

LITBOX 16

LITERATURE

African Rights 1995, Rwanda: 'A Waste of Hope': The United Nations Field Operation, London

Amnesty International, Peace-Keeping and Human Rights, January 1994, AI Index: IOR 40/01/94

Bell, Christine 2000, Peace Agreements and Human Rights, Oxford

Durch, William, J. (Ed.) 1993, The Evolution of UN Peacekeeping: Case Studies and Comparative Analysis, New York

Boutros-Ghali, Boutros 1992, An Agenda for Peace, Report of the Secretary-General pursuant to the statement adopted by the Summit Meeting of the Security Council on 31 January 1992, New York

Henkin, Alice H (Ed.) 1995, Honoring Human Rights and Keeping the Peace: Lessons from El Salvador, Cambodia and Haiti (Aspen I), Washington D.C.

Henkin, Alice H (Ed.) 1998, Honoring Human Rights: From Peace to Justice: Recommendations to the International Community (Aspen II), Washington D.C.

Henkin, Alice H (Ed.) 2000, Honoring Human Rights under International Mandates: Lessons from Bosnia, Kosovo and East Timor, Washington D.C.

Katayanagai, Mari 2002, Human Rights Functions of United Nations Peacekeeping Operations, The Hague

Martin, Ian 1998, A New Frontier: The Early Experience and Future of International Human Rights Field Operations, in: Netherlands Quarterly of Human Rights, Vol. 16, 121-139

Nowak, Manfred 2000, Lessons for the International Human Rights Regime from the Yugoslav Experience, in: Collected Courses of the Academy of European Law, Vol. VIII/2, 141-208

Otunnu, Olara and *Doyle*, Michael (Eds.) 1998, Peacekeeping and Peacemaking for the New Century, Lanham

INTERNET

www.un.org/Depts/dpko - UN Department of *Peace-keeping operations*

www.kosovocommission.org - Independent International Commission on Kosovo: The Kosovo Report

www.oscebih.org - OSZE-Mission in Bosnia and Herzegovina

www.ohr.int - Office of the High Representative in Bosnia and Herzegovina

www.aims.org.pk - Afghanistan Information Management Service (UNDP, OCHA)

17. CHALLENGES FOR THE FUTURE

Since the Second World War, the international community has developed an impressive **normative framework** of minimum standards and procedures for the universal and regional protection of human rights. **Empowerment** of the individual is the very essence of human rights, and participation, non-discrimination and accountability its most important elements. Through human rights, individuals can be empowered to participate in the decision-making processes, which are of direct relevance to their lives, to have equal and non-discriminatory access to those facilities, goods and services that are essential to live in dignity, and to hold governments and other power-holders accountable for not living up to their international obligations to respect, fulfil and protect their human rights. An increasing number of people in all regions of the world, including the poor and other socially excluded, vulnerable and marginalized segments of society, understand the power of the human rights approach as a means to solve their problems. In a global society, governments are no longer the only duty-holders. The so-called international community, consisting of governments, intergovernmental organizations, transnational corporations and the global civil society, has a common responsibility to prevent and to stop major human rights violations, wherever they occur.

The standard setting activities and development of traditional procedures for the international protection of human rights during the period of the Cold War had a major impact on the **global awareness of human rights**. Through this normative framework and its interpretation and application by human rights courts and other international monitoring bodies, we know today what our human rights are and which obligations derive from these rights. At the same time, these reporting, complaints, inquiry and fact-finding procedures (12.), notwithstanding many weaknesses and shortcomings (13.), together with the 'mobilization of shame' by NGOs (11.) and the media, assisted by a global information and communication network, enable us to have a fairly accurate insight into the factual situation of human rights all over the world. In the early days of human rights protection, governments, by simply dismissing allegations of human rights violations and denying international fact-finding missions entrance in their territory, had an opportunity to hide the real situation from the outside world and often even from the majority of their own people. Today, this is no longer possible. We know about the extent of human rights violations even in the remotest corners of our planet, and governments are aware of the fact that the international community knows what they are doing.

This **global knowledge** as such has a certain protective and preventive effect, at least on governments that care about their international reputation. After all, the combined efforts of domestic opposition forces and pressure from international human rights monitoring bodies, brought about many improvements even during the time of the Cold War. Apart from all the minor changes in most countries of the world as a result of judgments, decisions and reports of international human rights bodies, some more radical changes can be attributed, at least to some extent, to international human rights pressure: the dismantling of the Greek military regime in light of sanctions by the Council of Europe; of the apartheid system in southern Africa in light of UN sanctions, of many Latin American military regimes in reaction to pressure from the OAS and UN; and the 'velvet revolutions' in Central and Eastern Europe that were encouraged and facilitated by the Helsinki process of the CSCE. But at the same time, the human rights situation has deteriorated in many parts of the world without any effective action taken by the international community. Although the international system for the protection of human rights was developed in reaction to the Nazi holocaust, even further genocides have not been prevented, as the tragic events in Cambodia, Tibet, Bosnia and Herzegovina and Rwanda illustrate.

One of the major challenges for the international human rights regime in the 21st century, therefore, remains the **effective enforcement of human rights** against those governments that are not willing to comply with their international human rights obligations and respective decisions and recommendations of international human rights monitoring bodies. Since the end of the Cold War, binding economic and other sanctions have been adopted by the UN Security Council against an increasing number of those regimes that most systematically violate human rights (16.3.), and some of the worst regimes (in Haiti, the former Yugoslavia, Afghanistan and Iraq) have even been removed by international military force. If these measures were the result of a collective effort of the United Nations to protect the people of these countries against further systematic human rights violations, one could speak about a veritable break-through towards international enforcement of human rights. A closer look at these cases (16.11., 16.14., 16.15.) shows, however, that these events were usually the result of unilateral action by the United States (with only reluctant or no support from the UN) for a variety of motives, of which human rights were certainly not the decisive one. The real reasons seemed to be the prevention of refugee flows, economic interests (e.g. oil supply), military aims (e.g. preventing the development of weapons of mass destruction) or the fight against terrorism.

Economic sanctions and **humanitarian interventions** are legitimate measures of enforcing human rights against certain governments, but only under certain conditions:
- They should only be taken into account as a measure of last resort;
- They need the authorization of the UN Security Council under Chapter VII of the UN Charter; and
- They require a long-term involvement of international peace-keeping and peace-building efforts as a follow-up.

Whether unilateral action by the United States and other NATO states constitutes a violation of the UN Charter (as has been argued in the case of Kosovo in 1999 (16.14.) and Iraq in 2003), or not, it is in any case a strong indicator for an urgent need to reform the decision making structures of the United Nations. In fact, the Security Council has not lived up to its global responsibility of taking action against a considerable number of governments, which for many years have committed gross and systematic human rights violations and, thereby, constitute a threat to international peace and security. Following the recommendations of the Human Rights Commission, treaty-monitoring bodies, the High Commissioner for Human Rights, and others, the Security Council is the sole body that is empowered to take binding decisions under international law, and as such has the ultimate responsibility for enforcing human rights.

An effective collective enforcement of human rights against the will of the governments concerned would, of course, also serve as the strongest tool for the **prevention of human rights violations** in the future. As effective police work is not so much aimed at investigating crime and bringing the perpetrators to justice, but at preventing crime at the earliest possible stage by addressing its root causes, international coercive action should not only react to gross and systematic human rights violations but rather attempt to interfere at an early stage in order to prevent major escalations of conflicts and violations of human rights. In practice, most of the modern field operations with a human rights component so far carried out by the United Nations and other organizations (16.) were of a reactive nature, and the few preventive operations, such as in Burundi and Macedonia (14.1. and 14.2.), are far from encouraging. There is an urgent need to link the existing and, in principle, well functioning early warning mechanisms in the field of conflict prevention and human rights to the most powerful political bodies of inter-governmental organizations that are capable of taking effective early action for the prevention of human rights violations, including the authorization of preventive deployment forces.

Prevention also means to address the **root causes of systematic human rights violations**, such as misuse of power, corruption, impunity, lack of democratic structures based on the rule of law, poverty, nationalism, racism and religious intolerance leading to social, ethnic and religious tensions and violent conflicts. An analysis of these root causes illustrates the close relationship between human rights, peace, development, democracy, the rule of law and good governance (3.1.5. to 3.1.7.). It is an empirical fact that well-functioning democracies based on the rule of law are less likely to engage in armed conflicts with each other and usually provide a higher standard of human rights to their people compared with dictatorships and police states. An effective strategy of preventing human rights violations in the 21st century should, therefore, aim at **institution-building** in the fields of **democratization**, the **rule of law** (including the judiciary, the police and prison administration), **good governance** and special institutions for the protection of human rights, such as national human rights commissions, ombuds institutions, human rights courts, truth and reconciliation commissions etc.

Poverty is not only one of the most serious causes of human rights violations, but also constitutes a violation of a wide variety of human rights, including the rights to life, dignity, privacy, security, food, health, housing, clothing and education. Worldwide, roughly one billion people lack adequate shelter and access to safe drinking water, and approximately 800 million people are illiterate, malnourished and lack access to health services. The eradication of poverty, therefore, constitutes the biggest challenge for the credibility of the international

17. CHALLENGES FOR THE FUTURE

human rights regime. As reaffirmed in the **Millennium Development Goals** that were adopted by the world's leaders in 2000, the eradication of poverty constitutes today's overarching goal for the development policies of the United Nations, the World Bank, IMF, OECD, EU and bilateral development agencies (3.1.6., 4.4.8.7., 4.5.6.; 9.4.). The international community has set the goal for 2015 to reduce by half the proportion of people living in extreme poverty and suffering from hunger. The success or failure of this initiative will be a good test for the seriousness of the international community to comply with its own targets and benchmarks. There is no doubt that a **human rights approach to poverty reduction strategies**, as advocated by the UN High Commissioner for Human Rights, will enhance these strategies by providing them with a normative framework, consistency, sustainability and accountability mechanisms. The human rights approach also underlines that in a global society the eradication of poverty has become a global responsibility. As national governments are no longer the only power-holders responsible for the poverty of the people living on their territory, they are no longer the only actors to be held accountable for the gross and systematic human rights violations implied by extreme poverty. A concerted effort of governments in both rich and poor countries, inter-governmental organizations, transnational corporations and the global civil society will be necessary to achieve the ambitious Millennium Development Goals.

This brings us to another major challenge for the contemporary international human rights regime: How to hold **non-state actors** accountable for human rights violations? There are many reasons why human rights abuses by non-state actors are on the increase, and in certain countries far outnumber those committed by state actors. The globalization process driven by neo-liberalist forces necessarily leads to a decreasing importance of the traditional nation-state model as compared to global actors which range from inter-governmental organizations and international financial institutions via transnational corporations to global networks of organized crime, trafficking in drugs and human beings and terrorism. The phenomenon of the so-called 'failed states', above all in Africa (16.12.), is the most obvious example of this trend. But even in highly developed and democratic states, the neo-liberalist policies of deregulation and privatization have led to an erosion of governmental power and responsibilities and the taking over of essential governmental functions (in the field of educational institutions, health services, social security, but even of internal security, policing and prison administration) by non-state actors. Another reason for the increase of human rights abuses by non-state actors is the fact they take place in the context of internal armed conflicts based on ethnic, religious or nationalistic tensions and intolerance.

The strategies of holding non-state actors accountable, of course, depend on their nature. **Inter-governmental organizations** should at least be held responsible for complying with the human rights standards that they have adopted for their own member states. When the European Union organs violate human rights, by issuing regulations and directives that are directly binding in the member states, the victims should have the same remedies at their disposal against the EU as against its member states. The same holds true for human rights violations committed by organs of United Nations interim administrations, as in Kosovo or East Timor (16.10. and 16.14.), NATO and other peace-keeping, peace-building and peace-making forces, or the World Bank and similar inter-governmental organizations.

Transnational corporations (TNCs) and other business enterprises, which resort to practices of child labour, forced labour, discrimination, restrictions on freedom of association and similar human rights violations, might be held accountable by exerting pressure on the governments of their 'seat-states' as well as the states in which they operate. In practice, however, governmental efforts (in particular by the governments of the countries in which TNCs operate) to force TNCs to comply with minimum human rights standards, have not proven to be highly effective. Consumer boycotts and the 'mobilization of shame' by international NGOs sometimes had a stronger effect and also have led to the adoption of voluntary codes of conduct and similar initiatives towards corporate social responsibility by the respective companies. These initiatives have been encouraged and supported by international action, such as the UN Global Compact, the OECD Guidelines for Multinational Enterprises and the draft 'Human Rights Principles and Responsibilities for Transnational Corporations and Other Business Enterprises' prepared by the UN Sub-Commission on Human Rights (4.4.1.6., 4.5.7.). Nevertheless, despite a certain progress achieved by these voluntary initiatives, more efficient mechanisms need to be put in place to create directly binding legal obligations for TNCs and similar non-state actors. In a world where the budget of many TNCs by far exceeds that of middle-sized states, and where these organizations are in fact much more powerful than many governments, it seems somewhat anachronistic that states should remain the only subjects of international law capable of signing and ratifying international treaties and assuming direct obligations under international law.

Another possibility of holding non-state actors accountable is to shift from exclusive state responsibility to **individual responsibility**. In the field of environmental law, **civil liability** for environmental crimes and disasters seems to be one of the most powerful tools for holding respective companies and individuals accountable and, thereby, forcing them to improve their safety mechanisms (e.g. for oil tankers). If individual torturers, and others along the chain of command are held personally liable to the victims for all the costs of social, medical, legal and psychological torture rehabilitation measures, which might last in serious cases for many years, this might have a far greater deterrent effect than holding the government accountable before a traditional human rights monitoring body or court. In a judgment of July 2002, a United States District Court in Florida awarded to three Salvadorian torture victims a total of 54.6 million USD for punitive and compensatory damages in a civil lawsuit filed against two former Ministers of Defence of El Salvador presently living in retirement in Florida (*Romagoza et al* v. *Garcia*). These claims were based on the United States Alien Tort Claims Act of 1789, which was seldom used until a United States court in 1980 awarded to the family of a young Paraguayan, who had been tortured to death in Paraguay, over 10 million USD damages against the policeman responsible (*Filartiga* v. *Pelia-Irala*). The Alien Tort Claims Act can also be used against non-state actors, and in recent years at least 25 separate lawsuits have been initiated before United States courts against prominent TNCs, such as Coca Cola, Exxon Mobil, Del Monte and Unocal for allegedly resorting to forced labour in Myanmar, for murder and torture in Indonesia, for using anti-union death squads in Colombia and Guatemala, etc. Similarly, some of the collective legal actions taken against banks and other private companies in Germany and Austria allegedly responsible for forced labour and other major human rights violations committed during the Nazi Holocaust proved successful despite having been initiated more than 50 years after.

One of the biggest achievements of the last decade was the rapid development of **international criminal law** and its application to perpetrators of gross and systematic human rights violations. The practice of the International Criminal Tribunals for the former Yugoslavia and Rwanda shows that, in addition to heads of state and government and other state officials, non-state actors (members of the Bosnian Serb or Bosnian Croat armed forces and paramilitary forces, 'private' genocidaires in Rwanda) have also been accused and sentenced for war crimes, genocide and crimes against humanity (15.4. and 15.5.). These ad hoc tribunals or the International Criminal Court (ICC), of course, also have jurisdiction in relation to officials of inter-governmental organizations and business enterprises, as well as to individual members of criminal organizations, guerrilla movements or terrorist networks. The individual criminal responsibility for serious human rights violations seems, therefore, one of the most promising possibilities to deter future human rights violations and to hold also non-state actors accountable. It is, therefore, of utmost importance that the ICC will be enabled to perform its tasks with the full support of the international community and individual governments (speeding up of the ratification process, allocation of sufficient budgetary resources, arrest and extradition of persons indicted by the ICC, non-interference with the independence of the Court and its Prosecutor, etc). Whereas the European Union has adopted a Common Position in support of the ICC (9.4.1.), the present US administration is engaged in a multi-pronged campaign to exempt its nationals from the jurisdiction of the Court and to undermine its authority (15.6.). It is a major challenge for the international human rights community to convince the current or the future United States administrations that this policy is simply wrong and based on false assumptions (15.). Since the ICC is only competent to deal with the most serious and systematic human rights violations, there is also a need for domestic courts and prosecutors to live up to their responsibility of bringing human rights criminals to justice in accordance with the principles of territorial, personal, and universal jurisdiction (15.1. – 15.3.).

The terrorist attacks of 11 September 2001 on the World Trade Centre and the Pentagon finally made it clear that organized international **terrorism** constitutes one of the major threats and challenges to human rights and international security in the 21st century. The relationship between terrorism and human rights can be approached from different angles. Terrorist attacks against civilians are not only a serious violation of many human rights, including the right to life, by well-organized non-state actors, but also constitute a crime against humanity if committed as part of a widespread or systematic attack. If such attacks are launched on the territory or by a citizen of a state party to the ICC Statute as from 1 July 2002, the ICC is in principle competent to prosecute these crimes. The high degree of organization and professionalism that is characteristic of modern terrorist networks, such as Al-Qa'ida, as well as the broad support they enjoy among the population and governments in some Islamic and other countries, created the fear among the population in the potential target countries, above all in the United States and Europe, that the self-fulfilling prophecy of *Samuel Huntington*'s 'clash of civilizations' might become true. These fears were supported and to some extent incited by the United States policy and rhetoric of having to fight a virtual 'war against terrorism'. The term 'war' implies a continuing emergency situation, which might justify far-reaching measures of derogating from human rights obligations (3.2.4.). In the United States and some European countries, serious discussions have even been initiated about the legitimacy of using torture methods against suspected terrorists, and most countries have enacted anti-terrorist legislation which authorize the police, intelligence and security forces to broadly interfere with most human rights, including the rights to personal liberty, fair trial, privacy, freedom of association and assembly. In particular, the mere suspicion of belonging to or supporting of a terrorist organization might trigger off a series of legal consequences, including deprivation of liberty for a prolonged period of time. Most notorious in this respect is the detention of suspected Taliban fighters and Al-Qa'ida supporters at the US military Camp 'X-Ray' at Guantanamo Bay in Cuba. Suspected terrorists have been kept there in preventive detention, without any access to a court, without being indicted, and without any protection by the US Constitution or relevant international human rights monitoring bodies, for an unlimited period of time, i.e. until the 'war against terrorism' might be over. Under the standards of the ECHR, even in exceptional circumstances of terrorism, every arrested person must be brought before a court within four days after the arrest at the latest. At the time of this writing, most Guantanamo detainees have been in detention without access to a court for more than one and a half years! In addition, the conditions of detention at Guantanamo Bay (chains and cages, extremely harsh interrogation techniques, etc.) amount to inhuman and degrading treatment, if not torture.

The fight against terrorism certainly is a legitimate ground for restricting human rights and even derogating from international obligations, **anti-terrorist measures nevertheless have to be in accordance with international law**. In particular, no derogation is permitted from certain core rights, as the right to life and the prohibition of torture and ill-treatment. Secondly, derogation measures are only permitted after a state of emergency has been officially proclaimed and notified to the other states parties of the respective human rights treaties (CCPR, ECHR, ACHR). Thirdly, derogation measures are only permitted to the extent strictly required by the exigencies of the situation, i.e. proportional to the actual threat. The same **principle of proportionality** applies to **military responses** to terrorist attacks.

While military intervention by the United States and allied forces against the Taliban regime in Afghanistan was explicitly authorized by the UN Security Council as an act of self-defence in accordance with article 51 of the UN Charter (16.15.), this argument cannot be applied to other countries, where Al-Qa'ida still might have active cells. Finally, the response to the threat of terrorism should go beyond military and police action and address the **root causes** of the increasing use of terrorist methods. In addition to the unresolved conflicts in the Middle East and the denial of the right to self-determination to the people of Palestine, there seem to be many other causes of terrorism. **Poverty** and denial of human rights as a result of **globalization** driven by neo-liberalist policies certainly figures prominently among the root causes of present day terrorism. Perhaps it would be more in line with a future oriented universal human rights strategy to divert some of the resources used for the current 'war against terrorism' and to invest them into comprehensive poverty reduction strategies.

New developments in **science and technology** continue to pose new challenges to human rights, in particular the rights to human dignity and privacy. In the fight against organized crime and terrorism, modern police and intelligence agencies are using information and **surveillance technology**, including racial profiling, that potentially affects numerous innocent citizens and constitutes far-reaching interference with the right to privacy and data protection. Even more dangerous are new developments in **biotechnology and biomedicine**, as they enable human beings to modify the human genome and, thereby, to interfere with human rights of future generations. With the adoption of the European Convention on Human Rights and Biomedicine in 1997 and an AP on the Prohibition of Cloning Human Beings in 1998, the Council of Europe has assumed a pioneering role of human rights protection in a very sensitive area (5.7.). If we wish to protect human beings and future generations against **cloning** and other interventions on the human genome, much more far-reaching universal measures would be required. The extent of our interference and destruction of environmental resources also will have far-reaching consequences on the **human rights of future generations**, including the rights to health, food and the newly emerging human rights to clean water and a **satisfactory environment.**

In addition to these and other threats to human rights arising from progress in science and technology, many 'old' challenges remain. For example, we have come a long way in the gradual abolition of the **death penalty** under international law, but there are still roughly 70 retentionist countries in the world, including very powerful and influential states, such as China, India, Indonesia, Iran, Saudi Arabia, Nigeria and the United States. In Europe, South Africa and most Latin American states, the death penalty is considered as an inhuman punishment, and the European Union is pursuing an active policy of persuading third countries to move towards abolition. But it will still need stronger efforts of global awareness raising until the death penalty, corporal punishment, torture, female genital mutilation (FGM) and other forms of inhuman and degrading treatment and punishment will be eradicated worldwide.

17. CHALLENGES FOR THE FUTURE

For many people, human rights are still perceived as a fairly abstract legal concept, which seems only to be relevant in far-away countries. Much remains to be done in terms of **human rights education** and awareness raising in order to create a **universal human rights culture**, which might for once form the basis of a new and less violent world order. The UN Decade on Human Rights Education (1995 to 2004) as well as the UNESCO programme on a Culture for Peace and Non-violence for the Children of the World (2001 to 2010) represent two powerful initiatives at the global level (4.5.3.), but greater efforts need to be undertaken to implement these programmes at the national, local and individual level. Human rights should be imprinted on the hearts and minds of everyone in a process of life-long learning as well as being practiced in our day-to-day behaviour towards our fellow human beings.

This brief outline of issues, weaknesses and challenges shows that we are a long way from efficient and effective human rights protection. By the same token, we have achieved more in half a century than most people would care to believe. Many taboos have been broken, people's awareness has been raised, and the course has been set for effective protection measures and prevention of human rights violations. Now that states, and in principle non-state actors too, are obligated by a comprehensive set of international standards to respect, protect and fulfil human rights, we can be sure that this is not just a whim of the day, but a way of no return. As long as international law is understood as the normative basis for international relations, human rights will hold their ground as the only universally recognized and legally binding codified system of values, and as such will demand factual implementation by all of us.

ABBREVIATIONS

ACC	UN Administrative Committee on Coordination
ACHR	American Convention on Human Rights, 1969
ACP	African, Caribbean and Pacific States (EU)
AGP	Agreement on Government Procurement (WTO)
AI	Amnesty International
AP	Additional Protocol
ASEAN	Association of Southeast Asian Nations
AU	African Union
BiH	Bosnia and Herzegovina
CAT	Convention against Torture and Other Cruel, Inhuman or Degrading Treatment or Punishment, 1984
CCPR	International Covenant on Civil and Political Rights, 1966
CCR	Committee on Conventions and Recommendations (UNESCO)
CDDH	Committee of Ministers' Steering Committee for Human Rights (CoE)
CDF	Comprehensive Development Framework (World Bank)
CEB	UN System Chief Executive Board for Coordination
CEDAW	Convention on the Elimination of All Forms of Discrimination against Women, 1979
CERD	International Convention on the Elimination of All Forms of Racial Discrimination, 1965
CESCR	International Covenant on Economic, Social and Cultural Rights, 1966
CFSP	Common Foreign and Security Policy (EU)
CHR	UN Commission on Human Rights
CICP	UN Centre for International Crime Prevention
CIS	Commonwealth of Independent States
CoE	Council of Europe
CONADEP	Comision Nacional para los Desaparecidos (The National Commission on the Disappeared) (Argentina)
CPT	European Committee for the Prevention of Torture
CRC	Convention on the Rights of the Child, 1989
CSCE	Conference on Security and Cooperation in Europe
CTC	UN Counter-Terrorism Committee
DAW	UN Division for the Advancement of Women
DESA	UN Department of Economic and Social Affairs
DPA	UN Department for Political Affairs
DPKO	UN Department for Peace-Keeping Operations
DSB	Dispute Settlement Body (WTO)
EC	European Communities
ECHR	European Convention on Human Rights and Fundamental Freedoms, 1950
ECJ	European Court of Justice
ECOSOC	UN Economic and Social Council
ECPT	European Convention for the Prevention of Torture and Inhuman or Degrading Treatment or Punishment, 1987
ECRI	European Commission against Racism and Intolerance (CoE)
ECSC	European Coal and Steel Community
Ed.	Editor

Abbreviations

ed.	edition
EEC	European Economic Community
e.g.	for example
EIDHR	European Initiative for Democracy and Human Rights (EU)
ESC	European Social Charter, 1961
etc	et cetera
ETS	European Treaty System (CoE)
EU	European Union
EUMC	EU Monitoring Centre on Racism and Xenophobia
FAO	Food and Agriculture Organization
FGM	Female Genital Mutilation
FIAN	Food First Information and Action Network
FMLN	Frente Farabundo Marti para la Liberacion Nacional (El Salvador)
FRY	Federal Republic of Yugoslavia
FYROM	Former Yugoslav Republic of Macedonia
GA	UN General Assembly
GA Res.	Resolution of the UN General Assembly
GATT	General Agreement on Tariffs and Trade
HABITAT	UN Centre for Human Settlements
HCNM	OSCE High Commissioner on National Minorities
HIPC	Heavily Indebted Poor Countries
HRFOR	UNHCHR Field Operation in Rwanda
IAEA	International Atomic Energy Agency
IASC	Inter-Agency Standing Committee (UN)
IBRD	International Bank for Reconstruction and Development
ICC	International Criminal Court
ICJ	International Court of Justice
ICRC	International Committee of the Red Cross
ICTR	International Criminal Tribunal for Rwanda
ICTY	International Criminal Tribunal for the former Yugoslavia
IDA	International Development Association
IDP	Internally Displaced Persons
i.e.	that is to say
IFAD	International Fund for Agricultural Development
IFI	International Financial Institution
IFOR	Implementation Force (BiH)
IGO	Inter-Governmental Organization
ILC	International Law Commission
ILO	International Labour Organization
IMF	International Monetary Fund
INTERFET	International Force for East Timor
IPTF	International Police Task Force (BiH)
KFOR	Kosovo Force (NATO)
KLA	Kosovo Liberation Army
KVM	Kosovo Verification Mission (OSCE)
MDG	Millennium Development Goals
MINUGUA	Misión de Verificación de las Naciones Unidas en Guatemala (UN Verification Mission in Guatemala)

ABBREVIATIONS

MWC	International Convention on the Protection of the Rights of All Migrant Workers and Members of their Families, 1990
NATO	North Atlantic Treaty Organization
NGO	Non-governmental Organization
OAS	Organization of American States
OAU	Organization of African Unity
OCHA	UN Office for the Coordination of Humanitarian Affairs
ODCCP	UN Office for Drug Control and Crime Prevention
ODIHR	Office for Democratic Institutions and Human Rights (OSCE)
OECD	Organization for Economic Cooperation and Development
OIC	Organization of the Islamic Conference
OLA	UN Office for Legal Affairs
ONUSAL	Observadores de las Naciones Unidas en El Salvador (UN Observer Mission in El Salvador)
OP	Optional Protocol
OSCE	Organization for Security and Cooperation in Europe
PIC	Peace Implementation Council (BiH)
PRSP	Poverty Reduction Strategy Paper (World Bank)
Res.	Resolution
Rev ESC	Revised European Social Charter, 1996
RPF	Rwandese Patriotic Front
SAARC	South Asian Association for Regional Cooperation
SAP	Structural Adjustment Programme (World Bank)
SC	UN Security Council
SC Res.	Resolution of the UN Security Council
SFOR	Stabilization Force (BiH)
SG	Secretary General
Sub-Comm	UN Sub-Commission on the Promotion and Protection of Human Rights
TBT	Agreement on Technical Barriers to Trade (WTO)
TC	UN Trusteeship Council
TNC	Transnational Corporations
TRI	Agreement on Trade Related Investment Measures (WTO)
TRIPS	Agreement over Trade Related Aspects of Intellectual Property Rights (WTO)
UDHR	Universal Declaration of Human Rights, 1948
UN	United Nations
UNO	United Nations Organization
UNAMET	UN Mission in East Timor
UNAMIC	UN Advance Mission In Cambodia
UNAMIR	UN Assistance Mission for Rwanda
UNCTAD	UN Conference on Trade and Development
UNDCP	UN International Drug Control Programme
UNDP	UN Development Programme
UNEP	UN Environment Programme
UNESCO	UN Educational, Scientific and Cultural Organization
UNFICYP	UN Peacekeeping Force in Cyprus
UNFPA	UN Populations Fund
UNHCHR	UN High Commissioner for Human Rights
UNHCR	UN High Commissioner for Refugees

ABBREVIATIONS

UNICEF	United Nations Children Fund
UNIDIR	UN Institute for Disarmament Research
UNIDO	UN Industrial Development Organization
UNIFEM	UN Development Fund for Women
UNIKOM	UN Iraq-Kuwait Observation Mission
UNITAF	United Task Force (Somalia)
UNITAR	UN Institute for Training and Research
UNMIBH	UN Mission in Bosnia and Herzegovina
UNMIK	UN Transition Administration Mission in Kosovo
UNMISET	UN Mission of Support in East Timor
UNOCCP	UN Office for Drug Control and Crime Prevention
UNOPS	UN Office for Project Services
UNOSOM	UN Operation in Somalia
UNOV	UN Verification Office (El Salvador)
UNPREDEP	UN Preventive Deployment Force (Macedonia)
UNPROFOR	UN Protection Force (former Yugoslavia)
UNRISD	UN Research Institution for Social Development
UNSCOM	UN Special Commission (Iraq)
UNTAC	UN Transitional Authority in Cambodia
UNTAET	UN Transitional Administration in East Timor
UNU	United Nations University
UNV	United Nations Volunteers
USG	Under-Secretary General
USSR	Union of Soviet Socialist Republics
VCLT	Vienna Convention on the Law of Treaties
VDPA	Vienna Declaration and Programme of Action, 1993
vol.	volume
WFP	World Food Programme
WHO	World Health Organization
WTO	World Trade Organization

INDEX CASEBOXES

Casebox 1: Human Rights in Practice – Examples I (1.) (page 6)

Casebox 2: Human Rights in Practice – Examples II (1.) (page 7)

Casebox 3: UN Preventive Deployment Force in Macidonia (UNPREDEP) (14.1.) (page 278)

Casebox 4: Burundi Field Mission of the UN High Commissioner for Human Rights (14.2.) (page 280)

Casebox 5: OSCE High Commissioner on National Minorities: Case Studies Albania, Slovakia and Hungary (14.3.) (page 282)

Casebox 6: Austria and the European Committee for the Prevention of Torture (CPT) (14.5.) (page 286)

Casebox 7: The Struggle against Impunity at the National Level: The 'Dirty War' in Argentina (15.1.) (page 290)

Casebox 8: The Principle of Universal Jurisdiction and the UN Convention against Torture: The Case of *Hissèin Habré* in Senegal (15.2.) (page 291)

Casebox 9: Diplomatic Immunity *versus* Criminal Responsibility: The Case of *Pinochet* before the British House of Lords (15.3.) (page 293)

Casebox 10: UN Peacekeeping Force in Cyprus (UNFICYP) (16.5.) (page 319)

Casebox 11: UN Observer Mission in El Salvador (ONUSAL) (16.6.) (page 320)

Casebox 12: First Field Presence of the UN High Commissioner for Human Rights: UN Field Operation in Rwanda (HRFOR) (16.7.) (page 321)

Casebox 13: Between Peace-keeping and Protectorate: UN Transitional Authority in Cambodia (UNTAC) (16.8.) (page 322)

Casebox 14: Comprehensive Peace Operations: The International Community's Quasi Protectorate in Bosnia and Herzegovina (16.9.) (page 324)

Casebox 15: Self-determination and UN Transitional Administration in East Timor (16.10.) (page 326)

Casebox 16: Human Rights Protection by the Security Council as a Direct Consequence of International Peace Making: Case Study Iraq (16.11.) (page 328)

Casebox 17: Humanitarian Intervention for the Protection of Human Rights in *Failed States*: Case Study Somalia (16.12.) (page 330)

Casebox 18: The Tanzanian Intervention in Uganda in 1979: A 'Humanitarian Intervention'? (16.13.) (page 332)

Casebox 19: NATO Humanitarian Intervention for the Protection of Human Rights: Case Study Kosovo (16.14.) (page 334)

Casebox 20: Human Rights and the Fight against Terrorism: Case Study Afghanistan (16.15.) (page 336)

Name Index

Aga Khan, Sadruddin 136
Agosti, Orlando 290
Aidid, Mohamed Fahrah 330, 331, 332
Alfonsin, Raul 290, 291, 292
Allende, Salvador 289, 293
Amin, Idi 204, 273, 289, 309, 332, 333
Annan, Kofi 105, 123, 131, 133, 137, 138, 310
Aragona, Giancarlo 225
Ashdown, Paddy 324
Ayala Lasso, José 133, 313

Baby Doc 289
Bage, Lennart 140
Bassiouni, Cherif 63, 296
Bellamy, Carol 137, 140
Belo, Carlos 326
Bildt, Carl 324
Bin Laden, Osama 312, 336, 337
Blaskic, Tihomir 295
Bokassa, Bedel 204
Boutros-Ghali, Boutros 131, 133
Brahimi, Lakhdar 337
Breshnjev, 16
Brown, Mark Malloch 138, 140
Brundtland, Gro Harlem 140, 143
Bush, George Jr. 300

Cassese, Antonio 247
Cassin, René 76, 104
Ceauscescu, Nicolai 216
Churchill, Winston 22, 23
Clinton, Bill 300
Cutileiro, José 325

de Hoop Scheffer, Jakob 225
Debry, Idriss 291
Del Ponte, Carla 295, 297
Denktash, Rauf 310, 319
Dieng, Adama 297
Dienstbier, Jiri 325
Diouf, Jacques 140, 144
Dunant, Henri 17
Duve, Freimut 226, 228

Ekéus, Rolf 225, 227
El Baradei, Mohamed 140

Engels, Friedrich 13

Garzon, Balthasar 293
Gauthier, Jean-Jacques 176
Gil-Robles, Alvaro 159, 183
Gligorov, Kiro 278
Gorbachev, Michail 26, 215, 220
Gusmão, Xanana 326
Habibie, Bacharuddin Jusuf 326
Habré, Hissèin 291, 294
Hammarskjöld, Dag 131
Hartling, Poul 136
Havel, Vaclav 217
Hegel, Gottfried 2
Hitler, Adolf 23
Hocké, Jean-Pierre 136
Holbrooke, Richard 334
Holthius, Hans 295
Höynck, Wilhelm 225
Huntington, Samuel 345
Hussein, Saddam 328, 329

Imbert, Pierre-Henri 159
Izetbegovic, Alija 314

Jellinek, Georg 48

Kambanda, Jean 297, 300
Kant, Immanuel 10, 11
Karadzic, Radovan 295
Karzai, Hamid 337
Kirsch, Philippe 299
Köhler, Horst 140, 144
Korczak, Janusz 91
Kordic, Dario 295
Krajisnik, Momcilo 295
Kubis, Ján 225

Lalumière, Catherine 247
Lambruschini, Armando 290
Lassalle, Ferdinand 11
Letelier, Orlando 294
Leuprecht, Peter 247
Lie, Trygve 131
Lindt, Auguste R. 136
Locke, John 2, 9, 10
Lubbers, Ruud 136, 137, 140

Name Index

Lule, Yusuf 333

Magarinos, Carlos 140
Mahdi, Ali 330
Marx, Karl 11, 13
Massera, Emilio 290
Matsuura, Koichiro 140, 142
Mazowiecki, Tadeusz 114, 325
Meciar, Vladimir 239, 281
Menem, Carlos 290, 292
Meron, Theodor 295
Mill, John Stuart 11
Milosevic, Slobodan 279, 295, 300, 309, 314, 334, 335
Mladic, Ratko 295
Mobuto, Joseph Sese Seko 204
Mose, Erik 297
Museveni, Yoweri 333

Nansen, Fridtjof 136
Nowak, Manfred 325
Nyerere, Julius 205, 333

Obote, Milton 332, 333
Ocampo, Luis Moreno 299
Ogata, Sadako 136, 137
Paine, Thomas 9

Panitchpakdi, Supachai 147
Pérez de Cuéllar, Javier 131
Petritsch, Wolfgang 324
Pinochet Ugarte, Augusto 56, 273, 289, 291, 293, 294
Pol Pot 289

Ramos Horta, José 326
Rehn, Elisabeth 325
Robinson, Mary 27, 133, 247, 277
Roosevelt, Eleanor 75, 104
Roosevelt, Franklin D. 22, 23

Rousseau, Jean-Jacques 9, 12

Sahnoun, Mohamed 330
Schnyder, Félix 136
Schwimmer, Walter 159
Senghor, Leopold 205
Shah, Zahir 337
Siad Barre, Mohamed 330
Solana Madariaga, Javier 243, 247
Somavía, Juan 140, 142
Stalin, Joseph 16, 22
Stoltenberg, Thorvald 136
Straw, Jack 293, 294
Strohal, Christian 229
Suharto, Mohamed 317, 326

Thant, U 131
Taylor, Charles 300
Tudman, Franjo 314

van Boven, Theo 63
van der Stoel, Max 225, 227, 281
van Heuven Goedhart, G. J. 136
Vasak, Karel 23
Videla, Jorge 290, 292
Vieira de Mello, Sergio 105, 133, 134, 140
Viola, Eduardo 290, 292

Wade, Abdoulaye 291
Waldheim, Kurt 131
Wałęsa, Lech 217
Wedeye, Goukouni 291
Westendorp, Carlos 324
Wildhaber, Luzius 159
Wilhelm II, Emperor 296
Wilson, Woodrow 19
Wolfensohn, James 140, 144

Yeltsin, Boris 16

SUBJECT INDEX

Absolute human rights 56, 58
Accountability 53
Admission criteria 170, 238
Advisory Committee 181
Advisory jurisdiction 199
Advisory opinion 194
Advisory services 106
Affirmative action 86
Afghanistan 114, 309, 336
African Charter on Human and Peoples' Rights 205, 206
African Charter on the Rights and Welfare of the Child 211
African Commission on Human and Peoples' Rights 207
African Court on Human and Peoples' Rights 208
African Union (AU) 68, 203, 204
African values 205
Aggression 301
AIDS/HIV 143
Albania 282
Aliens 6
All human rights for all 13, 25
American Convention on Human Rights (ACHR) 191, 196
American Declaration of Independence, 1776 10
American Declaration of the Rights and Duties of Man 191
Amsterdam Treaty 236
Apartheid 106, 203
Apartheid Convention 95
Arab Charter on Human Rights 255
Arab League 255
Arab-Islamic area 254
Arbitrariness 61
Arbitrary executions 115
Argentina 290, 292
Argentina's dirty war 291
Armed conflicts 39, 281
Asia 68, 253
Asian values 253
Assembly of Heads of State and Government 210
Asylum 136, 240, 241
Atlantic Charter 22, 23

Austria 286
Aut dedere aut iudicare 90
Autonomous interpretation 66

Banishment 7
Banjul Charter 205, 206
Bassouni Commission 296
Beijing Platform for Action 150
Bill of rights 16
Biomedicine 181, 346
Biotechnology 181, 346
Bosnia and Herzegovina 279, 300, 314, 324
British House of Lords 293
Burundi 280
Burundi Field Mission of the UN High Commissioner for Human Rights 280

Cambodia 296, 311
Central and Eastern European countries 159
Chad 294
Challenges 339
Chapter VII UN Charter 129, 307
Charter based mechanisms 104, 192
Charter of Paris for a New Europe 220, 222
Child labour 94
Child pornography 94
Child prostitution 94
Children 91, 117, 127, 137, 186, 211, 212
Children in armed conflict 94
Children's rights 91
Chile 107, 114, 289, 293
China 246
Citizens' rights 4
Civil and political rights 23, 160, 259
Civil freedom 10
Civil liability 343
Civil rights 10
Classical human rights concept 12
Cloning 183
Cold War 23
Collective complaints 176, 267
Collective rights 4, 5, 24, 68, 205, 207
Collective security 129, 309
Colonialism 25, 152, 203, 205
Commission for Real Property Claims 316
Committee of Ministers (CoE) 161, 171, 173

357

Subject Index

Common Foreign and Security Policy (CFSP) 243, 245
Common positions 246
Common strategies 245
Commonwealth of Independent States (CIS) 254
Communications → individual complaints procedure
Compensation 63
Complaints procedure 99
Complementary jurisdiction 302
Complex peace operations 314
Comprehensive Development Framework (CDF) 145
Comprehensive peace operation 324
Comprehensive security concept 69, 222, 226, 309
Concluding observations 99
Conditionality of human rights 244
Conference on Security and Cooperation in Europe (CSCE) 215
Conference on the Human Dimension 219
Confidential procedure 108
Conflict prevention 229, 276
Constitutional law 4
Constitutionalism 14
Consultative status 258
Contentious jurisdiction 199
Convention 29
Convention against Torture and Other Cruel, Inhuman or Degrading Treatment or Punishment (CAT) 88, 284, 291, 292
Convention on the Elimination of All Forms of Discrimination against Women (CEDAW) 86
Convention on the Rights of the Child (CRC) 91, 137
Copenhagen Declaration on Social Development 152
Copenhagen Document 219
Corporal punishment 6
Cotonou Agreement 243, 245
Council of Europe 67, 157, 253
Country reports 195
Country specific mechanisms 110
Criminal justice 121
Crime prevention 121
Crimes against humanity 301
Criminal law 186

Croatia 300
Cross-cutting issue 132
Cultural rights 81, 142
Culture of Peace 142
Cyprus 166, 310, 319
Czechoslovakia 179

Data protection 186
Dayton Peace Agreement 314, 324
Death penalty 6, 196, 346
Debt relief 145
Declaration 29
Declaration of Human Rights for Islam 254
Declaration on the Elimination of Violence against Women 52
Declarations of interpretation 57
Democracy 9, 45, 157, 281
Democracy, right to 46
Democratic society 60
Democratization 341
Deregulation 275
Derogation 58
Detention 116, 178
Developing countries 82
Development 43, 117, 122, 137, 151
Development cooperation 43, 243, 244
Development, right to 44
Dignity → human dignity
Diplomatic immunity → Immunity
Dirty war 290
Disappearances 6, 115, 198, 283, 284
Discrimination 61, 179, 241
Discrimination against women 86
Divorce 7
Domestic jurisdiction 33
Dualism 36
Dublin Convention 240
Duties of the individual 205
Dynamic interpretation 66

Early warning system 277
Earth Summit of Rio 147
East Timor 309, 317, 326
Economic and Social Council → ECOSOC
Economic rights 81, 141
Economic sanctions → Sanctions
Economic, social and cultural rights 12, 19, 24, 62, 116, 151, 173, 195, 260
ECOSOC 122, 139

Subject Index

ECOSOC Resolution
- 728 (XXVIII) 107
- 1235 (XLII) 107
- 1503 (XLVIII) 107, 108

Education, right to 7
Effet utile 66
El Salvador 114, 310, 320
Emergency reports 99
Emergency session 107
Empowerment 2, 339
Enforceability 52
Enforced disappearances → Disappearances
Enforcement 171
Enforcement of human rights 28, 29, 340
Enlightenment 9
Environment 346
Equality 61
Equatorial Guinea 111, 114
EU Annual Report on Human Rights 247, 248
EU Charter of Fundamental Rights 240, 248, 249
EU external relations 242
EU Monitoring Centre on Racism and Xenophobia (EUMC) 185, 241, 242
EU network of independent experts on fundamental rights 241
European Charter for Regional and Minority Languages 181
European Commission against Racism and Intolerance (ECRI) 184
European Commission of Human Rights 161
European Commissioner for Human Rights 183
European Committee for the Prevention of Torture (CPT) 177, 286
European Committee of Social Rights 175
European Convention for the Prevention of Torture (ECPT) 176, 285
European Convention on Human Rights (ECHR) 160, 239
European Convention on Human Rights and Biomedicine 181
European Court of Human Rights 161, 170
European Court of Justice (ECJ) 239
European Framework Convention for the Protection of National Minorities 179

European Initiative for Democracy and Human Rights 245
European integration 236
European Social Charter (ESC) 173
European unification process 235
European Union (EU) 69, 157, 235
Experts 96

Fact-finding 117, 195, 258, 267, 269
Failed states 275, 330
Female genital mutilation (FGM) 7, 151
Field missions 230
Field presences 133, 321
Follow-up 101
Food and Agriculture Organization (FAO) 143
Food security 143
Food, right to 143
Freedom of expression 7
Freedom of information 7
Freedom of religion 19
French Déclaration des droits de l'homme et du citoyen, 1789 10, 11, 12, 15, 16
Friendly settlement 166, 211, 268
Functional commissions 123
Fundamental rights 4, 14, 249
Future generations 339
Future of human rights 339

Gender mainstreaming 150
General Agreement on Tariffs and Trade (GATT) 146
General comments 99
General recommendations 99
Generations of human rights 23
Genocide 21, 95, 279, 295, 301, 313
Global awareness of human rights 339
Global civil society 257
Globalization 146, 275, 346
Golden rule 9
Good governance 45, 281, 341
Grand Chamber 170
Greece 166
Gross and systematic human rights violations 107, 130
Guarantees of non-repetition 63
Guatemala 111, 114, 311

Habeas corpus 284

Subject Index

Haiti 111, 114, 309
Health, right to 143
Heavily Indebted Poor Countries (HIPCs) 145, 151
Helsinki Final Act 215
Helsinki Process 218
High Representative for Bosnia and Herzegovina 315, 316, 324
Historical antecedents of the international protection of human rights 16
History of human rights 9
Homosexuality 7
Horizontal effects of human rights 1
Human development 45
Human Development Reports 138
Human dignity 1, 88, 181
Human dimension 219
Human Dimension Mechanism 219, 221
Human rights
- definition 1, 9
- terminology 1
- universality 25
Human Rights Agenda for the European Union for the Year 2000 248
Human Rights Chamber for Bosnia and Herzegovina 316
Human rights clauses 243, 246
Human Rights Committee 80, 100, 102
Human rights defenders 260
Human rights education 142, 347
Human rights theory 48
Human security 310
Humanitarian intervention 308, 309, 318, 330, 332, 334, 340
Humanitarian law 17, 38, 54, 95
Hungary 282
Hunger 143

Immunity 17, 293, 294
Implementation of human rights 28, 29, 36
Impunity 55, 276, 284, 289, 290
Incorporation 37
Independence 261
Independent expert 111
Indigenous peoples 7, 117
Indigenous populations 119
Individual complaints 67, 200, 266, 273
- procedure 160, 168, 192, 194, 195, 210, 267

- admissibility criteria 194
Individual responsibility 289, 343
Individual rights 4
Indivisibility and interdependence of all human rights 14, 25
Indonesia 326
Initial reports 97
Inquiry procedure 103, 267, 268
Inspection Panel 145
Institution-building 341
Inter-Agency Standing Committee (IASC) 132
Inter-American Commission on Human Rights 191, 193
Inter-American Convention on the Forced Disappearance of Persons 201
Inter-American Convention on the Prevention, Punishment and Eradication of Violence against Women 201
Inter-American Convention to Prevent and Punish Torture 201
Inter-American Court of Human Rights 192, 199
Interference 57
Intergovernmental organizations 67, 275, 342
Interim measures 64
Internally displaced persons 39, 135
International Bill of Human Rights 106
International Committee of the Red Cross (Red Crescent) 18
International Convention on the Elimination of All Forms of Racial Discrimination (CERD) 83
International Convention on the Protection of the Rights of All Migrant Workers and Members of their Families (MWC) 94
International court of human rights 79, 275
International Covenant on Civil and Political Rights (CCPR) 78
International Covenant on Economic, Social and Cultural Rights (CESCR) 81
International Criminal Court (ICC) 55, 299, 300
International criminal law 289, 344
International Criminal Tribunal for Rwanda (ICTR) 55, 296, 297
International Criminal Tribunal for the Former Yugoslavia (ICTY) 55, 295, 296

Subject Index

International criminal tribunals 131
International financial institutions 144
International human rights system 67
International Labour Office 19
International Labour Organization (ILO) 141
International law 35, 52, 289
International Monetary Fund (IMF) 144
International war crimes tribunals of Nuremberg and Tokyo 296, 298
Interpretation of human rights treaties 64
Inter-state complaints procedure 100, 161, 165, 198, 209, 266, 274
Intolerance 152, 179
Investigation 111, 269
Iran 114
Iraq 114, 309, 328
Islamic law 253
Israel 107, 152

Joint actions 246
Justice to victims of human rights violations 292
Juveniles 93

Khmer Rouge genocide 322
Kosovo 230, 279, 300, 317, 334
Kuwait 328

Latin America 191
Lawful sanctions clause 89
League of Arab States 255
League of Nations 20
Legal claims 2
Liberalism 10, 11
Lieber Code 17
Limitation clause 59
Limitations of human rights 56
Linguistic diversity 181
Lomé Conventions 245
Long-term missions 228

Maastricht Treaty 236
Macedonia 278, 279
Mainstreaming human rights 75
Mandate Commission 20
Mandates system 21
Margin of appreciation 59
Marriage 95

Mechanisms 265
Media freedom 228
Medicine 181
Migrant workers 94, 186
Migration 240, 241
Military intervention 309
Military sanctions 129
Millennium Declaration 145, 152
Millennium Development Goals (MDG) 128, 342
Millennium summit 127
Minorities 18, 119, 179, 227
Minority Committee 21
Minority conflicts 281
Minority languages 181
Minority protection 21
Mobilization of shame 257, 258
Monism 36
Monitoring of human rights 28, 96
Moscow Declaration 22
Moscow Mechanism 220
Multilateral diplomacy 67

National law 52
National Socialism 21
National sovereignty → sovereignty of states
Nationalism 179, 184, 220
NATO 334
Nazi Holocaust 22
Neo-colonialist attitude of northern human rights policies 2
Neo-liberalism 146, 276
New problems 275
New world order 148
Nice Treaty 237
No power to take action doctrine 106
Non-governmental organizations (NGOs) 67, 149, 257
Non-intervention in domestic affairs 33
Non-refoulement → Refoulement, prohibition of
Non-state actors 54, 275, 276, 289, 342
Northern Ireland 166

OAS Charter 191
OAU Convention Governing Specific Aspects of Refugee Problems 211
Object and purpose of a treaty 65

361

Subject Index

Obligation to fulfil human rights 49, 86
Obligation to protect human rights 50
Obligation to respect human rights 49
Obligations of conduct 81
OECD Guidelines for Multinational Enterprises 146
Office for Democratic Institutions and Human Rights (ODIHR) 223, 229
Optional Protocol (OP)
- CAT 91, 285
- CCPR 103
- CEDAW 87, 88
- CESCR (draft) 83
- CRC 94
Opting out 103
Organization for Security and Cooperation in Europe (OSCE) 69, 158, 215, 253
Organization of African Unity (OAU) 68, 203
Organization of American States (OAS) 68, 189
Organization of the Islamic Conference (OIC) 254
Organized crime 121, 135 275
OSCE High Commissioner on National Minorities (HCNM) 224, 227, 281, 282
OSCE rapporteurs 226
OSCE Representative for Freedom of the Media 225, 228

Pacific area 253
Palestinians 152
Pan-American Union 189, 190
Participation 93
Peace 40, 122, 129, 307
Peace making 328
Peace operations 310
Peace-building operations 41
Peacekeeping operations 41, 130, 310
Peacemaking and peace-enforcement operations 42
Peoples' rights 4
Periodic reports 97
Personal liberty 7, 177
Personal security 53
Petitions → individual complaints procedure
Philosophical foundations 9
Political dialogue 246

Political freedom 9, 46
Political rights 10, 46
Political rights of women 95
Popular participation 45
Portugal 326
Poverty 7, 45, 127, 138, 151, 276, 281, 341, 346
Poverty reduction strategies 342
Poverty Reduction Strategy Papers (PRSPs) 145
Pressing social need 60
Prevention of armed conflicts 42
Prevention of crime 121
Prevention of human rights violations 27, 239, 276, 277, 341
Preventive system of visits to places of detention 176, 268, 270, 285
Privacy 183
Privatization 275
Procedural guarantees 47
Procedures 265
Progressive implementation 81
Progressive realization of human rights 50
Prohibition of abuse 59
Promotion of human rights 27, 73, 277
Proportionality 59, 345
Protection of human rights 27, 93, 277
Protectorate
UN Transitional Authority in Cambodia (UNTAC) 322
Provision 93
Provisional measures → interim measures 194

Quasi protectorate 324
Quasi-judicial monitoring body 80, 96

Racial discrimination 83
Racial incitement 85
Racism 152, 179, 203, 220
Racist violence 184
Rationalistic doctrine of natural law 9
Reaction to specific threats 273
Reactive and event-driven human rights policies 273
Reciprocity, principle of 35
Recommendations 99
Red Cross Movement 17
Referendum 317

Subject Index

Reform 274
Refoulement, prohibition of 6, 40, 90, 101, 136
Refugee law 38, 95, 135, 186, 211, 212
Regional commissions 123
Regional organizations 67, 253
Rehabilitation 63
Religious intolerance 115
Remedy 47, 56, 63
Reparation 101, 171, 194, 268
Reporting 269
Reservations 57, 63
Responsibility of parents 93
Restitutio in integrum 64
Restitution 63
Restrictions → limitation of human rights
Revised European Social Charter (RevESC) 175
Rights of peoples 24
Rome Statute for an International Criminal Court (ICC) 298
Root causes of human rights violations 276, 341, 346
Rule of law 45, 157, 235, 281, 341
Rwanda 279, 296, 298, 313, 321

Sale of children 94
Sanctions 312, 340
Satisfaction 63
Schengen Agreement 240
Science and technology 346
Scope of application 57
Secession 179
Security 129, 307
Self-defence 129
Self-determination, right of peoples of 19, 25, 124, 317, 326, 327
Senegal 291
Shortcomings of traditional procedures 273
Sierra Leone 296, 300, 309
Situations of gross and systematic human rights violations 108, 267
Slave trade 19, 20, 95
Slavery 19, 20, 95, 119, 152
Slovakia 282
Social matters 186
Social rights 81
Socialism 11, 13
Socialist human rights concept 12, 25

Soft law standards for criminal justice 121, 135
Somalia 309, 330
South Africa 106, 114, 152
Sovereignty of states 33
Soviet Union 179
Special Court for Sierra Leone 296
Special rapporteur 111, 115
Stabilization Force (SFOR) 314
State of emergency 58
State responsibility 54, 289
Stateless persons 95
Statelessness 95
States obligations 48
States reporting procedure 97, 265, 274
Strasbourg Mechanism 161
Structural adjustment programmes (SAPs) 144
Surveillance technology 346
Sustainable human development 138
Systematic pattern of gross and reliably attested violations of human rights 110, 208

Tanzania 333
Temporary protection 40, 136
Terrorism 275, 336, 344
Thematic mechanisms 115
Third party effect of human rights 53
Torture 6, 88, 115, 201, 268, 285
Transformation 36
Transitional administration 317, 318
Transnational corporations 54, 119, 146, 275, 343
Travaux préparatoires 65
Tripartite system 142
Truth and reconciliation commission 292
Turkey 166

Uganda 309, 332
UN Centre for International Crime Prevention (CICP) 135
UN Charter 73
UN Commission for Social Development 152
UN Commission on Crime Prevention and Criminal Justice 121
UN Commission on Human Rights 104

Subject Index

UN Commission on the Status of Women 119
UN Committee against Torture 90
UN Committee on Economic, Social and Cultural Rights 83
UN Committee on the Elimination of Discrimination against Women 87
UN Committee on the Elimination of Racial Discrimination 85
UN Committee on the Rights of the Child 93, 94
UN Congress on the Prevention of Crime and the Treatment of Offenders 121
UN Convention against Genocide 296
UN Covenants 78
UN Declaration on Human Rights Defenders 260, 262
UN Declaration on the Protection of All Persons form Enforced Disappearance 283, 284
UN Declaration on the Right to Development 44
UN Division for the Advancement of Women (DAW) 134
UN Economic and Social Council → ECOSOC
UN Educational, Scientific and Cultural Organization (UNESCO) 142
UN family 132, 139
UN Field Operation in Rwanda (HRFOR) 321
UN General Assembly 125
UN Global Compact 146
UN High Commissioner for Human Rights (UNHCHR) 75, 96, 133, 150, 279, 313, 321
UN High Commissioner for Refugees (UNHCR) 40, 135
UN Human Rights Commission → UN Commission on Human Rights
UN human rights treaties 78
UN Observer Mission in El Salvador (ONUSAL) 320
UN Peacekeeping Force in Cyprus (UNFICYP) 319
UN Preventive Deployment Force in Macedonia (UNPREDEP) 278
UN Secretary General 131
UN Security Council 129, 307, 308, 328
UN specialized agencies 139
UN Sub-Commission on the Promotion and Protection of Human Rights 117
UN Transitional Administration in East Timor (UNTAET) 326
UN treaty monitoring bodies 78
UN Trusteeship Council 124
UN Working Group on Enforced or Involuntary Disappearances 283
United Nations 23, 67, 73, 262
United Nations Children's Fund (UNICEF) 137
United Nations Development Programme (UNDP) 137
United Nations System Chief Executives Board for Coordination (CEB) 132
United States 10, 15, 16, 17, 190, 300, 344, 345
Uniting for peace resolution 126
Universal Declaration of Human Rights (UDHR) 14, 22, 75
Universal human rights culture 347
Universal jurisdiction 56, 90, 291, 292
Universalism 12, 14, 26
Universality of human rights 3, 25, 149
Universally recognized system of values 1, 347
Urgent actions 117

Velvet revolutions 26, 215
Versaille, Peace Treaty of 1919 20
Veto right 129
Vienna Concluding Document 216
Vienna Convention of the Law of Treaties (VCLT) 58, 64
Vienna Declaration and Programme of Action 26, 44, 149
Vienna Declaration of 10 December 1998 248
Vienna Mechanism 219
Violence against women 117, 134, 198
Violence in the family 51
Visits 270

War crimes 301
Women 62, 86, 119, 135, 206
Working groups 111
World Bank 144
World Conference Against Racism 152

SUBJECT INDEX

World Conference on Human Rights 26, 133, 148
World Conference on Women 135, 150
World Conferences 147
World Education Forum 142
World Health Organization (WHO) 143
World Social Summit 151
World Summit for Children 147
World Trade Organization (WTO) 146

Xenophobia 184, 221

Yugoslavia 114, 179, 279, 295, 309, 324